St. Louis Community College

Forest Park
Florissant Valley
Meramec

Instructional Resources
St. Louis, Missouri

BRAZILIAN WOMEN SPEAK

DAPHNE PATAI

RUTGERS UNIVERSITY PRESS   NEW BRUNSWICK AND LONDON

BRAZILIAN WOMEN SPEAK

CONTEMPORARY LIFE STORIES

Parts of the Introduction have appeared in somewhat
different form in the *International Journal of Oral
History* 8:1 (February 1987) and *Feminist Studies*
14:1 (Spring 1988). Chapter 1 appeared in *The
Massachusetts Review* 27:3–4 (Fall-Winter 1986).

Library of Congress Cataloging-in-Publication Data

Brazilian women speak
Includes Index
1. *Women—Brazil—Interviews.* I. *Patai, Daphne,*
1943–
HQ1542.B73 1988   305.4′0981   87-23498
ISBN 0-8135-1300-6
ISBN 0-8135-1301-4 (*pbk.*)

British Cataloging-in-Publication information available

For Joel
and for Neide

CONTENTS

A great many friends and acquaintances helped me throughout the years that I worked on this book. My greatest debt, of course, is to the women whose willingness to talk with me made the book possible, and this includes the many whose stories are not in the final manuscript. Because of my promise of anonymity to the women who granted me interviews, I cannot name them here. Nor can I name fully the Brazilians who provided help and hospitality during the summers of 1981 and 1983, since they often played a large part in enabling me to make contact and conduct interviews with others. But in particular I want to thank several friends: in the Northeast, Célia, Helena, Margarida, Mauro, Teresa, Valéria, and the other Margarida—with whom I had some wonderful talks and then, through my own fault, lost touch—as well as the members of their families; and, in Rio de Janeiro, Ângela, Eliane, Gervásio, Olga, and, most of all, Lúcia and Lauretta.

In the United States, a number of friends and colleagues helped me by providing information, corrections, and suggestions. These include Sandra Lauderdale Graham and Richard Graham, June Hahner, Robert Levine, James Malloy, Muriel Nazzari, and Paulann Sheets. Ellen McCracken read and corrected parts of the manuscript and discussed it with me extensively, taking time from her own work to do so. Catherine Kreyche made valuable comments on the next-to-the-last version of the manuscript. Claudia Van der Heuvel provided excellent research assistance at various stages in the preparation of this book.

The difficult work of transcribing the approximately sixty interviews I conducted in Brazil was done in the United States in bits and pieces by several individuals, but the lion's share was undertaken by Celina Cavalcanti, whose spirited remarks both on and in the transcripts were always of interest and of help, and also by Cristina Pedone. The University of Massachusetts at Amherst sponsored these transcriptions through a Faculty Research Grant.

Evelyn Kramer typed first drafts of some of the chapters. Carol Laudermilk put most of the chapters on a word processor and then was available for constant consultation as I learned how to use the word processor and took over this work myself. I am grateful to both of them for their help with this, as with my preceding book. Excellent working conditions were made available to me at the Institute for Advanced Study, at Indiana University, Bloomington, of which I was a

ACKNOWLEDGMENTS

Fellow throughout the 1986–1987 academic year. I would also like to thank the readers of the manuscript, whose comments aided my revisions, and especially Marlie Wasserman, editor-in-chief at Rutgers University Press, who first expressed enthusiasm for this project in 1984 and, happily, never gave up.

This book is dedicated to two old friends who began teaching me about Brazil nearly twenty years ago and have continued to do so to this day. In Brazil, they provided me with hospitality, introductions, and information. Although in our normal correspondence many months might elapse between letters, whenever I sent them desperate queries about aspects of Brazilian life and law, they always replied promptly and fully.

In this as in all my efforts of the past ten years, I have had the invaluable support of Gerald Strauss, my husband and friend.

July 1987

BRAZILIAN
WOMEN
SPEAK

This is a book about ordinary Brazilian women—domestic servants, secretaries, factory workers, nuns, hairdressers, prostitutes, seamstresses, students, businesswomen, homemakers; single, married, divorced, and widowed; Black and White and many in between; prepubescent and postmenopausal; rich and poor. How unpromising a theme this is thought to be was demonstrated to me by the difficulty colleagues in the United States had in grasping that this book is, indeed, about ordinary women. Again and again my project was transformed, on other people's lips, into a book about "prominent women" or about "women writers" in Brazil. Making a distinction between "ordinary" and "famous" may perhaps be justified, but ordinary does not mean insignificant. Quite a few of the women whose life stories appear in this book are, in fact, extraordinary human beings. And all are significant. It is misguided, I believe, to ask of a life story, "What's the point?" Our task is precisely to attend to the story in such a way that we move beyond this question. There are no pointless lives, and there are no pointless life stories. There are only life stories we have not (yet) bothered to consider and whose revelations (including, at times, those of staggering ordinariness) therefore remain hidden from our view.

In 1981 I decided to put my training and interest in Brazil to work on the problem of invisible women, that is, to move from writing texts about written texts (literary criticism as it is usually understood) to collecting, editing, and translating life stories of contemporary Brazilian women, women not usually heard from. Until recently the prism of androcentrism has distorted most of our knowledge about women, and the lives of ordinary women, even more than those of ordinary men, have been seen as unimportant, even trivial. One cause of this distorted view is that our image of women is most likely to be formed from the representations of privileged artists and scholars, usually male, for it is they who have had greater access to the public arena and who have formed and framed canons and curricula. But oral history itself does not necessarily escape these constraints. It does not come to us in an unadulterated form: people speaking their souls directly into our ears. Rather, oral history depends for its existence on the intervention of an

INTRODUCTION
CONSTRUCTING A SELF

interviewer who collects and presents a version of the stories gathered. Nor do the stories themselves exist pristine and unchanging in some sphere outside the vicissitudes of human interaction. Quite the contrary. Although I went to Brazil with tape recorder in hand and asked a few questions and mostly listened, the resulting tapes must be seen as a point of intersection between two subjectivities—theirs and mine, their cultural assumptions and mine, their memories and my questions, their sense of self and my own, their hesitations and my encouraging words or gestures (or sometimes vice versa), and much much more.

My aims in undertaking these interviews were to learn how these individuals' lives appeared to them and, starting with these life histories as subjective accounts, to gain a sense of the cultural constraints and pathways that provide structure and direction for women's lives in contemporary Brazil. I hope that readers of this book, in giving their attention to these life stories, will end with some sense of both the specific and the general. To William Runyan's observation that "a *fundamental* question about a culture is what kinds of lives its members are allowed to lead,"[1] I would add the equally fundamental question of how the individual self, constructed in a given society, in turn sustains that society's givens. At the same time, I see the individual life story as a unique and uniquely valuable document, one that we must not too readily leap over in our pursuit of generalization.

It is important to stress here that what I am calling "stories"—the life histories I gathered—are not folklore or traditional tales about the individual's culture (although their telling may indeed be influenced by traditional stories the women themselves have heard, as well as by their notion of what telling one's life story ought to be like). Rather, these are accounts constructed by individuals within the framework of the interview situation. It is therefore necessary for my readers to know how my interviews came to be conducted, the circumstances and constraints that shaped them, and my own role in what was, after all, a dialogue, not a monologue.

Given the vastness and diversity of Brazil, it was clear that I would have to limit my interviews geographically. I therefore decided to concentrate on the two areas with which I was most familiar: the traditionally agrarian and patriarchal Northeast—the area in which African slave labor created a prosperous sugar industry in the late sixteenth and early seventeenth centuries—and the more industrialized and modernized city of Rio de Janeiro, Brazil's capital for almost two hundred years—until Brasília was inaugurated as the new government center in 1960. I further restricted my interviews in the Northeast to urban women, that is, women now living in urban areas. In many cases, the women were born in rural or backland areas and migrated to the city, often as children or adolescents. Precisely this sort of migration has shifted the Brazilian population over the past few decades from a predominantly rural to a predominantly urban setting, and it is women's greater facility in finding work as domestic servants that explains the higher rural migration rates of women in comparison with those of men.[2]

I began my research in a state of relative ignorance and innocence, uncertain about what I would encounter. Perhaps I avoided certain difficulties because I represented no one, had no funding for the project, and went as nothing other than myself with my particular wish to hear what people were willing to tell me. Some of the problems I faced had self-evident solutions: it was clear that in the Brazil of the early 1980s, with the military still in power, I would have to take special care to protect the identity of political activists who had belonged to illegal leftist groups. In fact, although I promised anonymity to all the women, what surprised me was that few of them seemed very worried about this.

Many Brazilians helped me during the summers of 1981 and 1983, both by acting as intermediaries and arranging for me to meet a large number of women from various walks of life, and sometimes also by giving up hours of their time to accompany me to places I could not easily have found on my own. One Brazilian acquaintance in Rio, noting that a particular woman she knew was willing to talk to me but would have been less willing had I been Brazilian, disparaged this as yet another facet of "cultural imperialism." But she continued to assist me nonetheless. On another occasion a young man, who had been introduced to me through a mutual friend, met me in the evening at a bus stop and took me to the house of an acquaintance living in a hard-to-reach slum in the Northeastern city of Recife. Hours later, having spent the evening nearby waiting for me to finish the interview, he came back to get me. We walked down steep and narrow paths back to the avenue at the bottom of the hill, where I could catch a bus. When I thanked him, he said, "I don't give a damn about you or your research. I'm helping you because it's important for these people's stories to be told."

And, indeed, this traditional rationale for our appropriation of others' time and words was the viewpoint shared by many of the people who helped me or participated in the project. I explained my aims in simple terms: I wanted to learn about the lives of Brazilian women and put their words into a book so that people in my country, especially women, could read these stories. Of the more than sixty women I approached, only one in effect turned me down. At our initial meeting her distrust and discomfort were so intense that I suggested we forgo the interview. More common was the reaction of Marialice, an illiterate woman whose story appears in this introduction. As we were parting after the first interview, she said, "I'm glad you're doing this. We need to know one another." Cristina (Chapter 20), a major stockholder and one of the directors of a firm she had inherited, told me she had found it useful to talk about herself; it had made her aware of the paths her life had taken. Such comments were not in response to questions of mine about the interview; rather, they seemed to be spontaneous offerings as I was taking my leave.

Many researchers have noted that people often feel flattered and affirmed by an outsider's interest in their lives. The tape recorder, far from being a hindrance, is, from this point of view, a verification of the importance of what is said. One scholar, however, has commented on the fact that it is more difficult to interview "up" than "across" or "down," noting that wealthy people are likely to be less receptive to scholarly interest in their personal lives.[3] Certainly, wealthy or prominent people are often accustomed to constant attention and demands and have a more public persona to protect. As it happens, the only interview I did that was, in my view, of little use was with an influential woman who knew that her identity could not be concealed. She was the wife of a governor of one of the Northeastern states and, like most of the other women, had agreed to the interview when approached by an intermediary. At the governor's mansion, she spent several hours giving me a very official life story that portrayed her as concerned wife, mother, and part-time professional, and her husband as an enlightened politician. And yet, as she showed me about the grounds before my departure, this woman looked me in the eye and said, "Forgive me for not being able to tell you everything." Such a response, I believe, hints at a key element that made this project possible: a recognition by most of the women I interviewed of some sort of bond with other women, the potential readers of their stories, despite differences in race, class, nationality, and much else.

If my own agenda clearly derived from my interest in learning about women's lives in contemporary Brazil, the women themselves had other, quite different concerns. To Teresa (Chapter 8), a washerwoman who lived in a slum in Recife, the interview perhaps represented a momentary escape from the usual confines of her life, a link with the larger world, a symbolic rise in status. For after our talk (which was clearly difficult for her), as we walked down the hill we passed a neighbor leaning out of her window. As soon as we were out of earshot, Teresa told me that she had asked this woman if she, too, wanted to be interviewed, and the woman had refused. Smiling complicitously, Teresa commented: "gente sem cultura!"—people with no breeding. Dorotéia (Chapter 7) possibly wanted to impress upon me that she was not so narrow-minded or old-fashioned as she could guess her daughters, Norma and Glícia (Chapters 5 and 6), had made her out to be. Such concerns invariably influence an individual's account of her life and her self. The range of reasons for agreeing to an interview is enormous, but not least among them, in my experience, is that not much of this intense sort of listening seems to go on in daily life, so that the opportunity to talk at length about one's own life, and to have one's story recorded, becomes something of value.

"Official" histories of Brazil during this period are likely to present a very different version of reality from that which emerges in the following chapters. The dictatorship, for example, was not a significant event in the stories of most of the working-class women I spoke with; the prospect of redemocratization, a prominent theme among educated women, was simply not a common concern for women at the subsistence level. The economic crisis, however, and its translation into a struggle in each individual household, was a major theme raised by virtually everyone I interviewed. In fact, I was struck by the spirited responses and resourcefulness of most of the women as they confronted their situations. But, though I aimed at breadth and variety in selecting individuals to interview, and in selecting from among the complete transcripts the twenty stories that make up this book, it has to be recognized that the interview process itself may encourage the telling of dramatic tales. As a result, despite the compelling nature of many of the stories that follow, I want to warn readers against the easy assumption that the individual stories are "representative." Even though, taken together, they certainly evoke a sense of many aspects of the Brazilian scene, the fact remains that we cannot know those stories which genuinely silent people might disclose.

In the end I conducted about sixty interviews, a few of which lasted merely one hour while others extended over several days. I began the interviews with simple questions: Where were you born? How old are you? What is your religion? Are your parents alive? Usually, as one or another subject elicited her interest, the woman would start to elaborate on an answer without my prompting.

Very quickly a major distinction emerged between those interviews with poor (and usually uneducated) women and those with middle-class or wealthy women. Just as the latter had more, and more lavish, food, shelter, and clothing, so also, in many cases, did they have access to a larger vocabulary and—most important of all—to the time required to elaborate their stories. Typically, the middle-class and wealthy women talked to me at far greater length. It is easy to understand why. Working-class women usually stole moments from a workday over which they had little control (and I, in my very different time world, spent many hours waiting for those spare moments), and they often had to dart off to get back to their tasks. It was more difficult, also, to find a place where we could speak in private and undisturbed. The situation of telling their own stories became another luxury to which poor women had limited access. Marialice's story, part of which I will give below, was gathered in a situation very different from, for example, Cristina's. Cristina, busy as she was, is her own boss, and she made as much time for me as she herself wanted, in the middle of her workday. As she spoke, fluently, eloquently, almost without pause, one of her employees served us coffee. Marialice, thirty years old, born in the Brazilian Northeast to a Black mother and a White father, works as a cleaning woman in a government office. She had less time, less education, fewer words. Yet she, too, was eloquent. It was Marialice who said, describing why she could not be sure of her future with her husband, "A man's heart is a land where no one roams."

Perhaps because I was not trained in the social sciences and had no sense of identity as a "fieldworker," I was startled to discover the legitimizing function of "having a project," of appearing with instruments—tape recorder and pad of paper—that transformed what might have been considered offensive personal curiosity into something respectable. Certain things that I had worried about turned out to be assets: I was a foreigner and would not be sticking around, tempted to let other people on the block know what I had been told; my fluent-but-not-native Portuguese, my occasional groping for words and having to ask for elaboration of simple things, not only led to interesting and unpredictable explanations but seemed to help restore a needed balance between the researcher and the researched, especially in the case of poor and uneducated women. I also found that I was implicitly cast into different roles during these interviews: I became older woman, younger woman, friend, authority figure, peer, White woman, exotic visitor, professional woman, Jewish woman, political ally, childless woman, privileged woman—depending on the particular contrasts and similarities that the person I was interviewing perceived (often in response to her own questions) between herself and me. There is also, in the interview situation, a problem of raised expectations, a hope (rarely, in my experience, a demand) that the interviewer might solve a problem or know what to do. What is implicit here is the usual class distance between researcher and researched, which makes the interviewer appear as (and often be) a powerful person from the perspective of the interviewee. Nor is this a misperception, for considerable class privilege is usually necessary to undertake this type of work. Over time, I came to see that, given the structural inequalities that typically exist between the researcher and the researched, important ethical problems are raised by and about the process of doing oral history or collecting personal testimonies.

We ask of the people we interview the kind of revelation of their inner life that normally occurs in situations of great intimacy and within the private realm. Yet these revelations are to be made within the context of the public sphere—which is where, in an obvious sense, we situate ourselves when we appear with our tape recorders and note pads eager to work on our "projects." The asymmetries are further marked by the different level of disclosure that we expect to elicit in others and that we ourselves may be willing to make. Researchers are almost always less frank than they hope those they interview will be.

Although our informants agree to the interview and frequently seem to derive satisfaction from it, the fact remains that it is *we* who are using *them* for *our* projects. Furthermore, the collecting of personal narratives, when done with professional and publishing goals in mind, is invariably in part an economic matter. One aspect of the difficulty of establishing appropriate practices concerning the use of personal narratives may lie precisely in the odd transformation of usual economic roles that the process brings about. The person telling her or his own story can be construed, conventionally enough, to be in possession of raw material, material without which the entrepreneurial researcher could not perform the labor of producing a text. It is the researcher who owns or has access to the means of production capable of transforming the spoken words into a commodity. While this may not be the main function of oral histories, life history studies, or cultural histories using "native informants," it is certainly one of the functions of such texts.

What muddies this analogy—and this may be one reason why many researchers who use personal narratives in their work have only a narrow or formal sense of the ethical problems involved—is that the researcher plays the role not only of capitalist but also of laborer. This constant shifting of roles prevents us from developing a suitable model for understanding, analyzing, and assigning rights and duties in the personal interview situation. From the viewpoint of the working researcher, the life story appears to be a mere potentiality waiting to be harnessed. And the preparation of a text that utilizes a personal narrative indeed involves acquiring raw material and then transforming it—through the researcher's labor of turning spoken words into written ones, editing, translating if necessary, or studying and interpreting the stories. Whether she or he is construed as capitalist entrepreneur or as laborer, it is the researcher's time and investment that is acknowledged and rewarded.

If, however, we are feminists and/or socialists or otherwise committed to social transformation, we need to treat with utmost seriousness the nature of the implicit values we enact in pursuit of our varied goals. In particular, feminist scholars who profess commitments other than to the "pursuit of knowledge" and immediate professional advancement must seriously consider the problem of reproducing, through our research procedures and limited sense of obligation, the structures of inequality that make other women serve as the subjects of our books. Whenever someone is used as a means to another's ends, the dominant social paradigm is affirmed rather than challenged. As we go about our business, including our "professional" business of interviewing individuals, we too are either affirming the preexisting order of the world or helping to create new worlds. There is always a danger of re-creating the world we are attempting to remake. And it is extremely difficult to confront this challenge, precisely because routine practices are all around us and the tendency to embed our projects within these practices, which pass for ordinary reality, is almost irresistible.

In the case of collecting life histories, our abstract responsibilities in the world—toward, for example, people we do not know personally—become something quite different precisely because of our voluntarily assumed appearance and interference in other people's lives. And the problem is exacerbated, it seems to me, when the "objects" of this research are people of a different socioeconomic level or culture from that of the interviewer. Furthermore, collecting life stories is a fundamentally different business than collecting folktales or even personal narratives focused on particular aspects of one's life (as, say, Studs Terkel does in his books). A woman telling her life story is in a sense offering up her self for her own and her listener's scrutiny. The fact that the speaker *constructs* this self in the act of speaking does not alter the dimension of personal revelation and disclosure. Under these circumstances, how can we claim to be innocent bystanders, having only the minimal obligations expressed largely in negatives: *not* to do harm, *not* to deceive or misrepresent, *not* to coerce participation? Indeed, as far as they go, even these injunctions are far from being transparent. If those whom we interview had equal opportunity to tell their own stories and have them be heard, and felt empowered to do so, our appearance in their lives with our "projects," for which they are to furnish the materials, would be far less likely. We have special obligations to them because we are inviting disclosures and revelations that they may not otherwise be able to make in their own voices. I believe that to view our actions merely as furnishing opportunities for otherwise silenced people (although obviously they do so), is to distort our obligations, which must extend beyond the immediate situation to the structure that allows that situation to be perpetually reproduced. As Calvin Pryluck writes, in a discussion of the ethics of documentary filmmaking, "Ultimately, we are all outsiders in the lives of others. We can take our gear and go home; they have to continue their lives where they are."[4]

I do not, however, want to reduce the complex process of gathering life stories to these difficult ethical problems, for another dimension to the interview process also needs to be stressed: the sheer pleasure of listening to a person weave a tale. Oral history is seductive work, to the listener no less than to the speaker. For me, one of the most intriguing aspects of this project was that it involved a new kind of listening, an exceptionally intense form of concentration and openness, unlike the listening we usually do in everyday life. With the tape recorder doing its work and the rather unstructured type of interview I had decided upon (in order to let the women's own themes, rather than mine, emerge), I became aware of an inescapable quality to many of the interviews, as if they were occurring in a special time and place. Of course, my inexperience also meant that I did not have adequate defenses, or prepared reactions (as they may well be called), and so I would often leave troubled and overwhelmed, but also filled with admiration—for many of the stories were painful to tell and to hear. While it is impossible to convey in print the intensity of the interview situation, I hope I have succeeded in presenting these accounts honorably—without, that is, turning them into the exotica of "other" lives, picturesquely different from "ours."

The act of telling one's life story involves a rationalization of the past as it is projected and leads into an inevitable present. And, indeed, a particular version of one's life story may become an essential component in one's sense of identity at a given time. From the enormous store of memories and possible responses evoked by the interview situation, the person interviewed selects and organizes certain themes, incidents, and recollections, which are then communicated in a particular way. Memory itself is no doubt generated and structured in specific ways by the opportunity to tell one's life story and the circumstances of the situation in which this occurs. At another moment in one's life, or faced with a different interlocutor, quite a different story, with different emphases, is likely to emerge.

If earlier researchers, especially those utilizing oral history in pursuit of a "truth" about a given culture or historical moment, tended to adopt a naive attitude toward the story they gathered, viewing it as a transparency through which they would try to reproduce the reality "behind it," contemporary scholars have moved to correct this overly simple approach. Having become sensitized to the bias that totally disregarded the presence of the interviewer, these scholars rightly recognize that the interview situation involves two people and depends on an interaction.[5] But it is inaccurate to suppose for this reason that the interviewer, rather than the person interviewed, plays the determining role and is in the main "responsible" for the interview. Such a view falls too deeply into the opposing simplification and fails to acknowledge the authority and creativity of the speaker weaving her own text.

Thus, problematic though they are as texts gathered, edited, and translated by a foreigner, I still hold the conviction that these life stories should be seen as the identifiable and unique constructions of the individual women and not as creations of mine. Although I gave essentially the same explanation of my project to each woman I interviewed, I elicited strikingly different narratives. Maria Helena (Chapter 10), for example, to whom I had been sent by her son, spent much of her time complaining that he did not give her enough money. She told me her life story, certainly, heavily laden with the theme of her sacrifices and his ingratitude. It was obvious that she was at least in part speaking to him through me. She was not the sole individual in need of money to whom I was sent in this way, but she was the only one who chose this particular theme and approach in her interaction with me. By contrast, Carolina (Chapter 2), who also knew that I had extensive contact with her relatives and who had even less money than Maria Helena, mentioned finances only in passing. While we need to note and analyze the role of the interviewer in the gathering of the story, we must at the same time credit the autonomy of the speaker as she constructs her account. During the interview, a range of options is available to the speaker, who then selects and elaborates her themes. Marialice, for example, as we shall see, transforms my questions in ways I could not have foreseen. The interviewer's responses—of disapproval or approval, of encouragement or indifference, of more intense listening to some themes than to others—without doubt play a role, but the different stories elicited by the same interviewer depend, in the end, upon the interviewees. To situate the researcher at the center of the universe is a mistake. By doing so we are once again overvaluing our role as individuals "in charge."

For a related reason I have chosen to begin this book without extensive "contextualization"—without, that is, devoting much space to the norms of Brazilian society against which individual stories are to be read. One initiates such a project knowing something, and one finishes it knowing something else. There is no escaping the possibility that our preconceptions overdetermine the interview, although a more open and less directed interviewing style helps reduce their impact. But if one begins with generalizations about a culture, one is likely to find them confirmed by every interview, for each woman will be approached not as a person in her own right but as a manifestation of a culture already posited as a given, and in working over the transcripts the researcher is apt to impose or select for that preconceived meaning. We would certainly not accept such reductionism for ourselves if, priding ourselves on our individuality, we were subjected to it by some outside investigator.

That is why I have opted, instead, for a more speaker-centered approach: I listened to what was said and, by noting repetition, emphasis, and the features selected by—and therefore evidently important to—the speaker, developed a sense of what mattered to her. This then became the basis for my selection and organization from among the dozens and sometimes hundreds of pages of transcripts that resulted from each interview. In addition, I have tried to interfere as little as possible with the stories' own rhythms, and have confined contextual information to the notes. I have, however, introduced each chapter with such information (personal or general) as seemed indispensable or appropriate. The additional material contained in my notes may be of further help to the reader interested in setting individual comments within a broader framework. My principal effort throughout has been to communicate a sense of the women's subjective realities as they emerged in the process of narration. Toward this end readers may find it preferable to read the notes only after they have concluded a chapter. My concern with conveying something of the richness and complexity of subjective experience also explains why I have selected a smaller number of lengthy stories rather than a larger number of brief ones.

T hree conceptual and empirical categories organize experience and perception in Brazil: gender, class, and race. These are far from self-evident categories, and the subtleties of their expressions and interconnections go beyond the scope of this introduction. Gender is, however, the most fundamental distinction illustrated by the life stories that follow: they are by and about women in a patriarchal society. Not surprisingly, given my own position as a woman seeking to learn about other women, gender emerges again and again as a striking theme—a theme articulated in different ways at different levels of Brazilian society. The fruitful ground for a Brazilian women's movement is of course *there*, in the oppression experienced even by those women who do not name it. Indeed, such a movement already existed, in a reformist mode, in the nineteenth century, and it has reemerged after many vicissitudes in a very active feminist mode since 1975 and the United Nations International Women's Year. Yet Brazilian women, like other Latin American women, are in some respects privileged in that, as will become apparent, they have for decades possessed legal rights for which many other women (including those in the United States) must still struggle. In theory. The practice is something else, for exercise of these rights is very much a function of class—and, of course, education, itself closely linked to class.

Class is expressed by the women I interviewed, often unconsciously, as something that explains many features of their lives. It is part of the "natural" background, usually unquestioned but emerging with considerable clarity in their stories. Despite the enormous regional differences that shape women's lives in Brazil, class and its articulation as employment opportunity, income level, and cultural crucible, is a far more important element. Domestic servants in the Northeast, for example, have more in common with domestics in Rio de Janeiro than either do with their own mistresses.

But the third category, race, is perhaps the most difficult to come to terms with, given the Brazilian reality. Hundreds of racial terms exist in Brazil and it is virtually impossible to translate these into English, for they represent a racial coding specific to Brazilian culture and ambiguous even within that culture.[6]

As a White woman interviewing women of many skin tones, physical types, and economic situations, I was constantly reminded that while gender linked me to these women, class and race in many cases separated us. White women, recognizing me as another White woman, may have felt no particular need to discuss race; or it may have been invisible to them, as part of the very landscape of their lives as Brazilians. Women who are Black and Brown (official designations of color on the Brazilian census), on the other hand, may have been shy or wary of discussing this level of their experience with a White foreigner. Certainly very few women of color brought up the subject of race (whereas, for example, without my soliciting such revelations, most of the women talked about their unsatisfactory relationships with men and conveyed, even when not stating this explicitly, a sense of the constraints that patriarchal society imposed upon them). Yet race is a basic issue in Brazil, clearly intersecting with class in that Blacks typically are in a worse economic situation than Whites, and intersecting further with gender in that Black women suffer double discrimination (see Chapter 3). I have therefore identified the racial background of most of the women interviewed as part of the description that begins each chapter.

To clarify the matter further, I want to transcribe at this point part of a conversation I had with two sisters born to the same mother and father in a racially mixed Rio de Janeiro family. These women, Alma and Júlia, are highly educated feminists who had recently (when both were in their early thirties) moved out of their parents' apartment into a flat of their own. Alma, the older sister, is completely White in appearance; Júlia's physical type reflects the family's Black antecedents.

ALMA: Here in Brazil there's a very strong prejudice about physical traits, but it's not so much a matter of skin color, or only if you've got really black skin. But if you're *morena*, if you've got brownish skin, delicate features, and straight hair, you're considered to be within the norm, White, which is somewhat different from what goes on in the United States. Here there's this special characteristic—if you have light brown skin and delicate features, a thin nose and lips, you're not discriminated against or labeled as a Negro, no, you're not. Now if your skin is about the color of Júlia's, or even a bit darker, but you've got a flat nose, thick lips, and kinky hair, you're ridiculed.

JÚLIA: I have a thin nose, but I'm not seen as White.

ALMA: Júlia's physical type is called *sarará*. I'm not sure about the origin of the word but it's a pejorative term—brownish skin, kinky hair, possibly light eyes. But the hair is labeled "bad"—frizzy, coarse hair. There's a strong prejudice against that. Not so much the color of the skin, just certain Negro characteristics, above all the hair.

JÚLIA: Also the skin. And they identify people's smell by their color. For example, they say, "You stink. You've got an underarm odor just like a Negro." To this day people say this, seriously.

ALMA: The idea is that White people don't have that smell, only Blacks. Whites smell "good," of soap.

JÚLIA: And prejudice also turns up in everyday life. For example, Blacks don't just have a mouth, lips, they have *beiçola*—thick lips, which comes from *beiço*, the word used for an animal's lips. Blacks don't have a nose, they've got a *fornalha*, a furnace, which is wide open, not a thin nose, not pointed, but flat and with wide nostrils. It's the Negro race that has these characteristics, so these traits are turned into pejoratives—*fornalha* and *beiçola*.

ALMA: The hierarchy's like this: hair, nose, and mouth—these are the three major things—and skin color afterward. I've always noticed this about Brazil, I think it's a result of miscegenation, specific to this country. What has left the deepest mark in terms of negative views of Blacks, in practical terms, is really this business of the mouth, the thick lips, the flat nose, the kinky hair. If Júlia didn't have kinky hair, if it were straight, she'd never be identified as having Negro ancestry, right Júlia? No, because she's *morena*. In our household we have a living example of this situation, of how it marks people. For example: we live together, but at first people never believe we're sisters. Despite all the miscegenation in this country, people don't openly admit it. We've learned how to deal with it, and we have to, to this day. When I'm with her, "You're her sister!?" This happens all the time. "Yes, I am." Sometimes we explain; we say, "It's because there's a lot of miscegenation in our family." It's even worse when I'm with Augusto—it's very hard to get people to believe I'm his cousin, people think it's not possible. Augusto is a real mulatto. He looks just like my aunt, the oldest one. She's the blackest of my mother's sisters. It's something biological, which I don't know how to explain, but as the children were born their skin got lighter. So my oldest aunt is the darkest, and they got lighter and lighter until the last one, who's a blonde with hair straighter than mine and blue eyes. Augusto has typically Black features. He's the type that's rejected in our culture, and in fact my own family was upset when I started dating him. They pretended it was because he was my cousin, but that wasn't it, that's common enough here. His mother, my aunt, married a mulatto, but a mulatto with wavy hair, somewhat coarse but not very. Just look at the prejudice in my own family. They're very racist. They have Negro blood, but they're racist; they discriminate against their own brothers and sisters. For example, my great-aunt, my grandmother's sister, is Black, and she used to say that Augusto's mother had a "dirty womb," because all her children were mulatto or Black. This made a very strong impression on me and really confused me, because ever since I was a child I've always had totally White characteristics. When I was a baby I had blondish hair, not quite blonde but very light, with ringlets. This situation has left its mark on me to this day. It was difficult because my grandmother lived with us, my grandmother who was Black. So this whole business was very hard for my head. I had White features. When I was apart from my family, in school, people could never figure out how that woman could be my mother and that one my grandmother.

JÚLIA: But I, I was always considered more Black.

ALMA: Because Júlia had other features, whereas I took after my father's side.

JÚLIA: And I after my mother's.

ALMA: My hair's a bit wavier, but I have a face just like my Italian grandmother, all her features.

JÚLIA: Alma doesn't look much like a member of our family. It created problems between us, because I was considered the little Blackie and she was White. Like I was found in a garbage can.

ALMA: It's a very serious business, but it's difficult to restructure all this in my head, this problem of acknowledging the two sides. It's something we're going to have to face our whole lives.

JÚLIA: I always identified a lot with my mother, since I look more like her, but I wasn't always sure I was her daughter. They used to joke that I was found in a garbage can, because I was dark, I was small. Imagine the competition between the two of us! I used to think she was the legitimate daughter and I wasn't.

ALMA: It was a kind of stupid game we played when we were kids, because even the way we were spoken to, the pet names were already discriminatory. I was *branquinha*, the little White girl, and Júlia was *pretinha*, the little Black girl. My father had this habit of calling me "my *branquinha*" and Júlia "my *pretinha*."

JÚLIA: The level of competition between us was enormous.

ALMA: There were other dividing lines between us, too, which have stopped now. I was the White one, I was intelligent, I was well-behaved, the intellectual of the family. I was the good one. And she was the trouble-maker, mischievous, full of pranks. She was the naughty, rebellious kid, while I was the typical goody-goody. Throughout our whole life it was like that.

JÚLIA: I wouldn't stay home, I wouldn't play with dolls. We were opposites. I was always out in the street playing with the boys. You can still see the marks on my knees from all that playing out of doors. I played ball, I was the opposite of the feminine role. It was even a form of competition between us, the two sides of the world and of our house, she and I. I was the little Black kid who just about lives in the street, who's messy. . . . No, I don't know if it was on purpose, it's something we have to think about more. She was first in class, and I was last. Maybe I did it on purpose, but it doesn't feel like I did. Maybe it was an unconscious mechanism for challeng-ing her, but I can't say I was aware of that when I was little. I just didn't like to sit still, and to this day I can't. I lead a life that doesn't keep me at home much. The house is a kind of reference point, but I've never been able to spend much time just concentrating on the house.

ALMA: There's another distinction, going back to the business of racial mixing. Compared with, say, the United States or South Africa—especially compared with South Africa, which is a disgrace—there's an image here, an idealized image of this country as an ideal experiment in heavy miscegenation. That's widely peddled to this day. But those of us who live within this culture know that deep traces of discrimination exist, diffused in this culture. They're very prevalent, you see, in attitudes toward women, in relations between people. It's a very serious thing that people try to conceal. They even say, "In Brazil there's no color prejudice, there's just social [class] prejudice."[7] And they mention Pelé. Nobody discriminates against Pelé because he has money, so he's not discriminated against. But that's not the point, because in fact Blacks have got to prove, above all, that they're more intelligent, richer, more competent—so that afterward they can be accepted. This in itself shows that there really is color prejudice.

JÚLIA: Of course there's prejudice. Discrimination exists, not only of race but of sex, too. As far as racism is concerned, the most serious problem where you can see this reproduced is in the indifference of Brazilian society. Why are so many Blacks in the slums? Why is the number of Blacks much higher among the illiterate population? Why is it that important positions, even within the state, the government, aren't held by Blacks? In other words, there's a funneling, a crushing. They can't just come and ask for equality. It's a tremendous struggle.

This conversation illustrates something important about how racial division is experienced in Brazil by two women from the same household—specifically, its profound impact on those separated by it. The reader, of course, is likely to take these words as "information," and as such they can be disputed; Alma's and Júlia's experiences and views may be dismissed as idiosyncratic or biased. Although considerable evidence supports their representation of racial attitudes in Brazil, there is no unanimity. Lúcia (Chapter 19), for example, who has very dark skin and Negroid features, was adamant that she had never experienced racial discrimination. Such conflicting views remind us that life stories present us not with "reality" but, rather, with its verbal evocation by a particular individual in a specific situation. Something further must therefore be said about the process of gathering a life story and presenting a version of it in print.

There is a distance separating the spoken word from the written word that is insurmountable. The women I interviewed did not, of course, speak in neatly punctuated paragraphs, often not even in complete sentences. I have supplied these conventions in order to facilitate comprehension of their stories. To this inevitable distortion has been added, in my work, the problem of conveying in English what was spoken in Brazilian Portuguese; moreover, in a Portuguese having different regional and class characteristics. Early in this project I decided against catering to the sense of exoticism and class distance conveyed to the typical reader when speech is presented in "dialect," that is, as perceived deviation from a norm.[8] This is why I have opted for standard English while attempting to retain some sense of the individual woman's rhythms and ways of expressing herself.

Although I was intensely interested in the impact of gender, class, and race, I did not conduct the interviews armed with a protocol. My impression is that I was sensitive (perhaps too much so) to the mood of the encounter and to the particular way an individual engaged with me. Thus, for example, although I tried to collect a sexual and reproductive history, I did not invariably bring up the subject of abortion. Especially in the transcripts of women who had guided the interview and elaborated their own themes, I frequently omitted from the final stories comments that seemed to be reflections of my own intrusive questions rather than of the women's own concerns. Lúcia, for example, did give me an "opinion" on abortion and on racial prejudice, because I raised these issues, but in reviewing her story these seemed to stand out as comments not integral to her account and I therefore eliminated them. Space—always a consideration in preparing a manuscript—also influenced me in such decisions.

My own role in the interviews varied considerably. Some women (Sister Denise and Vera, for example) tended to take charge of the interview; others (Teresa and Alice) were reticent. For ease of reading and in an attempt to reproduce some of the intensity of the listening process, I have not included my questions and interruptions, but have usually retained clear traces of them. In each story I have done a certain amount of editing, rearranging, and altering of details, including names, in order to protect the identity of these individuals. Pauses in speech are signaled by three dots (. . .), which are often important indicators of changes in direction, self-interruptions for reflection or correction, or other features of speech.

The twenty chapters in this book are distributed among six parts. Part One, "Commitments," comprises the life stories of four women, each of whom in her own way emphasized a deep commitment as she spoke with me. Part Two, "Family Portrait," presents the stories of two sisters, sufficiently separated in age to constitute two generations, and their mother. Part Three, " 'Women's Work,' " focuses on six women, most of them poor, whose lives are characterized by daily routines and occupations of a traditional and typically female kind. In Part Four, "Revolutionaries," my particular interest in political activists' responses to the dictatorship emerges as two women are heard who participated in clandestine leftist groups. Part Five, "Good Girls," brings together two stories by young people who reflect in commonplace yet fascinating ways the absorption of many elements of a conventional gender ideology. This is as fully present in the budding self-awareness of Alice, a twelve-year-old schoolgirl, as it is in the aims and aspirations of Branca, a nineteen-year-old prostitute. Finally, Part Six, "Entrepreneurs," presents three wealthy women who are owners of their own businesses. The two White women in this section inherited their enterprises and property, while Lúcia, a Black woman, built hers from scratch.

These six divisions are intended as structuring devices only, not as self-contained compartments. Life stories often range across many themes and moods and therefore do not fit comfortably into narrow categories. Indeed, no perfect way exists either to gather or to present life stories, and the ease with which criticisms can be made on methodological grounds should be self-evident.[9] Much of the discomfort of both writers and critics of oral history seems to me to be the product of a commitment to "objectivity," an objectivity challenged and threatened by the complexities of the interview situation and the subsequent transformation of spoken words into written texts. This is a messy business—not designed to please scholars preoccupied with neatness.

M y work with Brazilian women did not begin as a literary project, nor is it intended to end as one. But the literariness of the narratives struck me soon enough. The problems I faced with the transcripts resembled in some respects those I have encountered translating fiction: how to retain the meaning, tone, style, and flavor of the original. However, I also did some things one would rarely do in translating a text already marked as "literary," that is, cutting, reorganizing, and shaping the material I had gathered. Although I did not realize it at the time, this was because I had assumed that the final written version would be a prose narrative whose primary function it was to convey information. In making this assumption, I was following the standard practices of anthropologists, sociologists, and historians who work with life histories. While using slightly varying terminology, they all agree that the merits of the life history as a document are primarily those of immediacy and vividness: it lets us see, or in effect hear, for ourselves. As the anthropologist Dennis Tedlock has observed, oral narratives usually *evoke* rather than *describe* emotions;[10] and they often evoke rather than describe the cultural context within which the speakers' lives are lived. One of the most fascinating aspects of this kind of research is the frequency with which scholars utilizing oral accounts talk about fiction. What they typically say is that the life history resembles a work of fiction in its depth and appeal to the imagination.

Certainly there is an obvious sense in which the telling of one's life story resembles the creation of a literary work. Although the medium in the chapters that follow was originally spoken rather than written language (and in some cases the speakers were illiterate), the stories often reveal a concern for structure and for the satisfaction of unexpressed formal demands. Some of the distortions of this type of text follow from the effort to meet such demands. It seemed to me, for example, that the speakers typically were striving to give a coherence, a unity, to their stories. They therefore tended to present them teleologically. This is not the way a life is usually lived, but it is the way we usually make sense of our lives. And it is, indeed, the way literary texts are frequently constructed. The very act of telling one's life story seems to invite structure—one rethinks the events of one's life so that they make sense. Thus, in the telling, a subject, in many respects constant over time, is created. Many of the women commented to me on this: they discovered patterns in their lives that they had not discerned until they found themselves telling their stories. It is obvious that this imposition of a structure raises problems for the interpretation of these texts—the first of which is "the truth" of the accounts. While I cannot address this issue with any certainty, I am satisfied that the women who talked to me were telling me a truth, which reveals what was important *for them*. This does not, of course, exclude the possibility of intentional misrepresentation, self-censorship, or unintentional replication of a given society's myths and cherished beliefs about the world, itself, or the roles that distinctive individuals or groups play.

A more important conclusion, however, can be arrived at from the recognition of these stories' "literariness": the purely conventional nature of our usual definition of the "literary." If we include oral accounts as literature (as in epic poetry and myths), if we admit that literature has not only the clear form of a beginning, middle, and end prescribed by traditional stories, but also the patterns, fragmentations, and confusions of modernist writings—then these life stories, too, are literature. If we reject the notion (as I think we must) that literature is verbal art created purely for its own sake, and ask instead how texts signify, then again it is clear that these texts, too, are literature. But most of all, we need to challenge the assumption that literary value automatically resides in "high" cultural texts and that other examples of verbal creativity are not contenders for the much-desired label of "literature."

In fact, though, little work has been done on life histories as verbal constructs.[11] Instead, scholars tend to treat such stories as tools, and what they aim for is usually to see through the story to a reality presumed to lie beyond or behind it. Most readers will, I expect, approach my book from precisely this perspective. I therefore want to devote some space here to suggesting an alternative view of the life stories that, adhering to convention, I have rendered as prose narratives in the chapters that follow.

In the early 1970s, Dennis Tedlock wrote compellingly of the distortion that occurs when the oral narratives we assume to be stories are transcribed as prose. Prose does not exist outside the written page, Tedlock argued, and cannot adequately render living speech because "there is no SILENCE in it." Tedlock wanted to convey not only the silences of oral narration but also its poetic and dramatic features, and he argued that spoken narratives are better understood as "dramatic poetry." Toward this end he developed some techniques for representing, in print, the nonverbal and paralinguistic features of oral narratives. But his most striking suggestion, for the purposes of oral history or life history studies, is that narratives be transcribed, following the pauses and inflections in the speaker's speech, in the form of free verse. He has even transcribed one of his own lectures using this device, to very interesting effect.[12] It is possible that the success of such transcription depends upon the particular narrative; but Tedlock's ideas have been of great value, allowing me to see precisely how much was lost by my need to turn lengthy transcripts into coherent prose narratives.

This is a long-winded way of saying what a few writers have always known: the designation of "literature" and the presentation of a text as "poetic" or "literary" have profound effects on the reader's experience of the text. A simple example can illustrate this point. Decades ago the Brazilian poet Manuel Bandeira (1886–1968) wrote "Poem Taken From a Newspaper Item":

Sweet Johnny was a porter in the open market and lived in a numberless shack on Babylon Hill
One night he went into Twentieth of November Bar
He drank
He sang
He danced
Then he threw himself into Rodrigo de Freitas lagoon and died drowned.[13]

Because this is a poem, and not a newspaper notice, we *attend* to it. It is not just the broken lines (though this helps) that create the obstacles causing us to devote prolonged attention to the poem.[14] I would argue that it is above all the fact that we approach the poem with the metatext "Poem" already firmly planted in our heads. Our reading is determined not so much by what inheres in the text—in this case easy enough to discern—but rather by the frame with which we approach a given text. The institutional concept of art, as elaborated by George Dickie, teaches us that the label "art" is not granted as a result of the qualities inhering in a given cultural text; rather, the "art object" is in effect created by the institutions and practices that are in a position to bestow the label, in accord with their norms, tastes, and canons.[15] By inviting us to focus on a text that, in the form of a newspaper notice, would never be admitted as verbal "art," Manuel Bandeira calls our attention to this mechanism. And once our attention is focused in this way, we begin to notice features that would not normally be visible. We notice a series of contrasts: the numberless shack in which this nearly nameless Johnny lives, as opposed to the bar that bears a number, a date, for its name; the open market (in Portuguese, *feira-livre*, or free market) where he works, in contrast to his own limited freedom—to work as a porter and live in a slum, in short, a mock-freedom, a distortion of the word "free" which is more aptly and grotesquely assigned to the market than to the man. We notice the ironic appropriateness of the name Babylon for the hillside slum where Johnny lives and the staccato rhythm and parallelisms in the poem's penultimate lines. And by presenting these lines as a "poem," Bandeira, without further comment on his part, conveys to us that this work constitutes an act of protest.

Tedlock has made the poet's point a methodological possibility: ordinary spoken words, like written words, can be arranged so as to call attention to their poetic and expressive dimensions—the very dimensions usually overlooked in our habitual reactions to speech. He further asserts that it is especially important to do so in the case of the spoken word, even when we are not dealing with traditional "folkloric" material.

This, then, is the story of how I came to retranscribe one of my tapes as verse, in a very simple form, by reproducing the pauses and inflections of Marialice's speech. Once I had done this, the taped interview ceased to have the simplicity of a transparent object, merely letting us look through it into the speaker's world, and began instead to take on a certain density and appear as what in fact it is: a verbal construction, a structured narration. The contradictions, the pauses, the false starts, the groping, the repetition of the same words and events—all those features which the prose version of a tape would tend to smooth over and falsify—now appear as part of the speaker's performance. Instead of merely learning the "facts" of this woman's life, we can now proceed with a very different task: that of trying to comprehend how a person verbally constructs an image of her life; how she creates a character for herself; how she becomes the protagonist of her own story. What we see, finally, is that we are in the presence of someone creatively using that specifically human instrument: language.

Marialice's talk, as the segments below indicate, moves lightly from one subject to another, weaving a connection that is palpable but that she rarely spells out. Her efforts to explain rely almost entirely on the word "because." More often than not, the final words of one sentence create the link to the next phrase. Notice how much ground she covers as she speaks. I asked, "Would you have married a White man?" She answered:

> It's all the same to me
> to me it's all the same
> White or Black

to me everything is important
I wanted him to bring me peace and comfort
that's what I think is important
what I always ask God for
we're a poor family
and we didn't have a good upbringing
because my mother wasn't in any shape to take care of us
to educate us
it wasn't possible
for any of us to get any training
to be something in life
a few of them
at home
were interested in signing their names
and learning a few things
and my husband too
he finished primary school
he began to teach me at home
and then he paid for a course
when I was grown up
he paid so I could study
and I went for a year
I finished one year
and then I didn't have the strength
the means to study
because I was suffering in my life
and I was suffering for my mother
because my mother
without my father
didn't have anyone to give her food
and I think that my mother
at fifty-six
isn't a woman who can do heavy work any more
my mother
I shed many a tear for her
my mother
she's everything in life
really
she's God
she's my mother

for me she's the most important person
like I told you
I married
I love my husband a lot
but I wouldn't trade my mother for any man
I couldn't spend the rest of my life with her
because if my fate was to marry
I had to marry
and if it was to be an old maid
I would have stayed one
but always taking care of her
I still help her
that's why I'm happy
because I can help my mother.

I said, "Is that what you think?" Marialice replied:

I think I'm happy
she's the most important person in my life
because she suffered for me
and I have to suffer for her
she had six sons and five daughters
I don't mean . . .
I mean . . .
she loves all her children
but she talks a lot about me
that I'm the one she likes best
because I'm the daughter who understands things
and tries to help
if she says
"Give me that blouse you're wearing"
'Yes, Mother, do you think it's pretty, Senhora?[16]
Take it, Senhora"
"No, my child, you mustn't do that"
I say "Take it, God will give me another"
and so every word I say
every thing I give to her
I think God is helping me
helping me to help.

In her answer to my initial question, "Would you have married a White man?" Marialice disregards the apparent meaning of my question and instead discusses marriage in terms of what is most significant to her about it: how it affects her relationship to her mother. When I asked Marialice if she went to church, she gave this long reply:

No
because I don't have time
I have little time
sometimes I go . . .
sometimes I go
because before I moved
I lived across from the church
and then I used to go to Mass almost every night
because it was right across from my house
but after I moved
it got too far
I can't get there
I get so tired
also I've been sick
I'm not well
I'm still in treatment
I had exhaustion, fatigue
I thought . . .
I'd gotten pregnant
but it wasn't pregnancy
it was a lump
a swelling
something I don't understand
you see?
you see?
the first child . . .
I was expecting my first child
and then it wasn't a child
and then I began to get treatment
I went to the medical service
and then there was a doctor
who didn't . . .
one declared it was a child
and the other declared it was sickness

he said I had some problems . . .
cancer in the head
but I didn't
and then I went . . .
that day I spoke . . .
I was very ashamed and bashful about speaking to Seu Jorge [her boss]
but I went
very nervous
my belly growing
preparing the baby's things
and still no baby
I could already feel it move
my legs were in agony
and then
I talked it over with a lady . . .
a poor person
because I didn't even understand
how a person has a baby
she went and explained to me
how did I feel?
to have a baby
and so on
how did it move?
I explained
I said
"It moves
I'm nauseated
I have cramps in my legs and everything"
and so I told her
and she said
"But it's not exactly like that"
she said it was vomiting . . .
she said it was other things
I said "But I feel it moving
and there are nights I can't even sleep
what with so much thudding in my belly" . . .
and so
when the ninth month was ending
in February of last year
one year ago this February

I got nervous
for the doctor couldn't figure out what it was
I went to various doctors
the doctor wasn't interested
you see?
I went to Seu Jorge
who has a son who's a doctor
and so I said "Seu Jorge
I wanted . . .
to tell you about a problem I'm having
I wanted to tell you"
and so I went and told it to Seu Jorge
"Seu Jorge I'm feeling bad . . .
something's moving in my belly
the doctors
one insists it's a baby
the other insists it isn't
they sent me to have my head X-rayed
and they told me it was cancer
in the head
I got very upset
but it wasn't cancer
I don't feel anything in my head
it's fine
what I feel is this motion in my belly
and pains in my legs"
and then he spoke
he said "I'll take you to see my son
tomorrow you come all prepared to go to my son"
and then I went to his son
I went there all shy too
and then he said
"Don't be ashamed to tell him
not to my son"
and then I spoke to his son
and he told me to lie down on the examining table
he examined me
internal and external exams
and then he said
"Look it's not a baby

no
it's not anything important . . .
it's a problem all women have when they want a child and can't have
one" . . .
also
all that time
I'd been taking contraceptive pills
I don't know if it was the pills
I explained everything to him
and he said
"It's not a baby
you understand?
but it's nothing to worry about
not at all" . . .
and I was thinking it was a baby . . .
because I had milk in my breasts
you see?
and the doctor was also kind of . . .
how is it possible?
and then I spoke with the woman
a lady
mother of six children
and she said no
after one month two months
I began to have milk in my breasts real milk
and it wasn't . . .
and then I spoke to Seu Jorge's son
he treated me
and then I went back recently
and I had a problem with inflammation
and so I said
"Dr. João Henrique
is it possible for me to have a child?"
he said "Yes"
and so I'm in treatment
the only thing I want is to have a child
if I don't have one
that's the fate that God has given me
not to have children
if . . .
I have this treatment . . .

and no baby
then that's fate
God doesn't want me to have a child
then I won't think about it any more
I won't even want to see those things
I won't even want to see a baby
or a picture . . .
those things . . .
it's enough to make you crazy
I pray to God a lot to have a baby
but if God doesn't want to give me one
there's nothing I can do
is there?
it's fate isn't it?
that's what I think [*and she stopped talking*].

Transcribing Marialice's story as literally as possible, without the editing and streamlining usually believed to be necessary because of our expectations of a prose text, allows me to retain the structure of her account and to see the way in which she establishes links that lead her far from my original questions. She begins and ends with the present tense. As she explains her answer to my question about going to church, she is drawn into a description of her health and in that context tells me about her false pregnancy. She tells me about her contact with the official medical service (to which she has access as a registered employee of an office-cleaning outfit) and the unsatisfactory treatment she got there. Marialice then introduces another character, Seu [Senhor] Jorge, her boss, to whom she eventually spoke about her problem. But she does not at this point describe her talk with him. Using a two-steps-forward, one-step-back narrative strategy—a foreshadowing and delaying tactic—Marialice backtracks to tell me about talking to another woman. Details that she mentioned as part of a description of her condition now reappear as direct dialogue with this woman. Then she returns to the subject of Seu Jorge, and this time elaborates on her meeting with him. She now makes explicit what was only implicit earlier—the contrast between the official world and its medical service and the familiar (paternalistic) world, in this case her reliance on her boss, whose son is a physician. In telling me what she said to Seu Jorge, Marialice repeats most of the information, again as direct discourse, that she had earlier elaborated. When she comes to the diagnosis and explanation offered by Seu Jorge's son, she adds another explanation for her mistaken belief that she was pregnant: she even had milk in her breasts. And, as if to authenticate this, she again brings in the woman to whom she had spoken concerning her pregnancy.

Then she returns to Seu Jorge's son and his verdict: that she could have a child. But she concludes her story with reflections on her situation, governed by fate (God's will), and plans her reactions to this possible fate.

Marialice uses storytelling devices found in oral cultures to indicate continuity within her story. She repeatedly begins a phrase with *aí*—and then, and so. But often what follows is an event that occurred earlier in the past, without her having signaled this clearly. She does not construct her story in perfect linear chronology. She does not introduce an earlier episode with "before that" or "earlier," nor does she use the past perfect, just the usual *aí*, and then she proceeds, leaving it to me to piece together. If we were reading this and assuming sophistication on the part of the narrator, we would note the way such narration demands our more active participation in reconstructing the relations between the parts of the story. But we expect an "ordinary" speaker to make sense, and we tend to be intolerant when she or he does not. This means we expect a speaker to make *our* kind of sense. We are prepared to work hard to decipher high-cultural texts— often we admire them more the more they make us work (which surely reveals something about the kind of moral imperatives hidden in much twentieth-century literary criticism)—yet we will cry out in impatience when an "ordinary speaker," a person such as Marialice, requires the same of us.

And yet, Marialice *is* making sense. What does it mean that she was taking contraceptive pills while so eager to have a child? She did not explain it to me in terms of cause and effect, but at a later point she told me she was taking the pills because she knew she could not afford to have a baby. She was already helping support the nine people in her mother's household. Thus, torn between her desire for a child and her sense of responsibility, she took the pill and imagined she was pregnant.

When we hear Marialice's words in their full version, instead of condensed and shaped to approximate some misguided model of prose narrative, certain features stand out that we might not otherwise notice. Walter J. Ong has argued that literate people speak literately, according to patterns learned from writing. My interviews with educated women bear out his observation. But Marialice, living on the margins of a literate society, had almost no schooling and that only as an adult. She reveals a very different speaking style, one that contains many of the features Ong attributes to oral cultures.[17] Her speech is, for example, additive rather than subordinative (she frequently says "and," "and then," or "and so," while avoiding subordinate clauses); it is aggregative rather than analytical (elements are clustered together, and many parallel clauses and terms appear); it is redundant or copious. Redundancy, Ong explains, keeps the speaker and hearer on track and moving ahead slowly, unlike our acts of reading, which are much more linear because we can refer back to preceding passages if we should lose our place. Marialice's speech is also "conservative" or "traditionalist," to use Ong's terms, in that she repeats what has been learned and valued over the ages. Throughout our talks Marialice frequently referred to the way her mother brought her up and to the values of the poor.

Oral cultures, Ong writes, are close to the human lifeworld. Events tend to be placed in the context of human relations. And, linked to this, oral cultures are empathetic and participatory rather than objectively distanced; they are situational rather than abstract.[18] Marialice shows precisely this characteristic in her answer to my question, "How do you imagine God? Can you describe God to me?"

> I feel very happy
> because whatever I ask him
> "Dear God, let me make my life better"
> that's what I got into my head
> I got into my head that I think we have to have some comfort
> because God made us that way
> my image of him . . .
> that's what it is
> that all the words I say
> "Dear God, let me have something" . . .
> today everything is easier for me
> nothing is difficult
> I'm very close to him
> and I always manage things when I ask God
> "Dear God, let me have something today" . . .
> and so I have this impression
> that he arranges to help me
> and whoever has lots of faith in him
> and talks to him.

Marialice here replies in terms of a relation and a situation, not in terms of either description or abstraction.

Another feature of oral cultures, Ong states, is that self-evaluation modulates into group evaluation. This is apparent in Marialice's frequent use of the expression *em ordem de pobre*—"in the order of the poor," that is, among the poor—a phrase she always uses in a positive sense, to situate her behavior within that of a group she sees as possessing special qualities and valuable ways of doing things and defining itself. For example, in describing her quarrels with her husband, Marialice said, "Among the poor, we don't have those high styles of fighting."

A prose rendition of Marialice's words, with the objective of presenting merely the content of her speech, is likely to require eliminating much that could be construed as repetitive or even boring. But it is precisely the repetitiveness, the reworking again and again of themes and phrases, that, when accepted and accorded the respect we generally bring to a "literary" text, provides us with important clues to the meaning of her account. Thematic repetition occurs primarily on the following subjects: Marialice's devotion to her mother; her desire for a child; her relationship with God; and, of equal importance in all my talks with her, her sense of responsibility, her goodness and willingness to work hard and—following from these—the fact that, as she puts it, "everybody likes me."

As examples of these last major themes in Marialice's construction of her life story, consider her description of how she started doing housework. While still a child, she had worked in the fields in the backlands where her family lived. Her father had abandoned the family, eleven children and his wife, when Marialice was an adolescent. Then, at age fifteen, she moved to the city and, through the help of a friend, found work as a maid. As she said: "I went to work in other people's houses, earning my living in other people's kitchens."

> I didn't like to see my family doing without
> I offered to work in any house
> I'd go saying
> "Do you want me to sweep this porch?
> Do you want me to wash the dishes?"
> wherever I'd be
> whatever corner I'd get into
> and so everybody got to like me
> and got to know I had the courage to work
> because when people come to a poor person's house
> when someone comes who's got a better deal than me
> they come
> and they spend their life looking
> just watching
> not interested in doing anything
> but if you want to get anywhere in life
> you have to take an interest
> volunteer
> make a deal
> dry the dishes
> go to another house
> sweep the house

you see how it is?
so I would volunteer
and people got to like me
and supported me
and then everybody tried to help me.

When I first met Marialice, she was also doing extra work on weekends, cleaning house for people from the office where she was employed full-time. This was the only way she managed to earn enough money to buy things for her mother, including food that she used to send by bus from the city, where it cost less, to the rural area where her mother still lived with nine other people, most of them unemployed. In 1981, when I interviewed Marialice for the first time, she was making the equivalent of U.S. $67 per month, that is, "one minimum salary" according to the Brazilian mode of calculation. By 1983, when I talked to her again, she was still making only one minimum salary per month, but the dollar equivalent came to a mere $45 per month, a result of Brazil's spiraling inflation and consecutive devaluations of the cruzeiro. Thus, Marialice was in greater need than ever of weekend jobs, for which she got $3 or $4 or $5—whatever people were willing to give her, she said—otherwise she would not have had any money to buy things for her mother. To put these dollar figures in some perspective, consider the following details. At the time that Marialice's wages were $67 a month, she lived in a rented room that cost $15 a month; a kilo of beans cost $1 in her part of the Northeast, a kilo of beef $2; a small container of yogurt cost 40 cents, and two oranges cost 10 cents. By 1983, the situation had worsened considerably, with salaries falling ever further behind the rise in prices and the devaluation of the currency (which, in a major overhaul, was renamed the cruzado in 1986).[19] But Marialice did not mind working for people from her office in their homes, she said, so long as they treated her right:

Because the only thing I want
is for people to treat me right
if they're mean to me
I'll tell them off too
but if the woman treats me right
then she can count on me
I'd even give my life
I don't mind working Saturdays and Sundays
I just want people to treat me right
so if they have something to say to me
they should call me aside and say it

they shouldn't scold me in front of everybody
because I feel bad about these things
that's the way my mother brought us up.

As all these examples show, a woman telling me her own story is not a passive or neutral transmitter but, quite the contrary, an agent actively and creatively shaping and constructing her narrative. Marialice's account, like other autobiographies, moves back in time as well as forward in the narration. In addition, Marialice specifically projects herself into the future, imagining future events and planning her reactions to them, so that we see her life as stretched along a continuum held together by her act of narration. Her memory is creative in that she discovers the patterns into which fall the events she selects for narration; by means of such ordering, she creates the significance of those events. Marialice creates a past that leads to her present self. Am I here saying that what she—and the other women in this book—told me is not "true"? Not at all, but out of the innumerable scenes, moments, words, images, and sensations of her life thus far, she focuses on those which allow a "self" to emerge that is congruent with her intent. The events she relates are not isolated occurrences but are part of a pattern expressing the very idea of a self, a reference point that unifies recollections in the act of selecting and presenting them in narration. Scattered events thus turn into a significant whole through the act of narration. Agnes Hankiss refers to this process in her article "Ontologies of the Self: On the Mythological Rearranging of One's Life-History." Narrating a life history endows certain episodes with a symbolic meaning that in effect turns them into myths; and this is a never-ending process, for an adult must constantly select new models or strategies of life. The transposition of reality into mythology plays an instrumental role in the symbiotic relationship between the old and the new.[20] A similar idea has been expressed in rather different language by Maria Lugones and Elizabeth Spelman: "Having the opportunity to talk about one's life, to give an account of it, to interpret it, is integral to leading that life rather than being led through it."[21]

Although Marialice does not comment on her own process of selection and construction, she is certainly aware of some of her acts of omission, as becomes clear when, at subsequent meetings, she tells me bits and pieces that belonged to her earlier narrative but that she apparently feared would make me see her in a negative light. Once she feels she can count on my understanding, she re-members these pieces and allows me to see how they, too, fit into her creative construction of her self.

Clifford Geertz, in his article " 'From the Native's Point of View': On the Nature of Anthropological Understanding," suggests that to see things from "the native's point of view" (a term he appropriately sets in quotation marks), one does not need psychological closeness but, rather, a focus on "symbolic forms—words, images, institutions, behaviors." For it is through such forms that we actually represent ourselves to ourselves and to each other. Geertz asks, "What do we claim when we claim to understand the semiotic means by which . . . persons are defined to one another? Are we claiming that we know words or that we know minds?" He does not answer the question but invites us to consider how inseparable are the two, words and minds. Understanding others' "inner life," he concludes, is *not* like achieving communion, but rather like "grasping a proverb, catching an allusion, seeing a joke," or, finally, like reading a poem.[22] The poem into which Marialice's narrative can be turned is, however, a special kind of poem—one that was originally vocalized and that, moving from the inside out, has the capacity to link two lives.[23]

To judge Marialice's story as an expression of Brazilian Catholicism and the passivity it inculcates (as one person suggested to me upon reading her account) is, I think, to see Marialice purely as a victim and, thus, to miss the point. Of course we can see her description of her work relations as an example of ideology, which, according to the view developed by Louis Althusser, "represents the imaginary relationship of individuals to their real conditions of existence."[24] Yet what strikes me in Marialice's story, once I begin to consider it as neither a static object nor a transparency, but as a narrative, which is always structured, is her heroic attempt to respond to her situation in a positive way and create a self that can confront the conditions of her life. This attempt is not misrepresentation, nor is it trivial conceit. It is the self-expression of a woman who is doing what we all do: struggling to make sense of events that are beyond her control and to establish a place for herself in terms of the things that are within her control, and doing so not only through her actions but also through her representation of those actions via language.

In Marialice's case, the material circumstances of her life are largely beyond her control. She cannot move into a higher income bracket, which is her first and greatest necessity. What she has done, instead, is to humanize her surroundings, to try to forge human relations within the situations that constrain her. And she is not unsuccessful at this: it is family ties and kin networks that make life tolerable at the poverty level, where the majority of Brazil's population is situated. And it is the remnants of paternalism, as exemplified by Marialice's employer, that still on occasion provide essential help. Such help can be dismissed as mystification, as the appearance beyond which real relations of exploitation continue to flourish, but this is not how it looks to Marialice. To hang on to a human version of events is, it seems to me, to protect an important value. If Marialice is exploited while doing this, if she refuses to acknowledge (at least to me) her real work relations, she is nonetheless also maintaining her humanity, her capacity to relate to people as people, rather than through the mediation of things. This is where her concepts of goodness—her own goodness, that is[25]—and "being liked" enter. Marialice sees the world as in part a setting beyond her control and in part responsive to the self she presents to that world. There is poignancy in all this, yes, but there is also heroism.

Against the contingencies of her life—her poverty; the drought in the backlands; the crisis in the Brazilian economy (probably the only way in which the actions of the military dictatorship impinged on Marialice); her separation from mother, siblings, even husband (he, too, worked in another town and helped support his parents and siblings)—Marialice takes her stand. By affirming the human relations that she puts at the core of her narrative, she attempts to diminish the hold of mere circumstances. It is this theme that is reiterated at the end of the narrative about her false pregnancy. In describing her sense of loss and disappointment if she cannot have a child, and cannot thus reproduce for herself the love and dedication she has directed toward her mother, Marialice again chooses an attitude and a path. She chooses from the narrow realm of reactions left available to her. Marialice's construction of her life story is a demonstration of the colossal effort required in the face of the overwhelming material problems that are her everyday reality. Her insistence on responsibility and goodness shows that these are *not* automatic features of her social context but are beleaguered traits she explicitly defends. Her very insistence suggests the presence of alternative modes of behavior—such as her father's.

We are not, however, likely to see Marialice's story as an activity, an example of a construction of a self, unless we surmount the barriers imposed by our usual academic and literary categories. The breaking down of old divisions, the valorization of such anomalous (though by no means new) forms as the testimonial or documentary novel, are important steps in this direction, as is the gathering and studying of life stories. Our acts of criticism and analysis honor and ennoble texts, as well as illuminate them. Those of us who have the opportunity to be heard must not conceal our own role in creating meaning, in defining reality.

In his autobiography, William Carlos Williams describes what his work as a physician contributed to his creation of poetry. He writes about those moments in routine encounters when a more profound language emerged from the ordinary language of the people who passed through his office. He calls this more profound language the "language of poetry" and says:

> It is that, we realize, which beyond all they have been saying is what they have been trying to say. . . . We begin to see that the underlying meaning of all they want to tell us and have always failed to communicate is the poem, the poem which their lives are lived to realize. No one will believe it. And it

is the actual words, as we hear them spoken under all circumstances, which contain it. It is actually there, in the life before us, every minute that we are listening, a rarest element—not in our imaginations but there, there in fact. It is that essence which is hidden in the very words which are going in at our ears and from which we must recover underlying meaning as realistically as we recover metal out of ore.

The poem that each is trying actually to communicate to us lies in the words. It is at least the words that make it articulate. It has always been so.[26]

So it is in the interview situation as well. Certainly we need to be sensitive to the contexts in which interviews are gathered, as ethnographers stress. But we need above all to be sensitive to the words themselves. The texts that follow are not transparencies; they are dense with their own sound even as they invite us to glimpse the world within which they take shape, the world of Brazilian women.

1

COMMITMENTS

The Northeast of Brazil comprises nine states and occupies close to one-fifth of the national territory. A largely agrarian area beset by cyclical droughts (the most recent began in 1979 and ended in 1985) and by social and economic conditions that produce starvation, homelessness, and migration, it is one of the poorest regions in the hemisphere. By tradition more conservative and patriarchal than the rest of Brazil, the Northeast is often said to stand in much the same relation to the industrialized and more prosperous Southeast (the Rio de Janeiro/São Paulo area) as an underdeveloped country does to a developed one. And this in a nation in which, with an estimated population of 135 million people in 1985, approximately 40 million people were living in marked poverty and another 30 million in absolute misery.[1]

On 15 January 1985, the very day that the late Tancredo Neves, representing the opposition PMDB (Partido do Movimento Democrático Brasileiro), won the indirect presidential election that ended twenty-one years of military rule in Brazil, a group of industrialists in the Northeastern state of Ceará published a full-page advertisement calling attention to the region's problems, as the Catholic Church had been doing for years. With a population of 38 million (more than one-fourth of the country), the ad pointed out, the *nordeste* receives only 14 percent of the national income: per capita income is half that of the rest of the country, and 54 percent of working people earn only up to one minimum salary per month (about U.S. $40 at the time), whereas for Brazil as a whole 31 percent of working people earn so little. The federal government allocates a mere 11.9 percent of its spending to the Northeast. The illiteracy rate is 55 percent among *nordestinos*, compared with 31 percent nationwide. Average calorie consumption is 1,900 per person per day in the *nordeste*, as against 2,500 (approximately the daily minimum requirement) for Brazil as a whole. Land ownership in the Northeast is highly concentrated: according to the 1980 census, 67 percent of the holdings covered only 5 percent of the land, while 0.6 percent of the holdings covered 32.6 percent of the land—much of it left idle. Between 1960 and

SISTER
DENISE

1980, that is, during two decades of predominantly military rule, the income share of the poorest 20 percent of *nordestinos* fell from 5.2 percent to 3.8 percent, while the share of the richest 1 percent of *nordestinos* increased from 10.5 percent to 29.3 percent.[2]

It is this situation, translated into human terms as hunger, misery, and powerlessness, that has caused the Church in Brazil to make agrarian reform and the problems of the Northeast its principal social commitment. In the Brazilian Northeast, the important work being done by women in the activist Roman Catholic Church could probably have been explained to me by many individuals, but I specifically wanted to learn about the experiences of an older nun, one whose life in the Church had begun before the arrival of liberation theology. Eventually I was led to the nun I call Sister Denise, a White woman in her late forties who was working in a poor community on the periphery of one of the Northeast's cities. The interview took place in August 1983.

———

I'm a real *nordestina*, my parents and grandparents all were from the Northeast, and I was born here in the Northeast. I came to this town seven years ago. Before that I worked in a convent school. You see, our congregation does three different kinds of work. There's education, for those sisters who like to teach. There's health work, in hospitals and clinics. And there are the small communities, for those sisters who want to work with the people. After Vatican II [Second Vatican Council, 1962–1965] many sisters, including me, began to ask questions: what answer can we give to those people who live marginalized lives, those people who are actually forgotten by society, who are humanity's leftovers? It's a call heard throughout Latin America, for it's not only here in Brazil that there are many very poor people and a small group of very rich people. So some of us decided to go outside of the comfortable school structure. Of course it used to be a more peaceful life for us—we devoted ourselves specifically to middle-class and upper-class children, very little to the poor. And so in the face of this mission that we accepted from the Church, we began to ask ourselves what answer we could make to the Church's call. And then a few sisters began to take the first step, to move to the outskirts of the city, the periphery, and to the rural areas. And as it happened, I came here in 1976. I came for a visit [*laughs*]. My health wasn't good, you see, from the work I was doing. And three of our sisters were already working here, and they happened to be friends of mine who'd taken this step first, and they invited me: "Denise, why don't you come for a visit and have a little rest at our house?"

And so I came, and a meeting was going on of those sisters who work here in the periphery and in the rural zone, because the Church had begun to make a radical option for the poor. Some bishops had made this option, and the Church had created an apostolate that gave us more support. We were actually searching, first of all, for churches that had already made this option, and by chance when I came here for a visit, to spend just a month here, the sisters were holding a meeting. They always had meetings, retreats, twice a year, and by coincidence I was able to participate in one of these meetings, and I felt . . . a kind of call toward this, you see?

I had already felt drawn toward pastoral work among ordinary people and that meeting made things clearer. It was a meeting of sisters who were experimenting with work among the people. They met twice a year to discuss their experiences in this new religious life, because it's a totally different life. When you're in a convent school, life is very structured, it's as if . . . the sisters were living on the margins, apart from real life. We were very . . . insulated, very little aware of what was happening, for our whole world was there, inside the convent. So that, when we left to work among the people, we had to dismantle the structures we carried within us, including our very clothing. Because we used to wear heavy habits. For fifteen years I myself wore a habit, eleven pieces of clothing [*laughs*]. We had to strip ourselves even of our manner of dressing, so we could adapt to the people's way of life. In any case, working with simple people we couldn't go on living in convents. And so we decided to live in small houses, just like the people. For the first few years it was a bit difficult, because, though we wanted to join the people, we carried our own culture within us, our language, our way of being. We still had that view . . . of teaching, of dominating, of giving orders. And then, through these meetings we held, we started to reconsider the steps we'd already taken. And little by little we began to notice that it was the people who were teaching us to follow a new path in the life of the Church. I mean, the people have their own knowledge. It's not what you learn in school, but they have their own knowledge. At first we used to talk like this: "Let's evangelize the people, they don't know anything, we've got to bring them the gospel." But as we had more experience with them we saw that the people live the gospel. They don't know the words, but they're living the gospel. And they taught us to go back to the reading of the gospel, to God's word.

I wasn't expecting that. Look, I began with a group of children. Sometimes they'd call me "teacher," because I was used to dealing with children in a class-room. But in those neighborhoods on the periphery, we didn't hold classes, what we did was form groups, friendship groups with the children, with young people, with adults. It was a different method, as one friend to another. But I'd often start acting like a teacher [*laughs*], and the kids would call me teacher. And when this would come up, we, as a community of sisters, would do some reflecting on how our method was unfolding or on our attitude toward the people. And since we were living as such a small community—we were four sisters—at the end of each month we'd reflect on the work we'd done that month, and sometimes we'd seek persons from the outside to help us reach a more profound reflection, on the social level, on the religious level, so that we could become more and more committed to serving the people. It's like that story—instead of giving the people fish, teach them how to fish, to get out of that welfare mentality in which we used to live. Like when we were in the convent school, once in a while we'd leave the schools to do catechism, and we'd see the situation of the poor. We used to feel pity for them, we'd always take some food, some clothing, and then we'd feel calmer, with a calmer conscience. But with the call of the Church, of Vatican II, we saw that we couldn't go on that way, given the system in which we're living, a capitalist system that wants the poor to continue always being poor so that the rich can constantly get richer. So we had to change our methods of working, too.

No, I didn't think in those terms when I first came here. As I told you, I just happened to go to this retreat for small communities, and the sisters had already been following this path for three or four years before me. They talked about these subjects—it was the first time I'd encountered an analysis of the system. I was over forty years old, and I found it very real. I felt it was more coherent, because as a religious you take vows of poverty, chastity, and obedience in order to serve the poor. It was more coherent to take this step. Also, I was no longer satisfied with my classes, for however hard I worked in the classroom, they were the children of well-off people. I wasn't satisfied anymore living such a disembodied religion, a religion only of learning. Like the biblical marathons we'd do sometimes, and afterward the girls would get a prize. It wasn't worthwhile. There was a conflict between the reality taking place around me and the one I was living. So I thought my coming here was a blessing of God, because I saw that the conflict I was experiencing, which at times seemed incoherent, was not. I saw the distance between what I professed and what I was actually living. When I came here it was a kind of discovery, and I right away made an option. I came to spend a month, and I've stayed for seven years already. I decided to stay in this work and not go back.

And another thing that I remember. I was born into a poor family, too, in a tiny town, to a very large family, a patriarchal family. My father married four times; he had forty-three children. I'm the twentieth child, the first of his third marriage. It was a very good experience for me to have all these families. When my father's wife would die, within a few months he'd remarry, because to his mind there always had to be a woman head of the family, too.

My father was a shopkeeper; he had a small workshop. He used to make saddles, suitcases, shoes. It was a small business. Then, when the large multinationals came, it was all lost, the small businesses fell apart. And he ended up poor. My father had a very interesting life. When he was young he spent some time with his father in the Amazon, collecting rubber—the adventures of a young man. After his father came back, he moved to another town, and there he married for the first time, a cousin of his. From that marriage he had nine children. And then she died in childbirth. In the interior of the state, health care was terrible. And three months later he married again. With that wife he had ten children, then she too died. I think it was of a miscarriage, for lack of a doctor. And there he was with those ten children. Five months later he married my mother. She had twelve children; I was the oldest. Some of my brothers and sisters died when they were very small. And my mother died in childbirth, too. She was thirty-six, and I wasn't quite thirteen. And then he married a cousin of my mother's, my second cousin. Fourth marriage, twelve children. All in all, forty-three children.

He died a few years ago, when he was ninety-seven years old, and lucid. He was a man who'd always had good health, I don't think he'd ever been sick. He led a very regular life. He got up early, and he loved to read, especially the Bible. In those days they didn't even go to primary school, let alone secondary. But he was a man who loved to read, to know about historical events. He used to buy books, simple ones that he enjoyed reading. The Bible above all. And when he was ninety-seven he still used to spend all day reading quietly; books were his distraction. When I'd go to visit him—I had a month's vacation in the summer—I would always take a book for him. In the end I was bringing him the Bible in picture books, so he wouldn't get too tired, because he read without glasses. And he died suddenly, of old age. We were already talking about his centenary, but one Christmas, by chance a beautiful and very religious day, my brother went to invite him to spend the day at his house, so the two of them could go to Mass; he used to like to go to Mass. And he got ready, he shaved, he prepared himself to go to Mass. But when he got into the car he didn't feel well. And my brother said, "What's wrong, Papa?" "It's nothing, my vision just got dark for a moment. Let's go."

Even as an old man, he always, always . . . he never lost his strength, his courage, his way of being the father, the patriarch, you see? Until the very end he was always *the father*. They gave him a glass of milk but he couldn't drink it. And then he was dying. They put him in bed, and he was ready. They sent me a message. So, you see, it was calm. He lived calmly, he died calmly. Very easily. A man full of health. My stepmother had married him when she was very young, he never married old people—interesting, never old people. When he died he had fifty grandchildren, and some great-grandchildren. But there aren't forty-three of us anymore, no. Many of us died, and died young. At around thirty-five or forty. We don't know the reason for it. Now there are only twenty-two of us left, living in various states, all over the country. But we have a good relationship because we all married people within the family, so we're all blood relatives.

No, I'm not the only one in my family to become a religious. I had a sister, from my father's second marriage, who died when she was thirty-five. I was a novice when she died. And two of my brothers, from my father's first marriage, entered the seminary. I never knew them, because at that time there was yellow fever here in Brazil and they died of it in their seminary. One of them was close to being ordained when he died.

When did I decide to become a religious? I think very early. My mother was very religious, and my father. When I was a girl I always used to talk about being a religious, you see, but when I turned eighteen I really wanted to. In my home town I went to primary school only [four years], because there was no middle school.³ It was a very small town, I think it had a population of only about two or three thousand. I don't want to forget that town or our history, I have a cousin who knows details of the family history, and I want to record it all. I began to do it when my father was still alive, but there's a lot to be added.

When my father married for the fourth time, some of us didn't want him to marry again. And I, who before that had been a shy girl—my mother was the one who did everything, I had nothing to worry about, we were still in a fairly good situation in those days—but when she died I resolved to take on the care of my younger brothers and sisters. There were seven of us children left, and I was only twelve and a half years old. So I created a bit of a problem with my stepmother, because what I felt was jealousy. Jealousy because she had taken my mother's place [laughs]. Despite her being my cousin. I was jealous when she sat at the table. We had a table more than six feet long, a big house, five bedrooms, an enormous corridor on the inside. And we sat, my father here, then my mother, and in chronological order all the children. The kind of father who prays before eating, who says grace, and then we'd all eat in silence, you see. So I got very jealous, and I didn't want her to touch my brothers and sisters.

But it happened that my sister who was a nun grew worried about so many children in the house not going to school, because there was no middle school, and since she was from the same congregation as I, she arranged for me to study at a boarding school run by sisters of our congregation. I was fourteen when I went away to school. And the sister I was raising, I don't know how it happened, I don't remember, but she'd begun to call me "Mother." She was still very young and she stayed in the care of my aunts. But I only did the fifth grade there, because I missed my brothers and sisters a lot, you see, most of all my little sister. I missed her a lot and I couldn't stand it, so I went back home. I gave up studying and went back to stay with them. But later, at eighteen, I felt that desire to be a nun. What to do? I had to break with my siblings once again, break with the family. And I did. Then, when the little one was eight years old, I got her a scholarship so she could study with me at the same school, since we were poor by then. So it was mother and daughter together [*laughs*]—our relationship was interesting. And we were at the same school. She was extremely intelligent, very lively. And when she reached the age of twelve, that's when I decided to go into the convent. It was hard because I didn't know how to prepare her for my departure, so my leaving her was very brusque and she suffered because of it. She used to say to me, "Mother, don't go." And I'd say, "I am going," though inside I felt the separation deeply.

But I went, I went, I left her. She stayed at the boarding school, and I was calm because after all she was in the school, studying, with sisters of my congregation. Then when she reached adolescence she started to rethink her whole history and she began to rebel against me, because she'd had no mother and I'd left her. Our relationship was difficult for a while, with her accusations against me, and I suffered quite a bit. I worked in another boarding school that we ran, and I was very dedicated to those children and felt some conflict within myself because I'd left my own—that's what I considered them. It was that struggle between dealing with my reality and realizing my vocation, two things clamoring at the same time. But then, through my experiences of life, of my own and others', which were difficult and real, I began to overcome it. I know that a time came when she was past adolescence, when she got to a more mature age and began to understand her own history, and we picked up the pieces. I went through a phase of exhaustion, I think because of the struggle, and she wrote me a beautiful letter acknowledging, "I know you're not my mother; it was life itself that put me in this position. You have your rights, too." Well, it was a kind of liberation. A liberation. Her reaction was normal, but one day she was bound to realize her own vocation, and I would have been frustrated if I hadn't realized mine.

I was already twenty-four, and I had to decide what path my life would take. Either marriage or becoming a religious. My choice was to be a religious. And in fact when she got to about twenty, as I recall, she too decided her path, and she got married. And so we picked up the pieces, and certain things in the past that we thought were negative turned out to be just a phase that we went through. And now we reread our past and even find it wonderful [*laughs*]. But I also think that I came here because I was overwhelmed by family problems; and slowly, over time, I've felt free of them. Not totally free, for you always carry some traces. What's important is to have your life in hand, you see? To learn to live with these problems. And I think I have learned.

When I was young and I knew I wanted to enter the convent—this was before the Vatican Council—I used to think, "But why can't a woman be a priest?" [*laughs*]. I used to say, "Why wasn't I born a man, so I could be a priest?" I had that need for dedication. But many things in this Church will have to change. Many. Starting with the priests. Why shouldn't the Church, in this day and age, let priests marry? The Church should leave people free. I think it's time, it's really time. And you can see that there are lots of ex-priests with wives, who work among the people. And with much more dedication than when they were celibate. I even have an uncle who waited eight years to see if the Church would change—in fact, he didn't want to leave the priesthood, he wanted to continue, but married. And after the Council, he waited and waited, for eight years, and then he couldn't stand to wait any longer and he left. He married; he now has two children. And he has some friends, priests who are close friends, who still let him take part in church, preaching, for example, or doing certain things, and he feels fine. He has a priest's heart, you see, although he's married. He really feels fine. So, I mean, seeing other people's reality, seeing this in my own family . . . because before I didn't used to think much about it, I didn't think priests ought to marry. And that's why I say . . . while you view things theoretically, you'll never be convinced. But when you *live* something in practice, this practice speaks to you much more. Seeing my uncle's reality, if you go to his house, you see the love he has for the Church and for his family; it's moving to see it, how dedicated he still is to this Church, though he can't exercise his ministry because of a law.

And I remember when I decided definitely to become a religious. I was very experienced at twenty-four, because of my mother dying in childbirth and my caring for my little brothers and sisters. To this day my sister, the one whose birth caused my mother's death, still calls me "Mother" [*laughs*]. You could even say I have a grandson. I never had any problem with communal life in the convent, because I'd already lived in a community. And I remember very clearly that when I took my vows—I don't know if you understand how it works, but you have to take public vows as a religious, in front of the altar, vows of poverty, chastity, and obedience. And I, a girl from a poor home, when I entered the convent, I thought I'd changed status. I mean, when I took the vow of poverty, when I came down from the altar dressed in the most beautiful vestments, which were imported from Europe where our congregation originates, then my cousin said to me: "Denise, while you were poor you never needed to take a public vow of poverty [*laughs*], but now you've vowed poverty and descended like a queen, and we're the ones who are going to carry out your vow of poverty." I thought that was wonderful, and I never got her comment on that day out of my head, never. And although I lived a better life than I used to, economically secure I mean, I always tried to hold on to my origins, to reject privilege. So her comment, this problem she fixed in my brain, has served me well.

And one day, with Vatican II, I was able to return to my origins, you see. I mean, during that period of fifteen years in the convent my status improved. I almost didn't talk about my family; at times I was embarrassed to. Because my family was poor. And then, when I went back to the kind of life I'm leading now, among the poor, then I began to sense again the value of my life when I used to be at home, that a person's value is in what they are, not in what they have or in their status and other such things. To value the riches that the poor person has in his experience, in the human values that he has. And then I began to make comparisons, I mean with the time I spent there. Fifteen years in the convent and what farces we lived, communicating with people of a higher status, so many lives lived superficially! But looking at it from this side, you see that the poor are like clear water. They are what they are, and they have nothing else to lose; they can reveal what they are. And so you begin to love them, to take a position, to get on the side of the poor, to try to work so that they can achieve their rights, so they don't become . . . because they're no longer just poor, you see, they're living in misery, tremendous misery. Tremendous. And the level of misery is increasing, not only in the Northeast but throughout Brazil.

At the beginning we used to work in a different area of the city. There were about forty thousand people living there, but now it's being invaded by the middle class, apartment complexes have already been constructed there. We did some reflection and decided to move to the poorest area, and so we went to a place outside the city where there's a *favela* [squatter community or shantytown] under the high-tension wires of a hydroelectric project. These people had no place to live. They had been evacuated from the interior of the state, and they lived under the wires, which is against the law—you have to be at least thirty meters' distance—but they have such confidence in God, they've got no place to live but God will take care of them, He won't let the wires fall, so they stay there. And we decided to move near that *favela*.

They built over a hundred houses there—mostly mud huts, sometimes with thatch-covered roofs, occasionally brick, or made entirely of straw, depending on their means. By now there are more. And then some poor people came who had settled in a private area in the city, and the mayor was supposed to get rid of them. He thought it best to move them, so he sent five trucks to collect these people and take them to the area where we were. They dumped them underneath the high-tension wires, you see? And there was a reaction to this, because where we're living there's a community, what we call an ecclesiastical base community,[4] simple people who've been meeting for twelve years. At first they used to meet in a small private house, nine years in that house. Now they've already got a small meeting hall, where they get together every Tuesday. Simple people, so that looking at them you'd say, "And liberation work is going to come out of that?" You can't believe that this force can have any influence in changing society.

But I was very impressed to see how the community reacted to this event, to these people just dumped beneath the high-tension wires, because they did react. What to do with these people who arrived at eleven one morning and in that dampness began to set up some slivers of wood to hold up their tents under the high-tension wires? At about three that afternoon some inspectors came from the town hall and ordered them to move, because they couldn't stay there; they had to take down everything they'd done and move further away. And then the community held a meeting to see what to do about this social problem. There were pregnant women, lots of children, some of them lighting fires against the damp. So the community got together and they decided to open their little meeting hall so that these pregnant women and children wouldn't have to sleep in the damp, and they began to gather a bit of food for a few days, until the problem of these *favelados* [squatters or shantytown dwellers] could be resolved. And that little community, which seemed so weak, made this decision, and they fed those people for a few days while waiting to hear from the mayor's office if the people were going to stay there or not.

Another idea was that the people in the community should invite the *favelados* to meet together with the community and mull over the problem. And so those men—they were mostly young families, each with his wife, his small children, they met and discussed the subject and decided to go together to the town hall. And then the people who'd helped out with money, with food, got some money and rented a truck and drove to the town hall to demand that the mayor come up with a better solution, because it just wasn't right. They hadn't been allowed to stay where they were, since private houses were going to be built there, but for some authority to grab them and set them down elsewhere—well, that was serious. And when the truckload of *favelados* appeared at the door of the town hall, the mayor said, "You can go home, we're going to take care of this matter immediately." Then he went to the community, with some officials from the town, to talk to them, and they complained about the *favelados*, that this small community couldn't continue to feed them, and they couldn't go out looking for a bit of work because if they left their few things there they'd be robbed.

So what to do? Then the mayor said he'd arrange for some food for them, and he'd open a school building—there was one nearby—and they could go there. And the community thought that as of that moment it was up to the mayor's office to deal with the problem because that had been the cause of it all. Then the mayor found a place in a lowland area and he said, "Look, I've been there, I've sent out some machinery; it's within the city limits, and we're going to move all of you there so that you'll have a safe place for yourselves." And then some of the *favelados*—because it's not the first time or even the second that they've been dumped somewhere, so they're more aware—they said, "Well, let's take a look at this place." And he said, "Fine, I'll send two trucks to take you to see it," and they went. It was a lowland that gets flooded when it rains. So on the trip back they got to thinking about what they'd seen. In fact, he'd actually had a tractor go over the land, but it wasn't the kind of place that he'd promised, that would be good for them. Well, the group divided up: half wanted to move, and about fifty families decided to stay; they didn't want to go there, first because in the rainy season the place gets flooded, and second because it was very far away and they don't have money to take the bus, which would make it really hard for them to get odd jobs. And there were also a few who had trades, who were stonecutters, and it would be very hard for them, too. What they really needed was some place nearer.

Then the community and the *favelados* reflected together, and they decided to leave everybody free, so those who wanted to move could do so. Our work here, you see, it's not up to us to push people into doing things. Our work is so that the people, with the values they have, discover that *they* are capable of dealing with their own situation. So they reflected: "Whoever wants to move there is free to go, but the place is such and so." And they explained it, "Whoever doesn't want to go, can stay here." Then the mayor said, "Look, I recognize that we caused the problem and we have to settle it. There's this place, you went there by truck, you can see what it's like. Now if you decide to stay here, it's no longer my problem." Okay. The group that stayed is still meeting, and there's a government project here, a *mutirão* [project done by many people collectively] for the *favelados*; their motto is "The *Favela* Is Our Problem," and they decided to rent a truck and go see what the governor's wife, who's involved in this project, could do for them. And about fifty families went and camped there, but the governor's wife asked them to leave and said the government would analyze the problem. Then, when it was time for her to report back to the people, she said that in the future she would not receive anybody from the Church, no nuns, no priests, because she thinks that the Church is interfering with the work of the State. Because we're concerned with things like human rights, and when there's nothing pretty to report in the newspapers they don't like it. The Church has been very courageous in analyzing this among the communities. The base communities are a kind of threat, you see? It's as if they were a subversive group—which they're not. Because we know . . . so long as the Church allied itself with the powerful, the rich, we were never considered communists. Now that the Church has made an option to be on the side of the poor, of those who suffer, now it's considered communist and is persecuted.[5]

All this work that we're doing in base communities, we know that it has consequences. But you have to be aware that you are doing this work because of the gospel, because Jesus Christ Himself bore witness. If you want to live the gospel radically, then you have to understand Jesus of Nazareth when He says, in Luke 4, He says, "I have come to announce good news to the poor." Right? "To release the captives." Based on the experience of Jesus of Nazareth, we want to give this answer. When you look at the gospel from the point of view of the oppressed, you discover that the gospel is alive. We were spiritualizing it too much, whereas the gospel is something radical; it's the story of someone who lived and shared with the poor and as a result they said, "This man is living with the masses and is raising up the masses." And Jesus Himself was arrested and killed because of this, wasn't He? There's even that matter of the coin, when Jesus said, "Give unto Caesar what is Caesar's, and unto God what is God's."

You see, when we work with the people, we begin to reread the Bible itself, reread the very history of Israel. For when we were on the other side, everything was spiritualized. We approached these things, but there was a dichotomy—you worked so that one day you'd go to heaven. You're suffering, and we'd come up and give advice: "Have patience, one day you'll get your reward." But when you're in the midst of the poor, you see that it was our own mistake to have created this dichotomy. Man's salvation isn't only the salvation of the soul. It's of the whole man, totally. It begins *here and now*, because here some have the right to live so well, squandering their enormous wealth, and others don't even have the right to live like human beings.

When you visit house after house in the *favela*, it's absurd: the houses are just the way they always were, an Indian's hut, perhaps even poorer, made entirely of straw, and inside one square room there's a father and a mother with ten children, sleeping on the floor, without even a mat, because the community can provide a few things, yes, but it can't provide everything, can it? So, living in the greatest hunger, in that enormous hunger that is their life, they sometimes quarrel, they turn on one another. But what really impresses me when I see the people's enormous poverty is that they are still so peaceloving, our people are very peaceloving. In the face of those supermarkets, in the face of all those objects, these people with all their hunger are still respectful.

I get to thinking, "What keeps such a people going?" Because when we pray, our prayer is always based on the events of that day we've just lived through; and one of my sisters one day left work and went to get some groceries, and she hadn't eaten any lunch, she'd been up since early morning. She said that when she got to the market and smelled the meat they had there, she experienced such a hunger, of such ferocity, that she had the impulse to grab a piece of meat and eat it. And thinking about this she said, "I don't know how the poor stand it." Because whatever little experience we've had of hunger is terrible. I think it's the worst disease in the world, in Latin America, it's that terrible hunger, even to spend one day hungry. How do these people withstand living in hunger? That's the great question. And how is it that these people who live in hunger, in misery, have so much faith? They never say anything against God; they're a very religious people, and they have enough resistance to survive. Years and years of hunger. And as a result, many, many children die before they get to be one year old. It's hard to watch. . . . You ask, "How many children did you have?" "Fourteen." "How many do you have now?" "Five." That's very common. "How many?" "Ten." "How many?" "Three—now. Many others were born, and many were taken by the Lord."[6]

So, given this whole problem, I don't think we can just stand there with our arms folded. We religious, we have a great task to carry out together with the people. Beginning with consciousness-raising, so that the people have an awareness of their value, of their reality, of their oppression, and become capable . . . the small need to believe in the small. But the power of oppression has been so introjected into the people, their dependency is so great, that it's difficult to do consciousness-raising work. The small don't believe in the small. In general, the small believe in the great. You can see that in the last elections.

The last elections [the 1982 congressional, state, and municipal elections, the first free nationwide elections in seventeen years], the Church had been working in this liberation line, the rights of the people, of the very poor, the option for the poor. And on the eve of the elections an incredible campaign started along the periphery, among the poorest towns, an electoral campaign of bringing food to the people. For three or four weeks, the last month before the election, the people lived well, they got food baskets, cars drove along distributing food, bricks to build houses, medical care, everything. Everything that the people needed was provided. And so the people learned: it's the government that's got the money, it's the government that can give them things. That whole illusion. As a result of those few good days, the results on election day were absurd! The people aren't aware yet of change; they live only for the present. Give them something and they show their gratitude on the ballot. That's why they say that the Northeast belongs to the PDS [Partido Democrático Social—the military's party, which governed until 1985].[7]

The suffering Northeast, the Northeast of Brazil . . . you see why there's not much interest in improving the lot of the *nordestinos*. They're a force, another force that sustains the system. You know, the majority know how to sign their name, at least that much. MOBRAL [Brazilian Literacy Movement] teaches them that, so they have the right to vote.[8] It's a literacy program, but not one that sticks. Many people go to MOBRAL, tired after a day's work, and they learn how to sign their name; they're satisfied with that, and that's where it ends. It's good for the people to stay illiterate, isn't it?

Right now this disastrous drought is going on in the Northeast; we've had three years of it already, and probably there'll be two more—five years of drought. If the country really had any interest in the Northeast, there's the São Francisco river basin; a major project could be done so that *nordestinos* wouldn't be deprived, wouldn't go hungry. Irrigation, so that at least the banks of the river could be cultivated, and there'd be no lack of food for the Northeast if they were cultivated, expropriated for the purpose of growing food. It's rich, the São Francisco basin. That's why I think they're not really interested in this disaster, and we all know that here in the Northeast there are many private interests, big landowners' interests in planting sugar cane, because of Proálcool [program begun in 1975 to provide fuel alcohol for vehicles]. And the *nordestinos* are being driven out because of this, while cane and more cane is being planted everywhere you look.[9]

Not far from here there's a sugar mill with I don't know how many thousands of hectares of land. You can travel through it for an hour and see nothing but cane, cane, and more cane. And alongside it is a thin strip, a few hectares, where perhaps sixty families lived. For the past three years these families have been persecuted to drive them off that land. But they've set up a community, there are families who are holding firm despite the attacks. More than once their homes have been burned, they've been beaten; but a group of about thirty-five or forty families has stayed, and in order to keep on staying they've set up an encampment to protect the others. And a while back, a group of them went and camped in front of the governor's palace for more than a month, demanding the expropriation of that land so they could stay there—people who've lived there for more than forty years. There are fruit trees and good earth, everything is good there. Well, since it was close to election time they didn't want them camping there till the elections, so an army unit guaranteed their safe return and they went back home. They're still there, but once again the persecution is starting up to make them leave that land. Here in the Northeast there are many such conflicts over land.[10]

Even in our own congregation there have been conflicts. When we opted for this kind of work, we weren't understood within our own congregation. We were almost pioneers, and our leaving rocked the whole system, the organization of the congregation itself, which began to ask itself, "The sisters are leaving to go elsewhere, how can we sustain our work?"—of schools, hospitals, and so on. But the conflict wasn't only material. It also affected the very structure of our religious life, which is based on obedience to a superior. Even the theology of religious life, the values that had come down to us from our superiors and that we were to carry out, all this was shaken. Even our prayers changed. We used to be obliged, for example, to recite the Office at certain times, to pray in chorus. But when you come to a small community, the type of prayer is different. You sit down, you look at what happened that day in the people's life, and beginning with those problems and hopes—hopes in the beautiful things you see in the people—you start your prayer. But the mothers superior wanted to maintain the old structure, and they questioned us; they said we were no longer obedient because we weren't following the norms of the congregation. Because everything had changed. It could no longer be a pyramid type of structure, it had to be a circle, that is, a fraternal community, from one brother to another. And here we didn't accept anyone as our superior. No one is superior to anyone else, we are all brothers in the service of those of our brothers who are poor. It was a great change for us.

At first it was very difficult; we spent some time more or less marginalized. Now what helped us hang on was that the four of us understood one another. The ideal that I had, the others had too, so there was a sense of security among us. Then, at times, the mothers superior would come to see us here, and they liked our work. They said, "You're doing fine work, but you're not obeying this, that, and the other." And they questioned us. Finally we stopped listening to this, we decided not to pay attention. Other times they invited us to meetings with them, and we'd ask questions and the same debate would start up again: we were creating conflicts and so on. But another thing that helped us adopt a serious position before the congregation is that it wasn't only the few of us. Various small communities already existed in this state, and in order to remain strong in our option we began to hold meetings together, of the whole diocese. And our congregation became that whole group, sisters from the various congregations who had the same aim of working with the people and who felt like one congregation. And this strengthened us.

Some of the sisters in the other congregations, in the face of the pressure that these congregations put on them, were leaving the order to lead their own lives. But we thought the reverse, the four of us, we said: "We won't leave, we want to be a stone in their shoes, yes we do" [laughs]. And, after all, we weren't children, we were all over thirty. We knew what we were doing. It wasn't an emotional choice, the heroism of youth. We were aware of what we wanted. Even if they had sent us a document to sign separating us from the congregation, we were determined not to sign it. That was the position we took. And we spent about four, five years like that, in this misery of not being able to commune with the others, because it was impossible. And then we made a decision: "Let's lead our life tied to the local church"; and then, studying the gospel, we said, "Instead of constantly explaining the whys of our life, we'll just live it, and whoever wants to can come here. Come to see, as Jesus said, come here and see. And in time they'll understand. If we're doing something good, it will remain. And if not, it will collapse, right?"

That was our attitude, and by now we are already accepted in the order, and they're giving every possible help to the small communities. New communities have already been set up. The congregation decided to divide into sectors— education, health, and small communities. So once again we can see our own identity as we work with the people. Things are calmer now, not totally calm, because there'll always be some questioning, but at least we're welcomed. And something new is happening: the young people who are entering the order, most of them have opted for the small communities; they no longer want to settle into the old framework. Also because the training they're getting now, in the order, isn't the way it used to be, each one closed off in her own congregation. There's an intercongregational network for the training of young women, and the content they get has to do with the Brazilian reality, a content of liberation theology, and they are consciously opting to work on the outside.

I think the old ways can't go on. It's absurd for us to maintain convent schools nowadays, absurd. You used to be involved in the school twenty-four hours a day, or in the hospital twenty-four hours a day, as if you owned it. We had almost become managers, and we had to go along with things that happened, which I now think is against our principles. So when we left that and came here, we became freer. For example, I work in a medical clinic, a private clinic. I get there at 7:30 and I leave at 12:30, so it's not *mine*, I'm not the manager. I'm an employee, just like the other employees. Now my activities there are as a religious—not the kind of religious who used to be so privileged, but one who wants to be equal, who does everything, who isn't trying to be the boss but who works with the others. It's another way of being.

For us, as religious, the four of us also became aware that we should maintain ourselves with our own labor, so we wouldn't be outside of reality like we used to be. We'd been regressing, receiving things [*laughs*]. So now we support ourselves through our own labor. We try as much as possible to work half-time only, so that we're available for pastoral work the rest of the time. When you're doing paid work, when you enter the world of work, you understand what's going on in society, you experience the same oppressions that the others, your colleagues, also experience, and you're no longer economically dependent on the congregation, or on the diocese. You're autonomous, so you feel freer to make demands. And where, in some small communities in the interior of the state, it's difficult to do paid work, the archdiocese helps support the sisters there—because the archdiocese in this state has also made an option for the poor.

We try to live the way the poor do. Our house is of mud, too. Of course we're not totally like them, however little we have in the house. It's our training to have everything neat, in order, so we're always a bit different. The way this all came about is interesting. When we left the convent school, the first sisters to move away went to live in the social center, which was also the church. In other words, they left a big convent for a little convent. But that was the first step [*laughs*]. Then, through this contact with the people and through reflecting, they began to ask themselves if it wouldn't be good for them to leave this social center so that laypeople could take it over, instead of us; otherwise, we'd be repeating on a smaller scale what we'd done in the schools. At first the people reacted against this: they're used to having things done for them, all set up, with the sisters taking care of everything—after all, they were the "owners." But then with our own people, in our own communities, we began to reflect on the meaning of our move, showing them that they had the qualities necessary to care for the house, and that we'd only been there temporarily.

And what with reflecting among ourselves and with the people, it came about. We rented a house on a nearby street, still a pretty good house, with a proper floor. Three bedrooms. And the people began to take over the center. They knocked down a wall in what had been a bedroom to make a large hall for meetings. Another room became the office for a doctor, and still another a typing classroom; and a team of people, with all their weaknesses, learned how to run everything. The sisters who had been directing the liturgy team, for worship and celebrations, stopped directing it and began instead to help them discover their own liturgy for themselves. That's how we moved to that second house. A few years later was when I arrived. They were already in that second house. And we began to notice that when people wanted to enter our house they'd first take off their shoes, because it was that sort of house, a bit different. Everything led us to reflect further, you see? We realized that our house still wasn't really the people's house, and that we wanted to have a house where they'd come in and get to know us better without any fuss.

So we began a second reflection, but we only acted when there was consensus among us. So long as one of us thought we still shouldn't act, we'd wait. We'd make our plans, review each year at its end and plan the next, and we had people who in a moment of crisis could help us, because we did have our moments of crisis, in our own relationship as well as with the people, which was something new. In a large community of twenty or thirty sisters, if you have a conflict with one you can still get along well with the others, but in a small community of four, you need maturity in order to live together, to get along. And we went through all those phases. We drew up a list of people we trusted to help us in moments of crisis. And at the end of each month we'd hold a retreat, a reflection of the community, and the moment we encountered a crisis: "Look, let's call so-and-so to help us, or so-and-so." And we'd invite those people . . . because when you're emotionally involved in a problem, at times it's difficult to see your way out of it, but other people from the outside, who aren't involved, can help. When we'd feel like that, fragile in the face of a problem, we'd ask someone to reflect with us, and then we'd continue on our path.

Well, once we had arrived at a consensus, we moved to another house on the same street, a mud house with only two rooms. Little by little . . . when we left the social center for that first house, we had to get rid of quite a few things that didn't fit in the house. And when we left that house for the second, we had to get rid of much more. In other words, we were slowly decreasing the number of things we'd brought from the convent. We used to have a wardrobe for each of us, but in the second house we had one wardrobe for all four of us [laughs]. There wasn't room for more, so we let them go.

And now we're doing a new kind of reflection. We think, the four of us, that we've followed a good path together. I'm nearly fifty, I'm the oldest, the others are a bit younger, and about two years ago we began to wonder if we should always stay together, the four of us, and grow old together, or if we should allow some new blood into our community—I mean, those young people who are appearing. Last year it was very hard for us to talk about separating, we struggled much, faced it, and now we understand one another, truly as one sister to another. If we experience a great truth, we're not afraid to speak to one another. And this year, finally, we've reached a consensus, that it would be good to separate, however hard [laughs]. It's sweet to live together, but we have to make space for the younger people. And also we don't want our way of dealing with young people to grow stagnant, so they have something to teach us, right? That's why next year I'm going to go to the interior of [another Northeastern state]; it's all settled. It'll be more than a day's drive from here. I know the area slightly. There's a community there of three young sisters, and I'll be the fourth. They haven't yet made their perpetual vows in the congregation. We always like to team up two or three with a sister who already has some experience, so I offered to go. Another sister is going to open a house with several other young ones. There are quite a few this year who want to pursue this kind of work in a small community. They're coming out of their novitiate, and they want to make an option for a small community. The other two sisters in my community are going to stay here for the moment, and two young ones are coming to join them.

Several years ago there was a regional meeting of all the sisters in the Northeast, a meeting that left its mark on us. It was after that meeting that I began to question whether it was good for us to continue together, so many young women arriving and the four of us staying together. But last year we still didn't have the courage to separate, and, as I told you, we only do something when we reach a consensus, so that we're inwardly at peace with our decision. Because before, when we were on a project, a transfer would appear without our being consulted, and we automatically had to leave, and this created conflicts. But now we feel free. *We're* the ones who decide the direction of our path, not I individually, feeling happy all alone, but I and my community. And, as for the community . . . after that meeting I was already talking about separating. So was Teresa, one of my companions, but there was still a conflict among the four of us. But this year Sister Conceição also saw our real need, that we were kind of pioneers in this work of opening a space for the younger women. And in the face of this missionary zeal . . . for we have to believe that these young women just beginning will continue our work as we pass on, she saw the need for this, especially in the interior. Well, I felt an impulse and I said, "Look, you know, if you agree, I want to take this step" [*laughs*]. And this time, when I said this, the reaction was quite different, that is, starting from our reality, the reality we're feeling and living, you see? This time it was different. And Sister Lurdes said, "Oh! What a shame! What a shame for us to separate, but there it is, we really must." I said, "Yes, but we'll get together every year."

And now I work with children, which is a very good experience. Just as you can work with adults, with young people, you can also work with the children of the poor, so that they have their own group and an experience of friendship and can come to terms with their own reality. We want to help them be creative, and have their own concerns respected, you see? And I've also worked with children on rereading the Bible, because we noticed that their parents had already incul-cated in them an alienating kind of religion, also because of their contact with some other religions, Protestant; some types of Protestantism here are quite alienating. The children in my group began to ask questions: "Look, those kids, those classmates of ours, they've been telling us that when we die we're going to hell, because of this or that," and they began to have doubts about religion, about the Bible. What could we do? It seemed like a good idea to get to know the Bible, and so we began to study the Bible with the children, at their level, in response to their questions. It's been a great experience, and now some books are even coming out for this purpose, about the Bible. And along with this group of children, other groups emerged, too, other children's groups that also needed this kind of experience. We call the people who lead these children's groups *animadores de criança* [children's animators]. The "animator" is different from what the "cate-chist" used to be. The catechist was someone who taught, who brought doctrine to the children. The *animador* is someone who *animates* the children's group, and starts off from the reality of that group, the needs and questions of that group; and it's the reality, the overall reality of the children, that's discussed.

And from our experience with the children's Bible group also arose a short Bible course for children's animators. We saw that the animators themselves needed to reread the Bible starting from the reality that we were living, so that it wouldn't be that highly spiritualized Bible but our own reality. And now, every Wednesday afternoon I give a Bible class for children's animators, and on Sundays there's another group taking this course with me. That goes on most of the year. It's a very positive experience, very hopeful. Because what we see is that our people *are* religious, if religion is taken as a living thing. Religion itself has to be incarnated; it has to be lived.

The children themselves have a different consciousness today. Even in the schools, they're no longer those dependent kids you used to see. Sometimes you'd have over fifty kids in one classroom in total silence, and you'd give and they would merely receive. A step has already been taken, but time will tell. We have to plant this seed, to help history along. And if we don't do this now, we're holding things back. We know . . . at least I know that we're not going to see the fruit of this work, but only tiny results. A small group is like a seed that mixes with many other seeds, and one day it'll burst forth. It can't fail to.

We've already had a very interesting example in an industrial area near here. The people there were totally dependent on a company that produced textiles and owned all that land, and they thought of the company as their father and mother, you know, and they were the good little slaves. Well, what happened? A group of sisters arrived, three sisters, to live with the people in that community in a very simple house, just like the other people. And that drew everyone's attention. What are these three girls doing there? The first people to come around in such a case are the children [*laughs*]! The children find out about things first; they're not afraid, they march right into the house, "Who are you?" And the children ended up finding out that they were three nuns, and as soon as nuns are mentioned their parents want to hear about catechism, because that's what nuns know how to do, right [*laughs*]? Catechize. So one of the sisters who got on well with kids said, "Where do you want us to meet?" "It can be right here in your house." "Fine." And when the number of kids grew a bit, they said, "Why don't we meet at so-and-so's house? There's a jaca tree or a mango tree there, and we can sit under the fruit trees." "Fine." And then the sister, with another aim already, and not just the catechism, said, "What do you want?" "We want catechism." "But why?" Which gave them a chance to express themselves. "We want to learn how to pray." "Okay, we'll learn how to pray, and you can tell me about the neighborhood here." And so they started to talk, about everything that was going on. You see, this awakens their interest, not just in catechism but to see the reality in which they're living.

And then, afterward, she said, "What's lacking in this neighborhood?" And at first there was total silence. Nobody knew what was lacking, because they were all used to receiving, to being dependent on various things, and they didn't notice the reality of what was lacking, they thought they had everything. Then, in that silence, the sister who was following the discussion said, "Look, why don't you think about what's lacking in this neighborhood, ask your parents what's lacking, and when shall we meet again? How about next Wednesday?" And when they got together again, when the kids returned, they already knew what was lacking: "My father says what we need here is water, that the water has to be bought." And they began to discuss the water, the water that had to be bought. And they reflected on the problem of the water; there was only one fountain, and each can of water cost I don't know what. Many families couldn't afford it, and some left off buying bread in order to buy water. And then those children began to talk: what to do so that the water wouldn't have to be bought? And in the end, forty children got together and sent a petition to the mayor's office asking that the water not be bought. And they got it!

It's always roughly the same technique, to form a base community. It's formed with groups of children, young people, adults. At first we got together only in separate groups: children alone, young people alone, adults alone. But we saw that although each group had its own needs, there were moments when they all needed to be together, like a family that brings together all its members.

This work of consciousness-raising, beginning with the children, is also felt by the whole family. The parents had strong reactions once they saw it wasn't that old catechism anymore. "What? Sending the kids to catechism lessons so that they can play? Can that be right? Real playing they do at home." So we had to undertake work with the parents, too. I often held meetings with the parents, the kids in the middle and the parents around them, to show what all this meant, to let them see our work. The parents, together with the children, would learn the Our Father, the Ave Maria. And then I asked myself, "How can we make this prayer incarnate?" To be able to say the Our Father, the first thing we ask the kids is, "Do you have a father?" Very often they don't. "What do you see in your parents that's good?" Or else, "What do you see in your best friend's father that's good?" Or, "Have you ever seen a father who's good?"

Once I had a group of sixteen boys and five girls. Only two of them liked their parents. Only two. And those two were brothers. The others, not a single one liked his parents. Especially their fathers, because the father comes home tired, yells at the kids, hits them a lot. I mean, the kids are always the outlet, for both the father and mother, above all the father. None of them liked his father. I thought, "How can we call God Our Father with this image of a father? How?" So it was almost like doing therapy there, in the small group, because the family had no alternatives, no way of working things out as a family, and only in the group could the kids have a different kind of experience. And they lay out their problems. Sometimes they even cry, and they're glad to be able to tell somebody else. And one helps the other.

There was a boy . . . that day that we talked about Our Father, he couldn't see anything good about his father, who was an alcoholic. He said terrible things about his father. Then the other kids said to him—his name was Clemente—"But Clemente, sure your father's an alcoholic, but he also has some good qualities. When he's not drinking, he helps my father." So they began to show him that although his father was an alcoholic, he also needed to be understood. Or, "You must know that your father is sick. He's an epileptic, right?" The boy got very upset and the other children helped him understand. He couldn't do anything about the problem of a father who's an alcoholic and an epileptic, but, confronting this problem, he can begin to find a direction for his life later on.

In relation to the young people, the adults also react, because the kids' behavior today, the freedom they have in relation to the new films, for example, their attitudes, are different from the adults' values. So there's a conflict between the generations. I mean, when the young people are alone, they have their own way of behaving, and the adults react. But the young people come there to reflect on drug problems, on dating, on everything they need. They have their own world, and the animator has to know how to . . . but it's not only the animator who does this work; among themselves they've set up a team that reflects, that helps them. It's hard to work with youth because of their attitudes toward adults. But among themselves they feel comfortable.

And as far as adults go, sometimes in the base communities you don't always manage to work with the whole family. Often it's the woman who goes and not her husband. We deal with them one by one. Each family has its own suffering. Sometimes the woman is the one who's sick, or she's being exploited. And we do consciousness-raising about birth control or even about a ligation. It depends on the case. But to give birth control pills to a famished people is very dangerous. We try to help them analyze the government program, BEMFAM [Family Welfare Society—in fact, a private organization that promotes family planning and distributes contraceptives], its methods, its objectives, because the government isn't trying to educate people but rather to limit the number of poor people.[11] Sometimes the women themselves decide not to take these pills, because it's strong medication on an empty stomach; it's dangerous. The poor, you know, the worse nourished, the more fertile. I myself knew a lady who had six children in three years, three pregnancies with twins, one after the other. Living in misery. Without being able to use birth control because her body couldn't take it.

It's an extremely complex problem, all this. I mean, the people need to have a place to live, they need to have their own families, to love like everybody else, to have their children. And they can't. . . . What's interesting is that, as poor as they are, when a child is born it's the joy of the family. The women don't die in childbirth so much any more, at least not on the periphery of the city—I don't know about the backlands. And they do have abortions. Next to our house was a house where they performed abortions with home remedies. But the women's health is damaged by it, and they sometimes end up in the hospital. Some of them are just girls, very young, sometimes at thirteen they're already pregnant. They abandon their babies, or leave them at the hospitals. And then they learn to take pills or, if they get pregnant, to have abortions.[12]

Thus far, the base communities have been small. For example, where I used to work, there were ten communities there initially. And they were organized by streets. They'd each take a separate name and try to hold meetings in their own areas, and the leaders or coordinators of those groups would also get together every week. It's good for the groups not to get too large. It's slow work, and hard, especially because now, with TV finding its way even into straw shacks, it's hard for the communities. The young people . . . for example, they get hooked on television, and sometimes even older people get very involved with the soap operas [in the evening], and that's one of the phenomena that has decreased the number of communities. And another thing is the excess of work that the people have—for example, a worker from a factory gets home late at night, tired, sometimes in no shape to come to the community, sometimes there are shifts in their working hours that seem intentional, so that they can't get together, you see? And so the communities are becoming smaller and smaller.

Let me tell you how the group I'm now in began. It's a group that's been going for more than twelve years now, a small community but very lively. This was a really deserted area, one house here, another further down. Few houses, poor houses. The center was still the social center, and there was a community group there, and they got to thinking about the other poorer areas and how the people liked processions a lot, the stations of the cross, and so they decided to have a procession into one of those areas. The priest—who by the way was a great friend of the people, he was from Europe but he knew how to get down to the people's level—he had a lot of experience with the people, and to this day they remember him. He knew everybody, one by one, family by family, because the first thing you have to do, when you come to a new area, is to make visits. First you have to create ties of friendship so the people will have confidence in you.

Well, they decided to have a procession, and the people liked it. When the last day of the procession was over—it took several days—a lady asked . . . because the procession was like this, there wasn't any church, there wasn't anything, they'd get to a house, stop, reflect together, get to another house, stop, reflect, say a prayer. And in the last house a lady said, "Wouldn't it be good if we could continue to get together?" In other words, this community was formed starting with that procession. Other communities sometimes start with a problem: for example, the problem about the water that I mentioned before. There are many ways to begin, and that one began with a religious event, and the priest said, "Wonderful idea." Then children, young people, men, women, began to get together in a little house that belonged to one of them, and in that house they used to meet once a week, for nine years in that little house! And later a small center was bought, to make a meeting hall, and now the community meets in that hall, they have their own hall that they also call a church.

Last month they celebrated their twelfth anniversary, and the young people who are part of the community did some research with the older ones, "How did it begin?" so they would know, and they put on a play about the history of the community [*laughs*], reliving those steps. That's something we very much like to do, to stir the people's memory, because the people have been lost to history, especially the Brazilian people; their history gets ever muddier. People move from one place to another. They lose their roots. But in the work we do, they remember their memories, they recapture their history. Because if the people don't get together to become a major force, then they're lost to history, you see.

2 Carolina, a sixty-seven-year-old *nordestina*, is the least educated member of a middle-class, mostly White family. Her maternal grandfather was Black, and traces of an Indian great-grandmother are also visible in her features. Never married, she lived for many years with a man. Her younger sister, Cláudia, a schoolteacher, had two children—a boy, Sérgio, and a girl, Ana. As a child, Ana had encephalitis and suffered extensive crippling and brain damage. When Cláudia died, several years before the interview, Carolina took over the care of Ana, her niece, who is nearly thirty years old and lies in a crib, apparently totally unaware of her surroundings. Carolina cares for her as for a baby. Ana's doctor (also a relative) says that without such care, first from Cláudia and now from Carolina, Ana would soon have died of infection.

Several of Carolina's relatives, to whom I also spoke, consider her "difficult," even not quite right in the head, and they seem to resent her periodic cadging for money from them. Carolina is treated and tolerated as the inevitable "poor relation" by her rather large family, and her standard of living is considerably lower than that of other members of the family, which condition seems to bother her not at all. She lives in a run-down house, in which burnt-out light bulbs hang from the high ceilings and the toilet has no seat. A maid and the maid's baby live with her, and former maids occasionally come by to visit. Out of an income of about $200 a month, derived from the rents of two small houses that she owns, Carolina pays the maid $20 a month. Carolina can read and write (with many errors) and speaks a kind of ungrammatical and disjointed Portuguese. She laughs easily and winks and clicks her teeth when talking about men, one of her favorite subjects.

———

M y mother had one paralyzed side—on account of the birth of her first child she ended up with a dead side. And when she died, I was just a kid; I'm not sure, but I think she was in her thirties then, when you're a kid you don't know things right. And my father

C A R O L I N A

wasn't a good husband, but he was a good father, so even today I can live independently. I live in this house because of taking care of my niece. My father was very rough toward my mother. And he had other women, and . . . for many years, they didn't have marital relations, she being sick . . . she used to have attacks. . . . I was very young still, and I didn't have any idea about life, like I do today, and as far as I was concerned our life was good, it was good. I was happy because I had everything I needed, as long as I lived with my parents. Now after my father passed away, I went through some things in life. And later I got to like this boy. The first time I saw him I took a liking to him immediately. He owned a shoestore—I mean, he and his brother were partners. And I was out with a girlfriend and I met him. I didn't know who his people were yet. I just took one look and said, "That one's a real sapling." The other two were just standing around, and I was all eyes; I said, "That one's a real cute boy." We stood on the corner and began to talk, to talk, and well, time passed, and I got home at 10:00 o'clock or 10:30, to my sister's house. My father had died already, and I was living in Maria's house. I think I must have been about twenty-eight, then, because now I'm about to turn sixty-six, I mean sixty-seven. And then we fought, because I got home late and they thought I was leading some Bohemian life out there, running around, that sort of thing, but I was just talking to him. I'm not sure, but I think I was about thirty at the time, and he was older. I know I was very young.

No, he wasn't my first boyfriend. I had . . . I had others. But the only one I loved in my life was that one. And so, then, then I left; I went to my stepmother's house and I stayed for a little while. And . . . afterwards I rented a little house, and I lived there for eight years, him and me. I mean, he'd go there and sometimes he'd sleep there, sometimes not. Then, when I moved to my own house, he came to live with me; he actually lived with me. Me, him, and my old Black nanny who raised us, and she also raised Maria and Cláudia, my sisters, and Maria's two boys, two generations. Her name was Chica, and . . . I think Mama fought with my father over her; I don't really know what happened, but she moved to Maria's house and she took care of Beto, my nephew. Then she had a hard time on account of Maria's jealousy, and problems came up and everybody had a different opinion, so she finally went away. I don't remember if she first went to her sister's house—because she had a sister who's still alive—and then she got jobs in two houses, and then she left the last house and went to live with my sister Cláudia, and I always went to visit her there. When I could, I'd take something for her . . . And then, after my sister died, Chica was working, she was doing laundry again, and when I went to see her she was standing there all wet and I felt so sorry. She was in her eighties. So I said to her, "Chica, do you want to come home with me?" . . . and she came and stayed with me, as a friend. She was like a mother to me, and I took care of her until the end. She died a few years ago. She went to work for my parents when I was nine months old, that's what they tell in my family, so I can say that when I tell the story. I was nine months old. My brother was about two, and Cláudia and Maria weren't born yet. I'm not sure, but I think Chica was fifteen when she came to our house. She was already living here in the city; her parents were very poor. So then she kept on living in my house, and she only left when Our Lord called her.

This is why I left school: I was just a baby, crawling, and my father took a picture and was developing it at home. Of the family. So he set up a tray to make the picture, and I pulled off the towel . . . the liquid all came down and became acid and I swallowed some. And I got very sick. The doctor was called and he ordered beaten eggs, because that works against poisons; so they gave that to me and I got well. And then . . . I'm intelligent, I know things, but my family never thought so. I only know my letters more or less because I didn't study more, but that has nothing to do with intelligence. Intelligence is something people have, with or without schooling, it's something else. So I never finished my schooling . . . because when my mother got sick, I mean when she got really sick, I was the oldest so I was the one who took care of her. I think she was thirty-something at the time. I was already a young lady [had started to menstruate] when I stopped going to school; I must have been about twelve or thirteen. I tried to learn, but I was a little slow, because of having swallowed that acid. I didn't go to school much. My life was mainly helping anyone who needed it.

My father was kind of . . . Bohemian. He married again, but not right after my mother's death. I'm not sure how long he spent, maybe a year or more, in mourning. Then, well, this girl that he married, she was from the country, and a cousin of hers lived here and she was there in the house. Well, he took a liking to her. She was engaged, engaged to a very poor boy. So he went right in and talked marriage. She was going home to prepare for her wedding, but my father talked to her and she accepted him. And my brother, the one who's sick in bed now, went to get her from her parent's house. He stole her away. I think she stayed at our house, I'm not certain. And Papa married her. She was very young . . . about the same age as Maria, my youngest sister. And I lived in the same house with them. Maria had already gotten married; she married when she was seventeen. And my brother, he married . . . he was the first to get married; then after him came Maria, and after Maria it was Cláudia. But not me. I never wanted to marry. You know why? Because I like my freedom. My father was like this: when I wanted to go some place, if my father permitted it, I would go, and if he didn't, I wouldn't go. I obeyed my father.

You see, I have this kind of outgoing spirit. I like what I like, and when you marry, especially that boy, Gilberto . . . if I'd married him, it wouldn't have worked out. Because I like to talk, to go out, I like parties, all kinds of amusements. And when a person marries, I mean, just once in a long while the husband turns out all right. I'm not sorry, either, for not having married. Besides . . . Gilberto didn't give me orders . . . because he was living off of me, so I said what was what at home. I was crazy about him, crazy about him.

No, I never worked other than at home. I mean, I did embroidery, but that was for fun; I never worked to support myself. I never wanted to. I didn't mind depending on my father and my mother, but not on anyone else. Not even on this boy I loved. I did what I wanted, I mean, I didn't do things that I saw might annoy him. I always liked to go out. Sometimes I'd go to the movies with him. Then, later, he had a grocery story in the center of town. I was already living in my own house, in my first house, I already had these two houses. They used to belong to my father. This one belonged to my sister Cláudia, Ana's mother; today it's Ana's. You see, when my father died this house needed some repairs, and at that time I couldn't do it and I didn't have anyone to help me, so I sold my part to my sister and bought two smaller houses, and that's what I live on still today; I support myself with this, with the two rents.

Sometimes you want to buy something, and then you shouldn't have to ask your husband. Maybe it's because I've been independent all my life. I mean, not while my father was alive, I wasn't independent then. But now, with the rents; it's not much, but I don't want for anything either. I've never in my whole life been greedy for anything, all my life I've been like this. To my way of thinking, everybody has their own way, right? I think women should run their own households, not work but stay at home and take care of their family. I'm used to doing things my way. Even when I loved that boy, I did just what I wanted, but not dumb things. We spent twenty-five years together, as if we were married. He worked during all that time, but I gave the orders [*laughs*]. Sometimes he'd say, "This is my house." "The house isn't yours, it's mine," I'd say; that's just my nature. When I was a girl, I was quieter, I wasn't as gay as I am today, but I always liked to have friends. But if you marry, you should obey your husband. Maybe that's why I didn't marry [*laughs*]. To my way of thinking, once you're married you should take care of your house and obey your husband, because that way there's unity. Otherwise there's misunderstanding. You should agree on things, some things, not all.

Once I went to talk to the priest about having a wedding. But I'm kind of a difficult sort. And it ended the way it ended. Gilberto's family wanted him to marry me, but he told me he was afraid to get married because of my temperament, because when I got angry I'd grab his clothing and throw it all outside. And then I'd go to see him and he wouldn't leave his room. And his sister would say, "But Carolina, stop being silly, you know what Gilberto's like," and then I'd have to make up with him. He wanted to, but . . . he didn't want his arm twisted. I missed him and I liked him a lot, so I'd make up with him and he'd come home. When he died I . . . I'd been very angry with him, I threw out all of his things. I mean, just before he died I made up with him, but before that . . . it was stupid, but he was very jealous of me; sometimes he'd say things he oughtn't have said and I'd get angry.

Yes, my family accepted that we weren't married. I mean, not at the beginning. I used to go to my sister's house, to all my sisters' houses, but he didn't. The only house he'd go to was this one, Cláudia's; he used to come here, he was friends with her. But Maria was always a little aloof. After many years, when I was already living in my own house with my Black nanny for company, then Maria finally began to visit us. Otherwise, I'd have to go to her house. But he and I never quarreled about that. He was single and so was I, I still am, and it wasn't important. I cared a lot for him.

I was very afraid of having children; I was afraid of the eleventh hour [*laughs*], really afraid. Of pregnancy and of the moment of having the child. And I never got pregnant . . . I mean, to be frank, I had two abortions, but they weren't his; with him I never got in the family way. It was someone else, just carelessness. It was before I met him. They were kind of difficult, the abortions. I nearly died. My family never found out. I didn't have money, but through a friend I heard about someone. The first time was at home; my father was still alive, but he never . . . he died without finding out. He didn't suspect a thing, nobody did. I was the only one who was worried. So I asked a lady who lived across from my parents' house, I said to her . . . I was always retching and feeling like I wanted to eat something, but constantly retching. So I asked her, I said, "Look Tereza, I'm retching all the time. Could I be pregnant?" And she said, "Carolina, it's very possible." I said, "For the love of God, don't say that." I was very upset, for fear of my father. I said, "If I get pregnant, my father's liable to throw me out of the house, and I don't have any place I can go." I didn't have enough schooling to get a job in business, only in a household, and I didn't have the nerve to face my family. I wasn't about to subject myself to being a maid in some household, either. So she gave me medication and I took it and aborted.

I had that abortion at home, and my father never knew. And afterward, I wasn't doing well, I had pains, everything, I'd . . . how do you say it? I'd lost a lot of blood. I was in the bathroom and my father heard me moaning. No, I left the bathroom and went to the bedroom, and my father said, "What's the matter, Carolina?" And I said, "Papa, I'm having pains," but I didn't say it was the abortion, I let him think it was my period, and he gave me some medication to relieve the pain.

Now the second one was with forceps. That was in Recife. That time, too, I nearly kicked the bucket. After that, I didn't have any others. I spent some time in Recife, at a lady's house, and I became pregnant. I was very frightened. No, that's wrong. I got pregnant here, by another boy, and I went to Recife. And then I noticed it. So I said to the lady where I was—it was a rooming house, but not for women of easy virtue, it was a family. My father knew the owner of the house, so I went there. Very scared. I said to her, "It looks like I'm pregnant." She said, "Carolina, let's go to a house I know and see . . . she can tell if you're pregnant or not." And I went. She said to me, "You're two months along, Senhora." I said, "*Ai,* Blessed Mary!" I was frightened, I was afraid of my father, I didn't have any branch to hang on to. I was really scared, and I went back there . . . she gave me an injection in my thigh, then she put this instrument in and started pulling.

My family never found out about it. My father died and never knew that I'd been in a family way. Then, after many years, I told my two sisters. They didn't say anything. I was so shy in front of my father, I was always afraid of him . . . even after I was a grown woman, I always feared my father. That time, I bought a ticket without telling him; then I said, "Papa, I'm going to Recife." He said, "What? To Recife. No, you're not." I said, "Papa, let me go, I've already bought the ticket." He said, "You can buy ten tickets, but you're not going. And if you do go, don't ever come back." Then I talked to my stepmother, I said, "Look, I've bought a ticket for Recife and I went to tell Papa and he said he wouldn't let me go. Talk to him so I can go." And she did talk to him. We always got along very well, and we still do. So then I said, "Well, what happened? Did Papa agree?" She said, "Go, Carolina, go." And I got ready and left.

Yes, I did tell the boys, both of them, when I got pregnant those two times. But they . . . neither of them accepted it. The first time he said that it wasn't his, and I knew that it was. And the second—no . . . I'm not really sure that I ever told him I was pregnant. I mean, both times I'd only been with them once and I got pregnant right away. I didn't know how to avoid a family. I was so foolish. I mean, I only went with them when I liked them; otherwise I wouldn't go. I've liked some others, too, but not like that.

Now after that last abortion I had some complications; I had a fibroid tumor, a lump, and I used to get sick twice a month, and when I had to go to the bathroom there were those pains and I'd get white, white, white. Then it would pass. Sometimes I would bleed and wouldn't know what it was. My father, my father was already dead by then. And it was getting worse. The most horrendous attacks, without knowing, so I spoke to my brother, my only brother, and I said, "Luiz, I want to go to a doctor because I'm in such pain it feels like it's going to finish me off." And he said, "Go, go to Doctor . . ." I can't remember the doctor's name. "I'll write you a note saying you're my sister and that he should treat you." So I went. When I got there, he wasn't in. I asked the nurse and she said, "He's only here on . . . he's out of town," and she gave me an appointment, I don't remember when. So I went, and when I got there the nurse called me and he came in. He asked me what I was feeling, and I said, "Look, before menstruating I feel such pain, pains that almost make me pass out." And he told the nurse to prepare me for examination to see what I had. Then he pressed on my stomach, he pressed, and he said, "That's a fibroma, Senhora, and you have to be operated on right away because it's very far advanced." So I left and went to tell my brother. I said, "Look, Luiz, I need an operation. You know that I can't manage it." He said, "No, that's no reason not to have the operation. I'll talk to him, and he'll do your operation." So he talked to him, and I did all the tests so I could be operated on, and I had my operation. My brother paid the doctor. Aside from this, I've always had good health; that was the only complication.

Thank God, when I was a girl, I wasn't like the girls today; they have too much freedom. I was very timid, you know, very shy. But I always wanted my freedom. Also I didn't understand life the way I do today. I thought that marriage was like friends living together . . . but not . . . I was very foolish, very silly, I didn't really know what would happen. I liked some other boys after Gilberto died, but I never had that passion like I felt for him. Now, after he died, years later, I got to like someone else, this was recently, and for this one I feel the same passion like I did for that first one. To this day.

You know, the last one . . . I really liked him. I mean, I thought that he wanted to live with me right to the end, or get married. That's what I always thought. Look, you can judge me by this boy; it's been a year since it ended, and I haven't been with anyone else. Let's see, the first time I was with a man . . . I must have been about twenty-six. I don't think I was even thirty . . . because now I'm going to be sixty-seven. Yes, I wasn't even thirty.

No, I don't think Gilberto wanted to have children. Because once I thought I was pregnant, and he got irritated: "Stop pretending, Carolina," he said. I said, "I'm pregnant." I really thought I was, but afterward my period came. But I was already sick, and then I couldn't have a family because something was wrong with my uterus. No, I didn't see a doctor about it, and I'm not really sure what it was. But I stopped getting my period after a while and that was that. I couldn't have had a family.

My first boyfriend was married, but I didn't know it until later. When my brother found out, he wanted to kill him. I was living in my brother's house when it happened. I didn't know anything about life. My mother never talked about certain things in front of us. I was very, very foolish, much too much. Then I spent some time scared. I didn't want to be near men at all, I mean, in that way—just to talk, but anything else scared me terribly. You see, I was so silly, very silly. I thought people married just to be together, to talk, to go out. Those other things . . . I just didn't know. I was dumb. My mother never told me about those things, not a word.

After my mother . . . the last one to die was my Black nanny, and then I came here to my sister's house. Sometimes I'd spend a week, but I was, I still am, very suspicious. I'd spend a few days here and I'd say, "Cláudia, I'm going home." She'd say, "You're going because you want to." I said, "No, I'm afraid I'm getting in your way." "No, you can stay here as long as you want." I was living alone then. I had my own house all set up, but this was at a time when Cláudia was sick and getting worse. So I stayed here with her, and I'd go to my house just to see that everything was all right. And then, after Cláudia, Ana's mother, died, I stayed here for good.

I first came here to live about three years ago. Cláudia had already had this ailment for quite a while, she had it but she didn't know what it was. Then she started to get worse: she had strong attacks and had to go to the emergency room and I'd stay. It turned out to be cancer. Sometimes I'd sleep here, but I still had my own house. And then . . . after she died . . . no, before she died, I talked to my nephew, Ana's brother, and I said, "Sérgio, I want you to do one thing for me, I want you to give me your sister to take care of." He said, "I will, Auntie." I said, "God bless you . . . I want you to know, it's not that I'm hoping . . . no, because she's blood of my blood, I don't hope Cláudia dies; but if she does pass away, I want you to give Ana to me, so I can take care of Ana," and he said, "I will, Auntie." I said, "Look, Sérgio, after she passes away, won't you give me Ana?" "Aren't I saying that I will, Auntie? I'll give her to you." Then she died, she died here at home. And I stayed on here. Afterward, afterward I . . . I went to fetch all my things, and I rented out the house. The other one was already rented, so I had the two rents. I've never needed more money, I've never paid any attention to all that, I just wanted to have enough to get by, to have my own things. I have money to buy what I want . . . this house is all fixed up, at my expense; everything you see here is mine. Cláudia's things were worn out, so I slowly replaced them. [*At this point Ana, who had been moaning softly, began to howl and Carolina went into the next room to attend to her, explaining as she went that Ana howled only when she needed to be changed or fed or was in pain. Carolina took a diaper from a drawerful of neatly pressed and stacked white diapers and T-shirts, and cleaned and changed Ana, all the while caressing her and cooing at her.*] Ana was so cute when she was little, and Cláudia really loved her. Then one night there was a terrible storm, and after that Ana got sick. She'd begun to talk by then, but after that night she just lay all curled up in bed and couldn't speak or walk any more. Cláudia was desperate: she took her for a treatment she heard about in São Paulo, and for a while it looked like she was improving, she began to be able to sit up again, but then it just didn't work. I still have . . . wait a minute. . . . [*She brings out several shoeboxes full of papers and looks through them until she finds an old, faded telegram.*] Here it is. When her husband found out that they couldn't do anything for Ana in that clinic in São Paulo, he sent her this telegram: "Very sorry STOP suggest amicable separation STOP otherwise you're on your own." So that's what happened. I still think it was the storm; she was never the same after that night.

My nephew Sérgio, my sister left him everything, and his father left him something, too. His father was a businessman. He had another family after he left Cláudia; he had two other children. If it weren't for this other family, everything would have gone to Sérgio and Ana. Her brother is her guardian; all I do is take care of her. My money is enough for me because my nephew gives us money just for food. All the rest I pay for. When she needs something, a doctor, anything, I let him know. He gives her whatever she needs, she doesn't go without. Sérgio is responsible for her, I just take care of her. But she has whatever she needs. He doesn't come here, though. She was sick recently, and I called . . . first I called the doctor . . . no, first I called Sérgio's house, then the doctor. He thought she had eyesores, she was groaning and moaning and had a fever. And he gave her some medicine for the fever and some medicine to put in her eyes, but it wasn't that. She was still moaning and I said, "My God, can it be an earache?" I had some medicine and I put it in, and then she got better. It was an earache. Because she can't speak, you see, and when she moans she's either wet or it's time for her meal, and after I take care of her I feel so happy, that's what I feel.

I'm Catholic, but I think the best way to serve God is by how we live. I do what I do for Ana with all my heart. I know what she needs. Now, this business of a person constantly running to church . . . I think that what I do, that I serve God more than if I go to church and do this, that, and the other thing. I go to Mass when I feel like it, or when it's a Mass for a friend who died, then I go. But to go every Sunday, no. That's just my way. When my mother died . . . she taught us to go to Mass every Sunday, and my father used to go, too. He was a Mason, did you know that? But he still went to Mass every single Sunday; so because of my parents I did, too, and I'd say novenas when it was time in the month of May. I'd go, more out of habit than really out of religion, I'd go to enjoy myself.

I'm not sure about *candomblé;*[1] sometimes I believe in it—because I had one experience. I was living in the other house and there was a lady . . . she wasn't exactly my neighbor, but she lived in a house next door to that other one of mine that I rented out. Well, one day my tenant's maid called me about some problems, something in the water pipes. I explained to her how to make it work, and she said, "Dona Carolina, when I need to use the water, [the neighbor] takes a rubber hose and fills up her tank." So I called her and I said, "Look, you should draw out the water only when they're not using it here; otherwise it ties up the flow. Then, afterward, if you want to, you can draw some." And more time passed, and after a while the neighbor came and I said to her, "Look, I have to tell you something. Tell your maid that she shouldn't draw water when they're using it here." And she said, "I've already told her." I said, "Look, you owe me more than you paid, just for all this water I've given you." So—I'm like that, kind of hasty that way—so I said, "Look, you're going to live to regret this, your rudeness to me," and that's where we left it.

I already knew all about her life, and I was sure—not that anyone had told me, but I was sure she wasn't faithful to her husband. I mean, marital life, nobody else should get involved in it; let everyone live their own life, right? But I got mad at her. I got mad and I spoke. Then I calmed down and at about eleven o'clock, or noon, when her husband came home, I called him over and told him the story. Then he went into the house, and things started buzzing. She came out to the fence and said, "You shouldn't have done that." So I repeated it to her face; I said, "It's your fault. I've lived with this man for twenty-five years, and I've never been unfaithful to him, and you, being married, still you're unfaithful to your husband. I say it and it's true. And I've got proof." Then my tenant, my tenant was in her neighbor's house when her husband grabbed her. She had a knife and wanted to come to my house to kill me, you see. She had a knife behind her back, and my tenant noticed this and said, "Penha, what's that for?" "To kill that woman." Then she said, "Penha, don't be a fool, don't do anything crazy." She took the knife away from her and [Penha] stayed home, but she complained about me at the police station and I had to appear. But nothing happened, and she swore she'd . . . get even.

Well, time passed on and on, and I began to get sick. Sick, sick, then . . . I couldn't even walk, truly. And sick, sick . . . I went to the doctor . . . I think Mário, my nephew who's a doctor, hadn't graduated yet, so I went to another doctor, and he examined me and said, "No, Senhora, there's nothing wrong with you." And me so sick, too sick even to walk straight. Then, at that time my brother had a companion and, she and I, we were friends; and I went there because I needed him and always got his help, so I went there and when I got there he wasn't home, but she was, his companion. And she said, "Carolina, what's the matter with you, Carolina?" I said, "I don't know. I just know I'm sick." She said, "I can't believe it, Carolina, you like this." I said, "Yes, I'm sick, I went to the doctor, I've taken medication, but I can't seem to get better." So she said, "Wait till Luiz gets home"—that's my brother—"wait till Luiz gets home, then we'll go to the right place." Then he arrived, she told him, and wouldn't you know? He went to this place, I went too, I mean, the three of us went, and she told them the story. Then the woman there said, "I can't start a session now, but since this involves a friend"—that was my brother—"I'll start one after all." And she started a session just for me.

Then she said, "Something was done against her, and we have to take care of it . . . or she might go from one hour to the next. You need to bring this and that," and she went through a list of things I had to bring to put a stop to it. And I bought it all and took it there, and she started. First she asked me for a black chicken, then she asked me for *dendê* [palm] oil, flour, and something else that I don't remember. And she cut the chicken's throat and she passed it over me, in a cross. Then there was another session, and I was present. And from all this business I got well. It sounds like a lie, but I got well, I didn't have anything wrong, and that's why sometimes I think it does exist, spells exist, you see? Now . . . this business of spirits descending, I believe and I don't believe. But I believe in these spells, I mean, I believe owing to this experience of mine, because there wasn't any medicine that could cure me. All this happened a long time ago; Gilberto was still alive, and he's been dead now for eight years. And that's why I believe that there are spells. I don't believe much in spiritualism, but I do think that witchcraft exists. I believe it because it happened to me—not to someone else, to me. There wasn't any medicine that could cure me. And after I got well again I was fine.

After Gilberto died, I liked another man, I mean, I did like him, but not to live with. I don't know how long it was . . . after his death I spent some time without liking anyone, you see? But I used to go to the post office, and I saw this boy. I went to buy stamps, and I knew a lady who worked with him. So I saw him and I said, "Who's that boy?" She said, "He works here." So I said, "Is he single?" She said, "Yes." I said, "He's really cute. A dark cutie." Well, color doesn't matter in a sincere friendship, but real black isn't for me. Golden brown is nice, though. Well, I started talking to him, while buying stamps, but I don't know if he'd noticed that I was interested in him, and I kept on going there to buy stamps. Then, one time, there was this program in São Paulo for arranging marriages, confidentially, and I wrote a letter and he said, "Carolina, do you know the address?" I said, "No, I don't," that's what I said to him. And he said, "You don't need to write to them . . . you can find somebody right here." And he stood there, talking to me; I was always good at conversing. Then finally, one day I wrote him a note inviting him to come here and have dinner with me—I was already living in this house. I'd been wanting to get to know him, but I was tongue-tied; but finally I invited him. I still have the letter he wrote back, accepting my invitation. We set a time, everything. And he came, and he kept on coming here.

Then I said to him, "You want to know something? This house isn't mine, so I'd better tell my nephew," and Sérgio said, "Aunt Carolina, are you sure this will work out?" I think he was worrying about Ana, you see. So I said, "I don't know,

I'm telling you because the house doesn't belong to me, and it seems that I should inform you of everything that goes on here." He said, "That's fine, Auntie, but I think this isn't going to work out." But I continued anyway. And the boy used to come here, sometimes he'd sleep here. And then I ended it because I heard a rumor that he'd found . . . I mean, a girl. He began to date this girl. He didn't say anything to me, but I found out. And I asked him. He denied it. And, after a while, I got disgusted with him. This was after seven months; I liked him for seven months. So I said, "Look, it's not going to work. I don't want to see you anymore." And I said some other things to him. About the girl, too. Nothing offensive, but he thought I was attacking her morals. So I said, "Well, that does it. Do me the favor of not coming anymore because I don't want you at all." And he . . . afterward he tried to make up with me, but I said, "I've already told you that I don't want anything more to do with you." I haven't seen him for some time. He's studying at the Law School. Once I saw him again at the post office where he worked, and I went to talk to him; but he was very rough, he grabbed my arm and squeezed it. I said, "Look, leave me alone. You seem to think you're number one. Well, you're very much mistaken. I only came to tell you this." That was that, and I got indifferent to him. I pretended not to see him.

How old was he? He told me that he was twenty-three or twenty-four. But I think he wasn't really that age. I'd say he's about thirty or thereabouts. My sister, Maria, she thinks I should like someone older, but, you see, I like them younger. And anyway, it's more who you're attracted to, isn't it? I mean, I met someone who wanted to marry me, but I didn't want to. He was a widower, I don't even know if he's still alive, but I never liked him. And another time, the man was too old. And I don't want to be yoked into marriage. I've always liked my freedom. Life in a prison isn't for me. Like my sister. You know, they're all against me, because he was younger than me.

Now Cláudia, my younger sister, she'd liked Antônio for a long time, I think eight years. Then she went to Recife to work. When she got married, my father had already died. He never wanted that marriage. But she wasn't in a family way yet. I think it happened when she was in Recife. Then she came to Maria's house, and when I saw her I had my doubts. And I think Maria's husband talked to him, but it wasn't a forced marriage, because they were both adults, so you couldn't force him to marry her. Well, they got married—just a few months before she gave birth to Sérgio, they finally married. He only wanted a civil ceremony. But Maria is very suspicious and she said, "No, we won't accept just a civil ceremony. Marry in the Church, too, not just the civil ceremony." And he said, "No, I'll have a religious ceremony later."[2] So they got married before Cláudia gave birth, and she was already married when her first child was born. Now, Maria, I think she was a virgin when she married. She got married in church, in white. I'm sure she was still a maiden. She was always a bit timid, you know.

But it is important to marry virgin. My case was different: it was just luck, because I wasn't one of those girls like now. I was always shy, and nobody ever kissed me until a boy who was going to marry me, he was the first to kiss me. The others were just flirting. We didn't marry because he was working in a bookstore that belonged to a relative of his. He was the clerk, and he was poor and very calculating. And then his relative died, and he got interested in the widow. I think I was about twenty at the time, twenty-something. Maybe twenty-two, twenty-three. And the widow was much older, she was old enough to be his mother. But she had money, you see. And at that time, my father's situation was neither here nor there, so he married her and that was that. After he broke it off I cried and went into the house crying, and my father asked, "Carolina, what's the matter, Carolina? Why are you crying?" And I told him; I said, "José's ended it, it's finished." He said, "My child, this isn't the end for you, you still have your whole life ahead of you. You still have your father. Forget about this, just forget about it." I spent some time without talking to him, or he to me. Then, after a while, he became a widower and I talked to him again, just to talk, but I didn't have anything else to do with him. He went one way and I went the other.

I don't know. It's hard to explain about virginity. I mean, for me all women have the same worth. If she's an honest woman, even if she's not a maiden, just being honest she has the same worth as a virgin. But a virgin is a different thing. Because she's a maiden, and a woman isn't a virgin anymore. That's the way I think, you see. If she's an honest woman, she's just as worthy. If she has a companion or a husband, I think she's worthy. And if people don't get along, then they should separate . . . I mean, before they have relations. They should separate, because you should live only with someone you care for. Otherwise it's better to separate. Whether it's a husband or a companion, they should each go their own way. But men don't need to be virgins. Women are one thing, but a man . . . a man can do anything and he's still the same man; a woman is different. That's my way of thinking. But if he has a wife, he shouldn't do anything else. Now if he doesn't have one, that's a different story. Men are men, but women are different. Once a woman marries or has a companion, she should always be with him; but if it doesn't work out, it's better to separate and each live their own life. But if they marry they should be faithful, because marriage is for making a home, having a child, having a house.

With Gilberto? Well, to be frank, I went wrong once, but to this day I regret it. And it was only because I was so upset with him, it wasn't because I wanted to. All my life I've been like this, I only like one man. It's been a year since I stopped seeing that boy, and I haven't even noticed any other man. That's the way I am; if I'm fond of one, I don't notice any others, he's the only one who exists for me. As for Gilberto, I think he was faithful, I never heard that he wasn't, that he was looking for someone, never . . . it's true I once saw him talking with a woman of easy virtue, but when I saw him I went right after him and I think I cured him of that. Because these women of easy virtue, they're the ones who chase after the men, aren't they? But I don't think he was ever unfaithful. And there were people who told me, afterward, "Dona Carolina, Seu [Senhor] Gilberto is devoted to you." I don't think women should go with a man for money, only because they like him and feel good together, feel happy with that person. But these women of easy virtue, they go just for the money, rarely out of fondness. I've done a lot of stupid things . . . because most men just want to know a woman, and once they know you they don't want to continue, you see. What can you do? And when you're young, your organism . . . at least in my case, I can't speak for others . . . some people can bear it and others can't, they feel sick.

When I lived with Gilberto, I did what I wanted and he didn't say anything about it. I mean, I didn't do things that might annoy him. He didn't like me to go out in a certain skirt and blouse, because he was jealous of me; but I liked it, though not to exhibit myself to anyone, just to show him, and I liked to go for walks, but he was jealous [laughs]. I think my life was good, I had . . . I lost my mother, but I had everything. My childhood was happy, it was normal; I never wanted for anything in all my life, never. After my father died, my life changed a lot because I had very little money, and when I needed something I had to ask my family. I always wanted to live the way I live now: I can go out, and I can do what I like. I'm very happy with my life now, especially since I started taking care of my niece. I'm not sorry that I've kept her with me. I don't have the freedom I used to have, I mean, to go out for the whole day. I do go out, but I worry about her. When I'm with her I don't worry at all, but when I leave her at home, I spend the whole day worrying that something might happen while I'm not here. I care for her as if she were my own daughter. I'm not sorry, and I'm not even sorry that my nephew doesn't reward me; I don't think about that. What I think about is how she's suffered in this life, and I do everything so that she'll never suffer, and as long as I live she's not going to suffer.

You know, I always celebrate Ana's birthday. I do it in my sister's memory, because she always did, and she'd invite us, the whole family. But you can tell when people really want to come, and now they're all against me, especially Maria. She said, "Carolina, Ana can't understand what you're doing. Why bother?" They did come last year, but without really wanting to. Last year I had a party for her, but this year I didn't, because I felt bad. I know Ana doesn't understand the celebration, but I do, and I wanted to do it for the sake of my understanding, not hers. I think she deserves everything in life. But the rest of the family don't agree. They don't invite us places . . . though you can take Ana anywhere, just like a baby. They're all like that. But I'm happy. So long as I can take care of her, I'm happy.

———

C A R O L I N A   D I E D of pneumonia three years after this interview. Ana was moved to her brother's house and died shortly thereafter.

3

The first time I met Vera, in August 1983, at the headquarters of an Afro-Brazilian cultural group of which she was an officer, she was wearing an African headdress that accentuated her striking features and intense look. She is a dark-skinned Black woman in her mid-forties who lives with her two grown children and her mother in a house in a working-class neighborhood in the North Zone of Rio de Janeiro. During the interview Vera's phone rang repeatedly, as one or another member of the groups with which she was involved called to discuss projects and meetings.

The disadvantageous position of Blacks in Brazil, as expressed through detailed comparisons with Whites, begins with their geographic distribution. Whereas 64 percent of the White population live in the Southeast—the most developed area of Brazil—nearly 70 percent of black- and brown-skinned people live in the rest of the country, especially in the states of the Northeast. The illiteracy rate of Blacks in recent years has been nearly twice that of Whites (40 percent vs. 22 percent).[1] A 1982 household survey revealed that whereas 20 percent of Whites have less than one year of education, among Blacks the figure is about 40 percent. A corresponding imbalance is seen among the more educated: 16 percent of Whites have nine or more years of education, as opposed to only 6 percent of Brown men (*pardos*—the official census designation for *mestiços* and/or mulattos) and 7 percent of Brown females (*pardas*). This reflects the recent tendency for women to have slightly higher rates of schooling than men. As skin darkens, level of education decreases: among Black men only 4 percent have more than nine years of school, as do 5 percent of Black women.[2] Research conducted in São Paulo by the secretary of education in conjunction with private groups concluded that Black children, regardless of the family's economic position, have fewer opportunities than Whites to attend and stay in school. In addition, Black students tend to go to poorer-quality schools, whether private or public. In terms of educational attainment, then, race rather than sex is the more salient characteristic.[3]

V E R A

In terms of employment, non-Whites are disproportionately concentrated in the service, farming, and construction sectors, which are the lowest paid and least prestigious. Not surprisingly, strong inequalities exist in the income received by Blacks and Whites. A 1976 national household survey revealed that nearly 60 percent of Blacks earned no more than one minimum salary, in comparison with a little over 23 percent of Whites located in the same low-income bracket. At the other extreme, more than 16 percent of Whites and only a little more than 4 percent of non-Whites had incomes above five minimum salaries.[4]

A more complex picture emerges from consideration of employment and income in terms of gender as well as race. Black women (except where otherwise noted, I use the term as does Vera in the following pages, to designate black- and brown-skinned women) work more and earn less than White women. But whether White or Black, women as a whole are discriminated against in the labor market, and their income is consistently lower than that of comparably educated men—with the income gap increasing as the level of education rises.[5] Although in recent years the number of women working in industry (where women earn 40 percent less than men earn for equal work) has risen, women workers still tend to be concentrated in the lowest-paid jobs in the tertiary sector. In 1983, 10 percent of economically active men earned only one-half the minimum salary, as compared with 23 percent of women workers.[6] By 1985, the percentage of men earning that little had dropped to 7.1, whereas among women workers the decline was much smaller—to 21.7 percent. Furthermore, the monthly earnings of men averaged 2.8 minimum salaries (U.S. $154) in 1985, while women's earnings averaged only 0.8 of the minimum salary ($44).[7] At the higher salary levels, 5.4 percent of employed men in 1983 earned between five and twenty times the minimum salary, as opposed to only 1.4 percent of employed women. And whereas men's representation in these higher-income brackets had increased by 0.1 percent since 1970, women's had decreased by 0.5 percent.[8]

But occupational segregation, a problem afflicting all women in Brazil, afflicts Black women in a very special way. Historically, the change from unpaid slave labor to wage labor did not substantially alter the working conditions and opportunities of urban Black women. Even after the abolition of slavery in 1888, Black women continued to work as maids, laundresses, cooks, nannies, street vendors, and prostitutes.[9] Furthermore, the largest single job category for women is that of domestic servant (see Part Three, below). This occupied nearly 27 percent of wage-earning women in 1970, decreasing in 1980 to 20 percent (i.e., approximately 3 million women by 1985), as more women found work in industry and as secretaries and shop clerks.[10] And among domestics today, 90 percent are Black women. It is still common to see job advertisements with the phrase *exige-se boa aparência* ("good appearance required," a code term for "no Blacks need apply"), as Black women continue to be excluded from work that brings them into contact with a "select" or "demanding" public (which one Black activist translates as "racist"). Eighty-seven percent of Black women workers, the majority of whom are not registered, do manual labor.[11]

The great beneficiaries of women's recent gains in the labor market, argues one writer, have been White women: "The White group reserves for itself the best places in the market; it reserves secondary functions for its subalterns. Thus we have White men as executives and White women as their secretaries. The left-overs are given to Black men, and only thereafter does the Black woman enter."[12]

The intertwining of race, class, and gender in Brazil is further demonstrated by the patterns of interracial marriages. When their level of education (and with it access to higher incomes) permits it, many Black men marry "up"—which means White. And they are more likely to do so as their educational attainments increase. Among higher-educated White men, however, the tendency to marry Black women decreases.[13] It would seem that the old (androcentric as well as racist) Brazilian saying still holds: "White woman for marriage, *mulata* for sex, Black woman for work."

Given the complexity of the Brazilian racial situation, it is hard to obtain reliable data about the racial composition of the population. The 1980 census, however, reported that approximately 54.8 percent of the population declared itself to be White, 38.4 percent Brown, and 5.9 percent Black. In view of the incentives toward "whitening" one's racial designation, however, it seems probable that, as Vera states further on, only a small minority of Brazilians today are of unmixed White ancestry. As one Black activist has written: "Power in Brazil may be White, but the true face of the people is not. Who, in this country, does not have one foot in the slave quarters?"[14]

———

I 'm the daughter of an unmarried mother. I only started to have a closer relationship with her, more mother-daughter, after my marriage, and just recently she came to live with me. I never knew my father.

When I was a baby, my mother lived in a tenement in São Paulo, and she used to leave me in a room alone while she went out to wash clothes and do cleaning. And when I was six months old, my mother says that I got my head caught in the bars of the crib and that someone passed by, heard my crying and wondered about it, and came in and saw me stuck. A few more minutes and I would have died. Maybe that would have been better, who knows? Afterward, when I was nearly two—I'd already started to walk—my mother was advised by some people to put me in the care of a friend of hers, and this family then moved to the interior of the state of São Paulo. That's where I was raised, loose in the street, running around barefoot, with no idea of cleanliness, no manners, nothing. I was a child, and this woman was suppposed to take care of me. She gave me food but only took good care of me when my mother was due for a visit or when my aunts, who lived in the same town, were coming to see me. Then they'd fix me up, give me a bath. I only started to take baths alone when I was already in school and my classmates talked about taking baths. I looked at myself, looked at the other girls, and noticed that I was really dirty.

My mother was always concerned about my schooling, but she wasn't around. At five I already knew how to read. For that town and that time, I was a genius, but it did me no good because . . . I was a little Black kid wandering the streets, with ugly skin, circulation problems, always going around with open sores. . . . Then later, my mother had a rooming house in São Paulo, for prostitutes, and that's how she had the money to support me. When I was eleven my mother got me into the best school in the state. But to get into that school I had to have a guardian because my mother, as a single mother, couldn't put her daughter in that kind of school. So my foster brother, who was already grown up and a successful businessman in that city, he was in a position to be my guardian. I thought that was unfair to my mother because she was the one making the sacrifice so I could go to that school, and she was the one paying for it. The governor's daughter studied there, and the mayor's, and for a time my mother's financial situation allowed her to keep me at the school. I was the only Black there, but I didn't get bent out of shape because of the racism, no. I was above all that. I always had a strong character, and I didn't let it affect me or my work at school. But a time came when it began to get to me, so then I decided to really be the black sheep. I thought, "I can't stay here being discriminated against, being mistreated even by the nuns." But I also couldn't tell my family about it, because they didn't understand me. They thought the mother superior *was* superior, adults were adults, and children should keep quiet and not complain. But I carried on so at school that the sister had my mother called and told her that she should transfer me from the school.

I was in that school for just eight months, and I was the only Black. When I left I went back to my foster family, but I couldn't really adapt to life there again, because all that I wanted to be—this is what I thought—was what I could be only at the school, among the people there. I'd noticed these kinds of distinctions before. For example, my aunts were washerwomen and I used to deliver the laundry, pick up new batches, and so on. And at Christmas I would deliver laundry to people's houses. One of my aunts also used to prepare banquets at the home of the richest family in town, big landowners who had exploited several generations of my family. I would deliver the laundry to their house, and I'd see the table laid out. But everything they had on their table, we also had on ours. We had walnuts, hazelnuts, raisins, turkey, suckling pig—because we also used to raise animals, and in those days we could buy what we wanted, not like today. But what we didn't have was that refinement. I didn't dress like their daughters, I didn't have those beautiful manners that they knew about, their way of behaving at the table or even the rest of the time. When they played, they never shouted. I used to shout a lot, I fought a lot. They didn't. They would work things out quietly. One had a doll and the other would take it perfectly calmly. There was no trouble, nothing. And it all got my head muddled. I used to say, "But why are they like that?"

And then I discovered the reason: because they used to sit in their father's lap, their mother's lap, their grandfather's, grandmother's, and they had that permanent support from all the members of the family. Those girls had all that intimacy within their family, while for me, my relationship with my aunts never produced any feeling of family intimacy. That would have required a mother, a father, grandparents. I had a mother, but she wasn't there with me. She was in the capital, and I was in the interior of the state. I could never understand why I was there with that foster mother, why my aunts were living in a different house. My cousins were treated differently by my aunts. And all these things were dancing around in my head. My foster parents never took me into their laps, and I was becoming more and more withdrawn, more cut off. Then one day I thought, "When I get to their house, I'm going to sit on my aunt's lap." And to my amazement she liked it. I was really too big by then, and I'd never done it before because I didn't live with them and by the time I was old enough to want to I was afraid of their reaction. My aunt used to spend the whole day at the washtub, and at night she'd iron; she'd spend night after night over that iron. But that day I sat on her lap, and she began to stroke my hair.

And then I started to become more manageable, and I wanted most of all to be with my aunt. People began to notice that I was changing, because when I first came back from school I felt discriminated against. My whole life was that discrimination—because I was Black, had poor manners, behaved differently from the other kids. But one thing I was always perfectly clear about: my mother never acted out of lack of love, or because I was a burden in her life, no. She always wanted the best for me. Then her situation got worse, and it looked like she wouldn't be able to continue to pay for my education. She tried to get me into a public school, but couldn't; and finally someone suggested she put me in this other place, from which I could transfer to a good school when a vacancy came up. But it never did.

The place wasn't a school, or even an orphanage or anything like that. It was an asylum, run by nuns. There was one wing for old people who could pay, men and women, and another for those who couldn't pay, indigent people. And there was a wing for children with disabilities—spastics, mental retards, all kinds of problems. I was already thirteen years old. It was a huge place. There was an enclosure where the nuns lived, a theater, a music room, an auditorium. In one wing, the disabled children lived downstairs, and there were sleeping quarters for the employees upstairs. There was a snack bar and two floors of nurses to take care of the old people, and a kitchen. And out front there was a school that children in the community could attend up to the fourth grade. Opposite that was the tuberculosis pavilion. At that time there were mainly young people with tuberculosis. And I used to run up to the sanatorium because that's where the healthy young people were—to me they seemed healthy, even if they had sick lungs, because their minds were fine. That's where I used to find people my own age to talk to.

I used to take care of a group of kids in the kindergarten of that school, and I worked with the sisters in the main office. I sang in the church choir and helped clean the church too. In exchange, I got room and board, clothing, and shoes. As far as food went, I was privileged. I ate with the nuns, three times a day, the best of everything. I've just always been skinny. I spent a lot of time with the nuns, and I learned good manners; but they only wanted to teach me about domestic work, so that I could be a highly qualified servant. There was one nun there—today I can see she was very progressive—who used to give me music lessons, art lessons. It was a very important phase in my life, on this pilgrimage of mine. But when I left the asylum, I didn't get into the other school, although my mother did her best.

It happened like this. I started having problems, not with the institution— because there I was extremely useful, in all kinds of ways. But my relationship with the disabled children began to trouble me. I'd keep thinking, "That girl is fourteen, just like me, and she can't even talk. How long can she live like that?" They all should have died, because none of them had any future at all. There was a retarded girl there who had a marvelous voice. She sang in the choir, she had perfect pitch, and this retarded girl gave me a slap. She was blonde, blind but with such eyes—one was deformed, but the other was a perfect clear blue. And I didn't see a retarded girl hitting me, I saw a White girl hitting me. She hit me and I hit her back. Then I panicked. I went to a sister and told her what I'd done, and she didn't reproach me. My head got even more muddled, I actually wanted to be punished for what I'd done. But the sister wasn't in the least concerned about it. And so I started to think, "My God, I've been looking upon this girl as an enemy, but that's not what she is at all. She's as needy, as discriminated against, as I am. I can't stay here because I don't have any solutions for these problems, for the old people"—at night I'd cover them up, and in the morning I'd go there thinking they'd be dead. Then I would see their blankets twisted up, their pillows flung to the floor, and I could see that they'd been struggling against death, trying to ask for help. But since they weren't paying, they didn't get the same care, because the personnel would stay by the bedside of the rich people, constantly bringing them medicines, but not these others.

Then a cousin of mine came to visit me, and she saw the disabled, the others, and she wrote to my mother that she should take me out of there. She acted out of good intentions, and so I came to this state, to the house of another cousin, who was married and had no children and was complaining about being lonely. She said I could keep her company and she'd send me to school, take me on outings, and so on. But that's not what she did. On the very first day I was at her house, she set me to waxing the floor. She'd had a party and when I got there the house was a mess, so I cleaned the living room. The next day, she told me I had to clean the bedrooms, the bathroom, and the kitchen. Next thing I knew I was her maid, without any payment. That's what it was about: "Do that, come here, that's not done right, neither is that." So I went to the house of the cousin who'd come to visit me. She was married by then, and I went to live with her and got a job in a dry-cleaning shop. My work papers said I was a clerk, but actually I was the manager. The owners were two Black twins. They used to show up, open the store, and disappear. I would deal with all the problems. And then I began to date my husband. I was just coming out of a very turbulent relationship. I was going with a fellow who was *desquitado* [legally separated from his wife], and in those days a man who was *desquitado* was seen as . . . heaven help us! And so my family rejected me. They laid down the law: "You can't live here if you go on seeing that man." And I thought it wasn't worth the trouble, just when I was beginning to feel stable. So I started to see this man I later married.

But one day I came home from work—I used to do all the housework for my cousin, or most of it. Not that she obliged me to, but she'd had two very difficult childbirths, and she'd had an attack of eclampsia [a type of convulsion associated with pregnancy and childbirth] and her whole nervous system was affected. I still like her to this day. Well, I thought I had to help her as much as possible and spare her any heavy work. I took care of her, I liked her a lot but, as I said, her nervous system was damaged and she'd have these sudden explosions. And on that day, I'd gone out and was seeing a friend off at the bus stop. We got to chatting about one thing and another and decided to go get a soda at a shop near the bus stop. And when I got home my cousin commented on how long I'd been out. The next day when my husband came, she turned to him and said, "You can say goodbye to this room because your fiancée's moving out." She'd had a really hard day, but I didn't take that into consideration. I thought only about what she'd told him, that I was moving. She hadn't said a word to me, hadn't asked me to move, nothing. And I was contributing to the household expenses. I thought, "I don't owe any explanations." But I also didn't have the money to support myself and to pay for a place to stay. My job was nearby; bus fare was minimal.

So I bought a newspaper and saw that a lady was looking for someone to keep her company, and I came to Rio to talk to her. My cousin had said that on a Saturday, and on Sunday here I was. And that lady really did need someone, not just to help with the housework but also with some embroidery that she did at home—a fabric that was sold already embroidered; that's what she used to do, and she needed someone to help with that, and to help her with the accounting for a restaurant she had. So I went to stay with her. It was a real experience for me, because I went through the greatest trials with her—of honesty, dishonesty, conflicts of interest, exploitation, everything. Not that I was exploited in my work, but she was exploited by her daughter and son-in-law. Her daughter was co-owner of the restaurant with her, and this daughter had a husband who didn't want a thing to do with work. He was just out for what he could get. She also had another really beautiful daughter, who was the lover of a politician—a blonde girl, tall, beautiful; and he was a tiny, ugly man. She'd get home and lie down and say to her mother, "Tell the restaurant to send me up some food." And the mother would do it! She was a strong woman, I don't know why she subjected herself to that. One woman exploiting another. The mother would get her food and give her money.

I was already engaged by then, and one day my employer came to me and said, "Look, Vera, you want to get married just so you can have your own house, but you don't really love your fiancé." I said, "No, I'm not madly in love, not like that business you see in the *fotonovelas* [photoromances—a popular form of mass culture, like comic books but with photos instead of drawings] and on the radio"—in those days there were a lot of soap operas on the radio—"but I like him enough to get married and build a life with him." Then she said this: "Look, it would be better if you went back to school, got a degree, and thought about having a family in the future. I see a gloomy future for you, even in setting up a family, because this boy can't provide you with a good standard of living, nor can he match that thirst for knowledge that you've got. You'll be able to go along side by side up to a certain point; but after that, once you wake up, you'll have some sense of what I'm trying to tell you." I said, "No, Senhora, you don't want me to marry because you want me to stay here, putting up with your daughter, solving your problems." That woman wasn't a soothsayer or anything, and I don't believe in fortunetelling anyway. All you need is a bit of psychology and imagination. You deal with people and try to understand them from the inside, and then you can even foresee what's in store for them. And in fact she was right about my husband, and years later—when I told him, "I want to go to university"—he said, "University? With two kids? What for? You should be taking care of your children."

A H ,   M Y   H U S B A N D. . . . First of all, he had a lung problem. He was tubercular. He got treatment, but he was someone who liked to drink and he didn't take care of his health, so he had to go back to the hospital. Then he had surgery; they took out three ribs, and it took a long time for him to recuperate. He got a heart disease and spent six months in the hospital with this cardiac problem, and eight months at home. And from that surgery he got bronchiectasis—it's an infection where the bronchial tubes get stopped up and cause a hemorrhage. So then he had that problem, too. It was getting worse as the years went by, and whenever he felt better he'd go out, drink, play pool, and stay up all night, that whole business. Things were going from bad to worse. Our relationship was being damaged by all this. I began to get really fed up because I saw that he wasn't taking care of himself, he showed no interest in the family. I was worrying about him while he was just spreading lots of insecurity to us.

And then he got very sick and spent nearly a year in the hospital, and during that time he really recuperated. He was a noncommissioned officer in the Navy— he's retired now—and their medical plan paid for it all. So he stayed a year and got well. When he got out, he decided to take up with someone else. He met a woman and started a relationship with her. He wanted to have that relationship and keep on living at home, but I . . . I don't accept that sort of thing. Why have him at my side just because he's my husband? Why should I stay with him for the rest of my life? Because of society? Because of my mother, my father? No! So we separated. And after that, he got steadily worse and he had two strokes. And recently he had surgery on his right lung and he came to my house. After six years of separation, he came to my house. And here he was treated like a . . . like a friend who needs help, but he was always making those nasty little comments of his. And he got better. The woman he'd been living with didn't care; that's why he had to go to the houses of relatives, friends, and ended up coming here. Now he's all right, and he's gone. He went to live in São Paulo with a cousin of his.

We lived together for eighteen years. Today I look on our separation as a perfectly natural thing, but at the time I felt a lot of turmoil that I hadn't been able to keep my family together. I judged myself to be a terrible wife, a terrible housewife, a terrible mother.

Because of my husband's poor health I had this fear of having children, and so I had two abortions. I already had one child—now I have two—and between the first and the second, I had two abortions. Afterward I regretted it. I should have had my four children. No, I didn't go to a doctor. It was a really unpleasant situation, I felt brutalized . . . because they stuck in what they call a sound [probe]. It's a kind of small plastic tube and they put medication on the end and insert it into the uterus. It's horrible, horrible, and yet I did it. And the first one was done with some drug, injections, I don't know what kind but they caused a hemorrhage. I got really sick both times, even the second time, with the sound, which I thought was supposed to be a better method than the first. My husband was really disgusted. He said that whatever happened to me was my own responsibility, that he wouldn't waste one cent on medicine for my fever, that I should look for a doctor to handle the situation, that I'd be badly treated by the doctors once they realized I'd caused the abortion. I hadn't told him in advance because I knew he wanted to have those children, but he was very sick. He used to stay for ages in the hospital, ages at home. So I was the one who had to take care of everything: my family, the family's problems, our problems, our children's problems, his family's problems, and my own. I thought there was no way we could raise four children, on top of everything else and the financial problems, too, there was no way. With the standard of living that we had, two children were fine, but if we had more than two I thought we wouldn't have been able to maintain that standard.

But these are things that people do when they're poorly informed. If it happened today, if I had the financial stability that I had in those days, I'd have my four children. It was stupidity really, lack of information, fear, insecurity. But today I'm not against abortion. I think women ought to decide, they ought to choose. Nothing should be forced on them. But, you know, the legalization of abortion here in Brazil is the subject of lots of disagreement, because the women of the . . . lower class, proletarian women, they haven't been consulted about this. There's a law already in the works in Brasilia, and nobody's asked if we want it or don't want it or what. But I don't think it will be legalized. There's a great deal of opposition to it, a great deal. On the part of women, too. It's interesting, because they all do it; but when it's time to legalize it, they're opposed. But also, to legalize abortion so that a minority has access to hospitals, to conditions for doing an abortion, I'm against that. It ought to be available to everyone, through the medical care programs, that's how it ought to be done. But, on the other hand, that frightens me a lot, because our medical care is awful, so we're in a bind. Lots of women die from illegal abortions. If it's not legalized, women do it anyway and die; and if it is legalized, you still can't trust in the care that poor women are going to get. You're damned if you do and damned if you don't.

The medical care that's provided by the government is stratified. If a patient, a worker from the slums, goes to the public clinics, he's treated one way. If he's middle class, suddenly, wham! He goes to the same doctors and they treat him in a different way. I know this because I've taken people to the clinics. Not long ago I took a woman from this neighborhood to a clinic for treatment, and they left us waiting there for ages. Then someone arrived, a well-known actress, as it happens, and she was taken care of immediately. We waited the whole morning. It was a Saturday; we got there at 8:30 and left at 2:00 in the afternoon. And even so, we got out at 2:00 only because I decided to protest. If you don't protest, you just keep on waiting; that's how things are here. Lots of times women don't even go to the doctor because of this, it's such a problem. They don't have anyone to leave their kids with. If they take them along, bus fare is high, a snack costs a lot—the kids get hungry so you've got to have money to get them a snack—so they just don't go. They take some tea, do something, go to the pharmacy—the pharmacists usually prescribe medicines—and that's how it is. There used to be horrendous lines, kilometers long. Now that's decreased, but even so, they wait for hours in a waiting corridor; it's not even a room. And that's at the INAMPS [National Institute for the Medical Care Aspects of Social Welfare][15] itself. In the state and municipal hospitals it's even worse. At this time of day, if you went to the hospital you'd see people in a room that's filthy, really filthy, waiting to be taken care of at the out-patient clinics. Those who are waiting in the emergency rooms, with a broken leg, say, they're there, too. The real emergency patients don't wait that long in that room, just long enough to give their data; but when they go upstairs, *there* they wait, and it's no use complaining, protesting. When I take people these days, they don't wait. They go up in the elevator, I look around and go up a back staircase and corner the doctor. I've done this four times already. I've said to the doctor, "You only respond to pressure, you're used to this. If you don't take care of that patient over there, I'm going to the press." They respect the presence of the press more than a broken leg. So many men worry about their image. Well, we've learned that, too.

M Y   S O N   I S twenty-two and my daughter is twenty. My daughter . . . it was funny, I decided to stop with this business of abortion. I was talking with some friends and I said, "I can't do it anymore. I feel mutilated"—that was exactly the sensation, you know. I was crying a lot, I'd gotten very depressed. So my friend said, "Well, that's it. It's damaging you, affecting you psychologically, too. You could even get mentally unhinged." So we went to talk to a doctor, and she taught me how to calculate my menstrual cycle, the rhythm method. And everything was going really well. Suddenly I got pregnant, with my daughter, and I used to say that I was going to name her Rhythm [*laughs*]. When she was born my son was two and a half. In that one year in between, I'd had two abortions. And after she was born I decided to take contraceptive pills. I went to the doctor, explained the situation; my husband's health was much worse then, so I was in no shape to help my husband and to have more children, even if I'd wanted them. But I always wanted to be the mother of four, five, or six children—any number, *and be able to educate them*, obviously, because I didn't want to have six illiterate kids.

All the time that he was sick, and to this day, he got his salary from the Navy.

Now *he* never worried about saving anything for the family's future, just the immediate present, right now—food. And he'd go shopping once or twice a year to buy clothing for the children. That was it. After we separated he contributed a small amount for the children. In fact, I've always said it's not that he gave it, it's that I managed to get it from the Navy. It was humiliating, this story of family support. There's a law about this, but it was humiliating because to have this right recognized you've got to fight for it. If it's the law, why did I have to go there and stand exposed before a lawyer? Isn't it the law? It was supposed to be automatically discounted from his salary, you see. We went there and he kept repeating, "I'm not going to give her a thing, because she's this, she's that"—offensive names, unpleasant things. I think women aren't respected in any way. All the rights that a woman has, she's won by virtue of a lot of sacrifice, of struggle, under so much humiliation, and if I could I wouldn't live on this support. Because I think he shouldn't have to pay me a thing. Why should I get a pension because I had a husband? After all, my years of marriage weren't eighteen years of sacrifice or terror. If they had been, I wouldn't have stayed married for even one year. There were good moments, too; and then we saw that the relationship was getting worse and we ended it. I still get the money. It's 30 percent of his salary, and now it comes directly to me. And my 100 percent is divided more or less into thirds. It comes to less than one minimum salary for each of us. And while he stayed here recuperating, he ate and drank, everything out of that same money.

When we separated my children were still in school, and we had a hard time. I was really naive, really stupid. Because I'd worked a lot but hadn't saved a thing. I invested all the money in making the house and my family comfortable. On account of his illness, to compensate for it, I always tried to get the best, and at that time I thought the best meant better clothing, better toys, things like that. One year before we separated I developed an allergy. I was a hairdresser and I couldn't work any more. I stayed at home and watched things wear out. This table that's still here, it dates back to my daughter's birth. He never replaced the furniture, and my things were wearing out—naturally, since the quality wasn't good. And when we separated I saw that I had nothing in the house, no blankets, no food. By the time we separated, he'd stopped shopping. I had to wait three months for the support money, with no supplies in the house, nothing but what I managed to scrounge up.

After my separation I had to survive somehow, didn't I? I couldn't pay the rent anymore on my house [in a middle-class neighborhood in greater metropolitan Rio]. Plus I wasn't feeling comfortable there, because I had no prospects at all. I was leading a closed little life, very neat and tidy, and people . . . they vacillate, their support depends on your status. If you fall, if there's some change, they don't want to see you. So I came to Rio looking for work, but I couldn't find any because I was already nearly forty. Here, until about age thirty, a woman can find a job. After that age it gets harder and harder. Then a friend of ours here said, "Look, I can't help you get a job because I don't know anyone, but I can cosign so you can rent a house. Move into it and sublet two rooms to make ends meet." I thought it was a good idea and so I came here, to a house not far from here, and I sublet part of it. At first I had a difficult time: I wasn't used to that kind of life, although my mother was also living in a house with sublets, but I never felt comfortable when I went to her house.

And that's how I started to have more direct contact with prostitutes, because I rented out a room to a woman who was a prostitute and had a child. And then one day she was gone, just like that, and left her child. Later I found out that she'd been arrested, and so I began to be aware of her struggle, of that difficult life the women lead. And I started hanging around, always trying to talk to people, above all to the prostitutes, to find out if their lives were all the same. And I started to see that even in prostitution there's a class distinction. There are those who work the best spots, the elite spots, and then there are the less elite ones, and so on down the line. The women who work in the South Zone [a higher-status area] of Rio are different from the women who work in Botafogo, from the women who work in Cinelândia, in Mangue, and so on. And as they work their way from the South Zone to here [in the North Zone], the class gets lower and lower. And that worried me a lot. I tried to see how I could help. I used to go to the [red-light] districts and take food, help them get documents, take them to a doctor—doing a kind of volunteer social work.

I didn't know about any research on this, but it was obvious that the majority of prostitutes are Black. If anyone has studied this, they've kept the results to themselves—which is another problem we have, of people who are concerned mainly with their research hanging on to the information. Later, when I got involved with some women's groups, it happened that we'd start talking and someone would come up and say, "No, it's such-and-such percent, there's a study . . ." and then you'd realize that the work exists, but it hasn't circulated.

In comparison with other jobs, lots of women are in prostitution. What we get here is three generations in prostitution—the grandmother, the mother, and the daughter. They become mothers very early, and that's the way it happens. You see women of forty-four, forty-five, with a daughter of thirty, thirty-one, and a granddaughter of fifteen, sixteen. They go into prostitution at an early age. When you go to the railroad station you see a huge number of prostitutes, most of them Black. Or if you go to Tiradentes Square, or to Frei Caneca Street—the spots where there are lots of men with little or no money, because in the South Zone things look a bit different.

Black women are exploited starting with the samba schools [samba groups that perform during Carnival], which parade them half-naked, and this attracts the attention of another kind of exploiter, the nightclub owner who puts on shows. We've got one here who's an incredible exploiter of Black women. He's gotten rich by staging a show with Black women, whom he calls *mulatas*—that old sexual mystique of the *mulata*.[16] You see, we're Black or White, and this label of *mulata* and *mulato* was created to hide the truth. We are Blacks, and Black women, when they go into these clubs, these shows, are labeled *mulatas* and, even worse, "the *mulatas* of so-and-so." They start having an owner, a master. And they are prostituted on the stage. The men in the audience have always wanted to prostitute these women, but the women might not be aware of this, and anyway they have to survive. I don't know if they earn much—they've never shown much interest in talking to us. They seem to think that if they say anything, they'll lose their jobs. What they do say is, "Well, if I weren't on the stage, I'd end up at some madam's house." Because Black women have few options, and lots of these women who go on the stage and expose themselves have hardly any education. They don't need to talk, just to wiggle. And when they get old, they beg. Those that make it. Lots of them die young—sick or murdered.

I wish I had a law degree. Not out of personal vanity or out of some whim, but I'd like to turn the profession upside-down. Why should the expert's voice count and not ours who *experience* the problems? I think that laws in this country are placed before necessities, and this is wrong. Laws should be created *starting from necessity*, as the need arises. Laws should come about in response to a necessity, and not the necessity mould itself to the law! To my mind, that's not right. We have a law here against racial discrimination.[17] I'm telling you frankly, I've never stopped to read that law, to study it, because to me it's a joke. I won't waste my time on it. What I want is to fight for a law that would really address this problem of racial discrimination. People are afraid of creating such a law, afraid that it would cause divisions. But the divisions are already there. What we've got to do is unite. We have to fight for equality, Whites don't. They have their rights, all their rights. We want our rights, in proportion to the duties that we have in this country. Because we're overloaded with duties, and we're blamed for everything that goes wrong in society. A holdup? A Black did it. If three people are standing on the corner talking, two Whites and a Black, the police won't search the Whites; they'll go directly to the Black. This has to be changed. If they've got to be searched, search them all, Whites and Blacks. Blacks and Whites live in the *favelas*, but the majority are Black. Burglars, drug dealers, and everything else—they've necessarily got to be Black! On principle it's the Black who's the rapist, who's the mugger. It's the Black woman who's the prostitute—and also the maid, because people have this image of domestic servants; they see it as a form of underemployment, so these women are marginalized, too. If a Black woman appears at an apartment house here, she has to go in by the service entrance because that's what all the servants use. I've had this experience visiting a friend who lives in the South Zone, I'm supposed to enter by the service door. Of course I don't do it. I argue with the doorman, threaten to make a scene in front of the building. And I get in. I don't understand why a maid has to go up by one elevator and the lady of the house by another. I can't understand this spatial discrimination.

In schools—I have personal experience of this—there's discrimination against Blacks. My son was studying in a public school, and he was discriminated against by the teachers themselves, and also by his classmates who already brought this discrimination from home with them, that's what they learned at home. And the teachers, who are supposed to change these things, continue the same pattern. One mother in the *favela* not far from here told me about a case. The teacher turned to her son and said, "Look, you're a *favelado*"—the boy was having a hard time with some subject—"You're not learning, you're stupid, you're a *favelado*. You'll end up on the streets." The Black *favelado* is discriminated against. If a man is a *nordestino*, he's discriminated against here for being *nordestino* and for being Black. But, on the other hand, the *nordestinos* themselves discriminate against Blacks, too. They themselves are oppressed, are discriminated against, and in turn they discriminate against the Black. If it's a woman, she suffers three kinds of discrimination. In the end, in people's minds, at the bottom of the whole social ladder are the Blacks, us. If a Black reaches a high professional level, or cultural, he doesn't stop being discriminated against on that account. It's racial discrimination here, not class discrimination as they say—though they try to pretend that's it. But we know perfectly well it's not that.

In the mass media you find the greatest discriminators, in terms of both employment and the message. All day long you're bombarded by endless commercials and appeals to buy, but the people who make this appeal, who are selling you these products, are all White. They're blond, they seem to belong to the middle class, they represent that class. The children who ask other children to buy chewing gum, cookies, a toy, to use a certain toothpaste, they're all children getting out of a comfortable bed, leaving their room and going into a luxurious bathroom, with a father who's also very well nourished, well groomed, successful, sending messages to the *favelados* to buy that particular brand of toothpaste.

There's a newspaper that advertises its classified pages on television. The commercial shows a head of the family who's unemployed. His wife's really sad, his kids look worried—they're sitting in a comfortable living room, watching a color TV. The husband hasn't shaved; he's reading the job ads. And the next day he goes and finds a job. Right away. Then he comes back, dinner's on the table, and the family is as happy and content as could be. Well, the *favelado* goes out with his paper under his arm and looks for work, but he doesn't find it. Our mass media situate

Blacks outside of reality. The standard of beauty you see on the soap operas is White. You can be short, skinny, whatever, but you've got to be White. Why can't they portray the life of a Black family, a real Black family? The reality of Blacks in this country isn't what they're trying to convey on TV.

Sometimes I feel like I'm going to explode, there's so much going on inside me. All around me I see our problems placed in the hands of people who are—they're not incompetent, they just have bad intentions. When people say our legislators are incompetent, they're wrong. They've just got bad intentions. And in their hands the problems just continue. These things are suffocating us.

W E L L ,   W H A T happened was that I used to talk with the women, the prostitutes, and I was already beginning to have larger goals; but I didn't have access to government offices, to any services. Then the neighborhood association started, and a neighbor asked me to participate in a meeting and I went. At the association, I met people who were militants in political parties, and I began to participate in one, too, the PT [Partido dos Trabalhadores, or Workers' Party, started in 1979].[18] We'd have meetings and discussions and I got to hear a lot of information from other states, other cities, other countries, and as things came up for discussion I'd be asking everybody about whatever I didn't understand. I'd ask the economists, the lawyers.

Then I began to participate in women's groups [these grew rapidly in number after 1975 and the United Nations International Women's Year], but they didn't satisfy me because they were elitist groups. Some were national; they had contacts with groups in other states. I got involved with them through the PT; there were women in the PT who invited me to participate in these meetings. This was several years ago, and at that time their vision was theoretical. Because to the extent that they were called upon to do practical, concrete work, I saw that they had some . . . reservations. There was some resistance on their part, resistance to taking part in the work. They'd keep postponing it. They thought with all that theory of theirs, which they were spreading through the press, through their meetings and debates, that they were already making a contribution, carrying out some task. And it's true, they were contributing, but only to a very small group of people, those who bought magazines, bought newspapers, and took part in those debates. They weren't reaching the people in general. There are some women in these groups who do work in the slums, in prisons, and so on, but it's on a very small scale. It wasn't more widespread, there wasn't any call for participants, because the groups that carried out these kinds of projects didn't invite others. They weren't open to outsiders. I'm not saying that they did this through any bad intentions, no. I think their intentions were good. It's just that in their minds—

and this is logical, they don't have the experience we have. They've learned a lot at home, in their childhood, in adolescence—their mothers giving old clothes to the maid, giving leftover food to the maid to take home. This can also happen at the cultural level of militants, that people act this way.

Yes, they were mainly White. There were one or two Black women, the minimum. Well, these White women, at the first meetings I just kept quiet because I didn't understand anything, not a thing. Today I think that I actually understood a fair amount, that's why I kept quiet. I didn't participate in their talk. I thought that the terms they used . . . you see, there are various ways of intimidating people, and speech is one way. If you hit someone, if you shove them against the wall and threaten them with a gun, you're doing something wrong. But if you threaten them with your way of speaking, what I hear in my ear isn't what she hears. She can say, "No, I didn't say anything wrong, I just said such-and-such." And I began to get irritated with this kind of behavior that these women had.

How did I start to notice this? Well, it was when they would refer to Blacks. They used to stammer, beat about the bush [*imitates their nervous laughter*], things like that, if there was a Black in the audience. If they said *faveladas*, it would come out sounding as if they were worried about offending someone. I don't even know how to explain to you how I managed to hear all this, because when you're reading, you can read between the lines since you have the opportunity of going back to the text many times. But listening, that's an immediate thing, and sometimes you don't even have time to think.

Something got to me, made me see that those women were on the wrong path, that we couldn't just leave things there. So I began to speak up. One day I said, "I'm going to speak up, whatever happens. Because if I keep quiet I'll just go on absorbing what they say." So I spoke. They'd begun to talk about this abortion business, abortion this, abortion that, proletarian women, who knows what else, that they needed this, they needed that. I said, "Fine, but where's the *favelada* here? Where's the Black woman? Why are you speaking for us?" And I told them what I thought.

Look, it's important to have intellectuals participating in social movements, even to express our ideas on paper. But why are there things we don't talk about? Why do we talk about abandoned minors and beggars when we can see that the abandoned minors are the children of prostitutes, that prostitutes beg. This word, "prostitute," it's not a word that should shock anybody. Since the fact is there, why should the word scare people?

But it's not only the government or the middle class that discriminates. Whites in the same social conditions as Blacks still discriminate, and Whites discriminate against Blacks even within prostitution. And Blacks also discriminate against prostitutes [*dry laughter*]. So it's hard to tackle this subject of prostitution; it's a whole train of thought. It's the product of this particular society, because it's been going on since the Empire; prostitution has existed since the beginning of the Empire. The plantation owners, the foremen, they prostituted the Black women in those days. It's an old, old story and it was brought here to Brazil. It wasn't invented by Brazilians, so why should we blame only our own society nowadays? But you can't run away from the problem, no. It's got to be faced, even on a political level.

Well, at the beginning, when I started to raise this issue of prostitution at meetings, the women were shocked and tried to avoid discussing it. They came to me and said, "Look, Vera, this path you're on is no good. You're going to be hurt by this, you'll get burned." This was said, usually, as we were leaving the room, talking things over, because not one woman ever had the courage to say this to me publicly.

They put me through a lot, but I put them through even more. I said to them, "I don't know the solution to this problem, this situation we're in. I really don't know. But there must be a solution, there must be, and all I'm doing is pointing out the problem, putting it on the table, because you all want to set out caviar, *salade niçoise*, who knows what else, but Brazilian food you don't want" [*laughs*]. Brazilian food, let me tell you, is made up of the worst ingredients. It's hard to digest Brazilian food! People didn't want to discuss it. To talk about foreign policy, that's terrific, but to discuss Brazilian defects, that's horrible: "Tomorrow we'll get into that. Right now we've got to deal with the IMF [International Monetary Fund] problem." And that's where we left it.

They listened to me, but they didn't like it. I could tell. But on the other hand, they didn't try to shut me up. They even invited me to other meetings and I showed up, at four or five others. I always came with some proposals for projects, and then they began to get interested because they were getting access to information they'd had only on a theoretical level—they had no contact with people who'd had that kind of experience. Then I began to notice that I was playing the "useful idiot" to them, that they had no interest in going ahead with any of the projects.

What kinds of projects? To visit the sites and, starting from these visits, to talk to people and do some concrete work. You see, they had the means to form a legal aid group, a medical aid group, educational aid, to create a group to pressure the state about the women's needs. At one of the last meetings I had with them, I said this: "I'm really sorry that you, who have in your hands all the elements to move the state to action, haven't got the slightest interest in doing this. You're working for a small group, you're not working for the collectivity." The women from the various women's groups in Rio, they were always the same women saying the same thing. Whenever a group is organized they want to lead the work, to direct it, and real understanding becomes difficult. I think their objectives really are different.

For example, when they talk about legalization of abortion. Fine, then the middle-class woman can have other relationships, aside from with her husband. This is the impression I got, but I've never heard a woman say it. And from that relationship, let's say a pregnancy results. She's got the means, so she goes to a clinic and gets this little nothing removed. She has the abortion, and things continue as they were. Now the proletarian women, are they going to understand the middle-class proposal? They'll never understand it. They'll say, "Great, I can get pregnant as often as I want since I can always get an abortion." What they don't see is the risks they're going to run, because, as I said before, they get a different kind of medical care than middle-class women. But the middle-class women *are aware* of this. When they preach legalization of abortion, they're much more emphatic about our freedom to use our bodies than about the state's obligations and responsibilities. And that's where there's this enormous difference, because we could even, in the future, think about the legalization of abortion—but only once we have decent medical care, once we have access to places in the schools, up to whatever grade we want to reach.

Because, right now, kids can't even finish primary school. The schools are much too crowded, and when the kids get to be twelve, thirteen, they've got to leave to try to help support the household. So they become underemployed, too. They sell peanuts, deliver papers, shine shoes. And they hang around with people who are already marginalized. Where's he going to sell peanuts? In Praça Quinze, in Tiradentes Square, where people hang out all night. And there they have access to thousands of things, they get all kinds of information. Somebody comes up and says, "Hey, go over there, take this package to that fellow who's standing there, and I'll give you a thousand cruzeiros." Well, to earn that much money he'd have to sell how many bags of peanuts? So he drops the peanuts and off he goes, not knowing what's in the package. And he's caught—caught with marijuana. And there, in front of the judge, the boy will start to see what he was doing. So now he knows, but he earned a thousand cruzeiros, and it was just bad luck that he got arrested, right? So he runs away and goes where? Right back. Only from then on he does it knowingly. That is what we've got to face; that's what the kids out there are like.

And their mothers are these women who've got no real medical care, no information. They go to the clinic and say, "Doctor, I've missed my period, I'm feeling such-and-so." They have a urine exam and find out they're pregnant. So then, "Senhora, you should come for prenatal care." And she goes, and on those visits she's hardly examined, because the doctor has twenty patients to see in two hours; he doesn't have time to spend giving patients information. And he's not interested either. It's great to have a son who's got a degree in medicine or engineering. To have a daughter who's a doctor gives you status. They study books, they get practical training; but social awareness they haven't got, they think that's for social workers. But even the social workers at the hospital are a nightmare. They treat people coldly, with total indifference; they're robots. So—how're you going to talk to these women about legalization of abortion, women who have three, four, six kids and have no rights to childcare, to schools?

And this campaign for breast-feeding, this group, Amigas do Peito [Bosom Friends—a women's group that promotes breast-feeding], that's another elitist outfit. Working-class women, *faveladas*, breast-feed their children because they can't afford to buy milk; it's very expensive. They breast-feed without all these stories, without needing a campaign, nothing. It's the middle-class women who don't want to breast-feed: they don't want to end up with sagging breasts, they don't want to be stuck there breast-feeding their child every three hours. It's the executive who can't leave her work for a minute, the television actress. Black women who work as domestic servants, they breast-feed, they take their children with them; somehow or other they manage it, or a neighbor will breast-feed them. I used to go to another part of the city to breast-feed a child whose mother was sick. Sometimes, if I got home late, my neighbor would breast-feed my son. Sure, women need information, but what they hear on television is the minimum; it's "You should breast-feed your children," and so on. We know that. But how will I get proper nourishment so that I can do it? That's what needs to be touched on, because I *know* I have to breast-feed my children and, even if I didn't want to, I know I won't have money for a can of milk.

We proletarian women, when we set out on the struggle for better conditions of life for women, for our men, for our children, we're not fighting against men, we're declaring war on the system, which in the end is made up of men [*laughs*]. And when women become part of this system, they have macho heads. Proletarian women don't distinguish between macho heads and feminist heads. I, who've come a step further, I've begun to grasp this, but in general what we see is a woman behaving like a bourgeois woman, a reactionary woman, who's taking part in the system.

A S   F A R   A S I've been aware, the Black movement here has been active for about the past ten years. But I know it has existed for a lot longer than that. In São Paulo we had, in about 1932—I hate to mention dates because I'm never sure of them, but I know there was a Black leader in São Paulo who managed to mobilize a great many Blacks. I don't remember his name, but he mobilized many Blacks around some political question; maybe it had to do with the Estado Novo.[19] But São Paulo is a state where there's a lot of discrimination against Blacks, more than in Rio. It's apparent at all levels, all the time. It's not camouflaged. As you go farther south—São Paulo, Paraná, Santa Catarina, Rio Grande do Sul—discrimination gets worse and the Blacks more silent. Because *cariocas* [residents of Rio], *bahianos* [residents of Bahia] are more outgoing. They show what they feel. But farther south, I think Blacks are often ashamed of even being Black. Sometimes they're not even conscious of this racial discrimination because of the notion, the image that people try to create, that there's no discrimination in Brazil.[20]

It's been demonstrated that the majority in this country are racially mixed, not Black or White. But Blacks can have light skin; that makes no difference. If my daughter gets home soon, you'll see that she's light-skinned, but she's still Black. My husband looks White, but he's descended from Blacks. In my family we're 100 percent Black, with no miscegenation. My husband, no, he's the grandson of Italians, the son of a *nordestino* who married the granddaughter of a Black woman here in the South. So in my children's heredity, the Black race predominates. Now my father, judging by what my mother has said, is mulatto, the son of a Portuguese man and a Black woman. We're all Blacks. This whole story of mulattos, mestizos, is nonsense. For us, mulattos are Blacks. Now *caboclos*, who are a mixture of Indian and White, that's something else. In the Northeast, a great many people are descended from Indians. But farther south there's more the influence of Germans, Italians—Europeans who were more careful about not miscegenating. It's easier in the South to find a person who's totally Black than here in Rio de Janeiro.

I used to see people from the Black movement in the streets, making speeches. I used to read about them in the papers, just the few things that were printed about this. And one day a fellow I know from an Afro-Brazilian cultural group that I belong to said to me, "Vera, go down to [an Afro-Brazilian center]. You're getting really preoccupied with the Black problem"—can you imagine, a Black telling me I'm "preoccupied with the Black problem"!? He said, "Go there, because they discuss these problems of ours. You'll like the place." I said, "But how can I go when I don't know a soul there? I've passed by their door and seen people there, but they seem really different." He said, "Go anyway. Join the group. You'll like it." When I got there, a group of Blacks were meeting to discuss something or other, and I felt like an outsider right away. Not that they said, "Get out, you don't belong here," no. It was the way they welcomed me. Because they were a group of Black intellectuals, and what they were doing was really research into Black cultures. Social problems could have fit into this, but that particular moment wasn't the right time for this discussion. Now I went there interested in culture, but also in a broader discussion of social problems and with the objective of going out and doing some work. I was really put off and for a long time I didn't go back, but I was always interested in what was happening there. This was a couple of years ago.

Then, in March of this year, the first meeting of Black women took place here in Rio, early in March. It was the first meeting of Black women in Brazil—at least, I'd never heard of anything like that happening before. At first I didn't identify myself because I understood that at a meeting of Black women all women could participate. But in the corridor I ran into a woman who immediately asked me if I was representing some group. I said no. She asked if I had a report to present. I said, "No. I'd like to know what the subject is, because I don't want to impose my own, but I need to know, so that in case there's nothing that really interests me— which seems unlikely—I won't participate. But the issue I'd like to raise is the problem of Black women in prostitution." Then she told me that she thought this was a very delicate subject, that I should raise it on another occasion. A Black woman, an intellectual, said this to me. And I thought, "If I don't overcome this barrier now, if I can't create some space here, I'm not going to have another chance, because I've been talking about this in various women's groups and nothing's happened. So it's got to be here." They told me they had sent invitations to neighborhood associations, so I said, "Well, I belong to one, and I didn't get an invitation. I just read about this in the paper this morning, and that's why I'm here." But I called the directors of our association and asked if I could represent the group at this meeting, and they authorized me to participate. And finally I raised that topic. There was no way they could prevent me, because I raised the issue in the plenary session. Two of the women there were running for the directorship of [the Afro-Brazilian center], and their slate contained a proposal for a project in conjunction with the community, to open the house to the community at large. These women thought my particpation and this issue I'd raised were interesting and important. And once I got this response, then I thought the moment had come to actually get into the Black movement. Although I'd been in this struggle for a few years then, fighting for this cause, I hadn't been affiliated with any group. And that's how I came to take part in that center, and now I'm one of the officers.

But, you know, for me the Black movement is the samba school, it's *candomblé*, it's *umbanda*.[21] The Black movement is the Blacks inside prisons. It's not directed, it just happens. But when there is leadership, it's not the right kind, because the leadership of these groups turns out to be in the hands of Whites, of capitalists, of people who are much more interested in earning money, becoming famous, occupying high positions than in changing our way of life and improving our conditions.

Just look what's happened with Carnival. It was a popular expression of our culture, and now it's been taken over by Whites, too. We're an underdeveloped country, full of illiterates, and people try to elitize things. Carnival . . . it was really our own stupidity. Everything that happens in Brazil, good or bad, starts in Rio de Janeiro. Well, the mayor came with this story of setting up grandstands on the Avenue [where the samba schools parade during Carnival], that it would be better, people would be more comfortable. This was some years ago. The *cariocas* thought it was a great idea. So did I [*laughing*]; I was alienated, too. I don't remember a single person objecting. I took my little cushion and went there and paid for a seat. Ah, that first Carnival with the grandstands on President Vargas Avenue was wonderful. People got to sit down, it was great. There were ten tiers, and you just climbed up. But, you see, it was cheap back then, really cheap. And if you couldn't afford it, there was still a lot of space cordoned off where people could stand and watch. But then what happened was that they saw this as a great source of income, and the following year they extended the grandstands and started to improve them, sophisticated improvements, even boxes just like in the theater [*laughs*]. You should have seen it this past year, there were boxes with cooks preparing food, serving imported champagne, whiskey, all that. The economic crisis is for most people, but not for everyone. And every year the stands grow. I wonder if people are that alienated, or just uninformed, naive. They don't seem to realize what's happening. Well, by now Carnival's turned into politics, politics and big business, and it's being taken over by Whites.[22]

Still, the Black movement is everywhere, and all that's lacking is the right leadership. My proposals within the social movement are always directed toward work with a practical result. I see that where specialists are involved, at least in the field of culture, they're often obliged to do this or that because of their professions. They have to fulfill that role. But those of us who are in the social movement as volunteers, who are genuinely voluntary volunteers [*laughs*], we have to raise these problems, to rouse people, to expose the problems and point them out to the government, regardless of what one or another group is doing.

At the moment my contacts with the prostitutes are through Marilene [a prostitute-activist], and also Dona Yolanda who has a pool hall in [a working-class section of Rio]. Just recently, the first meeting of women from the *favelas* and the periphery took place. There were women from various sectors, and I thought it important that prostitutes participate, because there are many prostitutes living in *favelas* and the periphery of the city. So we had to mobilize the women, to let them know what was happening, to show them that they had this opportunity to state their problems, to make their demands. So I went to Dona Yolanda and she gave us her pool hall and undertook to get in touch with the women. And we met.

But before that, I got a call from a woman in one of the social service agencies who'd heard about my contact with the prostitutes and that I wanted to carry out a project on behalf of these women. I went to see her, and she asked me what I thought needed to be done immediately, to serve the women's interests. I said, "Well, the way things look in my neighborhood, what seems most needed right now is a place for them to leave their children." Because here, in various parts of Rio de Janeiro, the women pay on average $3 a day for someone to watch their children—that would be in a house with other children. And sometimes they're not well cared for anyway. On the one hand, these people charge a lot; but, on the other, there are lots of mothers who don't pay, who let days pass without paying, who are arrested. And when these mothers are arrested, there are women who go right on giving the same care to the child. But others don't. Anyway, we can't judge these women who care for the children. They're not in a good position to support a child either, and in fact they don't know if the mother's going to show up or if they'll be stuck with that child. Sometimes they really get attached to the child, really start to love it, and don't want to give it up. They might even end up hiding the fact that the child was born to someone else and was abandoned in that house.

There's a huge shed up the street that's unused most of the year. It's for a samba school from another community. It does no good at all to this community, and it occupies all that space that could be transformed into a community center, to serve the entire community. I took the woman from the government office there and showed her the space. She asked me not to discuss it, so the project wouldn't be quashed before it even got off the ground, and I agreed. Then suddenly it appeared in the papers. There she was saying that the project was taking shape, bla-bla-bla bla-bla-bla. And the women began to complain—that this wasn't for real, that their main concern wasn't this, that their main demand wasn't for a community center since they didn't even know if they'd go on working in that location. They live with the constant prospect of being kicked out of their rooms. And there was a tremendous conflict, a terrible uncertainty among the women, because behind every government proposal all kinds of things are going on. And they began to think not about the possible benefits they'd get, but about the harm that might come to them.

I was in a strange position, because the women knew me but they didn't know that woman who'd talked to the papers, so they came to complain to me: "Look, Dona Vera, you talked with us, you motivated us to try to get some space, medical care, a daycare center, and now this whole thing has landed on top of us and we don't know what's going on. We don't want to learn how to sew, to knit, to crochet—none of that. We want a place where we can stay, have medical care, and not have the police show up all the time. We don't want to be exploited." Well, I let things cool down, there was no point talking further at that stage. I was really on the hotseat, and no interview with that woman was going to change that. Then the women who run the houses came to me and started pressuring me. They didn't understand what I was doing; they thought I wanted to give their houses to the women, to let them take over running the houses. It was crazy. And the organizing for the meeting of the women from the *favelas* and the periphery still had to be done. I was getting desperate because the women were disbanding, and I was afraid they'd lose confidence in me.

And then one woman told me that she'd voted for someone for the Chamber of Deputies, and I said, "Oh? What did he promise you?" "He promised to solve our problem." "Great, then let's go talk to him." So I located this deputy, and we got the women together for a meeting with him. We suggested they take part in this meeting and lay out their problems, which would be publicized by the press, with their demands coming from themselves and not from other people. And now we're trying to organize a work team and my function is to mobilize the women, to organize the team with specialists in the areas of social work, medical care, planning, housing construction, engineers, architects. It might seem like a large group of people to deal with, but it's not quite like that—one or two engineers, that's all, one architect, one doctor, one person in sanitation, one gynecologist, one pediatrician. That's what's needed. And a social worker—which is a serious business in this country because they leave a lot to be desired. I admire the profession, but I've never met a social worker I could really admire. I've made dozens of appeals, and what we've gotten are professionals wanting to do a master's, a doctorate, concerned about their thesis, and their participation is very paternalistic: "We'll find someone to give you food, to give you medicine, to give you clothes." And that's not how it should be, I think. I've already gotten in touch with people interested in participating in this work, and now Marilene, who used to live in a hotel, has moved into a house that she's rented, where the women can get together, can talk, and can get away from these people who want to come to our meetings to find out what's happening, people who are curious about things that are totally irrelevant. They want to hear about the prostitutes' sexuality. I say,"They're women. I think it's the same as other women's. These things don't change from class to class."

But it's hard to get the women together. They don't believe things can change. They need a guaranteed place to work, they need security, health, education. Now the other aspects that come up with prostitution—drugs, theft, violence, these things that surround prostitution—all that's the government's sphere, and they're always wanting us to testify about these things.

You know, the law doesn't say that selling your body is illegal. It says that inducing someone to sell her body is illegal, even if the money doesn't get back to the person who did the inducing. It's the *inducing* that's illegal, the pimping, but the law doesn't say that to *be* a prostitute is illegal. So, if being a prostitute isn't illegal, then they have the right to a place to work. That's our reasoning. Now look, the communities themselves create the space for prostitution. Prostitutes have space that's defined not by the law, the city, the state, but by the community itself. The city can't come along and say to them, "You've got to move because it's illegal to do this." So the women stay in Mem de Sá, in Frei Caneca, in Orla Marítima . . . but they're exposed to a whole range of repressions. Some days the police seem to be more aggressive, some days less. When they pick up a prostitute, there's no code, nothing. They try to get her for vagrancy, but they can't prove she's not a seamstress, a manicurist, and they've got to let her go. It's just a method of intimidation. The girls themselves often aren't aware of their rights, because they think they're in the wrong, they feel guilty.

Our ultimate objective? To make the profession official. As long as the profession isn't recognized, they don't have any rights to anything. And I think this would actually decrease the number of prostitutes. Because once they have better conditions, many of them will find some other way. But the way it's going, with the women not having the basic conditions of survival, it'll never end, only get worse. If these new generations, these kids, had medical care, had education, if they were really socialized, prostitution would stop. Women have to have other possibilities in life.

Yes, this implies a complete social change; but my struggle, my priority, is for a change in the situation of Blacks. If a large portion of people were taken out of their marginality and were able to move up, they'd help create more space for other people to move up, and we'd win. We're fighting for a general change directed first of all at the prostitute. And these are mostly Black women.

Y O U   W A N T   T O   K N O W about my standard of living [*laughs*]? It's getting worse every day! The support money I get isn't enough; it has to be supplemented. I sew once in a while, or I sell things. There's a possibility I could make sweets to sell. They're all temporary jobs. We've changed what we eat, but sometimes that's not enough and you have to eat less, too, because even if you buy different things, they end up costing the same amount. What I've been noticing lately is that we're running out of choices. Rice has gone up a lot, so some time ago we made beans every day in order to eat less rice. Nowadays we can't make either beans or rice much, because they now cost the same. A kilo of beans is almost ⊅1, and rice is nearly that much. Corn meal is over 20 cents a kilo and manioc flour, too. Spaghetti went up a lot all of a sudden—we'd been using that instead of rice. Soup—you can't make much soup these days because vegetables are expensive. The price of carrots varies a lot, it can go up to 90 cents, ⊅1 a kilo, or back down to 50 or 40 cents, never lower than that. Potatoes cost about $1 a kilo, too; that was another thing we used to have instead of rice, we'd make mashed potatoes, fried potatoes, and we can't have that anymore either. We're eating less fried foods in general anyway, because the price of cooking oil has gone up. So, all of a sudden we see that we can't make substitutions. What we have to do is decrease. I have meat once or twice a week. Today I bought a kilo of liver and was shocked to see it's gone up to $2 a kilo. Rump roast costs $2.40, not much more than liver—before, liver, tripe, all those things we call beef viscera, used to be a lot cheaper, but not anymore.

The rent on this house is very low; with building tax and water, it's about $70 a month. When you rent a house here you're responsible for everything—for insurance, fire insurance for the building. Your own belongings you've got to insure separately. Electricity costs a lot. I'm paying on average $9 a month, and I constantly economize. I don't turn on one bulb if another's burning. I turn off the light when I leave the room. Gas also, I'm paying about $1.00 to $1.20. Now I'm not including my phone in my expenses. I work especially to pay my phone bill, extra work because I need the phone but I don't think my family should make sacrifices for it. I don't decrease my other expenditures in the house in order to pay my phone bill. It's usually about $12 a month, but it's been as high as $40. I've even got a bill waiting to be paid. One of these days they'll cut it off. I've been waiting to get some money for a job I did, but I won't pay the phone bill out of my other expenses. If they cut it off, stay cool.

And yet, with everything that's going on in this country right now, and with all my experience, I consider myself to be in an excellent situation. I could even sit here in my house and not complain about a thing, because I have food. I have a roof over my head. And I'm in good health, thank God. That's also why I'm privileged, because I get medical care from the Navy, and it's excellent. My children are also privileged that way. I may be in a terrible situation, but relative to other people I'm really well off. Right in this neighborhood we've got a head of one family earning $60 a month and supporting them all. Why can't he find a way to supplement that income? Because he's already working from eight in the morning to eight at night. With this wave of unemployment, the bosses can do whatever they like with their employees. Just the specter of unemployment makes the employees submit. If he protests, the boss says, right to his face, cynically, "You want to leave? There are a thousand people lined up outside waiting to take your place." And it's true! We're in such a predicament; you're damned if you do and damned if you don't.

That's the portrait of our country now, one part of it, a small corner of that portrait. Because it gets much worse than that. Look at the Northeast, five years of drought with no letup. On television I saw the "work fronts" the government's created [for drought-stricken *nordestinos*]. They're giving the *nordestino* the indecent salary of $25 a month. You see them digging, God knows what, what can they be building there? How? These people don't even have the strength for this sort of work. They don't have food; they're eating wild rats, lizards, stuff that gives you the creeps. That's what they're resorting to. A woman cooking an ox head, she's been cooking that ox head for six months, making soup out of those bones. These women *procreate!* And these women are suffering. Nothing's done about this aspect of Brazil. To build nuclear power plants, that's not our reality. On television last week I saw a *nordestina* with six or eight children. She'd been walking twenty kilometers a day to get to work. When her husband saw their awful situation, he took off. Then she got some help from the government, and he came back and said he hadn't abandoned her, that he'd just gone looking for better days. But we know it wasn't that at all. They do abandon them; the number of abandoned women in the Northeast is growing every day.

I doubt that our problems can be solved by political parties. I don't believe in this opposition. The parties are made up mainly of people with bad intentions. I'll say it again: they're not incompetent, they've got bad intentions. Individuals elected with the vote of the people turn around and do the people a disservice. What we need is to have home-grown candidates. We need to get sufficiently politicized to install our own representatives; then things could change. We just want to collect our due, because we're fed up with owing, all we do is owe. Energy is more expensive, gas is more expensive. We've got to pay more for energy, for gas, to go without food, because the country is in debt and has to pay. It just so happens that when the country took on this debt, I got no benefit out of it whatsoever. We've got to say, "You did this against our will, and it's your problem to pay it." I don't know about these politicians. If they don't vote against this new proposal, to hold back 20 percent of the salary increases we're due,[23] then what's the point of having direct elections anyway? These men were elected directly by the people, so if they don't do what's right, who should we trust? They don't care how we live. We should break with the IMF; that would be the best solution. Because right now it's not we who have to be afraid of them, it's they who have to worry about us. We need to create a system for *us*, for this continent. We need to negotiate on the level of continents, because what's being pushed down our throats isn't isolated policies, they're continental policies.

I connect what's happening in my country with what's taking place in other countries. And outside of South America, too. When I see that they killed that Filipino leader [Aquino], I don't need the word of that Japanese reporter to know that he wasn't killed by any terrorist. And now the government's cracking down on the press, to intimidate the Filipinos. Brazilians hear that, and they're kind of slow anyway, but they hear that and think, "Better stay out of it, who knows what could happen?" And it shouldn't be like that. I, as a Black woman, discriminated against for being a woman, for being Black, for being working class, for being separated from my husband—with all this weighing on me, it still won't stop me. I'll go right on talking. It's no use telling me that story about our problem being economic. It is, but the economic problem is something the government has to solve. I didn't create this situation for the country. It's the country that created the situation for me, the government of this country, and it should resolve my situation and that of the other 130 million Brazilians. If they have direct elections, they're only doing what they're obliged to do. None of these men picked within the system is any good. We've got to have someone who'll govern *with* the people, not govern *the people*. There's a huge difference between governing *with* and governing *the*.

M Y   L I F E changed after the separation from my husband. What I did during all those years when my children were small . . . [*laughs*], it was worthwhile but so insignificant. Solving family problems. I thought, "I'm important because I have a mother-in-law, a sister-in-law, nieces and nephews." I thought, "This is the center of my life, and it's for them that I've got to fight." I was fighting for them, but they, ah! Each one was fighting just for himself [*laughs*]. Only afterward did I analyze it. But at the time, that's where I was, being fulfilled. I'd take my son to school, get him ready to have his first book, and I was working. I was a hairdresser. I had a middle-class clientele, and I worked at home full-time and took care of my children. I was always concerned about staying close to home. We lived in a residential neighborhood and I worked for this bourgeois clientele and I thought I liked that, too. I transferred myself to their world without knowing whether they accepted me or not.

In that community, I dealt constantly with those women and they befriended me. I took part in those middle-class programs—Catholic women's teas and so on. But I used to say, "I've got the feeling that something has to change, but I don't understand what, or how, or what's going on." Once I'd begun to cultivate my clients, they'd talk to me, and sometimes the women would say things I didn't understand, and I'd keep quiet. I didn't let them know I couldn't understand. I wouldn't agree or disagree, I'd just try to figure it out. I used to avoid having only one client in the house. It was better if several were there at the same time; then I could follow their talk, and it would become clearer. Then I began to see that for them a hairdresser, a seamstress, all are illiterates who don't know a thing. But I always listened to the news, and I read a lot—newspapers, books, magazines—and that helped me because I'd be able to make comments. I never walked in and said I couldn't understand something. I'd say, "Did you hear the news, Senhor? What do you think of it?" One man would do one analysis, another a different one. The women in my neighborhood weren't too interested in that sort of thing. They wanted to exchange recipes with me, discuss domestic problems, and I was very patient. When clients would come to my house and start to talk about domestic problems, I'd go along, but I also had clients who'd bring up other, more interesting subjects, and they were the ones who began to invite me to parties at their houses. When my son was a baby, some of them would hold him—they had small children, too. And when I was pregnant with my daughter, they brought me baby clothes, they kept me company. And so ties of friendship were formed, and when there's friendship, when the friendship is real, discrimination ends. That happened to me with several of my clients, that I started to participate in their everyday life and they in mine. We'd have parties when the children had a birthday. When my husband was sick and we didn't have a car, they would come to our house, take my husband to the hospital. They gave us a great deal of help, of companionship. I would never have had the money to go away on weekends, but they'd take me— to their ranches, to their country houses, their beach houses.

Today I see that this was all wrong, that I shouldn't have been benefiting from their wealth. What I should have been doing was fighting to change things. The hours we wasted playing cards and at their ranches, we should have been doing some work. Because these women I was associating with, they were open-minded, ready for real work. Though they were from a different class, their view of things, the way they treated their servants and other people, you could tell that all they needed was that slight push that I got—which woke me up and made me see.

But it's no good being happy because I'm sitting at a table with half a dozen people, all of us satiated. It's no longer a question of hunger—hunger can be satisfied with bread, and there you are eating milk and meat and much more. That's why I can state, the best moment in my life since the day I was born is now, now that I'm being useful. Without any pretension I can say that I'm being useful. And until a few years ago, until about four years ago, I was just one more woman who wasn't really there. Criticizing the dictatorship, criticizing this and that, but any real participation? My participation was the strictly paternalistic kind that's damaged the country so much. It's precisely the kind of thing that's led us to the point we've now reached. Because if instead of coming along with that story of distributing food and clothes at certain locales, in exchange for which they wanted votes, if they had taught people how to get their own food, if they'd provided people with basic conditions, we wouldn't have got to this point.

My story, this life, this struggle—if I had the opportunity to live, to choose a certain number of years of life with good health, a clear mind, I'd like forty more years, because until now I haven't taken part, I haven't contributed in any way. Although—are you a mother? Well, when you're a mother you think, "Wow!

Now I'm fulfilled. The best thing in my life is being a mother." It is very important, but to be an alienated mother, to be a mother separated from everything that's happening, to be mother only to your own children—that's very little. It's almost nothing. We have to be mother to all children, sister to them all, companion to them all. And we have to be mother to our ideas and defend them as if they were children of our flesh and blood that someone was trying to hurt. This is what we have to do, this is what's important. And so long as I defend the rights just of my children, I'll achieve a momentary satisfaction only. Because what am I defending? A place for my son in a school? Sure, I have a connection, I go there, pressure them, and he gets in. But my neighbor's son can't get in. So my son's going to school and he loses this contact with his playmate here, because now he's better off. And from then on I'll always want more for *my* son, *my* son, *my* son, until one day he'll get to a point in his life when he'll be a grown man, he'll marry and have his own family; and I'll have spent so long, so much time fighting so he can get ahead that I won't have noticed how I was being left behind, left alone, and my son will be moving in another sphere and won't accept me, won't accept my neighbor or my neighbor's children. We'll stay here while my son moves on. No, what I think is this, that my son has the same rights as my neighbor's children, and we all have to march together. And when I realized that up to now I hadn't done a thing, I got so upset. My God, forty years of idiocy, of watching the clouds drift by.

I'm just beginning to make a contribution. This is the most important time in my life.

Ângela, a tall and wiry twenty-seven-year-old with a very earnest manner, is the eldest child of working-class White parents who have some Indian and Black antecedents. Ângela lives in her parents' house with four of her six siblings. She has worked for many years as an optometrist's assistant and is now also studying public relations at a university in Rio de Janeiro in the evenings. Her father works in an automobile factory, and her mother works as a seamstress at home. Ângela considers herself a socialist and is eager to travel to Cuba and the USSR. The interview was conducted in 1981, at a time when Ângela was intensely involved in spiritualism.

Brazil is the world's largest and most populous Roman Catholic country. According to the 1980 census, 89 percent of Brazil's population of 119 million considered itself at least nominally Roman Catholic. Nonetheless, many Brazilians take part in some form of the syncretic Afro-Brazilian religious practices that were introduced into the different areas of Brazil toward the end of the sixteenth century. Interestingly, the 1980 census, which was the first to ask specifically about Afro-Brazilian religious participation (as opposed to the earlier more general designation of "spiritualist"), indicates that less than 0.6 percent of the population so declared itself—a gross underrepresentation. The census further reveals that in urban areas many more women than men declared adherence to Brazil's important minority religions (Protestantism and spiritualist sects), as compared to the relatively equal numbers of men and women who declared themselves to be Roman Catholic.[1]

From the mid-sixteenth to the mid-nineteenth century (when the slave trade was effectively abolished), a continuing supply of fresh slaves from Africa maintained and strengthened African religious practices in Brazil. As time passed, the individual identities of these practices, based on separate ethnic groups with their distinctive tribal characteristics, were lost. White slaveholders forbade African cults as part of an effort to convert the slaves to Christianity and separate them from their group and their past, but Catholicism and its saints instead came to be used by Blacks as a protective

ÂNGELA

screen for their own beliefs. Thus, different religious elements blended and coexisted in the Afro-Catholic rituals, which became new religions existing in different forms and under different names in the various regions of Brazil. With the abolition of slavery in 1888 and the proclamation of the Republic in 1889, the Afro-Brazilian cults experienced a wave of severe repression that altered but did not succeed in extinguishing them.[2]

Candomblé, sometimes used as a generic name for the Afro-Christian cults, is the oldest and most traditional of these practices and has the strongest ties to African ritual. Initially a means of maintaining and expressing group solidarity among uprooted Africans who had become slaves in Brazil, it also provided a way for Africans to retain their collective memory and, by commanding cosmic forces through the rituals, to overcome White domination. *Candomblé* is characterized by a variety of rituals focused on the worship of saints or divinities, called *orixás*, who are amalgams of African gods and Catholic saints. These *orixás* descend and take possession of initiates. Healing and problemsolving slowly became a major focus of many of the Afro-Brazilian religions. According to one interpretation, these religious practices are attempts by poor and marginalized people to resolve their problems—problems left unaddressed because of Brazil's economic and social inequalities and inadequate social services.[3]

In *macumba*, the form of *candomblé* developed in Rio de Janeiro during the early nineteenth century, ethnic identity seems not to have been a factor, and non-Africans could enter the priestly hierarchy and help their adherents resolve personal problems. Social or spiritual communion was no longer the main feature.

Umbanda, the spiritualist practice in which Ângela was engaged, is a newer form of Afro-Brazilian religion. It developed in the great urban centers of Rio and São Paulo in the 1920s and is an amalgam of *macumba* and the spiritualism of Allan Kardec (1804–1869), a French intellectual and investigator of occult phenomena whose 1857 Book of the Spirits set forth the basic tenets of spiritualism. *Umbanda* also unites the old solidarity of *candomblé* with the magic aspect of *macumba*. The progressive "whitening" already evident in *macumba* is even more apparent in *umbanda*, as is the hope of socioeconomic ascension. *Umbanda* quickly achieved great popularity throughout Brazil and, in the late 1970s, was estimated to have nearly 20 million adherents.

Initiation into *umbanda* is far more rapid than into *candomblé*—weeks rather than months—although its doctrines and rituals are more complex. The contradictory concepts of good and evil that imbue Christianity appear in *umbanda*, but evil can be domesticated and can even be made to serve the initiate's own purposes, although this is not without risk to future incarnations. A sense of ultimate moral purpose is thus aroused in the believer. *Umbanda* has been called "a rallying symbol for all races and all social classes."[4]

So long as several of us are working, the family isn't in too bad shape, but if one person had to support us all it would be very difficult. It's hard to say how much my mother earns, but my father's salary is ₣300. Plus he's retired from another job and gets a pension of ₣200, so his income is ₣500 a month. I started working in optometry in 1973, and since then I've worked for several firms. The longest I ever stayed in one job was three years, then I changed jobs—two years in one place, a year in another, but always in the same line of work. Now I'm frantic to get out of it, to do something else, because I'm fed up with this kind of work, grinding lenses, making glasses. It's a job that isn't much valued monetarily. I earn ₣200 a month for a forty-hour week. The possibilities for a job in public relations are minimal, but I'm trying by every means to get a foot in the door; and even if I can't, I want to switch to something else. Now would be the best time, because I haven't graduated yet, so I could take a job as a trainee or something, whereas once I have my degree it'll be even more difficult, if only because of the salary crisis and also because the market is really tiny. People who already have jobs aren't leaving the field, so others can't replace them, and there's almost no growth.

Before I started at the university I was interested in two professions: airline stewardess, since I'd love to travel, and modeling. But I couldn't do either one. I couldn't become a stewardess because I hadn't studied foreign languages—that stood in my way. Maybe if I'd taken a language course instead of going to the university I still could have done it. But I preferred the university. So, the two things I wanted to do, I couldn't get into. Right now I'm interested in working in public relations, but if nothing comes up in that line, I'll take any other job. It's important for me to feel good in my work, to like what I do. I'm tremendously adaptable and I think I could adapt to almost any kind of job, so long as it wasn't castrating—you know, having a boss looking over your shoulder and getting in your way all the time. If I were free to act, I think I'd easily adapt to any kind of job.

I ' M   T H E   O N L Y   M E M B E R of my family to go to university. My parents didn't encourage or discourage it. It was a real shock for me because I was the first one to go to university. I finished secondary school in 1973 and my brother finished in '74, and we just stopped studying because we didn't have the money to continue. We had all come from the interior of the state to Rio; that was nearly ten years ago. My brothers and sisters were small, so we had to get jobs in order to help support them. Then, a few years later, things got better: the kids were growing up, each one had some sort of job. My brother never went back to school, but in 1976 I started to take some courses, some free courses, like in accounting. And in '78 I decided to go to college. Some friends of mine even encouraged me, and when I passed the admission exam, my parents . . . I think they must have been pleased but I don't really know, they didn't say anything. When I got home: "Oh, I passed," and they went, "Okay." Even my brothers and sisters were happier than that. Sometimes I talk to my mother: "You know, when I finish this degree I'm going to go on studying." She goes, "Studying, what for? You're just wasting money studying." Because my mother hasn't had any education at all, not even primary school. She thinks it's ridiculous for me to want to go on studying, instead of staying at home nights with nothing to do. She thinks I should get off work and come home and rest, rather than go to school. But to actively discourage me, "Oh no, don't do that," they haven't acted that way. Neither did they encourage me. They just accepted it.

My mother doesn't know how to read. I think she really misses it a lot. She's constantly complaining. But she's also had a hearing problem since she was a child, and this makes learning very hard for her. She's a person who feels very . . . resentful. She's a good person, but you can feel her resentment because she can't hear. She thinks she can't learn things because she can't hear, even though she has a hearing aid. But she's also ashamed to wear it; she thinks it's disfiguring. When I was younger she tried studying at night, but then she felt too tired and she stopped. Today I always say, "Look, Mother, I'll teach you," but she doesn't want to. I figure she's ashamed to see me teaching her, so she's in a difficult position. She could actually learn to read a little. Now, numbers and things like that she knows very well. She gets around Rio alone, but picking up something and reading it, no. Sometimes she really complains, "Oh, if only I could read, I'd read this, I'd read that." But it's a routine—she complains, and then when I want to teach her she has kind of a negative reaction. It's a bit hard on me because I never know what to do.

My father went to primary school—he didn't finish, but he went. He can read well, but he's a very *machista* man, you see. I don't think he ever tried or even thought about sitting down and teaching my mother to read, which he could have done when we were small, couldn't he? Even when he married my mother, he could have done it; but possibly he thought it wasn't necessary, and we never discussed it at home, because in fact there's not much scope for us to discuss this kind of thing. It never was a subject that could be talked about at home, why he hasn't taught her.

What I mean by *machista* is that he's a man with all those ideas like, at home what the man says goes, without any discussion, without the woman even giving her opinion. My brothers are a bit *machista*, too, because of this, because they've always seen my father say what's what, and the few times that my mother did anything with us against my father's will, he got angry, and he still brings it up to this day. He thinks things have to be the way he wants because he's the head of the household.

No, he doesn't go out much without her; he's usually a homebody. Saturday morning sometimes he goes out—that's when he goes to visit people—but usually he never goes out at night, he's always at home. When they do go out together at night it's just to visit my grandmother, things like that. They never go downtown, to the movies, no. It's incredible, isn't it? Sometimes we say to them, "Go to the movies." "Oh no," because my mother has that mentality—she finds everything wrong, even television. If she sees a woman in a bikini on television, she thinks it's indecent. And movies today, what are they? They're mostly that, at least the Brazilian ones. So she'd rather not go.

Most women here think that they have to be faithful but the man doesn't, and my mother has even taken that position in conversation, that a woman can have only one man, not more than one, but a man, no. She says that a man is a man, but *not hers!* She accepts other husbands doing this, but not hers! And he's complied with that. When I was still a child, I once found out that my father had another woman, and my mother got very upset, to the point of actually objecting. Since then I've never heard anything, so I think he really accepted having only one woman in his life. I don't know, it could also have been more because of finances—he didn't have the financial resources to have two women, so I think he accepted this marriage. She really objected that time. But she still thinks a man can do that, just not *her* husband.

My view of marriage is very different from theirs. They get along well in the sense that at least they don't fight all the time. Yet they're not a very accommodating couple, and sometimes they get irritated over nothing, both of them, and then two, three days pass. Aftrerward they're all right again. They get so annoyed, it's not an atmosphere . . . not even after these twenty-eight years of marriage . . . but I think they've accepted the marriage, so even if they don't think it's a good marriage, they also wouldn't give it up. They're very dependent, both of them. And my mother can't accept any independence in marriage. If you talk to her about a marriage with two people who don't constantly interfere with one another, she thinks that's ridiculous, she says no, that once a woman is married she can go out of the house only with her husband, can do only the things he likes; she can't go to a bar with her friends, nor can her husband. It's that kind of marriage, on a leash. You feel that since she saw her mother's marriage and was brought up with that kind and has the same kind herself, she thinks it's her fate to live like that. That's what she taught us, and to this day she still does it. Just last Sunday I was talking to her about this and she was saying, "Look, you've got to get married, I don't know what's wrong with you, I really don't," that whole business. So I said, "No, Mother, I'm really afraid of marrying, for this reason, and this, and that," and

I explained it all to her. I said, "Look, I want to marry, but I don't want to totally give up my freedom. I want a marriage and a home, but not where we'd be slaves to one another." "Oh, but that can't be," and so on. . . . So, she's constantly telling us this; she even tells my married sister that she shouldn't let her husband go out alone, that she shouldn't go out alone.

WHEN WE WERE KIDS the boys could go out much more than I could. I remember when we moved to Rio, I was in a phase when I wanted to be more independent; I wanted to get out, to see things, and my father and I had horrible fights. I already used to argue with him in those days because he wouldn't allow me to go out at all. I'd say, "Look, I want to go out with friends, relatives, cousins. I go to school and I could skip school and go out, but I don't do that. I just want to go out on Saturdays and Sundays." But it took a long time for him to give in. Even today sometimes he still insinuates that I'm going out too much. This past Saturday night he said, "Ah, you just come here to sleep, you don't really live in this house." Because he was complaining about some neighbor's noise and I said, "It's just a child," so he said, "You don't mind it because you don't live here." To this day, when there's some opportunity for him to comment about my not staying home, he does it. But not that business of "You're not going out," that he can't do to me anymore.

My parents criticize me sometimes, like when my father says I'm never at home, that I live in the streets. No, I rarely spend a whole night out. Sometimes I go out and get home very late, but I do get back. First of all because they worry unless I tell them in advance, and we don't have a phone at home. So if I've told them in the morning that I'm not coming back that night, it's all right; but if I haven't, I normally try to get home so they won't worry. Now my youngest sister, she's sixteen, going on seventeen, and she's so full of life, she wants to try everything, but she lives practically chained up. If she goes out, "Where were you? Who were you with? Where are you going?" She used to study judo at night, and he tried everything to get her to stop going because she'd get home at 9:30 *p.m.* He was always complaining about it. And she's rather rebellious, she says what she thinks, but they still keep her on a leash. If she goes out with me, that's fine, but alone with her own friends, no, she rarely manages that. And sometimes they say I'm a bad example for her, because they think she wants freedom just because I have it, not because she needs it, too. My mother's come up to me and said, "You're setting a bad example, you don't come home early, you do this, you don't do that, you don't take your duties in the house seriously." Because they insist that she do things at home as if it were her own house. So it's kind of hard. I accept them, and I try to change things around in my own way. I don't usually ask permission when I go somewhere. I just say, "I'm leaving tomorrow," and I grab my bag and go. Even if they're not pleased, I go. There's none of that business of asking permission—I don't do that. I say, "I'm almost twenty-seven years old, I'm more than grown up, and I don't ask for permission." My father doesn't say much, he's not inclined to come up and talk, he keeps it to himself. But not my mother, she complains.

We grew up in a place with a lot of space. That's why sometimes I say, "My childhood was very good in that sense; we didn't have toys, we didn't have anything, but we had freedom." I went to school when I was four years old; they put me in school till noon, but freedom I had—I could play with boys, with girls, up to a certain age there was no difference. He never prevented me from playing with my brothers; we played boys' games, girls' games. There weren't any restrictions about being out in the street. Also it was a very small town, more like a village. We lived on a sugar plantation, and there were many children, a great many, and we had a large backyard. I played a lot in our own backyard. My father was a metallurgist at the sugar refinery.

Then, when I got a little older, I went to middle school. I was eleven, still a child—I was always really scrawny—and from then on it began to change. They insisted that I study, they thought I should spend more time studying, that I shouldn't play anymore; and at a certain point I started helping in the house, since I was the oldest daughter. So I'd get home from school and have my chores to do and my younger brothers and sisters to help look after, and that deprived me of my freedom to play. Even if I'd wanted to, I had other things to do that were my responsibilities, you see. To help at home, to help my mother.

No, the boys never had to do anything, not in my house, and that's why I tell my mother sometimes that it was the wrong upbringing . Because if you need them to go to the kitchen, to cook something, only one of them goes—the one who was in the Army; he learned there—but the others, no, and even that one thinks it's not really his job, that it's a woman's job, only women ought to do that, but if it's necessary he'll go. And the boys had more freedom: they could still go out and play till they were older, while I began to work very young.

When I was fifteen I graduated from middle school [eighth grade] and came to Rio. I stayed for one year. I was studying and working here in Rio. I worked in a sewing factory for a short while, but most of the time I didn't have a job. I stayed in my grandmother's house, but I didn't get on with the people there, so I went back to live with my parents. By then I was already sixteen and I really began to work, full-time, and to go to school at night, and I got involved in more activities. I'd already lost that whole childhood atmosphere. I was working to help out at home, from that time to this. I had my adolescence, and then I started working to help them, to help raise the others. The boys also started working young, at about fourteen, at any kind of job, just to help out and to learn how to do something. We all went to work very young, and from then on I went to night school, to this day.

Maybe my father never thought it important for us to play because of the way he was raised: at the age of nine he already had to work in the fields, you see. And my mother, too; she was born on a farm. Then, for example, my father—his father separated from his mother when she was expecting a child, so when my grandfather left her they all felt more responsibility to support the household. And my father actually went to work when he was nine years old. Well, since he started working at nine, he thought his children should do the same thing. I think he considered it important for our education, so he passed on to us more or less the same upbringing he'd had, the kind of life, of childhood that he had and that he wanted his children to have. But he was never the type . . . he's always been very good to us, really good. I still remember, when I was ten years old, a present he bought with the greatest joy and gave to us. It was a bicycle, for the three oldest. It was crazy, that bicycle; it was already ancient, but to him it was a great thing to get that for us, and for us too, because, you know, poor kids accept things more. So we were happy. He was never one to hit us; he's rarely hit us. Now my mother, no, my mother was more demanding, I don't know if it's because my father was gone so much. He'd leave in the morning and get home late, and he was more flexible, in the sense of not hitting us and so on. My mother wasn't, but she didn't hit us much either. And then it passed, the younger ones didn't have those experiences; they had a different childhood, very different.

My childhood was happy, I'd say. Sometimes I think back on it and it seems like a good childhood. Now youth was more . . . especially there where we used to live, until I was eighteen; except for the time I spent here in Rio, from fifteen to sixteen, I couldn't go out and I didn't. I didn't have a boyfriend. I wasn't even allowed to stand and talk with a boy at the front gate; I had to be inside the house, that's how things were. A while back it started to improve and I began to be a little more independent, but my childhood was better than my adolescence.

WHEN I STARTED MENSTRUATING I already knew all about it, since I've always been very curious. I had a friend who started long before me. I only got it at fifteen. I'd finished middle school, and I still wasn't a young woman. Well, this friend of mine told me things: what happens, what to do. So when I first got my period I didn't have any problems because I'd already learned about it from this friend. But my mother, no, she never told me a thing, no. She did take me to the gynecologist a few times, but to sit down and talk with me about sex, no. Not with my sisters either; I'm the one who passed on information to the other two, because I was the oldest. But we never discussed sex at home, never. I learned about sex from my friends, and a bit by reading. When you're in school you end up with some information, hearing your friends talk, and I've always liked to read. I used to read a lot, so I got some information about sex that way, not by talking to my mother.

I had my first boyfriend when I was fifteen, here in Rio. Then when I went home, I continued thinking about him, and I went right on liking him for four years without seeing him [laughs]. Later, here in Rio, I had another boyfriend, but my parents always wanted us to stay in the house, which I couldn't stand. There was nothing to do, we'd have to sit there and watch television with everybody, we couldn't even talk. Then when I got older I began to go out, to go to parties, to go out for a beer, to go serenading, and I met more people. I was eager to get to know people. And from then on I became more independent, I had boyfriends. When I was taking a course to prepare for the *vestibular* [university admission examination], I had a boyfriend, and my first sexual experience was with him. I was twenty-three; it was in 1978. But I already knew a lot about sex because I used to talk about it with a cousin of mine. We were very close friends and we talked about it all, so I already knew more or less what it was about. Afterward I spent about six or seven months without a boyfriend. Then I met another boy, and that's when I got pregnant.

When I had my first sexual experience, I began to take the pill; then I stopped because I wasn't seeing anyone. I have this view of sex—I think you should do it when you really want to and with the right person. Just because I'm not a virgin doesn't mean I'll go with any man. So, when I got to know this fellow and we started seeing each other, I wasn't taking the pill, and that's how I got pregnant. He didn't live alone either, so we'd go to a hotel. That's what usually happens here, since everybody lives at home, and the family, at least mine, wouldn't stand for such a thing. We used to go to a hotel—when we had money, a more expensive hotel; when we didn't have any, a cheap one. And that was when I had an abortion.

I felt I had to do it, although I'm not totally in favor of abortion—but I'm also not against it. It seems to me, if a child's going to be born and not have adequate conditions, it's better to have an abortion. So, when I found out—and our relationship was already in trouble; it wasn't a real commitment because he was into a million things. He was kind of crazy, but he was really nice. Well, when I went to him and told him, he was actually happy at the idea of being a father, but there was no way he could set up a house for us, and I couldn't stay at home, nor could we live at his house; so I said to him, "I think one solution would be an abortion," and he started to ask around about it. We went to one doctor but when we got there he didn't like the place, so he looked for another doctor, and I had it done—by a good doctor. Even today I sometimes go to him when I have some gynecological problem. At the time, I had some money; he didn't have any. It didn't cost much. He wasn't some famous doctor, but he was a good doctor.

And after that I went back to school, and our relationship cooled off a bit. My doctor advised me to take the pill: "Either take the pill or use an intrauterine device." I preferred the pill, and I'm still taking it; it hasn't caused me any problems. Sometimes I think about the abortion, to this day. I was . . . not upset, but I keep thinking, "If I'd been in a better situation, I'd have a child aged such-and-such now," you know. Because when I did it, my nephew had already been born—I have just one nephew, and I'd see him and wonder . . . it's just being a woman, because all women must think about having a child some day—at least I do. So at times I wonder, "Did I throw away my one chance?" But sometimes I also think, "And if I'd had it, would it be all right? Would I be psychologically capable of facing the world?" And then I think that at the time it was the right thing to do. Maybe not now; if it happened now, I might keep it. Yes, even if I were still single. But at that time I couldn't, not in my head and not financially; but it was a sad business. It shook me up, but I accepted it.

My mother never found out. I think they still believe I'm a virgin. They never ask, but from things that my mother says sometimes, I think she believes I'm a virgin. That time, I got sick, I was nauseated, but she never even suspected it could be pregnancy, she never mentioned the subject. She thinks that every girl should marry in a white veil and all that, and when I say that no, the day I marry it won't be . . . "But every girl has got to marry in white!"—that whole scene. So I think she thinks I'm a virgin. She's never come up to me and asked, and if she did I'd say that I'm not. But she's never asked, and I've never told her. She still brings up how when I was a child I wanted to marry with an immense veil, a beautiful gown. Well, I was a child then, now I'm an adult. As far as marriage goes, it hasn't been that long since I gave up those dreams; it must be only about four or five years ago, about when I started college. It was that experience, meeting people, I changed my ideas a bit. I don't disapprove of it, but I don't think it's necessary to have a wedding like that. It's not what I'd want. I would get married in a civil ceremony, if my husband insisted. I'd even get married in church if that was what he wanted; but I wouldn't wear a bridal gown, I'd get married in ordinary clothes. I'm not opposed to marriage, but I don't think only marriage makes you happy. I'd live with a man, yes, and I can also imagine being single all my life. I can even imagine that more than being married, because I have an incredible fear of change in my life and, for example, I know that marriage changes you a little, though I don't think it has to be a radical change.

So, as soon as I have my own house, whether I'm married or not I'll be responsible for my house, with or without a husband I'll have responsibilities. But

I'd like to have a very open relationship, so that my friends would go on being my friends even when I have a husband, and his friends, too, would be a part of our life. Because the day I feel the need to see my friend, "Oh, so-and-so, let's go get a beer, let's all go," if my husband wants to come, fine; but if he doesn't want to and I go, I wouldn't like him to be upset at my going. Very open and very independent, each should be independent of the other. There aren't that many men in Brazil like that, but the situation is much better than it used to be. I have friends like this, I spend time with people like this, who are liberal and so on, though some of them aren't, some are more *machista*.

I had a boyfriend last year . . . he was married, but we had a real affair. We ended it because of his family problems. It was getting very complicated, and I thought it better to stop. Brazilian men . . . there are some who are so *machista* that they think a woman has to depend on them her whole life long. He used to get really angry when I'd go for a beer with my friends. He'd start nagging, "Don't go, don't." He didn't like me to come near him smelling of beer, and at school that's something we do almost every day, go for a beer, and I'd go too, because I liked it. And I'd get mad because he wouldn't accept what for me was completely normal. Well, one day he called me, a long time afterward, wanting to see me. And I said no, that there was no point in our seeing each other again. So he asked me, "Do you have a new boyfriend?" I asked, "Why?" He said, "Because I don't want you to." You see? We'd broken up in September, and he still thought I had to be all alone, without anybody; and that's the kind of mentality, typical *machismo*, that you find around here. I don't know if it's the same elsewhere, because I've never traveled anywhere, but here it's like this. There are very few men who grant a woman this freedom, just a minority, but I think there are some.

I've always said, "I want to have a child when I'm about thirty." So if I get to thirty and I have a more or less stable life, and can support myself and at least have my own place to live and enough money, I think that I could take on a child, if it happened that way. And if what turns up is a relationship that I consider good for a marriage, I'd take that on, too, fine. But even if I had to be an unmarried mother, I would—provided it's the right time.

These days, the way things are going, it's very difficult for a man to support a household all alone on his money. Usually the woman has to work, too. But even if I didn't have to work, I'd want to. I think that's very important for a woman. No matter how well informed you are staying at home, you can be much more so working. Also, you don't get into that domestic rut. Women who work are more concerned with looking nice, with getting themselves together. As soon as a woman just has to stay at home she turns into a housewife, and I don't think that's good. We've got to be both things, a housewife and a normal person in society who knows what's going on, who can talk about things—what's happening in

Brazil, and the Brazilian family, and the country in general. The woman who just stays home isn't concerned with what's going on outside the house, only with what's happening inside. But as soon as she's out working, that already helps a lot.

I've thought about moving into an apartment. Once I spent a month out of the house, with a close friend of mine in Copacabana. I liked her a lot, but it was her house and I had to live her way. Sometimes I comment to my friends at school that you get to a point, at least I feel this way, where it's a necessity to have my own place, apart from my parents. I feel this need, and I was talking to my friends about whether a few of us who are very close couldn't rent a house and live together, because we spend a great deal of time together. I'd really like to have my own place, to leave my parents' house. I even think they themselves feel this need, too. Sometimes I feel I'm in their way, so they might like it, too. My father himself says, "I only feel responsible for your youngest sister, the rest of you are all grown up." And they want to have their own life, too, and live just on his pension, which he can't do now because he has other children at home and so he needs more money—although we all contribute, each of us, in one way or another. One pays one thing, another something else; and my mother also contributes, with her work. She spends whatever she earns on the household. So I'd really like to move out, but I'd first have to be well set up in a job; then I could make a commitment.

I ' M   A   S P I R I T U A L I S T. It's a kind of religion we have here in Rio; it's also called *macumba* or *umbanda*. I go once a month. The rest of the family are all Catholic, and I am too. I mean, when I feel like going to a Catholic church, I go, without reservations, but I don't go regularly like with the spiritualism. I don't have the same kind of commitment to Catholicism.

There's a session once a month, and several *orixás* come to us. I usually go in the morning and stay all day. We clean the center, then at night there's an herbal bath, which is to cleanse the body, and each month we commemorate one *orixá*, one saint. Each month we put on a skirt of a special color in honor of that saint. And then we go through the ritual of *macumba*, when the *orixás* come down, one at a time, and then there are songs and the whole spiritualist ritual. It usually begins at 10:30 at night and ends the next morning. It lasts six or seven hours; there's no fixed time for it to end. It's always the same ritual. Now, spiritualism has some divisions: for example, *candomblé*, things like that. Ours is more oriented toward *umbanda*, toward the *orixás*. *Candomblé* is a ritual that involves more singing. Ours isn't; it's more a ritual of work, of spirits, to assist people. People go there needing help, and the *orixás* work to help them. *Candomblé* has more singing, dancing; it's more a kind of a festival. *Umbanda*, no; it's more to help people.

It's more effective than Catholicism in the sense of helping people, although I think the Catholic Church is good. But it's more distant from people. I always thought the priest was very distant from me, whereas at the [umbanda] center, no. You go there, you talk to the orixá. He tries to comfort you, he tells you what's happening, he tries to help you. And also it's much more like a family, because not many people go and so the people in the community are more like a family, a second family. I like the Catholic Church, but in terms of helping people I think it's rather distant.

No, you don't speak to the orixá through someone. It's the orixá himself, because he takes possession of a person; he comes and incorporates in that person, and then he talks to you normally, just like you and I are talking now. And, when you don't understand what he says, usually someone stays at your side who does know and who explains to you what he's saying. But generally he talks to you alone; he listens to you and tells you everything you ought to do. You can talk to him yourself; you don't need a third person.

I started going about five years ago. One Sunday I got sick, and on Monday my mother went there—but I didn't know about it. She hid it from me because she knew I wouldn't like it. It's like when you know there's something you need to do, a commitment you have to take on, and you look the other way. That's the way it was for me, because at that time I liked going to parties and things like that, and if you make a commitment, then you're obligated, just like with school, with a job, and I was afraid of making this kind of commitment. So my mother went, and when she got there this orixá spoke to her. My mother hadn't said a word, and he turned to her and said, "Your daughter's sick, isn't she?" And my mother said, "Yes, she got sick yesterday," and he said, "I know she's sick." Then he told my mother to take me to a center, so I could have some baths and the people there could work on me. Because something had been done against me. They said it was a boyfriend of mine who'd put a spell on me so I'd get sick, and they undid it. I never tried to find out who it was, or how he'd done it. Because, for example, that's one thing about our religion, it can work both good and evil, and lots of people do things out of vengeance. They get someone to put a spell on someone else, and that's exactly what happened in my case. Someone wanted to make me sick or something like that, to get even with me.

That's what this orixá told my mother—he said, "It was an old boyfriend of hers who did this to her." And I'd gotten all swollen. I had welts all over my body. It looked like I'd been whipped, red welts; and I felt faint, I couldn't stand up. It happened overnight. I went to my grandmother's birthday party on Sunday, I had lunch at her house, I left there at about 3:00 o'clock and went to another house, and when I got home at 5:00 o'clock and went to the bathroom to take a shower, I noticed these streaks on my body. But I felt fine. I went, "What's this? Could it be something I ate at my grandmother's house?" Because I'd had lunch there; I'd eaten fish. I said, "Maybe it didn't agree with me, maybe it upset my liver or something like that." And I went to sleep. The next day, Monday, I got up to go to work, and I had completely swelled up. But nothing hurt; it was just the swelling. So my mother took me to the doctor, and he gave me a shot which had no effect. The doctors were puzzled; they had no idea what it was. So then my mother went to see this woman, and [afterward] my mother said to me, "Let's go to the center, let's go?" and so I did. It just came and went, without leaving any scars, without my feeling anything, just like that. Then I looked for a center I especially liked, where I felt comfortable, with friendly people. And I've gone there ever since. In my center it's about evenly divided between men and women. Usually the women go more, but right now there are a lot of men taking part in *umbanda*.

That was five years ago, and they've helped me with things since then. I feel good spiritually. I feel at peace, I'm not someone who rebels against things. I accept things as they are. I try to solve my problems without getting desperate. That's something I think they've helped me with. I go there, but I'm not a religious fanatic. I have responsibilities, I do the things I'm supposed to do— though sometimes not all that well; I don't always do them all. But I feel very good, and if a lot of time passes without my going there, I start to miss it. It's already a part of me, you see.

Before that, I used to go to a Catholic church, but not often. I mean, when I was a child, until I was fourteen, I used to go to church every day. Then I started rejecting it, because of my age and because my mother always used to take me. My mother is Catholic. Sometimes she goes to the center as a visitor, but not regularly, and she doesn't have any responsibilities there. She's more involved with the Catholic church, not that she goes there every Sunday either. She usually goes maybe once a month, or twice. Now my father no, my father almost never goes to church, but he calls himself a Catholic. Here in Brazil there are lots of people who are spiritualists and don't admit it: "I'm Catholic," because that's the religion of the Brazilian family, right? That's the religion with the most followers. In my house they all say they're Catholic, but none of them goes to church regularly.

In spiritualism there's real equality, equal participation, because, for example, when another entity incorporates in you, you're not yourself, you're something else; and I can receive a male *orixá*, just as a man can receive a female *orixá*, so everyone's on an equal footing, much more than in the Catholic Church. I don't know how the choice is made of which *orixá* will choose which person to work with. A woman can have various *orixás*, so I could have male and female *orixás*. From the moment the *orixá* incorporates, you're no longer yourself. You don't know what he's saying, you don't remember anything; and if there's something he has to say to you, other people will tell you afterward. It doesn't depend on your own will at all. For example, I still haven't received an *orixá*, but I go to the center and, if and when I do begin to, I'll always receive that same *orixá*, from then on. Now, I could have five different *orixás* and I could work with them for several years, and then a time might come when a certain *orixá* won't come to that person anymore. It usually depends a lot on your spiritual state. If you're very troubled or nervous or have some problems, it's more difficult because you can't concentrate. But when you can concentrate, then they usually come, they do what they've come to do and they leave, and you're back to normal. Whatever they drink or smoke you don't feel.

I feel good after these sessions. I feel kind of as if I'd come out of a bath, really clean, really good. It's hard to compare with the Church, because when I used to go to church it was more out of obligation to my mother: "You have to go to Mass." Nowadays, for example, I can go to church and I even feel good when I leave. Because, you see, *umbanda* and Catholicism, there are differences, but they have almost the same saints, just with different names; so I can go into a Catholic church and talk to the saints there just as I do at the center. I can pray and talk to them and say what I feel, and I feel good when I leave there, too. But I rarely go to church now.

The saints come down to us in *umbanda* but not in the Church because the Catholic Church has a different tradition. I think the Catholic Church doesn't believe in spiritual evolution. They don't believe in reincarnation after you die. And since they don't believe in reincarnation, they can't believe that spirits can come to us. But I believe they do. For example, the *orixás* we call "Old Blacks" were slaves many years ago and today they incorporate in us.

I think we've all had other lives, but we don't remember them. I believe that when we die our spirits pass over to another kind of life, to another evolution where they can learn things. It's a kind of education, and then they come back, not as an *orixá*, but, for example, I could be reincarnated in a newborn child, but more evolved. But no one will know that it's me. I believe in reincarnation. No, of course I'm not afraid to die. I'm afraid of getting sick unto death, of suffering and mortal illness, but not of death itself.

In the Catholic church we never took the time to talk about these things. It was more a matter of coming and going without any contact with anyone inside. We never discussed these things, and only after I got acquainted with spiritualism did I begin to think, to sit down and talk and learn about these things. I never had the opportunity in the Catholic church. I think the church is very cold, very one-sided. You're here and the priest is over there. He celebrates the Mass and you participate, but that's it. Then you leave, you go home. It's all very one-sided, not like at the center. Also, since the center is so much smaller—at least the one I go to—it's more on the basis of friendship. There must be only about twenty people there. Black and White, no discrimination, just like a family. In my center the people are all different. The economic level is more or less average, although there are some seamstresses who are having a hard time just surviving. There are a few teenagers, there's a young woman who's a ballet dancer, there's a dentist, there are some boys who live in Copacabana, there are all kinds of people.

We don't believe there's a hell, at least not in my conception of hell. I think that whatever you do here, you pay for it right here. Our own lives, our own suffering, already are a kind of payment for the things we do. For example, a person who's very bad here, I think that this person's spirit will need a great deal of work. I don't think you can die today and incarnate in another person tomorrow. No, you die, and your spirit will go through a period of training. A person who's very evil here, I think it's their spirit that's evil, and it will have to start at that point and learn, because there are evil spirits, just as there are good spirits. That has to exist; it's a kind of balance. I can't imagine how it would be if everyone were good or if everyone were evil.

No, I don't know anybody else at the university who's a spiritualist. We almost never talk about religion at school, so there could be some. There must be, actually, but I don't know any. My friends know that I am; and some of them don't think it's right, but they accept it. I've suggested to people to go to a center, when I know it could help that person, but that varies a lot, too. First of all, I try to find out if the person believes or not. Because if you don't believe . . . I think it depends a lot on having faith; you can accomplish a lot through faith. If people don't believe, it's unlikely they'll do what they're advised to do. When I first went, I didn't believe, but I also didn't go thinking it was worthless. I said, "I'll go, but I don't intend to stay too long." I never went there and said, "This I don't believe." I always respected it, and I think that respect is actually a form of belief.

I've become a much more secure person. Not totally secure, but much more than some time back. To make my own decisions, to decide about my life, to take responsibility for what I do, and to know what I want and don't want. Even to fight for what I want. And to say openly, "I don't like that, I don't want to be a part of that." I think it's very much a matter of . . . of confidence, I became more confident. I used to have very little confidence and a great deal of fear. Though, I think we're all afraid of certain things, and then we get used to them. It's all a matter of education, of experience of things. As time passes we get to know more. Our life is really a school, isn't it? And we go on learning constantly. We get to know one person today, another one tomorrow, and all of that is a school. Each experience gives you strength to go on to the next.

A Y E A R L A T E R, in a beautiful ceremony involving white robes and masses of flowers, Ângela got married at her *umbanda* center. With her new husband she moved into a small one-bedroom apartment in a building in the Copacabana section of Rio. By the time I saw her again in 1983 she was already separated from her husband but had managed to hang on to the apartment, which she was sharing with a woman friend. Ângela says that her parents believe marriage gives a woman freedom, so they didn't ask her to come back home after her separation. She had also left her job at the optometrist's and was working in a fashionable travel agency in Copacabana, not far from her apartment. *Umbanda* continued to play a major role in her life.

Norma. Glícia. Dorotéia. Three members of one family: two daughters, a generation apart in age, and their mother. Each provides a sense of the context in which the other two lives have also been lived, and all are in transition. Together they express different points on the continuum of women's lives in the urban areas of the Northeast. Norma, the oldest daughter, struggling with her parents and her society, emerges whole and strong—but also strained and overworked. Glícia, her youngest sister, born in the same year the military took power, is cynical and depressed. She rejects the hard life she sees Norma leading and will attempt to use her sexual attractiveness to find a way out—a rational decision in the face of the available options as she perceives them. Dorotéia, their mother, an elegant-looking woman still intensely involved with her family, has had a bitter education at the hands of her husband, now retired from the military police, and her children. The contradictory aspects of her self-presentation convey the clashes of past with present in a rapidly changing society. In different ways these three women try to mediate between their public and private worlds.

Dorotéia's mother was descended from Portuguese and Brazilians; her father was the son of Indians. She married a man whose father was a *caboclo*—a mixture of Indian and White—and whose mother was from a predominantly White family with some Black antecedents. Both Dorotéia and her husband come from poor families in the backlands of the Northeast. They met in the city and married after a courtship of four months. Thanks to one richer aunt (from whom Norma later inherited the house she was living in when I visited her in 1981), the whole family moved to a larger city when Norma was five years old. "If it hadn't been for this aunt," Norma wrote to me later, "my vision of the world and of life would have been far more limited, living in a provincial city."

FAMILY PORTRAIT

Norma, thirty-five years old, lives in a small three-bedroom house in Recife with her three children, aged four years, three years, and one month, and her husband, a man of thirty-two who only recently found a job again, as a clerk in a record store. Norma has worked for years as an executive secretary and is the main financial support of her family. At the time of the interview (August 1981) she was still on maternity leave and planned shortly to return to her job at a factory outside the city, necessitating a bus trip of one and a half hours each way. Once again she would have to leave her house at 6:00 *a.m.* and would return at 7:00 *p.m.* Norma says, "Every Brazilian woman who holds a job and has children deserves a statue—she's a heroine!"

———

I work at [a factory] that's a subsidiary of an American company. The main Brazilian branch is in São Paulo, and there are branches in other states, too, not just Pernambuco, and still more are being built. I'm secretary to one of the directors.

There are about eight hundred workers in the factory, all men. My impression is that it's very heavy work, and there's a rotation system, with three shifts. At any time you can be put on a shift that starts at midnight, so it would be very inconvenient for a woman, plus it's very far away. The workers are all men and they earn more than the minimum salary, so it's a job that's much sought after. Everybody wants to earn more than the minimum. The minimum salary in this state is now about $70 a month, and at the factory they start at $110. It's not much of a difference, but it helps.

There's a man working there who has . . . I think it's eight children. When you go to his house—they're all little, you see, and you go there and find this pile of people, all of them really small; and on top of that he supports two nieces, one is seventeen and the other eighteen, but both already have children, fathers unknown, and they all live with him and he supports them, too. But when you talk to this man, he's so peaceful, so calm. So one day I said to him, "Don't you ever get the urge to run away? Don't you get crazy? Desparate?" And he said, "No." Then I

N O R M A

found out, of course it makes sense, that he's Protestant, so God's grace sustains him and his family, you see. Well, one day I went to his house. I was looking for someone to help me on weekends. I was pregnant at the time, and really tired, and I had asked him if he knew a girl who could work here on weekends, wash the bathroom, things like that. He said he knew a girl of fourteen, that I could stop by his house—he gave me the address—and take this girl home with me. So I went to his house . . . this is very painful . . . though it was interesting. Among the poor classes, you see some strange things. There are lots of mulattos, and lots of blondes, very fair and very white. And when I got to his house, I couldn't imagine that they were his children, all of them were really blond and white. He himself was a pale brown. And . . . and all those children had running noses, all of them were on the floor undressed, little boys and girls without any underwear. There wasn't a real floor, nothing, just mud. Mud. There was no table, not a single table on which to cut a piece of bread. I didn't see the rest of the house, but there was a sofa and a very large television, the same size as mine, an immense television. Well, that shocked me. When I saw the television, I stood there thinking: how incredible, how can this be? Going hungry and with such a TV.

And then I saw a girl dragging herself along the ground, a girl who looked about ten, judging by her face, but her body looked about six, more or less. With one normal leg and the other withered up, and she was dragging that leg along and crawling like a baby. I asked the woman, her mother, "What's the matter with that child?" Because in the factory everybody has medical care, complete medical care, for anything, for an operation, for surgery, everything is paid for, with the best doctors. It makes no difference who you go to, the workers can go to the same doctor as I do, or the same doctor the boss goes to, and the medications are 60 percent paid for by the company. So it seemed absurd to me to see that child dragging herself along the ground like that, and I said, "What's the matter with that child?" And she said to me, "Oh, she had *frieira*." Do you know what that is? It's a skin ailment [chilblain] that you get by going barefoot in muddy areas, a kind of eczema. I think it's some sort of microbe that gets in between the toes and then they get inflamed, and you can end up in bed because the toes get all open and raw. She said, "She had *frieira*, and since I couldn't get any medicine, it moved up into her leg." I mean, it was absurd, unbelievable, it could never have gone into her leg. It was a typical case of infantile paralysis, you see. You only had to look at the girl and you could see it was infantile paralysis and the leg had totally atrophied. Her kneecap was twisted to the right, instead of being straight like ours, and it looked like soon she wouldn't be able to move at all, not even by dragging herself.

Then I said, "Senhora, you have to take this child to the doctor." "Ah, but it's so difficult," and she started about the doctor, and God protecting them, and so on. I said, "Look, it's not as difficult as all that. There's a clinic very near here." "Ah, but I don't have a car, how can I take her without a car?" Creating all these obstacles in order to avoid doing what was necessary, what was essential, and it was more important to spend all day watching television. Like when I arrived, from the moment I arrived to the moment I left they were all sitting there in that mud watching TV. So I said, "The clinic is free, the doctors are free, it'll all be free. Don't you have money to take the bus?" "Yes, we can manage the money." I said, "Tomorrow, go to the factory and as soon as you get there have me called, and I'll arrange for a car to take you." There was no social worker at that time, she was in the process of being hired, but I talked with the head of the general services department and told him about this case and asked him to have a car take this child to the doctor. "Of course, for sure, we'll take her." I waited two days, and the woman didn't show up with the child. Then I called the father. "Look, what's going on? The child's in such shape and no one's going to take her to the doctor?" "Oh yes, we are," and so on. I said, "Look, tomorrow please bring the child." And then I threatened, "If you don't do it, I'll bring this to the attention of the head of your department." And that terrified him, and the next day they did bring her. The doctor said they had to operate on her and reset her knee; it actually was infantile paralysis. Well, they seemed headed in the right direction so I didn't follow up on it further. I assumed that he, as a father, would make all the necessary arrangements.

About then the social worker started her job—by now she's a good friend of mine—and I talked to her about this case, to see if she could do a follow-up. And . . . this is incredible. She went to talk to the person who'd first looked into the matter, and this girl came to me and said, "Norma, I wanted to explain something to you. There's no point your trying to do anything for those people. It's useless." I was furious; at first I thought it was sheer prejudice. Then she said, "I want to tell you something, but don't mention it to anyone. About three months ago that man came here and asked for a loan of $125 to take the child to the doctor and pay for her complete treatment. I arranged for the loan for him, to be paid back slowly, over a six-month period, as he was able to, because the child was in a drastic condition." Then I said to her, "But the child's the same as before." She said, "Are you sure?" "Yes. I was there recently, I saw her."

So she got in a car and went to see the child, who was in exactly the same shape as before, and then she called in the father and mother to talk it over and find out what had happened. Since they'd gotten the money, why hadn't the child's leg been fixed? And this is what they said: they'd taken the money, but they got to thinking that it wasn't so important to do anything about the girl's leg; it might improve on its own. After all, God's grace could lend a hand, right? And so they bought a used television, which was much more important to have in the house. Well, she thought of having the man fired because he'd been dishonest, but that would mean going from bad to worse, to fire someone in such a situation. So she talked with him, really told him off. She said that he hadn't acted like a man, he hadn't kept his word, he didn't deserve to be called a father, he was irresponsible. She really demolished him. He went out of there in tears, and she said that if she ever found out about anything like that again, she'd have him fired no matter what anyone else said, and that from then on she wanted to be informed of what was being done for the child. The last I heard about it she was in • the hospital and was going to be operated on.

You know, that man was supporting all those people on his own. Even the two girls, the nieces, don't do a thing. There's such apathy. But I understand why they preferred the television. There are people here who know what's going on. When I came back from Rio, I remember, in various parts of the city I'd see graffiti: "TV turns you into an idiot." It's true, it's a real opiate.

Poverty in the South is different. The poor there are rich compared to the poor here. Here it's misery, utter misery. There it's just poverty. Maybe the situation's changed a little, for the worse. Ten years ago, when I was still at the university, I was involved in some research about the cost of living. Every three months I had to go back and ask the same people how much they were paying for beans, for whatever. Some cases I'll never forget. There was a sad one in a *favela* rather near here; I think it doesn't exist anymore because they tore down all those slums and told the poor people they could go to hell, to cover things up a bit. Well, in one house there was a man, very white, very pale, who had a table, a chair, and a small bed. Just that. And this man had a little boy, just one. So I began to ask him questions about what he was buying, bla-bla-bla, bla-bla-bla. He bought the bare minimum, of course. You couldn't even ask about all the items on the questionnaire. He bought the minimum—beans, rice, manioc flour, and so on. Then I asked him why he was always in bed, and he told me he had tuberculosis and he had no family; the little boy used to do his shopping. And I made a date to return another time because I hadn't completed his questionnaire. It was getting late, it was after 6:00 *p.m.*, and he said, "It's late, it's not good for you to stay here." I said, "All right. Then I'll come back another day, I'll come back in a week, to complete this questionnaire." He said, "No, don't come in a week, come in two weeks." I said, "But that's too far off . . . it won't work that way." He said, "You see, it's the moon"—I don't know what phase it was. "We're in such and such a phase of the moon, and next week there's going to be a flood, and the following week the tide will have gone down and then you can come back." I said, "I don't understand what you mean." Then he said, "It's like this, next week no one can come in the house, I have to stay in bed the whole week, only the people from these parts can get around. Because the water will be up to the foot of my bed." And I thought . . . the man has tuberculosis, right? He lives in this wretched dampness without being able to get out of bed, and has no one. Later I saw many such cases. Even worse ones. In another *favela* I saw a man who earned 30 cruzeiros a month [U.S. $6 at a time when the minimum wage in the Northeast was 144 cruzeiros, i.e., $29 a month] . . . ten years ago . . . let's say that would be 1,000 cruzeiros a month today [$10], perhaps even less, because of the inflation. At that time it was absurd to earn 30 cruzeiros a month. He was a peasant, and he earned money only when they needed him to clean something up. And he lived praying to God to send him things to clean up.

That other man, in the house with the television, there was electricity, obviously, but no running water, just wells, the kind that bring the water up all brown, and there was no water treatment. In the factory, too, there's only well water, but naturally there's a chemical treatment for it. Still it doesn't kill all the bacteria. I don't drink water when I'm at work. Not water or coffee, nothing. I drink only coconut water—they have lots of coconuts there. At lunchtime there's soda, but I don't drink it because it's mixed on the premises. All these places just have well water. You see mud houses, covered with palm leaves, without real floors. And behind the house there's another tiny hut all made out of palm leaves, with a hole in the ground, and that's where people shit, and they cover it up with earth and more earth. When you pass by there you feel like you're being contaminated by all the bacteria of the entire community. Until I did that work, that research, I'd had no direct contact with that sort of life, although I knew it existed. You always know about it, unless you go around with your eyes closed or want not to see, because the misery is all around here. . . .Look, just a few weeks ago, a man came by here who always shows up to do odd jobs. He came here and asked, "Senhora, isn't there anything I could do for you?" I said, "No, Seu [Senhor] Mário, there's nothing right now." "Couldn't you find something for me to do? I just need to earn 100 cruzeiros [$1] so I can take some food home."

You know, when these things happen, sometimes you feel you're going crazy, you can't coordinate your thoughts. When he said that to me, I told him to send over his daughter, who's twelve years old, so she could play with my two oldest children, because when I got back from the maternity ward a month ago they were so jealous it was crazy; they were on top of me all the time. So I had his daughter come and play with them. And while she played, I could rest or get on with the housework. She stayed here for a week, and I gave her 800 cruzeiros [$8]. In a way I wanted her to come back, but she also goes to school. But then she . . . it's incredible, she's twelve years old and she has such a high level of need that you just can't say no. In that one week she stole so many things that . . . and on top of it all she was stupid. She stole some of my clothing, but mainly the children's clothes, for her little sister. I'd been thinking about giving her some, but before I got around to it she'd already taken a lot. I pretended I didn't notice. Then, one day . . . I don't know, it's total ignorance I guess, her mother came here and she came wearing some of the clothing that had been stolen. Another time someone broke in here. You'd never believe what was stolen—a broom, some diapers, things like that!

M Y   S A L A R Y is very high for a woman—it's almost $700 a month gross, but most of it goes for food. I'd have to earn twice as much in order to live decently. Yes, it would have to double. Because, look, I don't have to pay rent; my aunt left me this house. If I did have to rent a house, even an old one in the shape this one's in, it would cost at least $150 a month. And to eat the way I think we should, within the normal standards of good nutrition, I'd have to earn twice what I do. Because it's like this. We're how many here? Two children who eat regular food, plus two adults, and the maid. That's five. One kilo of beef costs $3.50. Just the meat would come to a lot of money each month. Milk, for example, a large can of milk that would last a week costs $9, so four times nine, that's $36 just for milk for the children, plus for the baby it will be another $10. I won't do without milk. I can get along without other things, but the milk is sacred. At least until they're six years old I think they have to have a lot of milk. And the price of food is going up constantly.

My salary is adjusted twice a year. For example, salaries will be adjusted now, in September. The INPC [National Consumer Price Index] has fixed the cost-of-living increase at a bit over 36 percent, that's for the year, from last September to this September.[1] Government statistics set the inflation rate at about 110 percent. But in general people think it's more like 200 percent or 250 percent. So you see, while salaries will go up based on the government's figures, the inflation is more like 200 percent in reality. As far as merit raises go, they never reach the government index. A factory isn't likely to give more than a 40 percent increase, above what the INPC sets. Because, apart from all this, they also have to contain expenses. There's no market, so how can they raise the salaries 50 percent, 100 percent? The result is that the longer you work, the less you earn. In real terms I'm only earning as much now as I was five years ago, and that's with all the raises.

As for being a working mother, there's a law stipulating that every firm with more than thirty women in their reproductive years is obliged to maintain a nursery, but this is almost never done.[2] Working mothers here live with an incredible level of daily stress as a result of this situation. I suspect that's why each year the number of women having strokes increases. Look, the cheapest childcare center nowadays costs more than the minimum salary. If I didn't have a maid, if I had to pay for childcare for my three children, even not counting the transportation costs and food, I'd be spending almost three-fourths of my net salary, so I wouldn't even have enough for my own food or clothing. That's why I'm thinking of moving into my mother's house. Then I could do without a maid. In the morning they could stay at my sister's kindergarten—she wouldn't charge me. And I could rent out this house and have a bit more money.

As it is, we're constantly short of money. That's also why José Carlos's salary is so important. When he finds a job, he hangs on to it, even if he doesn't like it. Because it's a necessity, and also because of his pride. He . . . it's a matter of pride, so he can pay for his own expenses. For example, buy cigarettes, deodorant, things like that. Or get drunk in a bar with his own money, you see? I think that's as it should be. It's hard for him to spend my money; it makes him feel bad. If it were the reverse, if it were he who earned the better salary, I wouldn't have the courage either, to go to a bar and spend a pile of money on a beer when I'd be aware that I hadn't earned that money. So it's the same thing.

We've been together for nearly eight years and, until he found this job in the record store, he'd been out of work for the past two. He's never stayed at any job for very long. Something always happens, either the place goes bankrupt or it moves elsewhere, things like that. When we were in the South he worked for two weeks at a time and stayed home for two weeks. He was working on a petroleum platform in the ocean, as an aide in the geology division. He collected samples. It was an excellent job. Then they moved, and it was just about impossible to get a job where they were drilling. So we went to Rio, and he spent his time doing silkscreens on T-shirts and selling them. He's very talented that way. It didn't bring in much money, but it was enough for his basic needs, and he felt very satisfied.

I F I H A D it to do over again . . . I think I would be a bit more ambitious, and I'd think twice before getting married. It was really an accident that we got married. This is very private. [*She closes the door of the living room.*] It was ridiculous, José Carlos was arrested because he had no money. He was caught smoking pot, and it was the first time he'd had anything to do with the police. Brazilian law mandates that a person who's arrested for the first time cannot be kept in a cell with other people, but there's a crisis over space in the prisons. They're even freeing people because they don't have enough space. If you behave yourself for two or three years, you're released; they give you a chance to become reintegrated. So, he shouldn't have been put in a cell with others, that was one thing. And, because it was for smoking and it was his first time, he would never have been sentenced if he'd had a good lawyer. Because what normally happens is this: you get arrested smoking pot, you go to the police station before they write it all up and you pay them some money, 5,000 cruzeiros sometimes, or 10,000, and then you just leave. Since he didn't have any money, he also didn't have a good lawyer—his lawyer was an indecent man, totally indecent. On the day of the sentencing he didn't show up, so José Carlos was condemned. This lawyer had been recommended by friends: "Go to so-and-so, he's good," and so on. The lawyer should have been prosecuted, but that would take money, too. Well, anyway, he spent nearly a year in jail. We'd known each other for two years at the time.

When José Carlos was arrested, I had just found out that I was three months pregnant. So, since I was pregnant and he was in jail, his family thought it would be good, and he thought so, too, for me to go visit him at the prison—my mother doesn't know anything about this, no one in my family knows this story—and since I was going to visit him in jail and I was pregnant, it seemed like a good idea for me to get married so the child would be born with a legitimate father, and all that. I didn't think three times about it, or even twice. I thought . . . I'd always thought that marriage is here today and gone tomorrow, that I could get a separation later. The fact of being married or not simply wasn't important to me, so I got married. I'm not sure of the year—you know why? I simply blocked out that phase because I thought it so terrible and sad, to be restricted to two visits a week to the prison. Everybody stares at you. They take everything out of your purse to see what you're bringing. It's a very sad business. That was about six or seven years ago.

What happened is incredible. I didn't realize that I was pregnant the first time, because I go right on menstruating for the first three months. In the third month, although my abdomen was slightly distended, I still wasn't sure about the pregnancy, but I had a test done and it came back positive. Then I went to the INPS [National Social Security Institute][3] and asked for a letter certifying the extent of my pregnancy. Brazilian law says that a woman's marrying or becoming pregnant is not grounds for firing her, and I'd heard that if she's more than three months pregnant the employer must pay during the entire pregnancy, but I wasn't really sure.[4] Then I went to the personnel department and said that I was three months pregnant but had no desire to stop working. I even thought that work would be the best therapy for getting through the rest of the pregnancy, especially because it was my first child. I told them that I intended to stay. Well, I went back to work the next day, punched in, and no one gave me anything to do. So I got fed up and talked to a friend of mine whose father had been in the Ministry of Labor, and they told me that although the law does not clearly state that the employer should pay the remaining six months and the following maternity leave [of eight weeks], there had been a number of Supreme Court judgments in favor of the woman in similar cases. Brazilian jurisprudence—I took courses in law one year—is based on written laws, digests, and precedents established in earlier cases. I then asked them for some photocopies of these precedents and returned to the personnel department.

Well, I told them I wanted to go on working, and they said the work was too demanding and there was no place in the company for a pregnant woman. So I showed them the Xerox copies of the law and told them I'd leave only if they paid me the entire nine months, the six remaining months of my pregnancy and the three months of maternity leave to which I was entitled, otherwise I'd go to the Ministry of Labor. A few days later, they phoned and offered me a settlement of 70 percent and I accepted, since I'd have had to spend a great deal of money taking a company like that to court. Even the 70 percent was a lot of money in those days, I don't remember just how much. But in fact I wanted to continue working. Then I went to various firms where I knew people. I even tried to get a part-time job, but, although they knew me well and knew how competent I was, nobody was inclined to hire a pregnant woman. So I ended up with no work at all.

Then, when I was in the seventh month of my pregnancy, I woke up one day with a rat nibbling at me. It gave me a terrible scare, although I think it hadn't actually bitten me yet. It was just a tiny rat walking down my arm, but I gave such a start that it obviously got provoked and bit me on my fingertip. I called my in-laws—I was living with them at the time, this was in Rio—and they killed the rat. I asked them to keep the animal for analysis later on. Then I went to the hospital to find out if I really needed to take tetanus and rabies shots, and the idiot doctor who took care of me immediately gave me a tetanus shot, without even testing me for an allergic reaction. I told him that the rat was at home, dead, and asked if he wanted to examine it. He said it would just be a waste of time and anyway that was no place for examining animals, I should go to the first aid center to take the rabies shot. That afternoon I began to hemorrhage as a result of an allergic reaction to the tetanus shot and, although I was seven months pregnant, I was advised to take the rabies shots, which are given through the belly. I was put in the hospital and spent two weeks taking the damned injections plus medication to keep the fetus, but I miscarried just the same. I still think they killed the fetus out of sheer incompetence and disregard for its life.

At that time I was so much in love I was nearly blind. Then when I got pregnant again, with Júlia; I wanted to have an abortion—the same old financial problems. But I didn't have money for an abortion, so I couldn't. Later, when I was pregnant with my second child, José Carlos wanted me to have an abortion, but I thought it wasn't right to have just one child—it makes everything more difficult, for the child and for the parents. The parents get very self-centered and are constantly after the child. And, although he kept pressuring me, I had the second baby anyway. And this last one I didn't want to have, but I had to because the abortion would have cost hundreds of dollars, most of my [monthly] salary. I mean, if there were . . . not completely free abortion, but if, for example, the government contributed to some good medical care, I think that this one wouldn't have been born.

According to Brazilian labor law, working women are protected both before and after their pregnancy. In each of my pregnancies—there were five in all, but only three to term—I took advantage of the law, and got my maternity leave and my salary. Actually, the firms are reimbursed for these salaries by the government. As far as nursing goes, by law we have the right to two half-hour periods off from work per day to breast-feed; but very few women know the law and demand their rights, or, if they do know the law, they're probably afraid of losing their jobs if they demand their rights. The law also gives the woman "job stability" for three months after the maternity leave ends. But it's obvious that if you begin to insist on your rights, you're likely to get fired afterward. And then, laws have some odd consequences. A friend of mine told me that, in one factory she knew of, the women workers had to show proof of their menstrual flow every month to the personnel department, and when they were ten days late, they had to take a pregnancy test immediately. If the results were positive, they were kicked out. No, I don't really know how it's done.[5]

In my jobs, I used to make a copy of the text of the law and enclose it with my letter requesting leave for nursing. Each time the personnel department did give me time off—in fact, two consecutive hours [including the lunch hour], although the law only mentions two half-hour periods. The firms where I worked always agreed. But it still wasn't really possible to breast-feed during that time because, after being at work all day without nursing, it's very hard to produce a reasonable quantity of milk, and aside from this there's a danger of fever, headaches, and mastitis—all of which I've had because I couldn't nurse at the right times. So, in short, the usual thing is to take an injection to dry up the milk when the baby is three months old, because there's no other way. Yet the government goes right on, in newspapers, radio, and television—and wasting an incredible amount of money!—urging women to breast-feed their babies. They even make it seem as if it's the mothers who are refusing to nurse, when the truth is quite the opposite.

I don't know . . . perhaps if I hadn't had Júlia, the first one, I wouldn't have had the others either, because then I would have had more time to think through my feelings about having or not having children. For a long time I was very inconsistent and didn't think things through. I was blinded by passion. You know, passion is a very sad business sometimes, because it's not just emotional passion. If you're really passionate about something . . . if you get into a semifanatic state about anything, you become nearly blind. Look at that case of Jim Jones [Guyana,

October 1978], people totally blind. Well, I think that during that period of my life I was completely blinded.

And something else I forgot to mention: during that time I was always smoking pot, and that weakens you; you don't think, you don't analyze, you just feel . . . apathetic. Things go right by you, you hardly feel it. That might also be due to this process of . . . I think of disintegration, of not wanting to face reality and instead just hanging on, "love and peace," like they said. The '70s. That was really it. The 1970s here in Brazil were like that. Everybody was into this, "Hey, love and peace, pal, everything's cool, everything's going to be okay." Still, I began to come out of it even before Júlia was born. But I think you have to need to wake up. Some people manage to. Hell, most of the young people who went through that process did manage to get free of drugs and that total indolence. Here in Recife it was a bit different: society here is more closed, and at that time . . . although there have always been drugs, pot, cocaine, everything, it was more among the elite, it didn't really reach the masses. But in Rio . . . any party you went to, it was sociable to smoke pot. It wasn't done as a crime, it was just available socially, like having a gin and tonic.

José Carlos was the first man I was really passionate about, but now I don't know what I feel. We're long past that stage of discovery, and sometimes I think it's all over. He wanted me to go on being the way I was. Irresponsible. But how, with a family? It's not just the three children; we're a family, you see? But at the same time, he thinks that if he hadn't met a stable person like me, he would have got much deeper into drugs, he could have ended up as a pusher. Because, you know, prison is a very good school for everything that's rotten.

I C A N R E M E M B E R when I first realized I was on a collision course with my parents. Until I was fifteen, I used to play with dolls. My present for my fifteenth birthday, when all the other girls were going out to parties, beginning to date, the present I asked for was a doll that could walk. I was still very much a child at fifteen. At seventeen I started university. Normally it's at eighteen, but I started at seventeen. I was a little ahead in school, in everything else, but as a result of the highly traditional upbringing I'd had, where the word "sex" was more than sacred, I was simply incapable of thinking about it. So, although it's hard to believe, I started university at the age of seventeen without knowing . . . without ever having seen a photograph of a naked man. Without knowing that a man had a penis, testicles, nothing about this. I'd never even seen an anatomy book. So I didn't know anything about anything. I didn't know what pregnancy was. I still believed—it seems incredible now—that the stork brought babies. I never masturbated. But this entire period in my life, as far as sex was concerned, was lived as a kind of dream.

Today I know how much of all this was revealed through my dreams. I remember those dreams, I remember having sexual feelings, but they were all . . . I didn't know what to attribute them to. It was just a dream. I often dreamt about playing with little boys, it was very much sexual play, but on a completely unconscious level. We'd be playing in the woods, cowboys and other games—there would always be a boy who was Tarzan and I was always Jane, or he'd be Captain Marvel and I'd be Mary Marvel. There really was something between us, but we didn't know what it was; it wasn't channeled. I used to have the most unbelievable dreams. He was Prince Charming and I had found him, and we would get married in my dream. But I never discussed this with anyone, or showed any sign. And I'd never even heard of masturbation.

My mother never let us play with boys. When we'd play with boys she'd hit us. From the time I was very little, about two years old. Today she has the same ideas about Júlia, who's four. If I'm not at home, she won't let her play with boys, only with her cousins because they're brought up practically in the same house. I was completely ignorant of everything. My parents didn't get along well, they were always fighting and disagreeing. I don't remember . . . ever seeing them hugging or kissing. Never.

I started menstruating when I was ten, but I didn't know what it meant. The only explanation I had was that I was getting to be a young lady. Young ladies have breasts and that business down there. I just didn't know its name. Júlia already knows almost everything, thank God. She's only four, and she already knows the most basic things; it's just not verbalized. She has a little book that explains everything, sexual relations, everything. It shows a rooster screwing with a hen, two little dogs, it shows a father and a mother, kissing, embracing. She knows that the baby grows in the mother's belly, how it's born. The only thing she still hasn't asked about is how it got there in the first place. But she knows how it comes out.

Well, when I was seventeen I went on an outing organized by the university. . . . My mother had to go with me—no other mother went, only mine. So everyone considered me a retarded imbecile, naturally [laughs]. And people didn't want to talk with me because they thought I was crazy. On that outing I met a very interesting boy, and . . . it was kind of love at first sight. A friend of mine who was also very innocent, just like me, she also met a boy and fell in love at first sight. The two boys were close friends. Well, when we got back to Recife, we made a date to go to the movies. And we went. Secretly. My mother didn't know. I'd go to class, and from class I'd go to the movies. I wouldn't let him hold my hand, my mother said I shouldn't do that, that "if you give a man your hand, he wants your foot." I'll never forget that, that phrase is engraved in my head forever: when you give a man your hand, he wants your foot. Men, in her very words, "A man is like a dog; he'll take anything he can get, any old bone." Well [laughs], this all seems so funny now, so fantastic. . . .

With this boy, we'd go out, we'd leave school and go walking in a park. One time he stopped for a moment, put his hand on mine and gave me a kiss on the cheek, here near my mouth. And I started crying and went running home. When I got home he called asking what had happened, but I couldn't tell him on the phone. So I called this friend of mine who was also very innocent but must have already known something, and I told her that I was pregnant. And she said, "How come? Where did you go?" That was her first question. I said, "In such and such a park." She: "It's impossible to get pregnant there" [laughs]! So then I spoke to the boy, that I didn't want to go out with him ever again, that he was indecent, immoral, and . . . a whole scene on the phone. And he said he wanted to meet me again just to explain something to me. So I went to meet him and told him that I was pregnant. He said, "Who was it?" I said, "Don't you know? Wasn't it you?" and God knows what else. "Look, you're crazy, you're nuts, you don't know what you're saying. This has got nothing to do with me." He was really shocked, so then [laughs] . . . when I began to cry and he saw that I was really desperate about being pregnant, he asked how I'd gotten pregnant. And I said, "When you kissed me." He was stupefied, of course. How could anybody believe such a thing in this day and age? And he said, "Look, I like you a lot, I think you're very interesting, but I'm not going to see you again until you've read a book I have at home, so that you can understand what's going on. I can't believe that someone your age can have such ideas. . . ."

So he gave me that book, something about the sexual life and so on. He was very sensitive, very intelligent, wasn't he? He said to me, "If you have any problems, call me, but I don't want to see you, I'm not interested." Well, when I read the description of the sex act, it was like being clobbered over the head! I couldn't sleep for three nights. . . . Bestial! Horrible! Pathetic! How could anyone tolerate such a thing? How shameless! How indecent! My mother couldn't possibly ever have done such a thing! That was my worst horror, you see [laughs]? What a shock. It's really a nightmare to have such a shock. Then I got terrified. . . . I couldn't speak to my mother, she'd have said the boy was a son of a bitch, right? That he was trying to bamboozle me so he could take advantage of me in the future. Well . . . at least I was intelligent. I read everything, and when there were some things that I couldn't quite understand I'd call him and he'd explain it to me. And then we made a date, to clarify things.

By the way, that book is still widely used in Brazil; it's a very biased book, the woman is totally subservient, she's there just for the man's pleasure. Right then I felt the possibility of being just an object. Women were to be used sexually . . . I don't know if it actually said that, but I reached the conclusion that the woman, even if she didn't want to, had to be available to her husband. That was the idea that stayed with me, that she had to be available. It's a very shocking idea, isn't it? Well, I went to talk to him about a bunch of things, and he explained them to me. He was a very tactful boy, not much older than I was, but very tactful and well informed. And in spite of everything he didn't try to take advantage of my ingenuousness, not at all. He didn't go beyond . . . just a few kisses. He didn't really touch me.

When he finally did, it was because I wanted him to and told him so. I already wanted to, you see? And it was with him that I had intercourse for the first time. He wasn't that eager. I thought it was all marvelous: it started an entire process, a touch here, a touch there, and I thought it all delightful, terrific, marvelous. It didn't seem at all immoral, I couldn't think it immoral, it felt so good; it *was* good. And there were other things, too. He was very respectful and I think that influenced me a lot, even though I had this idea that men are no good, immoral. The first time he touched my breast, the next day he was at my door. Every Saturday he'd come to the house to pay his respects to my mother and father. He was always talking about marriage, he really wanted to get married. Thank God I didn't want to. And my mother never found out about anything. I'd skip classes and go to meet him. We'd make love on the beach—there were lots of deserted beaches in those days. I was very lucky. Something else about this boy, he felt very responsible toward me; and when I wanted to end it, he still wanted to get married, but I said no.

I didn't marry him for one reason. He was very jealous. Logical, he'd made me into a woman, so naturally he thought—look how strong this prejudice is!—that since I'd slept with him, as soon as I'd meet other men I'd have sex with them, too. So he used to say to me, "When we get married you'll stay home, you'll never have to work because I'll earn enough" . . . things that shocked me. He was an engineer: "I'll earn enough to keep us, and you won't have to work and you won't have to go to school because you'll be done with that already." And I used to say, "I'm going to stay home all day with nothing to do?" He'd say, "Later on you'll have lots of children, lots and lots of children." And that idea horrified me. I'd say, "But that's ridiculous." And I'd think: "This is why I've learned so much? All for nothing? What'll I do at home all day?" Then I'd say, "All right, if I can't go out of the house, I'll call my friends and we'll stay home and chat, play cards." And he'd say, "Girlfriends, yes. Men friends, no. I'll *never* let another man enter my house when I'm not home." And I said, "But look, let's take an example. If one day there's no meat for us to eat, what'll I do? Can't I phone one of your friends and ask him to bring some over?" And he'd say, "No, we'll do without it, we'll eat eggs. In my house no other man enters, just me." Well, I thought that was ridiculous.

How could I see the absurdity of my mother's ideas so quickly? Look, the moment I met a man who wasn't a dog, who didn't try to get to me with sordid ideas, then it was apparent that there would exist other men like him, right? Once the basic thing that my mother told me was challenged, everything else could be, too. I was bound to discover this sooner or later. It worked out very well, don't you think? Now I see I was really lucky to meet such a sensitive person, because I might still be full of complexes, disturbed. Well, when he talked about marriage, I told him he would have to reconsider his own ideas, otherwise we would break up. He said he wouldn't change, he'd never change. That was what he thought. And for a long time he stayed that way. We spent four years like that. Then, long afterward, I ran into him. He was still a bachelor, but he was living with a girl who had two children. So you see, he'd turned my head around, and I'd turned his. It was a symbiosis.

Then, when I was about twenty, going on twenty-one, I met Bill; it was toward the end of my relationship with Mauro, my first lover. That whole period of my life was just palpable, physical sensations, but not real pleasure. And when I met Bill, he showed me this other side. Of course, he was more experienced; he'd already been married, he knew about women's needs on an empirical level, not like my first boyfriend, who'd only known prostitutes. Always. I was the first girl from a good family, with traditions like his, so naturally he fell for me, and he felt very responsible and thought he could never leave me because I'd end up a prostitute if he didn't marry me. But with Bill it was that sensation. . . . He and all the other Americans—this was during Castelo Branco's presidency [1964–1967]⁶—I think they were all forced to leave the country, the entire company. He never said they were, but I think that's what happened. And he began to write to me, saying I should go to him. He wanted me to go to school, to study, to get my B.A., and we would marry when his divorce was final.

But then . . . it was during that phase of anti-Americanism at the university. Everybody was against Americans, and I felt like a traitor to my country. And so I didn't go. Ideologically, I couldn't do it. I would have liked to stay friends, but he was so crushed. [*The baby starts crying, and Norma picks him up.*] Did you know that if you put a tape of a baby crying in a nursery, all the others start to cry, too? It's a sympathetic reation. In my sister's kindergarten, when one starts to cry, they all do. How's that for solidarity! Twenty at a time.

As long as I lived at home, I never openly went out with a man; it was always in secret. It's always possible to go to a girlfriend's house for dinner, or to go to someone's house to study, to do some work together that goes on till very late. My mother must have known, obviously, but she pretended not to, like a hypocrite. There's a lot of hyprocrisy in this phony morality, isn't there? Now, as far as accepting responsibility for going out, that I couldn't do because I might have been kicked out of the house, and I was afraid of that. The job I had didn't pay enough for me to live on. When I finally did start to live alone, I was earning very little money, the bare minimum.

For a long time my mother used to call me a whore, in front of the neighbors. I think she was making a point of fixing it in my head that I might become one, if I wasn't already. I must have had a lot of will power not to end up as one. Today my father's doing the same thing with my sister Glicia, the youngest one. At the beginning she was shocked, because she began to hear this sort of thing when she was only twelve, all because if her boyfriend stood in front of the house and dared to touch her, she was already a whore. You're only supposed to let him put his arms around you when you're about to get married, when you've set the date. Or maybe if she were twenty years old already. But if you're twelve, then you've got no shame. "She's shameless, she's got no respect for anyone and stands there in front of everybody with some fellow putting his hands on her!" It's unreal, isn't it?

I remember, when I turned twenty-one . . . Bill thought that dropping me off at the corner, as I'd always asked him to do, showed a lack of respect—given the culture he came from, right? And that day he said, "No, today I'm taking you home." When we got there, my mother was standing in the doorway and all the neighbors were around, too, and she shouted that I was a whore, "*Puta! Puta!*" I also remember how sometimes I used to come home and hide, waiting to be able to enter the house. And sometimes . . . this was after Bill . . . I would get home at 5:00 in the morning and, if someone would appear, I'd pretend that I was just going out to Mass. Then she'd shout, "Are you just getting in?" "No, Mama, I'm going to Mass, I just got up," and I'd go to Mass.

And yet I was already radicalized by then. All you need is to see the suffering of the majority and you become sensitive to things, unless you're determined not to see. . . . for example, I was telling you about these people who knock on your door looking for work. But this isn't just once or twice, it happens many, many times. The other day a man came here with a shovel and asked if he could clean the cesspool. Do you know what kind of a job that is? There's no sewer here, there are just holes where the shit goes, and he wanted to clean out the shit. So, if you really want not to see, you can manage to, but it's hard. Just pay a bit of attention and you see that everything's all wrong.

I was eighteen when the military coup occurred in 1964. I remember throwing stones at the horses. I used to go to political rallies; I remember Dom Helder's rallies,[7] and others by Gilberto Gil[8] who was very active politically at that time. And the soldiers . . . do you know what happened? The soldiers on their horses charged against the people! My father was always interested in politics, always against the government. In the revolution of 1930 he was locked in the sewers. He wasn't a political prisoner; he was protected because he was in the military. All the others he worked with at that time eventually got into positions of command, but not him. Because he took part in the revolution against the government.[9] In 1964 he was already in the reserves. But he . . . you see, he's not an educated person, I don't know that he even finished primary school, but he's very sensitive about social issues, so he thought it ridiculous that the president had to be a military man. Just that, he already thought ridiculous. My mother went to school through the fourth grade, but she's intelligent, she's always been able to cover up this lack. People who talk to her get the impression that she had more formal education.

I T   W A S   A F T E R   Bill left the country that I first moved out of the house. At that time a friend of mine who worked with me was renting an apartment on the same floor, so he helped me with the papers—there were so many new things that I knew nothing about: how to do the contract, how to find people as guarantors. And he helped me. You know what I did? I just left the house one day with the clothes I was wearing, the clothes on my back, and I didn't return. I didn't say anything, and I didn't send for my clothes. The next day my parents phoned me at work, but I didn't answer; I had a friend of mine answer. And she said, "She's not going back home." My mother cried, she said it was the end of the world, she fainted. But even before this . . . when I began to cause more trouble, my mother would have nervous attacks; she would faint, she would cry, she'd sit on the bed shaking. At that time she was seeing a psychoanalyst or a psychologist, I don't remember which he was, and one day I made an appointment to see her analyst and I told him I was having these problems at home and that I'd decided to move out of the house, and could he tell me what were the chances that my mother would die, because she always used to say that one day she'd be dead on my account. Well, he said that it wasn't important for me to know whether she would die or not. The important thing was to know what would make me happy, and he didn't think it likely that someone would die because a daughter left home; but I should accept the risk and, if something did happen, I was doing the right thing anyway. I thought he was right, that it was a good move.

Then I went to see Padre Tomas, who taught at the university and was a friend of mine. We talked, I explained everything—because there had been a time when I wanted to do some theater. I was always very interested in that, and for a while I was in a play; the rehearsals were on Saturday afternoons. All of a sudden they couldn't be in the afternoon anymore, so we had to meet at night; and it was midnight or later when we'd finish and everybody went home, and nobody lived near me or could give me a lift home. But even if someone could have, my mother wouldn't have let me, you see. When I told Padre Tomas that I was going to have to stop because my mother wouldn't let me go to evening rehearsals, he thought that was ridiculous. I did give it up, but he got me thinking. Oh, another time I'd been on the school volleyball team, and I had to give that up, too, becuse we'd practice late in the evening. All the other girls could go, but not me.

Well, I talked to him and explained that I'd wanted to be on the volleyball team and couldn't, I'd wanted to do theater and couldn't, that I wanted to go out at night to parties, to the movies, and she wouldn't let me, and that I was thinking about leaving home. What did he think? Could he give me some advice? And he told me the same thing, that he believed in me. I thought that was lovely—I've always liked him a lot; he's still alive. He believed in me, that I had good intentions, and he thought I cared about my mother—if I didn't, I wouldn't have been so worried. He said it was very sensible of me to seek out older people to talk to about what I ought to do, and he thought I should go ahead and do it, otherwise I'd start getting really nervous and upset and might even become so unhappy that I'd end up quitting school. Well, after that I stopped worrying and was ready to act, because I felt that I was supported by various people I trusted. So I started to live alone. I didn't see anything wrong with it. I used to think that living alone would be tiresome, lonely, hard. Of course there were lonely moments. But that it was awful, that you felt insecure? Not at all. I felt much more secure, much more in control of my life.

At that time I was working for an American company. I would go to work; I'd have lunch there; I'd go and come back on the company bus, which was free. I'd have tea and toast for breakfast, and tea and crackers with cheese and milk for dinner. So I really only had to pay for food on Saturdays and Sundays. All my money went for the rent and for those breakfasts. I didn't buy clothing; my friends gave me clothing. Rosa brought me a dress, another friend gave me shoes. Sometimes on weekends, when I was hungry and couldn't buy food, I'd tell one of my friends. Once in a while Rosa would say, "Do you have food for lunch today?" I'd say, "No, I don't." "I'll drop by later and bring something." Someone would bring me food, or they'd invite me to have lunch at their house.

I lived in that apartment for nearly a year. It had a living room, a bedroom, a bath, and a small kitchen. Then my mother came to get me. She said she accepted the way I was and that she'd heard through other people that I'd behaved very well, that men didn't go to my apartment. It was true: when men came they were always with someone else; for example, Lucinha would come with her husband, or Rosa with her boyfriend, and it happened that at this time I began to date the boy who lived in the next apartment, so in fact men really weren't coming to see me. So her information was all good, that I went around with

Lucinha, Rosa, Flávia, that I wasn't running wild. I think she'd imagined that just because I was living alone there'd be orgies, naked women in the windows, marching into the lobby naked, men peeing out the window and so on. And she saw that nothing like that was going on. Then, when I went back home, I said to her, "Look, you[10] have to rely on the upbringing you gave me. You brought me up right and I'll always have that, no one can take that from me." And she said that she accepted me, that she wouldn't be so intransigent, that I could go out at night with people she knew, and so on.

For some time she did approve, but then my father put too much pressure on her. I lived at home for two more years, and my father was always creating problems. He thought I was a whore and that it was a disgrace to have a whore in the house, you see? And so, after a while I said, "There's no way I can go on living in Recife, no way." I already had my B.A. So I quit my job and said, "I'm getting out of here." And I went to Rio, alone, without knowing anyone and with almost no money.

I went by bus, and on the bus I read the [Rio] newspaper I'd bought and I saw an ad, "Room for Rent." I went straight there and rented the room, in a girl's house. It could have turned out badly, because in Rio there are some horrible places, but it worked out pretty well. It was the first time I'd been to Rio, and I lived in a room in this girl's house. She didn't have a boyfriend; she was a rather nutty person, didn't seem to care about much. She lived alone and we shared the whole apartment, except that she had a series of fixed rules. For example, I wasn't supposed to turn on the radio. And when I was in the kitchen, if I left even a crumb of bread she'd rush by me to clean it up. A bit of a maniac. Things like that. But I'd leave in the morning and come back at night.

I found a job as a bilingual secretary [Portuguese/English] after two days. At that time you had your choice of jobs; I could have chosen any one of three that day. I began to earn double what I'd been earning here, so it was enough for me to live on, comfortably. I ate out all the time and wore nice clothes. But I felt very much alone. For six months I hardly spoke to a soul, except at the office. Then a lady who was also a secretary in my office invited me to her house for a birthday party, and there I met some other people and slowly . . . I created a circle of friends. But the first six months were really sad. At that time I used to like to drink *cachaça* [a cheap, strong liquor made of sugar cane], pure *cachaça*. But I never got drunk, never. It was just to get to that point, kind of lightheaded. At night, when I'd get home from work, I'd have it as an apéritif and I'd read—I've always liked to read. And then next thing I'd know it would be time to go to sleep, 10:00 or 10:30, and that's how I spent my time, always reading, reading, reading.

In Rio it was considered perfectly normal and natural for a girl to live alone, not like here. No one asked questions, no one wondered about you. At that time

I also go to know a girl, Moema, who was very good for me. She, too, was in a process of personal development, and we spent a lot of time together. They were all people like me, living alone, starting out in life and struggling to establish themselves. And today they're all doing well, all of them. That was about the time I started to smoke pot, too. Because everybody was smoking; it was the "in" thing to do. Everybody.

Then I met José Carlos, at a party. It was that passion. . . . Our life didn't change that much when Júlia was born. Getting around was still rather easy, with just one child. Even if you're going some place far away, with just one child and two people to share the work it's not so difficult. And, with Júlia, he really did share the work. I even have photographs of him—which now seem unbelievable— hanging out the laundry, washing clothes. But after Cláudio was born . . . you see, *one* was still easy, but two he found inconvenient, so he gave up. I wasn't prepared for that, I thought he'd continue. . . . Now with this new baby, I knew it would be like this, but I couldn't do anything about it. But, for example, when Cláudio [the second child] was born, my mother came south to help me. She got the news that he was born one day, and the next day she was there. It was fantastic, because it had been really heavy going, because José Carlos refused . . . he went through a deep rejection. For about six months, he almost never held Cláudio in his arms; he didn't even want to see him.

When Cláudio was born, it was still during that good phase in the South; he had that good job. Later, when we were in Rio, he was unemployed. When he was out of work he was really depressed, and very resentful. So depressed that he asked me whether I could put aside something from our budget so he could go to a psychologist to figure out what was happening, what kind of a mental state he was getting into. There were days when he thought he was really going crazy. I realized he wasn't to blame for not having a job; I even thought it normal given the general situation in the country. But I thought he should share the housework. Since he wasn't working, he should share the tasks. Or, even if it wasn't sharing, at least he should take care of the children more, since during that period in Rio I couldn't put them in a nursery because it was too expensive. So, seeing that he had twenty-four hours a day free, at least for half the day he should take them to the beach, or to the park or to a friend's house—or do something, anything, together with the two children so they wouldn't spend twenty-four hours a day locked in the tenth floor of the building. I don't think it was unreasonable of me to ask such a thing of a person who had all day free. But he'd spend his time at friends' houses, in bars . . . and a maid who'd been with me for a long time took care of the children.

And then . . . at that time I'd have said that this didn't influence our sexual relationship, but today I recognize that it did because, whether you like it or not, you slowly lose interest. Sexual stimulation isn't just in the flesh, it's in the head, too; it's an entire mental process. You have to feel an interest in the person himself in order to express yourself sexually. And the moment you lose . . . certain interests, and see that the other person's concerns aren't the same as yours, you don't feel attracted as you did before. Well, that's what I think was happening. . . . I don't know . . . I was losing interest little by little, and sometimes I even used to think I was becoming frigid, that there were serious problems. . . . Then I began to read, I'd pick up books on frigidity and so on, and I saw that it had nothing to do with that. . . .

José Carlos only went through the seventh grade, I think he repeated some grades, and he left school when he was about fifteen. I've done everything I could think of to get him to go back to school, but he's not interested. At the beginning it was like—I always think of that phase as our frivolous phase, our "hippie" phase. And since then I've tried to understand, I've asked myself these questions. But everything seemed perfect in that phase, our interests were the same. We'd go to parties, get high, enjoy life, watch the sunrise, watch the sunset, do yoga on the beach, wander around in clothing that was far out—the whole counterculture scene. We'd walk barefoot in the streets . . . so, we were really well matched then.

And now I'm always wondering . . . sometimes I think, "If he doesn't change, we'll have to separate." The main thing now is that he doesn't help with the children. I've talked to him about this, and he says I'm not making any sense, that he's a terrific father. And he is affectionate with them, it's true, but he doesn't share in the work. Affectionate he really is, without a doubt. Maybe his eyes will open, maybe . . . I'm trying to give him a chance. I told him so. Because sometimes you go through a crisis and you overcome it; you go through it and overcome it, again and again. And other times there are crises that you just can't tolerate anymore. Yesterday, for example, I said that it was absurd for him not to understand that he has a wife and children in the house and to still think it's my obligation to put the children to bed every night. That used to be a pleasure, but it got monotonous, routine, and now it's one more wretched task for me. But he thinks he's a perfectly normal father, because in fact his behavior is typical of Brazilian men.

Sometimes I'm afraid when . . . projecting into the future. I can't imagine meeting anyone and having a really solid relationship, only casual ones . . . not solid, and I'll get to be sixty years old, the children will all be married and I'll be alone.

I'm still recovering from this last baby, and he intends—I wish he'd done it before this one was born—to have a vasectomy. He's wanted to do it for some time but didn't have the opportunity. I didn't have my tubes tied because my delivery was very difficult, and there was no way it could be done at the same time.[11] So now we're going to start looking . . . for him to have the operation. Now we're going to start having relations again. I don't want to take the pill, so it'll have to be . . . but I'm breast-feeding, and normally I don't menstruate while I'm breast-feeding. But it's not sure, so we'll have to . . . I don't know, keep track of my cycle and maybe use a condom. Or abstain. He's the only man I've slept with since I first met him. But I don't think fidelity is important so long as it's not a solid affair. For example, an affair that goes on for three months or that divides the house, that's a mess. But a casual relationship, it wouldn't bother me to hear about that, and I'd even like to have one myself. I just haven't had the opportunity, it just hasn't happened.

I F   I   H A D   my life to do over again . . . I'd want not to have gone to work; I'd want to continue in school, to do a master's, a doctorate, and work within the university, not in business. This is one of my great frustrations. Even today . . . if there were some sort of financial support, I'd just want to study. I don't want to go on living like this. Study and then teach, that would be my dream, to be able to teach. When I came back to Recife I even thought about going in with my sister at her kindergarten, but she couldn't pay me. What really matters to me is to pass on knowledge. The level doesn't matter, it could be grade school, high school, college. . . . The transmission of knowledge is what counts, and the contact with younger people. I feel very restricted in my office.

If José Carlos earned enough, I'd stop working and go back to school, but I could never just be a housewife, I'm not cut out for that. It would have to be half and half, or I could be a housewife and give private lessons, in English or Portuguese, teach Portuguese to foreigners, but I couldn't tolerate the daily routine of just housework. But as it is, I'm not just a superwoman, I'm a superman, which is even worse. One of the things that really annoys me is this business that if there's no toilet paper, it's my responsibility; if one of the children is sick, that's my responsibility, too. For example, something happened that I think is typical, which drives me crazy. Cláudio was sick right after the baby was born, and the idiot doctor thought he might have tuberculosis, so the day I got home, José Carlos said to me, "They want to take an X-ray of his chest, and the doctor thinks that you . . ." and I was wiped out! It was unbelievable, a three-year-old with tuberculosis and a newborn baby in the house, and the doctor needed to talk to *me* because the mother has to take care of these things! So I sent him a note saying I'd just come back from the maternity ward and couldn't go to talk things over with him, and I wrote out . . . on such and such a day his temperature was this high, medication taken, a complete report.

Well, it turned out that the key question, the key to the whole business, was,

"Has he been vaccinated against tuberculosis?" And José Carlos hadn't been able to answer this. Which I think is real negligence. This is typical Brazilian male behavior. Fine, great, but it's still a profound case of negligence for a father not to know what vaccines his child has had. It's an utter lack of knowledge and interest in his child, because there's a vaccination card, and he as a father ought to feel an obligation to know where that vaccination card is. He should be able to come home, without consulting me, get the card, and say, "Look, here, he was vaccinated." But everything depends on me. The children were vaccinated for everything, every time. This is a very important point—just ask other women. Has any father missed a day at work to take a child to get vaccinated? It's the mother who has to miss work, no matter what happens. So look, during the first year, the mother misses one day of work every month. Which has negative repercussions. . . . The father doesn't deign to go to work and say, "Today I have to take my son to get vaccinated." Because that's just not a man's job, it's a woman's obligation whether she works or not. A father can't do it. And that's absurd, ridiculous. There's no doubt that the fathers could influence their own employers. The father could say, "I'll be a little late today because I have to take my son to be vaccinated." If they all started to do this, there's a much greater likelihood that people would begin to see this as a normal thing. Or, for example, consider this business of verminosis. The kids have to be tested for worms constantly. Lately I've begun to insist that he do it: "Look, Zé [José], today's the day for the stool exam for Júlia, you've got to take the specimen to the doctor." Because I used to have to take her stool and urine, and miss work for that. So now I say, "Look, you do it because you have more time." It was absurd, even when he wasn't working, he'd go to the beach, and I had to miss work to take the specimens!

Well, enough. Not anymore. Now he does it, he takes it, he picks up the results of the test and brings them home, but he doesn't do anything on his own. He picks up the results, but he's incapable of going back to the doctor to find out what medication to give them. He's incapable of giving them the medication. For example, this medicine that I have to give them three times a day. If he had to do it, it doesn't really matter to him, sometimes he'd do it, sometimes he wouldn't. When they're on antibiotics, it has to be every eight hours and you have to wake them at 2:00 in the morning, I always wake them at 2:00. Zé would never get up at 2:00 a.m. to give the children medicine, but he's quite capable of watching TV until 2:00 a.m. This is killing my feeling for him. I'm exhausted, drained, but I know that this is the typical behavior of a Brazilian male; he just can't do things for his children. The mother has to kill herself, give up sleep, everything. And it makes me furious, I get into incredible rages over this. . . . Once, just to see what would happen, I didn't buy bread. For three days there was no bread in the house. It never occurred to him just to go out and get the bread.

I don't know . . . I just don't know what will happen. There are days when I think my life would be easier alone, I would support the children, just as I do now—I'm going back to work in a month, as soon as my maternity leave is over—I'd still support the children, but it's almost as if I'd have one less child to worry about. Sometimes it seems that he's just one more responsibility, and I don't know how much longer I can stand it.

———

NORMA RETURNED to her job at the end of her maternity leave. As soon as her three months of "job stability" were up, she was fired. At a time of deep recession and increasing unemployment, she was fortunate to find another job—at much lower pay. The following year, having separated from her husband, Norma had to rent out the house left to her by her aunt and move into in a small apartment, still near her mother's house, with her three children and a maid. By August 1983, when I saw her again, an estimated 10 million Brazilians were unemployed.[12] Norma's salary at that point came to about $250 a month.

Glícia, Norma's youngest sister, is a small and slender sixteen-year-old who smoked continuously throughout out the interview and often coughed. Although Glícia is aware that she has benefited from Norma's struggles with their parents a generation earlier, she still finds life in her parents' household intolerable and is looking for an escape route.

6

———

M y parents don't give me an allowance, but they give me just about everything I need. When I need money, I just ask for it and get it. My mother, not my father. I can always ask, and mostly she gives it to me, whenever she can. My mother, because my father I don't talk to, I don't get along with him. He's a lot older than I am—I mean, I'm sixteen and he's nearly eighty. We don't agree about anything. Mama must be about sixty. She takes care of most everything, about 90 percent of the time. Him? He does *nothing*; as far as I'm concerned he's not a father, he doesn't know how to bring up children, at least not me. If only he'd

talk to me, treat me like a friend. If he doesn't like being a father, he doesn't have to be, if he'd just be a friend, but he's no father and no friend either.

I'm not sure how a father should act, but he should give a daughter some support. He never wants to know how I am, how things are going at school; he's not interested—where I've been, when I get home, who I'm with, he's not interested in any of that. He doesn't have the slightest regard for me, and I don't for him either. I mean, if he wants me to respect him, he's got to respect me, too, right? I don't like him. My mother's difficult to deal with, but I like her. I have to, right? I've been living with her for a long time, and, whether you want to or not, you start to care for people. But sometimes she's kind of a pain. She forbids all sorts of things; everything is a scandal to her, wrong. Like, a girl going out alone with her boyfriend, that's the end. So I never do, officially. I have to accept what she says. She doesn't seem to know what I really do, but I think she should let me. There's nothing wrong with it. If she never lets

GLÍCIA

me do anything, sooner or later I'll manage to do it anyway, so it's pointless for mothers to forbid everything. I already know what's right and what's wrong, what's good and bad, so why fuss? Sometimes I think that she's refusing to see that I'm grown up, that I already know how to behave. I don't think she should act like this, but what can I do?

I know I have a lot more freedom than Norma did. I'm allowed to go out on weekends, and I can come in at three in the morning; but it has to be *with* someone, some friend, and not just my boyfriend. I can go out, but not alone with him. Of course you can send the third person away for a while—I used to do that a lot, but now I think it's not worth the trouble; so now when we go out with a friend, we stay together. It's easier. Anyway, they're people who have the same tastes I do, who like to do the same things, so that doesn't really interfere with my plans.

No, we never talked about sex at home. Norma told me things, but never my mother. I started menstruating when I was very young, not quite ten, and I already knew about it from talking with my friends—you know, those little gab sessions that girls have. So when I got my period I wasn't shocked, but they never sat me down and talked about this; only Norma did. She always talked to me about everything. But not my mother, much less my father. If my mother couldn't bring herself to talk about it, then my father—God forbid, never!

I don't think they're happy, no. They just put up with one another. Ever since I was little I've had that impression. They don't love each other, they just each put up with the other. I guess they stayed together because of the children, the six of us, and now he's so old, it's not worth the trouble anymore to change things. When they should have done it they didn't want to—I mean, that was before I was born, this goes a long way back. My father is really gross, you know, really stupid. What he thinks goes, nobody else has the right to have an opinion, everybody else is wrong, but not him, get it? And, in spite of everything, my mother is very understanding toward him. I really don't think much of their marriage, it never was much. I think maybe they wanted to separate once, but they already had children. I mean, my mother doesn't have a degree, she didn't know what to do, "How am I going to live?" so she stayed. She shut up, she doesn't talk much, and they've just tolerated one another to this day. But I think that even though it's late, there's still time for her to live her own life and him to live his. I don't really know how she feels about it now. I don't talk much with her, we're not real friends. I'm not close to her, because she's horrified at most things and just says, "Oh!" about everything, anything you can imagine. A girl sitting on a boy's lap, that's all wrong. Things that I think are fine.

Yes, I've done drugs, pot and pills. I used to take pills for headaches, in large quantities. Like twenty at a time. I tried it various times and got kind of high. But other times I got very sick, vomiting . . . it was awful. I didn't like it. I wouldn't advise anyone to try that. Or pot. I'm not into that anymore. I tried it when I was about thirteen, and kept it up for a while. Then I had a boyfriend who was into it, so we continued, and then when I broke up with him, last year, I gave it up. I saw it wasn't doing me any good. I prefer to drink—I drink beer and wine now.

I started with drugs because of my friends' influence, at school. It was very common there. At that time I was living in Rio with my sister, and she gave me money for school, for snacks, to buy things. I was already smoking, so she gave me money for cigarettes, too. But often people would give me stuff, a friend would come around and offer it. It's easy to get your hands on it, when you want to. Especially for a woman, I think. At least for me it was always easy. But I didn't like it, and I wouldn't advise it. It messed up my head—first you smoke because it's cool, because everybody smokes, then because you like it, and finally out of necessity. I mean, when it gets to be a need, that's bad. If you went on smoking just because it felt good . . . like drinking, I only drink on weekends, and if I don't drink, that's okay, too. But if I needed it, that already makes it bad. No one should need these things, see? Now I smoke cigarettes, I can't manage to quit—I mean, I prefer cigarettes, a thousand times. Naturally, sometimes it makes me sick, but I just don't want to quit. I like it, I don't intend to quit, unless I die first [*laughs*].

AH, MY FIRST BOYFRIEND . . . we used to hold hands. I was ten. It only lasted a week. My first real boyfriend was Márcio. We dated for two years, from the time I was . . . let's see . . . eleven years old. And the first time I made love with him was when I was twelve. He was sixteen, a lot older. I was very developed, I had the same body I have now. We both wanted to do it, but I didn't enjoy it and I was sorry afterward. Not sorry about having done it, but I think the timing wasn't right. I should have waited a little longer, or maybe I could have done it then but with somebody different. It went on for another year. We never spent a real night together, we never had the chance—it was always very fast, very secret. Maybe that's why I never really got to like it. I had a completely different image—you know, a sea of roses . . . and it was all so different. I'm not sorry . . . I think it was worth doing. Every experience is valid, right? I mean, it could have been different, but that's the way it happened, so what can I do about it? But I never liked it much. I took birth control pills. . . . No, I don't take them anymore because . . . I'm engaged now and I don't make love with my fiancé.

Well, after I broke up with Márcio I had several silly boyfriends. We fought, he made my life hell. I don't know if he really loved me or just wanted to own me, if he was really crazy about me or if he thought of me as an object that just was his because he'd done it—but he pursued me for a long time. I went south, he came after me. I went to Rio, alone—my mother sent me to my sister's house—and he came after me. I mean, he pursued me like crazy, and I began to get angry, disgusted, see, so I broke it off. But he persisted, for quite a while. Sometimes I'd go back to him, but it didn't work out. I no longer loved him. So we broke up, and afterward I started dating Roberto. I mean, I had lots of boyfriends, but the only really serious thing was with Roberto. I ended up running away with him to Rio. We hitched rides on trucks, and we only let my parents know after we'd been gone for nine days. See, they didn't want to let us date, because of that business about him smoking pot. My mother never found out that I smoked, too. But they wouldn't let us go out. It was horrible: she was constantly at me, fights going on at home all day long. And I was getting fed up, so the day he brought it up, I agreed right then and there. And we took off, hitchhiking. It was very tiring, really exhausting. We stayed at his grandfather's house [in Rio]. Then, just after Christmas, this was this past year, we came back.

Of course, by then my mother knew we'd had sex. She was really, really outraged and constantly complained. See, I was . . . especially for people in this part of the country, a girl who makes love with her boyfriend is kind of . . . a whore. That's what my mother thinks, of course. I tried to explain things to her, that I couldn't stand it anymore, that I'd done it just because I was so fed up. And I ended up sorry about the whole business because things only got worse at home. They . . . they began to treat me even more coldly, more remotely. They thought I was really headed down the path of prostitution. I mean, it was terrible. And they put so much pressure on me that I couldn't stand it, and I broke off with Roberto. And while I was still dating Roberto, there was a boy, the type of ideal boy that families always love, who was after me. I wasn't interested in him at all, until I began to date him. Now I'm engaged to him.

Now, my second sexual experience was much better than the first, much better [laughs]. I was . . . you see, I was more prepared. Maybe I'd done it the first time around just to know how it was, just to see if it was really like everybody said. The second time was much better. I'm not sorry about it. Well, then I began to date Luis—this was about seven months ago. He's nineteen. Roberto was seventeen when I was fifteen. Luis is nineteen, so he's ideal as far as the family's concerned. Good purchasing power. Describe him? Good purchasing power . . . he's getting two degrees, he loves going to school, he's doing data processing and also accounting. He works in computing with his father. The family is rich; they've got good purchasing power, enough so that by today's standards he's rich.

I met him here, on this street, with some friends. It was last November . . . just about the time I was beginning to date Roberto. But I hated him, I wouldn't even speak to him. When I came back from Rio, I went on dating Roberto until the beginning of January, then I broke it off. And Luis got my phone number and began calling me, asking me out. . . . And my mother wanted me to go out with him. I mean, it was like going from water to wine, see? To a good wine, as far as she was concerned. So I started going out with him . . . and we still are. I mean, I . . . it's impossible, you see, not to like him. He's a very sensitive person, very refined, educated, everything you could want . . . sometimes even too much. Whatever you ask him for, he'll give you. If he can, he will. He'll do anything to see me smile. He's . . . I adore him, but I don't think I love him enough to marry. But I'm going to marry him, to get out of this house. We'll get married in about a year. He knows I don't get along well with my father, with my mother . . . and I think he knows that I don't love him. . . . That mad passion, I don't feel that kind of love for him. But he wants to marry me anyway. I like him a lot, and I think that, in time, who knows? It's a matter of time. If our relationship continues the way it is, probably I'll end up loving him. A lot even.

I don't make love with him because I haven't really felt like it. Yes, he knows about my other experiences. I thought that . . . I didn't have the right to deceive him. He's a person who really doesn't deserve to be deceived, he's very sincere. I don't think he deserves it. Right now, he's my only friend . . . when I'm happy, when I'm sad. . . . I like him . . . he's really a marvelous person; and he's never pushed me, he's never asked me, "Why don't you want to make love with me?" Actually, I think I'm a little bit afraid. I was very sad, really very sad, when I broke up with Roberto. I mean, maybe if I made love with Luis I'd feel a thousand times more attached to him, much closer to him than I do now. And I don't really want to be very close to him. Because what if we suddenly separate? It won't be good for me, you see. And also for fear that my mother would find out. I don't want to mess up my head anymore, I've had enough. Everything's fine just as it is.

I know that seventeen is young to get married, but I'm going to do it just the same. I think we'll have a good life. In the first place, you need understanding and love. And in the second place, money. Because money buys everything today, even people, everything except happiness. So, if I have love and understanding *and* money with him . . . it doesn't matter that it's his money, I don't mind depending on someone. The only thing I want is to get out of the house, because I just can't take any more. And he . . . maybe he's a bit old-fashioned, but he doesn't want me to work, so he knows that he's going to have to support me for the rest of my life.

Yes, I want to have children, and I want to adopt one, too. I don't know why . . . I'd like to adopt a child, that's all. Several people have told me that I was adopted. I mean, sometimes . . . I've never been certain and I always have this doubt. People who could have told me whether it was true or not told me that I really was adopted. And my mother, the only person who could tell me for sure, says that it's a lie. I've asked Norma, too, but she won't tell me. I think she felt she wasn't the right person to tell me who my mother was, so she wouldn't. She says it's a lie, but I feel sure it's true. I mean . . . I have to live with this doubt all the time, not knowing whether it's a lie or the truth. But I think it's true.

A friend of my mother's who's lived here for many years . . . just recently I was at her house and we were talking about this—all her children are adopted, too, because she has an undeveloped uterus. She said that I was left at the door. My mother was living in that building over there. I was left at the door. I've tried to tell my mother that I need to know, but she thinks it's not important. Or maybe she's also afraid that I'll leave her. It could be that. I think that in spite of everything she loves me, but in a very peculiar way. It's a crazy kind of love. . . . I don't know . . . it might be better if she didn't love me. If she loves me but won't tell me the truth, I wish she'd not love me but tell me instead. Maybe she doesn't even know who my parents are, but it wouldn't hurt her to tell me the truth, would it? "This is what happened, and I don't know who your parents are." That wouldn't hurt her, but she won't do it. She won't tell me, no way. There's no point in thinking about it a lot, but I imagine I'll find out eventually. I mean, lots of people who could know for sure have said it's true, but I wanted to hear it from her, you see? From her, and she won't speak. It's no use asking my father. If I did, I'm sure he'd say it's none of my business [laughs]. I don't talk to him, and when I do open my mouth he curses me out or I curse him out. He's always saying I'm no good. Given his ideas about life, I'm already a prostitute, right? That's how it is at home. Nobody wants to know . . . nobody cares if I'm intelligent, if I'm educated, if I'm studious—which I'm not, I was once, but not anymore—if I'm pretty, if I'm ugly. What they think is, "If you behave yourself you're a great girl, and if you don't, you're worthless."

Of course, a man's different. A man's a man, right? A man is superior. A man can do whatever he likes and it's all right, he's a man. There was always this difference; from the time I was very small, my mother always thought, "If a man is with a different woman every day, he's a man," right? He's proving that he's really a man. "And if a woman does this she's a prostitute," you see? Everyone'll gossip about her. I wouldn't bring up my children like that. I'd give them the same education: whatever freedom he has, she has, too, except that unfortunately she'll have to control herself because of the society we live in, where men will always be better than women. No matter how much women struggle to prove otherwise, men will always be better than women. Look, ever since Christ appeared, it's been like this. If it was going to change, it would have changed by now. It would have. From every point of view, physical strength, too. Society will always consider men superior to women. I'll try to bring my kids up the same, teach them what's right and wrong, and they'll have to figure out for themselves whether it's really right or wrong. But bring them up differently? Never!

W H A T   W I L L   I   D O   when I marry? Take some courses, take exercise classes, go on studying. I don't know about going to college. I detest studying. I just hate it totally. Of course school is necessary, but you can get along fine without it, too. I don't think it's obligatory to go to school, but everybody talks about it like it is. I don't know. I still have a long time to decide, three more years of high school. If I don't go . . . I'm not sure what I'll do. Work . . . something like that. Maybe in a store. No, I really have no idea whether I'd like that. I'm just so lazy [laughs]. I've only had one job—during my vacation this year, I worked in a shoe boutique. It was full-time, from 8:00 to 12:30 and from 2:00 till 8:00 p.m. I wanted to earn some money, but I got fed up and left after a while. It was really tiring, too tiring.

Luis would rather I didn't work, but if I want to, I can, just like if he didn't want me to do lots of other things; but if I want to I can, because I have my own wishes, too. He has his and I have mine. It's just that if I can do what he asks, great. If not, too bad. The same thing goes the other way, too: if he can do what I ask, great. If not, too bad. I like him a lot—he's a terrific person, very generous. It's just that there are certain things he asks and if I can do them he'll be very grateful; but if not, he won't force me, he won't insist. So far, that's the only thing he's asked. He's not concerned about what I do, so long as it fits in with society, because unfortunately we depend on it, whether we like it or not. Like, if I'm married to him and I go out alone and get in at 4:00 in the morning, the next day everyone will be saying that I was with another man, even if I was at a girlfriend's house talking. Well, I have to accept these rules, don't I? I've learned that it's no use fighting all alone against the whole world. It's not worth the trouble. Whether you like it or not, whether you want it or not, you've got to stay within society. If you don't, you'd better know in advance what you'll have to go through, suffering all the consequences, even being cast aside by other people. That's something I loathe, couldn't tolerate. . . . Especially here in Recife, here in the Northeast, women are really marginalized. I wouldn't want that. I mean, I tried doing everything the opposite, but all it brought me was trouble, beginning with the people right in my own home. So, I mean, it's not worth the trouble to fight any more. Fight, fight, I think it's a waste of time.

When I was in Rio, I don't know if life seemed much freer there because I was living with Norma, or if it really was freer. Probably both things. Because she's so much nearer my own age, and understands my life more, so we got along better than with my mother. My mother is really a serious case. My sisters, aside from

Norma, all have the same kind of life, just the same. I mean, they're terrific people, but, you know, they're all the same—same, same, same. They all had the same upbringing; they never left here, never traveled any place in the whole world. There are six of us: Norma is the oldest, she's thirty-five; then Diana, she's thirty-three; then João, he's thirty-two; and Neusa, she's thirty; and then Edilton, he's twenty-nine. They're all a lot older than me. But it's like Norma and me against the others. Because of the way she sees things, and so do I. I think we're closer than the others—like, she and I are heading north, and the others are heading south. There's no way we can agree.

Once I marry, I don't want to have too much to do with my family. I want to go on living here, in this neighborhood, but me in my house and they in theirs. Obviously. And we can visit once a month! Well, that's a manner of speaking . . . maybe every two weeks, but I don't want them interfering in my life with Luis.

He's going to finish his degree in two years, but he's working already and earns a good salary, and he's saving money. If he earns, let's say $1,000 or $1,200 a month, I think you can live pretty well in Recife on that. We'd be all set. He might even earn more . . . because his father's leaving, and he'll be taking his place. He's in computing . . . he does the accounting for some car manufacturers. Now, when we get married, I won't be able to have my own bank account because I'm still a minor, so it'll be like I said: "At the end of the month, so that I don't have to constantly ask for money if I'm not working, you give me a certain amount, let's say $500, just as if I were working and got a salary." You see? And that's the end of it. So long as I don't work, I'll get a certain amount a month. We could divide his salary 50 percent for him, 50 percent for me. We've already discussed it. Or let's say, 30 percent for me, 30 percent for him, and the rest for the house. I think it'll all be cool; and then when I'm twenty-one, I can have a joint account with him.

If I don't grow to love him? I'm going to marry him anyway. I'm going to do everything not to hurt him, because he's a person who doesn't deserve to be hurt. But if it doesn't work out, too bad, each of us will have to go his own way. But I will try, I really will. If it doesn't work out . . . and I'm going to try everything so that it does work, everything, but if it doesn't work . . . I can't do a thing about it. But I think, not that I'm much of an optimist, but I think it will work. Our temperaments . . . unless he changes, that seems unlikely. And if I change, I hope it'll be for the better [laughs]. Still, it could be for the worse, right? But I hope it'll work. I'll really try. Maybe he's a kind of lifeboat, you know, because my mother thinks that since I made love with other boyfriends, nobody will want to marry me. She's scared to death I'll be an old maid. No, I'm not afraid of that, I don't think that's all there is to life.

No, I've never been pregnant, but I have friends who've had abortions. In the first place, it's damaging from the point of view of your health, so I think it's wrong for a person. And, second, in terms of your self-respect, I think a person would feel torn apart, because I'd do anything rather than kill a child of mine, you see? In fact, I'm dying to have a child, but just not right now. If I were pregnant now, I'm sure the only solution for me would be to have an abortion, maybe to get married, but I wouldn't want to get married now; we haven't been together very long, just seven months, so that wouldn't be a good solution and might ruin a marriage that could be good in the future if we didn't have a child. But I don't approve of abortion. I approve if, for example, it's really necessary, if the child would be damaged in the future or the parents would be. If you can have it, fine, but I think it's disgusting not to have it just out of selfishness and not wanting to give up going out at night on account of the baby. I think that's really disgusting. Like, let's say, a couple who live comfortably, she gets pregnant and doesn't want to have the baby just because she doesn't want to, it's too much responsibility. I think that's disgusting. Now somebody who really can't manage it, let's say a poor person who hardly has enough to live on, to bring a baby into the world and not be able to take care of it—no, it's better to get rid of it as soon as possible. Or in cases of illness, obviously. A friend of mine caught the measles while she was pregnant, and had to have an abortion. But not when it's just this disgusting business of getting rid of it because it's inconvenient. I think that's really the end, I just can't go along with that.

I don't want to have children right away. Maybe after about three years. Having a baby when you're seventeen isn't so good, especially at the beginning of a marriage . . . because first of all I have to get used to him, naturally. We've only been together for seven months, though we're together a fair amount of the time. On weekends we're together twelve hours a day, but we see each other just about every day, if only for an hour, half an hour. And . . . we have to get used to one another—waking up, going to bed together, seeing someone twenty-four hours a day. No matter how much you like one another and have things in common, a thousand things will come up, right? And you've got to know how to rise above them. Having a baby just then isn't a good idea. Especially if you're seventeen. I think three to five years later would be ideal.

Yes, fidelity is very important. Especially because I'm extremely jealous [*laughs*]. I'm even jealous of the wind! Frankness is much better than infidelity. That's my view, and I think it's his, too. It's worth trying to talk about it, instead of being unfaithful. It's so much more work, you know? I'm very practical; that's how I like things. Aside from this, there's something else, too: I couldn't stand my husband being with another woman; I'd want to kill them both [*laughs*]. I mean, I just wouldn't accept it. But if it happens, of course . . . and it could happen to either of us—I think it's more likely to happen to me, because I think he loves me more than I do him. But if I fall for—no, I mean, if it happens, I'll tell him. I think he's perfectly capable of understanding. No one is obligated to stay with anyone. You stay as long as you want to, until you don't want to. And from the moment you feel obligated, it's no good anymore. . . . If it happens, I'll talk to him. Everyone should act that way; it's much easier. If you talk about it, you might work things out, but not talking only makes it worse. That wouldn't be good for either of us.

I think we'll share all the decisions, equally . . . about everything. I'll give my opinion, he'll give his. If we don't agree, we'll come to an understanding about what we should do. If we do only what I want or only what he wants, it's not going to be good, although we have lots of things in common. Our tastes are very much alike. About where to live, how to dress, and so on.

I D O N ' T K N O W if I'm religious. . . . Sometimes I believe in God, when I need to. I never go to church, I hate priests and nuns. I think that God existed, really existed, because only a person with a lot of power could create nature, the sea, man, all these things. But He came to an end, and I think He goes on living only because of belief. You know . . . it's much easier to believe in a greater being than to believe in yourself. "Oh, God, help me, I need this!" That's what people usually do, right? I go, "No, Glícia, you've got to help yourself and that's it!"

I've never really thought much about why He stopped existing. I think these things are too complicated. Everything ends eventually. Nothing in this world is eternal; it all has to end. People, places, things, all change and new ones are born, so I think that God also ended, like everything else.

How do I imagine God? Well, physically, like this: a tall man, rather thin, with a beard, a moustache, long hair. I mean, it's the traditional image of Christ, you see? Or maybe as a kind of spirit. But I never stop and sit down and pray—maybe I might even stop to talk, if He really exists, or maybe I'm not talking to anyone. But at the same time, if He really does exist, it could be that He hears me. I'd like Him to exist. But the churches should end, they're totally phony. Right now, one of the richest things in the world is the Church, right? And so many poor people are dying of hunger. Nobody lives with as much luxury as the pope. And people are dying of hunger. I mean, if God is so good, why not share some of His wealth with the people, see? Why isn't there some for building houses for these people, for finding work, for doing something like that for them?

No, I'm not interested in politics. I think the current government of Brazil is shit [laughs]. That's why I don't usually talk about this, because people call me a communist. Just because I don't agree with the government at all. In the first place, I think that the military should leave. Just not having a military man in power would already be a great step. Not a military man, a sensible fellow who would think about the people and not just about himself. I don't think that

Figueiredo[1] really thinks about the people. Maybe he thinks more about himself, his own purchasing power, than about the people. And the country's foreign debt should be paid off. That would be a great thing, too. Everything should be done to make that possible . . . while instead they're borrowing more money all the time without being able to repay it. That's why there's so much hunger. But first of all we have to have a man in power who isn't in the military. This regime has got to end. I detest the military. They're the most insensitive, gross, stupid people. I judge by my father; he was in the military. But actually, I prefer not to talk about politics. I like to pretend it doesn't even exist, though I know it really does. I keep quiet about it. That's the best way, because if I do talk, it won't change a thing, no matter how much I dance. It ought to change, and I don't think it's ever going to, because no one's going to have the courage to make a change, to get up and speak for it. People are accommodating. For the ones that have money it's all dandy. They're reconciled: "Let's leave things the way they are." And those that don't have any—what can they do?

We never talk politics at home. Parents here teach their kids, "The government is excellent." My mother never discusses politics. I've learned from reading—I like to read newspapers—and from paying attention to the things that happen in front of my nose. But there are people who pretend they're blind, who don't want to see. And people who criticized the government just up and disappeared. The other day—my fiancé is studying here at the university, and sometimes I go with him to his classes. Well, there was a fellow, when we got there, selling a leftist newspaper and he was saying, "Figueiredo is an idiot, he's no good, the government is shit." No one went near him. Everybody left, and he stood there talking all alone, because everyone knows that he could be arrested then and there and never be seen again. Then, on the beach the other day, a fellow was talking about the bomb in Riocentro[2] . . . and nobody said a word. The beach was crowded, everybody packed together, all silent, and he and a few friends of his were talking all alone. Everybody's afraid of opening their mouths. I don't open mine either. What's the point of somebody fighting all alone? You know it's going to end badly. It's just no use. So the best thing is to try to live well and shut up. It's no use talking. I think that anybody who gets involved in talking about these things alone is dumb. Because it's going to end badly. I mean, if all the people in Brazil would revolt, fine. But just one! There are 120 million people here! It's no use, it's just asking for trouble.

SURE, I'VE HEARD about the women's movement. I have a friend who's very much a feminist. I don't go along with it. I think that women can't just rise up all alone. They need men's help, like men need their help. Because there are some things a woman . . . from my point of view, a woman can't get involved in constructing a building. As a construction worker, on the job, piling up bricks . . . I mean, I don't think a woman can do this kind of work. Being a feminist isn't worth the bother.

I think their aim is to have women be equal to men, and not depend on men. But women depend on men and men depend on women, too. So they are equal. The feminist movement, on the other hand—they want to be superior to men. If he's been superior until now, why shouldn't she be superior? But I think neither one is superior to the other. Some things a man can't do, and there are also some things a woman can't do. For example, he can't be a mother; only a woman. . . . And building construction, I think only a man can do that. Not designing the building or being an engineer, just piling on the bricks and making the building. But a man can cook, wash, clean, iron—why not? Just like a woman can help with certain kinds of work. I think that a woman could be president, depending on the woman. Women are capable, just as men are. But it has to be a woman who really has the abilities to do it, not any woman. Some can and others can't. The same with men. But I don't think that only a woman should be president. Any time a woman is in a leadership position, it's immediately reported in some magazine, Visão or Veja [news weeklies]. Immediately. Why? Why aren't they treated just the same as men? If a man can be a leader, why not a woman? But a woman can never be better than a man. No. Neither can a man be better than a woman. And the feminists want to be better than men, which I don't agree with. I'd never get involved in their rallies . . . [laughs]. I think feminists are all imbeciles.

Dorotéia, a distinguished-looking sixty-year-old woman with silvery white hair, has four other children in addition to Norma and Glícia. Most of her six children still live on the same street in Recife on which they all grew up. Dorotéia was quite willing to be interviewed but seemed reticent and uncomfortable as she spoke, with both anger and nostalgia, about her past and present.

———

7

B oth my parents were Brazilian, and my mother's parents were Portuguese and Brazilian. My father was a mechanic at a naval base here in the Northeast, and my mother was a housewife. There were nine children in the family—I was more or less in the middle. My family has always been Catholic, but now I rarely go to church. It's too far for me to walk—I have a bad leg—and I'd have to depend on my children to take me. They don't go often, so I stopped going, but I'm Catholic.

I went to school until I was—about eighteen. And I got married when I was twenty-two. My husband was in the military police; he was a captain.

Up to my marriage I worked as a cashier in a pharmacy. I worked there for four years, but I gave it up as soon as I married. Why? Because my husband thought I shouldn't work. I wanted to go on, but he was the one who thought I shouldn't. At that time women were really fools. At home men gave the orders, and the women accepted out of sheer stupidity. So I never had a real job again. Now I'm working at my daughter's kindergarten. Before that, we had a little snack bar on the corner of the road over there, before they built all those apartments, and I used to run it. And then I had a small shop, here in this building. That lasted about four years, then I closed it and started working in the kindergarten. I love to work; I don't like to sit around and do nothing. I have to have some sort of activity. It's tremendously important for women to work, mainly because of communication. Communication is essential, a life of talking only to your husband and the maid isn't enough. There are other friendships, other ways of communicating with people outside. And also for financial reasons. A woman's help is essential; I think it's

D O R O T É I A

essential for the whole family that she work, so they don't have to depend on just one person. And even so that she herself doesn't have to depend on her husband. It's true this can create problems, but she shouldn't pay attention to that, she's got to carry on, she's got to be independent, because . . . it's not enough; I don't know, . . . you each have to have your own life.

In the days when I had my children it was already difficult to raise them, but now it's even worse. At that time, they obeyed their parents more. . . . For example, when I was growing up, when I was little, we never talked back to our parents. If they were talking, we didn't interrupt, we didn't hang around, we had no part in their conversation. . . . We felt respect and love, I think we felt a great deal of love for our parents. Which doesn't occur today. With my children there was already less, and with my children's children, I can feel that it's kind of ending. Respect, that love for one's parents, I think it's ending. Everybody acts as if they don't have a father or mother. It's horrible. It was better before . . . in some ways it was better before, because there was more love, there was more closeness with the children, and more respect for the parents. And right now independence is finishing off this dedication, this love that one had for parents, and parents for their children.

I don't at all approve of the freedom women have today. I approve of some, but not as much as there is now. It's gone too far, I think women are going much too far. Young people, they're abusing this freedom. Girls ten or twelve years old go out alone with a boy, come home at all hours and . . . I don't approve of this, no. I think if a girl is grown up, she can go out with her boyfriend without a companion, if she wants to. An eighteen-year-old girl nowadays knows her own mind; and if she falls into error, it's because she wants to. But up to eighteen she shouldn't go out alone because she's easily influenced; she isn't fully formed yet, and she can do foolish things. At eighteen she already knows what she wants, and she can go out with a boy alone and come home in the morning; and if she goes wrong, it's because she wants to.

Girls always have to be more careful. With men, I don't know . . . I've always told my girls that women have to be much more careful than men. Even today, they have to behave differently, because nobody truly accepts anything else. Few girls who aren't virgins marry, it's harder for them to marry; most of them . . . people talk about them: "So-and-so's a . . . this and that." They talk about her, and then nobody wants to marry her; that's why they ought to think a bit more. If there were perfect equality, then this wouldn't matter. Women should have freedom, too, but I don't think that's going to happen here in Brazil. Especially here in the North, the situation is still very precarious. It's not that I want to go back to the old attitudes. I think that right now it's . . . I just don't approve of . . . you see, family life, caring for your neighbors, your friends . . . that doesn't exist anymore. I think that nowadays it's every man for himself. It's like a kind of ambition, a selfishness; everybody's out for himself, nobody cares about the next person. Right now we're in a bad situation because of this. But if there were understanding, love, respect for one another, then girls should have freedom, too.

Marriage isn't that important—not for men or women. Because marriage is still a kind of . . . I don't know, I'm not good at explaining things; it's a kind of . . . a subservience of the woman to the man. I mean, the married woman is subservient to the man. The man has complete freedom, to go out, to chat, to come home at whatever time he wants. The woman, no, she's got to be there. When he comes home, he expects to find her there. Most men think she has to be at home. Even if she had to go out for something very important, she can't be late, no matter what. Well, I don't think that's right. If the men have the freedom to go out, to get home whenever they want, whether they're doing things right or wrong, then women have the same right, whether they're doing things right or wrong, they have the same right. I don't approve of marriage, at least not the way it's been. I think people should try some other way . . . like, if I'm a man and you're a woman, then let's go to live together and see if we get along. If not, there could be an understanding that each of us goes his own way, to put a stop to this business of men's arrogance. They think they're worth more than the woman, because they're playing that *machão* [big macho] role, and the poor woman is always "the woman" and she's the one that's got to be under his thumb.

I don't much like it—but I mean I don't have this problem with mine because I put a stop to this whole business. You see, when I married I was a big fool. If I went out and he got home and I'd gone to a neighbor's house, even for something I really needed, he'd really sulk, and then when I'd get home he'd be furious, like a dog, a beast, a lion. But then I got to seeing what life was like. I got a little smarter, I learned more things, and I thought that I had my rights, too; and that was the end of that. I knew I was right. I knew I wasn't acting in bad faith. I wasn't behaving badly. . . . Then for a while I tried to talk to him, but he never even paid attention, and so it just slowly came to an end, to the point where today I'm me and he's he. We each do what we want. But I went through a lot with this whole business. Even when I made a dress, he had to comment on it, if it was too short, too tight, and I accepted that for a while. Then I got to talking with some neighbors, some friends, and I started to see that it was just no use tolerating that situation . . . it would only get worse.

But nowadays lots of women still put up with this sort of thing. I think it's mostly out of ignorance, and egoism. Brazilian men are really egoists, especially men from the Northeast, they're still such egoists. They think their wives have to be just their wives, and no man from the neighborhood had better say hello to her. I know lots of people like this: "What! That neighbor talked to my wife!" . . .

Just next door here there was a newlywed couple; the poor girl didn't have the right to stick her head out the window or to say hello to any neighbors. If she did, when he'd get home he'd beat her up, but such a beating . . . he'd give her such a beating that . . . I know that one day she went running out of here to the police station to report him. She went out one way, he went out the other. She went to the police station, and I don't know what happened there, but afterward they came back arm in arm. It was impossible to get any rest at night here. I was living in this house, all the children were little, and we'd wake up in the middle of the night with their noise, their fighting: "I know you were at such and such a place . . ." and he'd end by beating her up. I actually had to go and talk to him; I said, "You can't go on like this, you're disturbing the whole neighborhood." Well, eventually they moved. Poor folks.

My husband is much older than I am, nearly twenty years older. I think that's one reason why I was very afraid of him. I felt a lot of terror; he had tremendous influence, all of that. A lot older, you see. I was such a big fool. If I had it to do over again, it would be different. I think that my daughters have overcome this for the most part. None of them accepts the sorts of things I accepted. That's why I approve of divorce, completely. To marry and die, like in this very building . . . there was a woman here, her husband mistreated her, he was very bad to her. Her mother-in-law used to say that he was a drug addict, that he'd take shots of all sorts of drugs, and he forced her to put up with it, everything; and when he used to travel—he was an officer in the Air Force—when he would travel she'd go running to the neighbors. She would run into my house, to another neighbor here, to beg us for the love of God to buy some things she had at home, a bicycle . . . a sewing machine, to buy it so she'd have some money and could run away to Rio to her family's house and when he'd return she'd be gone already. But we were all afraid of getting involved; the whole neighborhood was afraid of getting involved in this. Nobody wanted to buy anything. Finally one day he set her on fire. She burned to death. A young woman, so pretty. Nothing happened to him, he wasn't arrested. He was an officer in the Air Force; the lawyers were, too, and at first they were disgusted with him, such a scene, and he tried to run away, but afterward they made up with him because they were all colleagues, and they supported him totally. The police weren't allowed to go into their apartment to investigate, in short . . . she's the one that died. But that's common enough.[1]

Abortion? I think it's barbarous. Why should you deprive an innocent, who's not guilty of anything, of life? Except where there's a risk of death: if the woman's risking her life, then, yes, let's end the pregnancy, because the woman can always have another, and a child needs so many things . . . but, except in cases like that, I don't approve of abortion. Not ever. It's barbarous to kill a child. Women should take care not to get pregnant, they should use contraceptives, anything, just so they don't get pregnant. If you're pregnant, you should have the child.

If a woman's a mother, poor thing, she'll get so tired. The man will also come home tired, but why shouldn't they share the work? Why shouldn't the man do housework? Is he better than the poor woman? If she spends all day working and he gets home after working in the city, why shouldn't he lift a finger to get his own sandals, or give a child a bath? Why? He's a father just as she's a mother, isn't he? But men in the Northeast are very *machão*. They think that if they come home and help their wives or give a baby a bath they won't seem as *machão* as they want. People in the South are more likely to accept this, but not the *nordestino*. You rarely meet one who helps his wife. I think women should insist, they should fight until they reach a point where it's sink or swim, as they say. If it doesn't work out, they should separate, but he, as a father, has the same rights that she has as a mother. So the obligations that one has, the other has, too. Of course, it's hard, because there's so little understanding. It's not just women who have the obligations of raising children!

I wouldn't want to see my daughters in an old-fashioned marriage, submitting to a man. . . . Better not to marry at all. A woman can even be single and have children, they don't all have to go through a Church ceremony, you can be single and have children. What's so odd about that? If you're going to marry a monster, and live like his slave, better to find a man, have a child if you want a child. If you want to say "I'm a mother," then have a child! You know, if I had thought years ago the way I do now, I'd never have married. I'd have stayed single, worked, had a good time. I might even have had children, but not "I'm married! I have my husband!" A husband who's no good, just to be able to say, "I'm married and have a husband!" I'd rather be single.

That's one reason I always wanted my girls to go to school. My husband never paid any attention, he never even went to the school to find out if his children got good or bad grades. He was never interested in buying them books. He never asked if they needed anything. Indifference. He never paid the slightest attention. I always took care of those things, but he never even noticed. Then, when one of them would get a bad grade at the end of the year, it was, "What?" And the noise would begin, totally ridiculous. Since when his children needed help he never showed any interest, then at the end of the year he also shouldn't pay attention. But not complain. But, thank God, they never had too many problems. They were always good students, they always passed; but I struggled so they would get their degrees. And I'm satisfied. But, you know, they've given me a lot of headaches, a lot.

Much of the work routinely done by women in a patriarchal society is invisible. **3** For census purposes, the very label "housewife"—which most Brazilian women are likely to apply to themselves—translates into "economically inactive." The failure both to distinguish between "work" and "employment" and to note the existence of part-time and house-based employment compounds the oversight.[1] If women's work in their own households were measured, one researcher has pointed out, it would have a staggering effect on labor statistics. The 1976 rate of economically active Brazilian women, for example, would jump from 28 percent to more than 75 percent. Even so, the figures would still hide one persistent feature of many women's lives: the double workday, a common experience for most wage-earning women. If "official" figures tend to disguise the extent of women's work, so do they also conceal the diversity of women's daily routines, which typically involve childcare, preparation and care of food and clothing, housework, and contributions to family subsistence via wage-earning and/or gardening and animal husbandry.[2]

More than one hundred years ago, women's official participation in the Brazilian labor force was at approximately the same level as it is today. The 1872 census, Brazil's first, found more than 37 percent of the economically active population to be female, and by 1900 this figure had risen to above 45 percent. Half of these women were concentrated in domestic service, while one-quarter were in the agricultural sector. But women were also found in large numbers in textile production. Over the next few decades, as factory production of textiles replaced home-based production, male workers replaced females, and the proportion of women in manufacturing—as well as in other types of paid labor—fell. By 1920, only 15 percent of the total labor force were female. Women's participation in the paid workforce has grown slowly since then, and with it has come a slight redistribution in women's work. Yet, although the number of women in industry grew by more than 180 percent between 1970 and 1980, most wage-earning women are still concentrated in the lowest-paying parts of the tertiary sector.[3]

"WOMEN'S WORK"

In 1983, more than 33 percent of the Brazilian labor force were female, and more than 36 percent of the female population over the age of ten were wage-earners. This amounted to some 16 million women (up from 6 million in 1970).[4] By 1985, the participation of women in the workforce had risen to 37 percent, with 18.4 million women working outside their homes.[5] The Brazilian Constitution of 1934 prohibited discrimination in employment. However, when the first minimum salaries were set in 1940, women's salary was fixed at a lower level than men's. The 1967 Constitution, produced after the military coup, affirmed the principle of contractual equality, which was reinforced by Law no. 5.473 of 1968, specifically prohibiting any form of sexual discrimination in employment.[6] Nonetheless, in practice, such discrimination continues to be widespread, as does occupational segregation (see the introduction to Chapter 3, above).

Doing laundry, cleaning, sewing, housekeeping—these are the traditionally female jobs of most of the women whose stories follow. Nearly a quarter of all wage-earning women are employed as domestic servants, while farming, the second largest single area utilizing female labor, today absorbs about 13 percent of the female labor force. These figures represent considerable declines since 1970, but farming and domestic work still carry the lowest status and least remuneration in the labor market. They are also areas in which it is hard to gauge labor participation.[7] The percentage of women engaged in farmwork, in particular, is exceedingly difficult to establish. Some of the domestic workers whose stories are included in this section began life in the backlands; they worked as children, and their labor, like that of their mothers, is likely to have been unrecorded and unremunerated. In 1980, 39 percent of the adult women economically active in agriculture were not remunerated. But even paid laborers have little access to minimum workers' protection: of the women working in farming in 1983, 94 percent were not registered workers. Moreover, women farmworkers, even when registered, are not covered by the protective legislation applying to nondomestic urban women workers.[8]

A woman who is a registered worker in Brazil already occupies a relatively privileged position. With the acquisition of a worker identification card, issued by the INPS (National Social Security Institute) and signed by the employer, an employee becomes legally entitled to the minimum wage, the "family wage" (an additional 5 percent for each child younger than fourteen; if both mother and father are employed, each is entitled to this 5 percent), medical care, maternity benefits, disability and unemployment insurance, pension, and other benefits—for which a contribution of 8 percent is collected from both the employer and the employee and deposited with the INPS. Retirement with a pension is available to men after thirty-five years of work and to women after thirty years, regardless of age. Yet, more than 70 percent of the women working outside their homes in the mid-1980s were not registered employees. Quite apart from the loss of significant workers' benefits, these women receive salaries considerably below those of men in similar jobs.[9] Moreover, the average income even of registered women workers was less than half that of men workers in recent years.[10]

The first associations of domestic servants were formed in 1962 in Rio de Janeiro and São Paulo. Until 1985, however, few serious efforts were made to recruit members, and even today the membership figures are low. The enormous difficulty of organizing workers isolated in individual households is easy to understand. Only since 1973 have domestic workers been eligible to become officially registered workers, but the law is not enforceable. Furthermore, the benefits and protection they receive as registered workers are more limited than those of other workers: twenty days of vacation (rather than the usual thirty) after twelve uninterrupted months of work for the same employer; medical care; and retirement benefits. Registered domestic workers, however, unlike other registered workers, are not entitled to the minimum wage, to a thirteenth month's salary every year, to paid maternity leave, to unemployment compensation, or to a paid day off each week; nor is there any limit to

their hours of work. About 35 percent of all domestic servants were registered workers in the mid-1970s. From 1981 to 1984, during the recession, 75 percent of the domestics who were officially registered lost that status when they accepted jobs as dayworkers. Thus, the majority of domestics, of whom more than 95 percent are female, do not have access even to such legal protection as does exist.[11]

But women's domestic work is not only a matter of economics. It is also a significant element in perpetuating distinct gender identities (as revealed in Chapter 11, below); for domestic workers often serve to attenuate gender conflicts about household responsibilities and life roles by "freeing" the women they work for, to some extent at least, from traditionally female tasks. In substituting one woman's labor for that of another, no challenge need be posed to a gendered division of labor. At the same time, women themselves reproduce patriarchy's gender ideology in the way they rear their children, thus passing on to the next generation the problem of women engaged in "women's work."

Domestic service, the archetypal form of "women's work," paid or unpaid, is the easiest kind of job for women to get and the one they are most likely to fall back on (as shown in Chapter 13, below) when better-paid positions are closed off to them. It is also the line of work that most clearly exposes the class and race divisions separating women.

Teresa is a Black woman living in a slum in the city of Recife. She is about 4' 10" tall, has almost no teeth, and, with her thin and frail build, looks much older than her forty-four years. One afternoon, after she had finished her day's work doing laundry at the home of some White acquaintances of mine, we took the bus back to her house and trudged up the hillside leading to her wooden shack, which was surrounded by a low, rickety fence. Teresa carefully twisted open the metal wire holding the gate closed and led the way into her house—two rooms and an alcove for the kitchen, with electricity, but no running water and no indoor toilet. We sat around a large table in the front room, between walls decorated with paintings and statues of Christ and the Virgin Mary and magazine photos of soccer players and of naked women. Although there was almost no food in the house, Teresa insisted on giving me something to eat and drink. She was very shy and spoke hesitantly.

I'm a widow. My husband died a year and a half ago. He was a construction worker, fifty years old when he died. I have one son who's twenty-six. I had another son, but he died right after he was born. When I was ten years old I went to school, but only for a few months. No, I hardly know how to read. Both my parents are dead—my father died before I was born, and my mother when she was sixty-three. She worked as a maid. I have three sisters and four brothers—they all live here in Recife, all seven of them. And they have children, too. We're a very large family.

I have lots of friends here on the hill. I like living here. My aunt gave me this house, and I've lived here for twenty-five years. I started working when I was very young, about eight or nine. I worked in the fields in a village in the backlands, planting beans, manioc, corn. My mother did the same work, and all my brothers and sisters, too. When my mother died—I was about twelve then—my sister said that we couldn't stay on there, so we came to the city. I came with one brother and one sister, and we lived alone. They both got jobs and we lived in a little house, and I stayed home while they worked.

TERESA

Then I started working as a laundress. I met my husband at a party, and after we'd known each other for about a year, we got married. No, I wasn't a virgin when I married, I'd already suffered. My son's father wasn't the man I married; he was another man, and he died, too. I was about twenty-two when I got married, and I already had a baby. My husband hadn't been married before. We had a son, too, the one who died—that was his legitimate son. That was my only other pregnancy. Yes, I know lots of women who've gotten rid of babies; most of them around here do it, not with a doctor, just on their own. But I think it's a crime . . . because once you've gotten pregnant . . . if you can't bring it up, give it away, but don't kill it. Give it to whoever wants it; lots of people want babies. That's better than killing it, once you're pregnant. If you can't manage to raise it, give it away to someone who can, but don't kill it. It's a horrible crime. There was a woman here who did it in her fifth month. It was fully formed, everything.

After I got married, I stayed at home. My husband worked and supported us— there were only two of us, just me and my son. Then, about ten years ago, before my husband died, I went back to work because I needed the money. I wanted to buy some things, and we didn't have the money. You see, his money was enough for everything, but not for the things I wanted. I wanted . . . to buy things for the house. Since I wanted to buy things, I thought I ought to make the sacrifice to be able to buy them. I worked in various houses, and now for the last five years I've been working for Dona Glória. She pays me $5 a week. I go there twice a week and earn $5. I have to pay for the bus out of that. While my husband was alive, he earned very little; his salary was very low, not even 300 cruzeiros a week [U.S. $10 in 1979] for full-time work. He worked very hard, and he died of a hemorrhage, at work. He'd had it once before, and I took him to the doctor and the doctor gave him an injection and he got better. He was feeling better, so he began to work again, but at a lighter job. My husband and my son always got along. When I married him, my son was just five. He considered my husband his father. He was a good man. We got along fine.

My son went to school starting when he was five years old. He can read a little, but he doesn't have a good memory for studies. He went through the fourth grade. If I had my way, he'd still be in school; but he doesn't want to . . . I can't force him. He used to work in a garage, washing cars, but he didn't like it, so he left. He had to have an operation. He took a test for a job in a factory, but just then he had to have an operation and he lost the job. He had a hernia. He had two operations and then he got well. INPS [National Social Security Institute] paid for it. After that, he began to work, last year. He likes it where he is now; it's very good. He works six days a week, in a department store. He earns a good salary, the minimum wage [about $70 a month]. He lives here, and he contributes. If he marries, he'll . . . set up his own house, and I'll stay here.

I wish I'd had other children. . . . I was pregnant again, you know; I got pregnant again [*laughs*], this last February. But I didn't want to have it. It was just at the beginning, and I didn't want to have it: it would have been a big problem for me, not so much on account of the money, but on account of my living here, because of my son. I didn't want him to see [*laughs*]. I took some tea and it came out, some crazy tea, you see. I knew how to fix it [*laughs*]. And it came out without any problems; it was very early, you see. Now, if it had been further along, I'd have let it be, I wouldn't have done this. But it was only about a month. . . . Yes, the father knew about it, and he agreed with me. He said, "You work, and you want to work, so there's no way, right?" We're still together, but I can't get married again or I'll lose my pension. We could live together, but we have to wait a while; he wants to wait a while, and I'm willing. He's a good person, like my husband. I've been lucky [*happy laugh*]. But he's a little bit jealous, I don't know why. I'm never jealous. I'd prefer to live with him, instead of alone. I want to stop working, when things get better, and when my son gets married. It would be better for me. Dona Glória is very good to me, but it's better to have your own money instead of having to wait for other people to give it to you.

I get a widow's pension now; it's $40.52 a month, and on top of that I have my salary. That's the only money I have, so not having enough money is my biggest problem, especially when you don't have a husband. At the end of the month there's never any money left over. Nothing. I pay for everything, for the electricity, everything. The electricity here costs $5.40 a month. The water costs $2.40 for two months. Gas costs $4.20. That's just for the stove. Clothing isn't something you have to buy every day. And fixing up the house. I buy one thing and, when I finish paying for it, I buy something else. All these things here I bought on the installment plan. My husband bought that television. He bought it just for me, so I wouldn't go off to other houses to watch television. I like to watch the soap operas in the evening.

No, I wouldn't want to work more than two days a week, because of the house. You need time to take care of other problems, to buy food for lunch, to buy meat . . . to pay the electric bill. Sometimes I need to go to the hospital, and then I go to work and have to leave everything messy in the house. I need the other days to take care of the house, to wash clothes. On weekends I make lunch, wash the dishes, and then on Mondays I go to Dona Glória's house. Doing laundry is easier than working in the fields, but I get very tired when I work at Dona Glória's house. It takes a lot out of you. I usually go there at about 8:00 or 8:30, I have lunch there, and I work until 6:30.

My nephew sleeps on the sofa [in the front room]. His parents live far away, and so he's staying with me. He's been here for several months. He's about thirty, he's not married, and he doesn't work. I don't mind supporting him, but what's hard is that he drinks, his friends take him out drinking. Right now he's at his father's house. I sleep in the other room, my son too, in the big bed. My nephew didn't used to drink, but now he does; and I told him that it couldn't go on like that, because he's not working and now he gets into such a state . . . I can't be sure of him. I go to Dona Glória's house, and he goes out drinking and leaves the door open so people might come in and steal whatever I've got. A person who drinks isn't reliable; anyone can come in and take your things. It's already happened once—they took a radio and a camera that belonged to my son. Yes, I pay for all the food, and I take care of all our clothing. My son helps at home, he helps with the cooking, too; but not my nephew. He used to work for a TV station, but since it closed down he hasn't worked. That was about a year ago. He's been looking for other work, but till now he hasn't found anything. It's really hard to find work, especially for a man. He liked the job he had, and he thinks that if he took another one it would be harder. I complain about his drinking. Maybe he'll go back to his father's house, where he went today. I don't want him to stay here. I've told him I don't like his going out to drink. Then, when he comes home, he picks things up and drops them . . . he does stupid things.

My son always comes home for dinner, and he's here at night. He has a girlfriend. I think he wants to get married. I'd like to, also, if only I wouldn't lose my husband's pension.

Yes, I go to church, when I can. I've never gone to *candomblé*. I don't like it, I just don't think it's right. I've never been, but I don't like it. It's just not for me.

The revolution [the coup] in 1964? . . . Yes, I sure remember it. It was kind of hard . . . it was something I'd never seen before. A revolution, you know, it's kind of like a war, isn't it? They thought they could do it. And now it's better, because we can go out in the streets without worrying.

T E R E S A   D I E D suddenly of a heart attack a few months after this interview.

Carmen, sixty-two years old at the time of the interview, is a large Black woman with a strong face and a forthright manner. We talked in the wooden shack belonging to her neighbor, Teresa (preceding chapter). The smell of sewage wafted in through the window as the afternoon wore on.

Carmen often refers to life as a *luta*, a struggle, full of *sofrimento*, suffering—words that also appear prominently in the vocabulary of other poor women I spoke with.

I was born here in Pernambuco, in the backlands. My parents? They were both Brazilian. I don't know when they died. I never knew either my father or my mother. An aunt brought me up, from the time I was small. No, I don't have any brothers or sisters. I never had much schooling, just six months. I can read a little, and sign my name. I read a little, but I can't write much.

When I was fourteen I got married. Yes, my husband's still alive, and we still live together. He's ten years older than I am and he's retired. We have two sons; one is forty and the other's twenty-nine. My third child died, of asthma, when he was thirty-three.

I used to work in a factory. I started a few years after I got married, and I worked for ten years. Then I got sick . . . I'm not sure, I think it was . . . I started losing blood, spitting up blood, and the doctor diagnosed it and I had an operation. It was a vein broken in my esophagus. But I keep having to go back to the hospital because I get sick a lot. And I've had another operation since then. Who pays for them? The INPS [National Social Security Institute]. But they don't pay for the medicines. When you're in the hospital, yes, but not the rest of the time. They send you home with a prescription, a remedy you have to buy, a prepared remedy, but who can afford it anymore? I can't, there's not enough money. Sometimes you have to ask them at the hospital to give you the medicines, and if they have it, they give it to you. If they don't, you don't get it. The INPS lets us stay in the hospital for eight days. You go in one day and are operated on the

CARMEN

next. You hardly have time to recuperate. I myself, after my operation, the shaking of the bus made my stitches open and I had to go back, but I didn't stay. They treated it and sent me home because the INPS wouldn't pay anymore. Then I had to stay in bed and my niece took care of the house. No, my husband didn't set foot in the kitchen even then. Once in a while, when I'm sick, he goes, gets his milk, drinks it, and that's all. Because he's sick, too, in his stomach, and just drinks milk.

Why did I get married so young [laughs]? Because in the backlands we work hard and marry young. We start working very young in the backlands, and then a likely prospect appears and we get married. I was working in the fields—just like Teresa used to—planting, gathering, things like that. I started when I was seven, that's when the struggle usually begins. And I kept on working after our marriage. Then when we came here to Recife, I went to work in the factory. We came here because in the backlands life is bad, much harder than here. We went without food, without clothing . . . we didn't have anything, there just wasn't enough.

I didn't have trouble finding a job here; I was even lucky in some ways. I was lucky and found a job right away. It wasn't a good salary, but it was better than the backlands. I still didn't earn enough, but it was more than in the backlands. It was a textile factory, and I ran a machine. Both men and women worked there, and we got paid per piece, so if you got more work done you earned more. Then, after I got sick, I had to leave the factory, and I stayed home, just doing people's laundry. Poor people have to work, right? I worked for two families, and every week I'd go fetch the clothes, I'd wash them at home, and then take them back. I don't do it any more, I can't, not even my own; now my granddaughters do our laundry.

My sons? They're both married, and I have fourteen grandchildren; one son has two children, and the other has twelve. One of my grandsons is married already, and I've got one great-granddaughter, too. My son works as a chauffeur for the city hall, and his wife works, too, at the hospital, cleaning. My granddaughters also work already . . . some are working and others are newlyweds.

My sons went to school, they sure did. I washed a lot of clothes, but they went to school and they learned. I always wanted them to. One, the younger one, studied accounting; he's got a better job. Now the older one . . . he just went to grade school, he's the chauffeur. I wanted them to go to school. We're getting old, the children have to help out. Isn't that the way it should be? And they do help, when they can. If anything's wrong, they're always there. If I go to their house and say, "I want this," they give it to me, you see? It may be a sacrifice, but they give it to me.

We own our house; we bought it thirty-five years ago. I once lived in this house, too, long before Teresa came here, until we bought our own. Right now three of my granddaughters are living with us, because our grandchildren like us better than their own parents, you see. Two of them got married, and then three more moved in. If I didn't like their being there, they wouldn't stay. Sure, we support them all; there's not enough, but it's got to go around. My husband and I each get a pension, right now it's about $66 a month. And nobody goes hungry. We have breakfast, a midday meal, and a snack in the evening.

I'm Catholic, but I don't always go to church. I'm constantly sick, you see, and I don't even have time to go. I tried *candomblé*, but I don't like it, I just don't. My law's the Catholic one.

Who's the boss? My husband. I like it that way. The husband has to say what's what, right? And it's the same in my sons' homes. When they're not around, we give the orders, but when they're home, it's up to them. That's the best way.

No, my husband never helped with housework; he never even set foot in the kitchen, and I never asked him to. I struggled all alone . . . and now I already have a great-granddaughter. My two granddaughters who got married don't have children yet.

My husband likes politics, but I don't. Politics is for men, not women. . . . I can't talk about it because I don't know too much, I don't understand it. As far as I'm concerned it's like this: it's fine whoever wins, because sometimes you vote for one and the other wins and then you have to put up with him. So I think, let the ones that do it best manage it. What can we do? We're poor, so what can we do? Nothing. But the government ought to help the poor more, they really ought to, but they don't. Look, right now it's like this . . . we used to eat bananas, now we don't anymore. We used to get something sweet when we went to the market, for a treat, now we don't since there's not enough money. That's what this government is doing. It's been really hard for about the past two years; before that, it wasn't so bad. We'd go to the market and bring back fruit, bananas, oranges, something for the children, but not now. Now we've only enough to buy rice, manioc flour, and beans—and hardly enough of those. Just these past two years.

I think it's the government's fault. Aren't they the ones running things? Don't they run everything? Why are they doing this? Can you imagine, a bottle of gas [for cooking] costs more than $4, and you're supposed to afford that out of your pension? Old people, earning so little. And food costs more all the time. It's getting worse every day. A kilo of beans costs more than $1; a kilo of beef is $2. That's why we don't eat much fruit any more, we just can't stretch the money that far. So we eat beans, rice, manioc flour, a little beef, very little because it costs too much. And once in a while vegetables, not every day, we can't anymore. I know we should eat fruit—oranges have vitamins, right? But . . . they're two for 10 cents. How can you make orange juice when they're two for 10 cents? And in a year it'll be even worse, the way the government's going. Is it as bad as this in your country?

But you see, here in this house you've at least got a chair to sit down on. There are plenty of places around here that are just like rattraps, where there's no place to sit down even, they're that poor. Houses full of children.

No, no, they shouldn't have abortions; if they get an abortion, they'll suffer. The women always get sick from it, and they'll have to go to the hospital. Sometimes they don't even have INPS, they're all on their own. They've got to avoid it somehow, some other way, but not have an abortion. It's the husband's fault they've got so many children. . . . There was a woman here, she's gone or I'd take you to see her. There are husbands who don't let their wives do anything; they want the children even though they've got no way of supporting them. They just want to have them. Seu [Senhor] Antônio down the block, he had eleven. Eleven children. He was as carefree as he could be. He worked, but he found himself another woman and spent all his money and that was the end of that. We all fed his kids, a little here, a little there, so they wouldn't go dying of hunger. His wife couldn't do a thing. If she gave a bit of clothing to one of the kids, he didn't like it. He didn't want her to give them anything. I really think they would have died of hunger. If it were me, I'd leave him, yes I would. But . . . she, with eleven children, where could she go? She tried to go to her brother's house, but he didn't want her. She couldn't get a job with all those children twelve years old and younger.

My granddaughters got married two years ago. It'll be two years soon, and they've avoided it so far. I told them, "Don't get pregnant, it's so hard with a baby. Wait a while, till things get better, then have one or two. This son of mine, the younger one, if his wife turns up pregnant, I'll send her to get her tubes tied so she won't . . . I don't want her to kill it, I don't want her to arrange some abortion, no. It's a sacrifice, but I'll do everything, I'll even go hungry, if she can get them tied. I'll give her my last penny, but she's got to get them tied so she won't have any more. But killing the child! The trick is to avoid it. I never had to avoid it. I only got pregnant those three times. I never avoided it, never took anything for it, never.

Fidelity? If everything works out, if they're right for each other, its great; but if they're not, it's truly an abyss. If there's no other way, you have to leave, find someone else or live alone [laughs]. I don't think it's so bad for a woman to live alone, a working woman, it's not bad. If she has her work, living alone isn't so bad. It's ten times better than living with a rotten husband [laughs]. If you don't have children, it's easier. But even if you have them, I'd never stand for being beaten. Somehow or other you've got to find work. If you're healthy, work. Some of these men even kill their wives. This week a man killed his wife not far from here . . . no, he killed the man who was with her, her lover. Here in this neighborhood there aren't too many cases of men beating their wives. I think there was one on this street. Of course it happens, it always happens, but this is a quiet street. I wouldn't stand for it, I'd rather go begging. I'd say, "I'll beg first, but I won't put up with this." I'd work for free for whoever turned up, just for food, but stand for that? Never. And now that I'm old, I have my sons. I won't put up with that. I have my grandchildren and my sons.

Yes, we have a television at home, I like to watch it; I watch the news, to see what's happening in the world. It seems to be going from bad to worse [laughs]. I think war's going to start soon, or did it start already? Everything's rotten. We got the TV not because we could afford it, but we still have credit and we're paying it off in tiny installments, bit by bit. They give you credit, so even we can buy it. I've been paying it off for seven years now. If it breaks down, we'll never be able to buy another one. Nowadays the installments would be about $40 a month, so if you're just earning $60, how could you ever do it? Everything's going up, the cost of electricity, gas, water, everything. My pension went up just a drop; it's hardly changed. You end up going short of food so you can pay the electricity, the water. Some of the houses here have running water, not all of them. This one doesn't. She gets it next door. Mine has, and I give some to my neighbor. And somebody else gives some to another house. Then, when the bill comes, you split it, you say, "You give me this much in exchange for that." But now it's harder, people haven't got a thing.

Yes, those kids out in the street go to school, public school. If I were younger, I'd get some more schooling; but I was too old when I came here, and I couldn't study because I had to work. I came running here from the backlands, but when I got here I had to go to work. Here you had to buy everything, so I couldn't go to school. Then the years passed, I've gotten older and older. . . . I can sort of write, but sometimes I leave out lots of letters. You've got to be able to sign your name to vote. Yes, in the latest elections I voted, against the government [laughs]. And then I said I'd never vote again. Because the government always wins. They put up two candidates against one: even so, he won; but they pulled some fraud and so he lost. Two against one! And he almost won, and they still got the votes away from him. So why bother voting? If other people feel like it, let them vote. So-and-so's going to be elected? Fine, so much the better. Why should we worry about all that?[1]

At election time the politicians come around, they promise all sorts of things: they'll pave the streets, run water into every house. So where is it? It's so much prattle, that's all, and you see the shape the streets are in. . . . Sometimes people come here in a car, like when a child is sick, and the driver doesn't want to go up this hill: "I'm not going, I'll never be able to turn around in that wretched street."

The politicians only come around when there's an election. When you see a politician's face, you know it's election time [*laughs*]. You see those men only at election time, and then they're so good! They promise everything, promise, sure, and give nothing.

What? If a woman were president [*laughs*]!? She'd have to help us, wouldn't she? Because we're all women. We're the ones who know how much food costs, we know what's going on at home. The husband's off at work, and what's to eat? What can you give the kids at noon? What's left? Tell me. A woman knows; she goes into the kitchen, and she sees what's needed.

If I were young now, I'd become a soldier, to have a job and to defend the Fatherland. Women should do all sorts of things. Isn't it lovely to see a woman doctor? A federal deputy? And there should be a woman president, and a governor. There haven't been any until now because the president won't allow it [*laughs*], I mean, men, most of them, don't want it.

Yes, I've seen news about the women's movement on television. Isn't it lovely? To see all those women struggling, rising up, just like men, isn't it lovely? It really is. That's what I think. They have to insist they're equal to men. Are men the only ones who work? They've got to insist on being equal. No, I've never heard the word "feminist." What is it?[2]

Sorry, I've got to go, my great-granddaughter is at my house now; she stays with me much of the time. She's three years old now. Her mother works every day, all day, from 7:00 till 6:00 at night. She lives so far away, you can't imagine. On weekends she comes here, sometimes she sleeps here, and she takes my great-granddaughter back home with her on Saturday and brings her back here on Monday. No, they don't pay for her food, they earn too little. Her mother works so hard and only earns the minimum salary. The bus fare alone is 28 cents each way. Three of my grandchildren live with me, too; they're fourteen, fifteen, and eighteen. I take care of them all, even though I'm sick. You see how my limbs are puffed up? I make our meals, I straighten up the house. There's always work to do in the house, there's no end to it. The girls are growing up, they all study. . . . I don't want them to leave school; they can't study and then run to the kitchen to cook or wash clothes. So I do what I can for them. It's a lot of suffering. I've got to go now.

"I Never Won Anything, Not the Lottery or Anything Else"

Maria Helena, a short, sturdy, seventy-year-old woman with copper-colored hair, was born in a small town in the state of Minas Gerais. Her family was predominantly White, with some Black and Indian traces going back several generations. Maria Helena's mother had given birth to fourteen children, ten of whom survived into adulthood. Maria Helena was one of the youngest. She married at the age of twenty-two and had five children, most of them still young when her husband committed suicide at age forty. Maria Helena's son, Gil, who had done graduate work in the United States, had arranged for me to meet his mother. The interview was conducted in 1981 in the modest two-bedroom apartment, located in the North Zone of Rio de Janeiro, that Maria Helena shares with her eldest son, José, forty-four years old; her only daughter, Fátima, thirty-five; and Fátima's small daughter.

10

I only went to school until the third grade. Should I tell you why? Well, in my class there were two Maria Helenas; the other one had blond hair, and I had black hair. One day an inspector came to the school, and when it was time to ask questions like they do, he said, "White Maria Helena and Black Maria Helena, come here." Well, when my father heard about this, he got very offended. He thought it was humiliating to talk about White Maria Helena and Black Maria Helena, so he took me out of school. And then I didn't have a chance to go back. We moved to Rio then, and we had a hard time, and I never could go back to school.

My mother made sausages to sell, and meat pies. It was a very difficult life, but things are even more difficult today, aren't they? We always had money problems, always. My father worked in a stone quarry, with dynamite. The mayor of our town was my uncle, and he gave him that job; not only him, some other friends of his, too. They all worked in the quarry with dynamite, to get the stones to pave the city. My sister was a seamstress and I was, too. While she was still single she helped support the family—she's the oldest, she's nearly ninety now. When my husband died he didn't leave me a thing! And . . . I was a seamstress,

MARIA HELENA

too—the machine's over there, it's broken, you see? I have to get it fixed, but I don't sew much anymore, though I still know how, I can still make things. But I supported us after he died. . . . He died a tragic death; he killed himself. He was mentally ill. He'd come to a clinic here in Rio, for a cure, but that's all he could think about; he just wanted to die, he wanted to die. I don't know why. He had problems. He'd always been very nervous, you know? He put me through the wringer, he did.

He was a dentist, with a degree. He worked right up to the end, but very badly. He was impatient: for no reason at all he'd tell his patients to get out of the chair. He'd hurt them when he touched them, and he never let them complain. He'd just tell them to get out of the chair: "Get out and don't come back here again!" . . . Then he died, here in Rio, and was buried here, and I went back to my home town to get on with my life. My children were all in school, but one of them managed to get a job. His godfather helped him, and now he works in the mayor's office. He had to leave school so he doesn't earn much now. And José, the oldest, he's got a psychiatric problem, he's been hospitalized. He's the only one of them who lives with me now, aside from my daughter. He's crazy to get married, he's got a little girlfriend. He just hasn't married because he doesn't earn enough. And I . . . I got on with my life like this . . . sewing. I didn't lack for anything. Life was cheap than, with 15 cruzeiros you could lay in groceries for an entire month.

And I'd start to sew at the crack of dawn. I used to get up at 4:00 in the morning and work at the machine all day long. While I was married, too—I had a nanny, a washerwoman, everything was cheap then, but still I used to sew. I'd have a one-month-old baby next to the machine; I'd hang up some toys for him to play with, give him a pacifier, and get back to the sewing. So much that my vision began to go bad. Dona Angélica, my neighbor, used to say, "Maria Helena, you're being stupid. You're ruining your eyesight. It's too much . . . you'll end up half-blind." I didn't wear glasses then, but now I have two pair. My vision's very bad now. But I used to get up at dawn, at 4:00 o'clock, and in the dark I'd watch the workers going to the factory—I'd already be at my machine, sewing. I managed to get a scholarship for the two youngest boys, Alberto and Gil. They ought to be much more grateful to me today, you know. Gil, for example, he's really well off now, very well fixed, and all he pays here is the rent, and yet he says he won't even pay the maintenance. The rent is ₮150 a month; it's going up to ₮200 in September. It's a lot of money, but he earns more than ₮3,000 a month, you see.

So I live like this, constantly upset. They almost never come here anymore, because I can't put on a good meal for them with the variety of things like I used to. They're ungrateful! Ungrateful! Now my daughter, this little girl of hers . . . she's not married, but she managed to have this child, and I'm helping her, trying to bring her up the right way. I'm old now, I ought to be taking it easy, and the girl is really naughty. But I take care of her, I give her baths, I feed her. We all share this room. That's her crib over there, this is my bed, and Fátima's is over there. My son has the other bedroom.

The little one's nearly three now, and she's really a handful. She's constantly climbing up on the table, on chairs; she knocks things over, next time you look they're on the floor; she turns on the television—I find the chair leaning up against the television so she can reach it. Now she's in this phase of climbing on top of everything. . . . Her father? He didn't want to have anything to do with her. He phoned when she was born, he wanted to see her; but he didn't have a job at the time, and Fátima said, "You can come if you're ready to take on the responsibility. Otherwise. . . . What I need is money, to bring up my daughter." Well, he was unemployed, he couldn't give her any money, or anything else, so he didn't show up, he never came around. She had her baptized, registered, everything in her own name, my parents' name.

When she realized she was pregnant, she tried to get rid of it; she tried various things, but nothing worked. No, she didn't go to a doctor—it's very expensive, you see. It was all such a shock, finding out she was pregnant. Carlos [the middle son] was still a bachelor. He was dead set against it. They never got along much. It was hell in the house; Carlos wanted to get married immediately, just to get out of the house. He had a girlfriend, he was already engaged to Neide and he suddenly married her. He's an electrical engineer; he gets a good salary, too, and you know how much he gives me now? Just $80 a month! My total income? They give me a pittance . . . it's disgraceful. Let's see, $75, now it's $80—that's from Carlos. Gil pays the rent, not including maintenance and things like that, which now comes to another $40, and he used to give me $50 extra. He says he won't do that anymore—that now that the rent's going up, he won't give me the extra money. My daughter works full-time, and she pays for the maid; that's $40 a month. And she gives me another $40 on top of that. I pay for everything out of all this. Everything. Yesterday, for example, I had almost no money and I had to pay the rent, so I asked Gil, "Gil, please pay the maintenance for me, because I'm really short on cash." And he said, "All right, I'll give you another $20." But, you see, the position he's in—he earns so much. You won't tell him what I said, will you? I've been through so much, I'm constantly depressed . . . I almost live on tranquilizers. I'm constantly depressed and upset.

Sure it was different before. Life was cheaper. A kilo of beef used to cost 3 cruzeiros, but not anymore. Now if you want meat on the table, it costs $6 at the very least—that's for Saturdays when my son comes to dinner. During the week now I just buy a little beef, some ground beef for dinner. For lunch we have eggs, vegetables, and that's it. I don't think they're repaying me for all that I did for them, not the way they should. . . .

I've always worked at home. I never had any social security, my husband was always against it. I had a brother-in-law, Pedro, and one day he came to our house and brought a man with him to talk it over: "Dr. Jorge, you really should do this. It's security for your wife, and right now it's very cheap, the monthly contributions." And he: "No, no, I won't." He didn't want to, and so he didn't. He never gave a thought to what would happen afterward, God rest his soul. . . .

For more than twenty years I worked at sewing, to support the family, and, you know, if it weren't for having to keep an eye on my granddaughter now— she's a real fireball—I'd still take on some sewing, I'd go back to it. Look, do you want to see some things I made, a long time ago? It's not in fashion anymore, but just look at this dress, I made it! And these skirts. They're old, but I made them all. I always liked sewing, even when it was a lot of work. I always had maids, a nanny and another one. Look at this blouse, it's old too. I made them all, all these things, and it wasn't easy. I had so many customers, they'd wait in line to get in to see me! I made all these things, but that was long ago; they're old now.

I learned by watching, and I used to buy a fashion magazine and copy the patterns. Even before I got married I already used to sew. Then, once I married, I did twice as much, and after I became a widow. Didn't I mention that I used to get up at dawn? I didn't have time to eat, to sleep, to do anything else. At 8:00 o'clock, 7:00 o'clock, I'd put the children to bed and go back to the machine. I turned his office into a sewing room—it was on the other side of the house, his dental office, so the noise wouldn't carry, and I'd sew there. I sold his practice when he died. It was very cheap at the time—20,000 cruzeiros. That was more than thirty years ago.

It was different for my sister. My oldest sister, she's eighty-nine and she looks young. She's pretty; she has smooth skin, smoother than mine, and she's very vain. She once broke her leg. She's widowed, too, and she has one daughter who treats her wonderfully, gives her everything. The next one is also a widow; and the youngest, she's younger than I am, she's separated from her husband. There were six of us, six girls and four boys—one of them died just recently. We went to a Mass for him a few days ago. My mother had fourteen children; the other four died. She had the last one in her mid-forties, just before menopause. She tried to hide it from us, because we were all old enough to know by then. She must have married very young to have had so many children . . . She died in her eighties. If I could just write the story of my life, I could make some money, but I wouldn't know how to write it. I've always said, "If I could find a writer and I'd dictate and he could write it down and put the book in a bookstore, then I could earn some money." It wasn't easy . . . and what I still have to go through . . . because they're so ungrateful, they just don't appreciate what I did for them. They're rich, they live in mansions, they have good salaries, and when the time comes . . . that pittance! What's $80? Out of that $80 I have to pay the electric bill, the gas, telephone, water—maybe there's $40 left. Do you realize how much the phone costs nowadays? One phone call, if it goes on for a while... the units are so expensive. Here at home it's like a war, if someone stays on the phone, I get furious: "You pay the phone bill! If you want to carry on a romance by phone, you'd better pay the bill." But they don't.

My oldest son has always lived with me, but now he wants to leave. He has a girlfriend, and he says he's going to move out. No, he never went to college, just through high school. But Alberto and Gil did. Not my daughter either, she just went through middle school. But she can always get a job easily because she's an excellent typist, on an electric typewriter. She gets a reasonable salary. Right now she's due for a raise, in September. She earns about $180 a month; and in September, when there's a salary adjustment, she'll get $260. She works full-time, from 9:00 to 6:00.

My parents were very good to me, but I had one sister, the oldest one, who was really outlandish. She bossed us all around, even my parents. So I got engaged, to the deceased; but it was more just to get out of the house, because I saw... there was a home waiting for me. They'd built a house; it didn't belong to him, but the rent was very low and he intended to buy it later on. It was a little bungalow, very pretty, in the best part of town, and I saw that house and said to myself, "I'm going to get free." Well, I liked a friend of his, and they used to walk down my street and I'd go to the window to get a look at this other man, but he thought I was looking at him. Because I was very pretty, I was almost a beauty queen. I could show you a photo I have here, in that album.... Look! Just to see this album now! Well, I talked to him and I thought, "I've got to get out of this prison." When we'd been engaged for five days he gave me this machine, with an electric motor, so that I could earn money sewing! He was already calculating, but he said it was so that I could learn to make my own clothes. So then I sewed, while I was still single, for the maids, and I'd see to all my sisters' clothes, too, first theirs and then mine, you see? I also used to help my mother in the kitchen because we didn't have our own maid; so I'd give my mother a hand—she used to make sausages and meat pies, and my brother would sell them.

Well, one day he showed up at the house: "Today I'm going to pay a call on your family." And he went to ask for my hand. And without asking me, without anything, they said yes. In fact, the person who agreed, because he was there, too, was my uncle, Joaquim. He was a doctor and he lived near us. So my Uncle Joaquim said, "You can't reject him, he's a good match." And I didn't even like him! But it was a good match because he was a dentist, he'd already graduated. And I said, "No, I don't want to." But he wrote the letter saying yes, you see? It was all arranged by letter. And one Sunday... I was coming back from a place I used to go on Sundays, to get oranges at the house of another relative of mine, and I got home all messy, all unkempt, and I got there and it was the day of my engagement. They were all there, and I didn't even know about it. Isn't it like a novel? And I had to agree, I couldn't refuse. . . . Also, I was eager to get out of the house, to be free of my sister, her bossiness, you see. So I thought, "Ah! I'll have my own house. I'll stay there, in my own home, independent." Let me tell you, was I punished! He had such a temperament . . . it was frightening. Anything, anything at all, made him shout, yell. Fátima is exactly like him, even more so. For the least little thing she yells, she shouts. My God, if she comes home and finds the little girl with her hands dirty, or food on her clothing . . . she's like that—her clothing, everything, I have to take care of it. I'm her slave!

Complain? What's the point? She still has to work. She can't hire a nanny, and I don't even want one—just one more person in the house adding to the expenses. You see, my life . . . no, I'm not crying. These tears, it's just conjunctivitis, in my eyes. Not that I haven't cried plenty, but I'm not crying now. Sometimes I think . . . this life . . . it's too much work. . . . We got a new maid because I couldn't stand it. I can't manage without her, and if she leaves, what'll I do? The shopping, taking care of the child, cooking, washing the clothes. . . .

Did I mention that José contributes some money? No, nothing else. His ex-fianceé, the one he broke up with when it was almost their wedding day, he used to say to her, "I'll set you straight, I'll tell you what's what, you'll see." He's very demanding. He comes home: "Where's my food?" If the food is too . . . "Fry me two eggs, make an omelet, I want some vegetables." I said to him, "Look, son, thank God for what you've got." But just recently he's started saying, "I want a special diet, I want more vegetables, I want this, I want that." "Then give me the money to go to the market, to buy vegetables; they cost twice as much." He works for the state; he's a civil servant. He earns about $300 a month, that's more than my daughter gets. She pays for the maid, but nothing other than that, neither of them. On weekends Fátima helps with the little girl, but she complains a lot; she says how tired she is, that she wants to hire a baby sitter on Saturdays and Sundays because she can't take any more, she's so tired. There's constant pressure at her job. It's hard to spend all day typing—she has to do entire books. She works at the university, and they're always under pressure. If she'd only win something in the lottery, she keeps saying. I played once, too, but I never won anything, not in the lottery or anything else. I never pocketed a penny, never! I ought to win, just to show these . . . the thanks these tightfisted kids have given me!

To live the way I want to I'd need $200 a month just for food, and that's not even a lot, the way the price of food has gone up. So, $200 just for food. I could live with Fátima, as nervous as she is, if it were only with her, or only with José, but not the two of them together. They're constantly fighting. She's very angry, and he's quiet all the time; he just lets her talk on and on. It was her fault that Carlos got married so suddenly; she never got along with him either. So now he says, "I'll come over, but I don't want to see Fátima." It's hard, isn't it? Especially when you've got a son who earns a lot, when you know your son is rich—you've seen the apartment Gil bought. Isn't it gorgeous? I know how much he earns because his pay stubs used to come here. And I haven't even gone to a doctor for a long time, though I need to, but what's the point of going when medicine costs so much. No, I don't tell him I need to go, what's the point? I'm not well, I know I ought to go to the doctor, but the sooner I die the better. He . . . I know his salary from those stubs, and he's going to get a raise now, too. What would it hurt him to pay the rent and the maintenance for me? The maintenance is expensive now; it must come to about $60 a month. What would it cost him to give me another $50? Why bother asking? The rent is going up to $200, I've already found out, and that's not even much, because it's very expensive to live here in Rio. Even in the outskirts of the city the rents are high; and that wouldn't help anyway, because you'd end up spending the difference on transportation. . . . But Gil really should give me more than Carlos; he earns much more. He's an economist, he has a doctorate.

His wife? She's very good about all this. I like my daughters-in-law, although one of them isn't quite . . . but Marta, no, she doesn't get involved in all this. I don't think she has much influence on Gil about these things. Now Neide, that's Carlos's wife, she butts in, and now she's five months pregnant and she's still working, so she thinks it's not fair—that she works and I don't. Work at my age? But even with a child a woman can work, if she has a nanny. Neide, for example, she doesn't even need to hire a nanny, because her mother lives nearby and she's going to take care of the baby. She doesn't want to have a maid, just a cleaning woman, although it seems to me she could at least have one maid. But she said she doesn't like to go out and leave the maid all alone in the house. You know, when Gil was about to marry, I tried everything to get him to buy me a small apartment with just one bedroom, everything! It was cheap at the time, but he wouldn't do it. If I just had a one-bedroom apartment of my own, there wouldn't be this constant problem with the rent, with food. . . .

Yes, yes, he could have done it, he already had plenty of money. Men should have more responsibility for their parents—don't they have the opportunity to earn more? They don't have children—I mean, they have to pay for their education, but they don't raise them; the woman does that. For example, Fátima, if I didn't watch her little girl for her, she would have been smashed to pieces on the pavement below ages ago, because there aren't any bars on that window and she's always climbing up on chairs, on the table, on anything that can be climbed onto, on the beds, and she's always dragging things down on top of her. It's like that all day long; I constantly go running after her, closing the doors to keep her in. And when she takes a nap I sometimes go out to the bakery, to buy milk, to pick up some meat, because this girl who's supposed to watch her is no good. She's supposed to take care of the little one just when I go out. I tell her, "If she wakes up, watch her, drop everything else, whatever you're doing in the kitchen, close this door, and stay with her. Watch her. Don't leave that window open." Fátima is extremely worried: "Mama, I haven't got the money to install bars. What can we do? If only we had an apartment lower down." But I say, "Fátima, where could I find another apartment? They're all so expensive; moving is expensive, too."

I F O N L Y I had it to do over again. . . . I was such a fool. I was young, pretty, I had offers, good ones too, but I didn't want to marry again; I was afraid of a stepfather beating or hurting my children, you see. I was afraid of involving another man in my children's lives, abusing them, kicking them out of the house. I even had an offer: "You're still so young, Senhora, so pretty." But I never really liked any other man, either. There were two men, both of them married, and their wives were my close friends. Those men liked me a lot! My friends never realized it, and one of them still writes to me, asking me to go to live with her. She's a widow now, too, and she misses him a lot. Look at this album; these are photos of when I was young, a young widow with five children. See, I used to go around in high-heeled shoes, I was well dressed. One time, after I got engaged to Jorge, a friend of his said, "Jorge, you've caught one of the prettiest girls in town." That's how I was. I wasn't bad looking at all. But now I don't care . . . I don't even put cream on my face, I pay no attention. Up to the day before yesterday my hair was all white. Then Fátima said, "Mama, that looks awful. I'll call up a friend of mine," and she came and dyed my hair. I like this reddish color, and she only charged me for the materials, but even so it cost $15. That would be $15 a month if I did it regularly. Fátima paid her, to make things easier; otherwise, I'd have left my hair all white. It just costs too much. I know how to dye it myself, but just the dye costs a fortune.

I worked for a while, in a clothing shop, and I earned just enough for my own clothes, for shoes, and the rest I'd give to my parents for the household. That's much better than having to ask for money. Are you married? Do you ask your husband for money? But I had no choice: I got married, I had children. At that time there was no way to avoid it. They didn't have the things you can get today. There used to be some sort of tablet you could put into your vagina, but it didn't usually work. Can you believe that whenever I had intercourse I'd go running out and wash myself! I didn't even boil the water, I'd just take it straight from the tap, I'd like back in the tub and wash myself. And even so I got pregnant, one after the other. I lost the first one, but later I had the others. That first one took a long time to be born. I had a midwife who did those idiotic things they used to do, made me get into all sorts of positions, washed me with soap, made me take baths. And then my father, who lived near me, went and got the doctor at 3:00 in the morning. The doctor was my Uncle Joaquim, so he wouldn't charge anything, and he came and began to boil his instruments and he said to my husband, "Jorge, I want your permission, we may have to decide, I'm going to have to pull it out." And he did everything very skillfully. He gave me an injection, and finally the baby came out; but it was unconscious, it looked terrible. It wouldn't cry, even though they kept slapping him. I shed lots of tears over that baby.

I've got aortitis. It's an inflammation of the aorta, and I have to take pills three times a day, otherwise I might go "boom!" I only take the pills when I feel a stabbing pain. Whenever I get very upset I start to feel it, and I have to run to take the pill. I always carry them with me when I go out, though lately I've been getting careless. But it doesn't seem to matter much anymore.

No, I don't have any friends here. In this neighborhood there's nothing but a bunch of nasty women. Heaven preserve me from getting involved with them! There used to be one here who was nice, and when I wanted to have a chat I'd go to her . . . Raquel . . . but she left, and now there's a nasty woman. God preserve me from ever needing anything urgently. But I'm not lonely, I don't pay much attention to all that. Sometimes I go downstairs to the playground with the little one, so she can get some sun; but they're all nasty people here, *mulatas* married to White men, you see? One day one of them came running at Fátima with a broom in her hand and almost beat her with it, all because Fátima had accidently closed the gate on her when she was arriving. Fátima had the baby in her arms and was trying to protect her little head. Crazy woman! She was supposed to have an operation, she was in such a state of nerves. She'd had two pregnancies and each one was twins, first a boy and a girl and then two boys. So she had four children to look after. She had a nanny, but one nanny for four children!

One time I thought of having an abortion, but I wouldn't want Carlos to find out. I came to Rio to get it done, but my brother, the one who died recently, said, "I'm crazy to have a child, and you want to get rid of one!" I went to the doctor, and he said to me, "You'll have to stay overnight in my clinic, Senhora. I won't take any responsibility for you if you go straight home"; and I said, "Then I won't do it. I'll keep it, I'll raise it." I didn't really want to go through with it by then, and my sister-in-law—the one who's separated from my brother, because he caught her with another man, with our brother-in-law, she ruined two households—well, she said, "Just go back home," and that's what I did. My husband said, "You won't be sorry." But I don't think abortion should be legal. It ought to be avoided. Only if a person is really very poor and can't take care of it, then. . . . Fátima, for example, she tried everything to get rid of this baby; but when she saw that it was no use, she stopped. Yes, I knew what she was doing. At first I was shocked about her pregnancy, not for myself but because of my sons, because they would disapprove if she had a child. I didn't feel that way, but I did think it would be better for her not to have it because of their reaction. But when I saw what she was trying to do I said, "You know something, Fátima, don't take anything else. Let the baby be born."

She used to run around a lot, and she got involved with this man who was always on marijuana. She went to live with him. She left home without saying a word, she just took a whole pile of things, even her bed, the bedclothes; and when I saw that she was really going, I went out and bought her all sorts of things, to help her get set up. His parents gave him a lot of things, too; they were eager to get rid of him. So she brought one bed, and he brought the other. She also took a record player which at that time was worth a lot of money. Gil gave her a little television set. But she lost everything when she tried to get free of him. He used to lock her in the house, and then one day he forgot the key in the door and she went down, grabbed it, got some of her clothes together real fast, left everything else there, got on a bus, and came back here. Thank God. That man . . . she says that the other day she saw him from a distance. He's still somewhere around, but he's never showed up here. He used to spend all day smoking marijuana; he'd come home filthy, like a pig, and would want to go straight to bed with her, without even washing. People should separate if they're incompatible, that's why divorce is a good thing.

I'm very, very sorry I didn't marry again. It's been difficult living alone for so long, not because of sex but . . . because of the financial help he used to give me, willingly or not. He was very stingy, but even so he'd give me something, or I would take it without his noticing. I'd get his key, because he was very distracted. My sisters-in-law taught me how to do that. Do you know that once he won a good deal of money in the lottery, but out of sheer stubbornness, against my will, he put it in a bank and it went bankrupt, so I lost all that money. It's always been like that. Now this president we've got, I don't much like him. After he came along everything got much more expensive, inflation got much worse. I never used to vote, and I don't think I ever will. I don't work, I don't get anything from the government, so why should I vote?

YES, I GO TO CHURCH; I'm Catholic, but I've lapsed a bit. I don't go every week, but I really should. I used to go to Mass every Sunday, but now on Sundays Fátima wants to go out and the maid isn't here—she goes away on Saturday, at noon or 2:00 o'clock. She finishes her work here and goes running home, so I can't go out. But religion has given me a lot of comfort, a lot! I keep a picture here of my mother and my father. They say we shouldn't kiss it, that we should pray and ask them to watch over it, but I kiss it anyway, even though I know we're not supposed to. You see that portrait of them [in the living room]? I go up to it and I say a Hail Mary and I ask them to watch over me, over all of us. I take Communion. Now there's that group Communion, and you don't need to confess first—just repent of your sins, if you have any, and receive the host. They put the host into your hands nowadays, and then you swallow it. Yes, there are lots of people here who are spiritualists. I don't really understand what they believe in, but it's not God. Some crazy thing. I went once, but never again! There was this dreadful singing . . . dancing in every direction; there were some animals. There's a center just down this street, and I went in one day because I had these marks all over my body, like a lizard, shingles all over. So I went there, and then a woman came here to bless me, but it did no good. How I suffered! I had boils all over; even today I have some scars. Want to see? All over, and everything itching, full of boils. Good heavens! I threw out all the clothes I was wearing at that time, and I washed everything else; but their prayers didn't do any good, and I never went back.

W H E N   I   W A S   M A R R I E D my husband always liked to tell me what to do, but I wouldn't let him. For example, he didn't want our boys to go to school; he didn't want the extra expense. I said, "Look, this is what I'm going to do. You don't want to pay? Then I'll write to my parents. I'll pay half and my parents will pay half, but schooling they're going to get." When he died most of them were already in secondary school. He died here in Rio, but I went back to my home town and I went to the mayor, who was a relative of ours, and asked for a scholarship for the boys. "Ah, Dona Maria Helena, it's not possible, the town's grown too big . . . all the places are already taken." So I went to the school and talked to the director. There were two scholarships available, for two vacancies, and I said I wanted to sign up Alberto and Gil for those two places. "But Dona Maria Helena, a woman like you, a seamstress who earns money, who's well dressed, you don't need this." I said, "Need has nothing to do with it. The scholarships are for whoever does best on the exam." And the boys won those scholarships! Well, one day Professor Humberto announced, "The widow's two boys won the scholarships"; and I had a godmother who was there, and she came running to tell me: "Maria Helena, your sons won! Professor Humberto announced it today, 'The widow's sons won!' " And I rushed to get dressed and went out. I'd taken out my teeth, because they had to be worked on—it was after his death, so I went to another dentist, because they were so bad—and I went running to the church, just as I was: "Professor Humberto, please excuse me. I'm so happy, I came running. My boys won the scholarships, right?" "Yes, Dona Maria Helena, one of them really won." I said, "One? No! Both of them!" They were already trying to steal one back. He said, "Yes, I haven't actually seen the letter, but you must be right, they both won." And I was so relieved, because at least the boys could study.

But, you see, they never thanked me for this, for what they are today. My customers used to say to me that my sons didn't need a scholarship, because I was earning so much with my sewing, and I'd say, "I know my own situation. If I'm earning a lot, it's because of my efforts; otherwise, I wouldn't earn a thing." I wish Fátima had had more schooling, too, but it wasn't for my not wanting her to. She finished middle school because I stood in line with her and made her take the test, otherwise she wouldn't even have gone that far. She's so rebellious: she was always running away from school, skipping classes, the classes that I was paying to send her to. I always insisted that she go!

TOWARD THE END, I knew my husband was in bad shape. Terrible. He tried every possible way to kill himself. I used to hide things from him; I'd take his belt, I took everything. He ended up fooling them in the clinic. They used to keep an eye on him, but they were all having lunch and he got up and took his belt and tied it to the bedpost, and when they came running he was dead, he had just died. He was in that clinic for twenty days. But even before that, for months he'd been trying to kill himself. At home he'd drink things. I had to hide everything. I'd take medicines out of the cabinet and hide them, and he'd get furious with me: "Where's this?... Where's that?" I'd say, "I've hidden it." I never knew why he was so unhappy. It's... his whole family was very high-strung. He wasn't the only one; there was another case, too.

No, I never came to love him. I never liked sex with him, I never felt any pleasure. Obviously, since I didn't love him. You live together and you adapt, but love? No, I never felt any. When he died I didn't miss him. I felt... the separation... but I didn't miss him, because he was never affectionate to me. He'd constantly yell at me and fight with me... and if I was fitting a dress on a customer, I'd be unbearably ashamed; he'd go into the kitchen and pinch the maid. My customer would say, "Maria Helena, you've got your head in the clouds! Putting up with this!" I used to say to him, "For the love of God, when I have a customer here..." society ladies, you see, "When I'm doing a fitting, don't do this, Jorge." But he'd choose exactly that moment. God rest his soul, I don't want to say anything bad about him. God rest his soul.

Marta, a vigorous and attractive White woman with a degree in political science, was thirty-five at the time of the interview. She teaches part-time in a private elementary school, is still thinking about going back to complete her master's degree, and is very active in the local neighborhood association. Marta is married to Maria Helena's son Gil, an economist. They have a daughter nearly three years old.

When I first went to Brazil, in 1968, I was struck by the frequency with which middle-class women complain about their servants. I also noticed that men often ridiculed and criticized women for this talk, which they seemed to judge as empty chatter or frivolous complaining. Marta's account, like that of Conceição, her current maid, in the subsequent chapter, helps clarify some of the complexities of the relationship between maids and mistresses, an important and much-misunderstood subject.

The interview took place in the comfortable three-bedroom apartment that Marta and Gil own in a residential area of Rio de Janeiro.

I wanted to tell you about my marriage. From my perspective it's a marriage that can be considered . . . not just bearable, but successful. It's a good marriage. For example, my personal sexual relationship with my husband is fine. If you were to ask me if I have problems in bed, I don't have problems in bed. We're very good together, we're both satisfied. Whenever we want to, whether it's his initiative or mine, if one of us approaches the other, everything's fine. So it's a marriage that can be considered satisfying, happy. Now, when it's a question of dealing with everyday tasks, the struggle to bring up our child, the struggle to maintain a household, all these things . . . that's where you really get into an absurd contradiction. Because theoretically even my husband acknowledges that he has defects along these lines, but he says I provoke these defects in him, that I'm so efficient that I provoke him to be a lazy person, you see? But this efficiency of mine . . . it's almost been imposed on me, precisely by the experience that I've had of our life.

MARTA

At the beginning of our life together, when we didn't have a child, he still used to do some of the household tasks—for example, washing dishes and sweeping the house, or straightening up his papers—but basically the bulk of the housework was always my responsibility. It's not that I was or wasn't busy with a full-time job outside the house. When we began living together I had the same work schedule as he did, with one difference: I used to get home forty minutes before him, because I had more direct transportation. And I had all the concerns that any intellectual at that time had. I was trying to finish my courses. I had papers to hand in on certain dates. I was doing a research project that was extremely interesting. And I used to do the housework—I mean, to be immodest, I was a good cook. I've always liked cooking, I enjoy food. I like to make food for other people; it's never been a problem for me. And now he says to me, "You've never minded doing this." It's true. I haven't. But, as of the moment that this became an obligation, delegated to me by the simple fact that I am a woman, then, really, I got very, very depressed.

At the beginning we'd divide things: I'd be in charge of the food, and he'd be in charge of cleaning up the kitchen. And that was fine, because actually I preferred to eat the food that I made, since, in fact, what could he cook? He'd fry some eggs, and make a soup with piles of vegetables and no salt. And I just couldn't eat that several times a week. It wasn't a problem, and it still wouldn't be today, if we were still in the same situation, without a third person. But now he comes home for dinner and right away wants to play with Clara. He gets her wide awake when it's her bedtime, so what do I have to do? Leave the kitchen, change her, make her a bottle, put her back in bed, and wait for her to fall asleep so I can get back to the kitchen. And after we have dinner, instead of his going to the kitchen to clean up whatever's dirty, if I don't do it it'll just sit there for me to do the next day, and if I don't do it that day, then on the third or fourth day I'll have to pay someone to come up and do it. I've already had the experience of leaving things for four or five days, and it upset me.

Long before we had a child I always used to tell him, "Look, I like this universe I call my home. I like taking care of my house, cooking, choosing whether I want to eat meat or fish. I'll never hand over my refrigerator to a maid and let her decide what I should eat." This is part of my biotype, of feeling good. I even used to say to him, "Don't you want to decide these things for yourself?" He'd say, "Yes, but I can't really think about these things. I'm not used to having to do the work to satisfy my wishes, because I've always had someone else do it for me, and I don't intend to give that up." Because he's out working eight hours a day, or six, or seven—who knows how much he works? In fact, with his teaching at the university and his research job, his schedule is rather irregular. He said, "I don't give a second thought to having to get home to make something to eat because I *know* that's your obligation." That's what he said last night. So that means he doesn't even consider the possibility that he might feel better doing something for himself.

I have the impression that all this business is deeply related, at its roots, to the structure of Brazilian society, which was always a slaveholding society, and whether you like it or not, with or without the freeing of the slaves, this ideology continues. At the end of the twentieth century it's still a patriarchal slaveholding society in terms of the kind of relationship you can have with your domestic servants. If you consider yourself to be a good employer, let's say by Brazilian middle-class standards, the most you do for them is act paternalistic and not establish a real work relationship. That's the source of my great difficulty in dealing with domestic servants here in the house. For me it would be much better if I could just set her tasks and she could do them perfectly, or at least satisfactorily, and then go away, but that's not the way it is. And precisely because it's not like that, the relationship between maid and mistress is highly deteriorated. In fact, the relationship the maid maintains with her mistress is one of total dependency, even emotionally.

If you're nice to her, if you do whatever she wants, she's always in a good mood and ready to do any kind of job for you. And then she uses your house and every single item in it—for example, the telephone, the television, the refrigerator; the consumption of food isn't watched, it's never regulated. She eats everything, she tries everything, she enters any room at any hour, she uses all the domestic appliances. And, on the other hand, she thinks that you have an obligation to provide her with social security, with health care. For example, all the maids who have been here have gone to my doctors or to my daughter's doctors. They've never even had to buy an aspririn for a headache. I've always given them *everything*: aspirin, soap, toothpaste, talc, perfume, deodorant, sanitary napkins. In other words, this goes far beyond a work relationship. The relationship is so deteriorated that the maids in fact expect this type of behavior, and if the mistress doesn't come through with it, they'll definitely leave and start to gossip. They leave and hurl accusations at your house and up and down the street, so that all the maids on the block get to hear that you're a wretch, and all the mistresses learn that you're someone without a heart, that you're inhuman, and so on!

And you've got to try constantly to keep her happy, because it's dreadful to have a stranger in your house and on top of that to have to put up with bad moods. Look what happened with Rosa, who was with me for two and a half years. Once she had to go to the doctor, the same woman I was going to, and she asked me to pay for the visit, and I went there and paid. Well, I'd asked her to do something—I think it was when my little girl was sick, and I couldn't count on my husband to help early in the morning and during the night, so I asked her help:

"Look, make her a bottle at dawn and keep your ears open so if I call you, you can come and change her diaper for me." Clara was vomiting at night, and all the sheets would get soaked, too. But in exchange I always had to give her presents, because if I didn't, she was always in a bad mood. So what happens is that even if you were to give the maid a better salary and expected her to provide for herself, in practice it's more or less irreversible, because you always end up owing her something. It still seems to me that this is all tied in with Brazilian social structure, as I was saying before, a patriarchal and slaveholding structure, because it seems that you, as the mistress—I, in any case, always have a feeling of guilt about exploiting someone in my house and, at the same time, I have a feeling of aversion about feeling this guilt, because I consider myself to be a good mistress, because I share the work with the maid, on an equal footing. But inasmuch as she's a stranger, she's of a differeeet color than I am, she's in a social situation worse than mine, other things come into play. . . . It's like this: the relationship between maid and mistress might even seem to be mediated like formal work relations, but you can't help getting to a point where this relationship slides into an emotional one because you end up living with this person twenty-four hours a day, and she transmits her emotions to you and you transmit your emotions to her.

And this is what I find so difficult in being her mistress. This is a profound difficulty for me, and it creates a conflict with my husband. He always puts it like this: "Well, I need a maid because you don't want to do anything. You say you'd rather not have a maid because you prefer to do it yourself, but when you do it, you always complain." And I say, "I complan about the way you're exploiting me, because if we didn't have a maid and shared the work half and half, wonderful, I wouldn't want to have a maid in the house." It's even a situation that makes me feel bad. I feel invaded, as if my house were split, with a foreign universe that isn't mine, and that makes me feel constrained. Then he always says, "Well, you spoil the maid because you don't know how to be a mistress, you don't know how to yell at her, how to give her orders." I say, "Nonsense, you pay her salary, you have the right to do these things; but the minute a maid doesn't iron your shirt right, instead of going to her and complaining about the shirt, you come *to me*, and you try to put it into my head that I ought to treat the maid in this way or that. But the fact is that I can't behave the way you do for the simple reason that we're two different people. I'm not going to fight with the maid just because she ironed your shirt badly, because on that day she told me she wasn't feeling well, she had menstrual cramps and wanted to lie down, and I let her lie down and I always will." So then what happens is that when we don't have a maid he doesn't want to do any of the work, and when we do have one he insists that I maintain purely formal work relations with her, when the truth is that's not possible when you're living with her in the same house. It just can't be done.

So if you ask me right now how I've resolved in my own mind my role as a mother, I don't want to make a value judgment, to say that I'm a good mother or an awful mother, it's not that. I've taken on this role, it was something I really wanted. I had my child, I'm taking care of her, I think it's great. But another factor enters the situation, which is that at certain times I need someone to help me. Naturally—I'm a human being, I get tired, I get worn out; sometimes I just don't want to face any children, I want a bit of time to myself, and in order to have these things I have to give up my privacy and tolerate a maid. And the result is I lose—let's say 50 percent of my possibilities for being myself in my own house. When a maid's in the house I lose half of my freedom, because there's another person there and I have to get along with her, which is difficult for me. I don't know how to be authoritarian with a maid, and at the same time I can't stand it if she acts sluggish and leaves all the work for me to do. I don't know how to tolerate that because, since I'm paying her, I want to receive something in exchange.

Well, you can see from all this that it's a difficult situation to resolve, this problem of running a household in Brazil; at least that's my experience, and I've seen my friends go through much the same thing. My friend Julieta, who's a biologist, says to me, "When I don't have a maid I go crazy, because then things don't get done at home, and I have to go to the university to give my classes. But if I do have a maid, I can't have a consistent relationship with her because I have to be away from home, I have to go to work. And my husband, who stays at home more, doesn't know how to give the maid orders, so when I get home he unloads it all on me. . . . 'The maid did this wrong, and that, and the next thing,' and he gives me messages that I'm supposed to pass on to the maid, which is very difficult for me because I can't transmit to the maid an emotion I haven't felt." Since he's paying her salary, why can't he talk to her directly? Even this, even dealing with a servant, has to be the woman's job. The woman has to take on not just the management of the house, but even the relationship with the servant, although the husband benefits from the servant's work. You always have to be supervising her so the work gets done right; otherwise, what will come up in your relationship with your husband is this: "The maid isn't any good because you're a lousy mistress." All this really hurts me.

No, I don't think it's more a problem for my generation. Well . . . my mother's not a good example because she's Italian, and my father is Portuguese, so they, as immigrants, always had to struggle, and they always helped each other. They met in Brazil—he was twenty and she was sixteen at the time. But culturally they're not like us; they weren't born in a house with servants. They were born in a house where they had to manage for themselves to survive, so it's already a great departure from middle-class Brazilians. But I've seen the same problem in other people, older people. In fact, I met a woman of about sixty who said to me, "My dear, how many years have you been married?" "Four." So she said, "I've been married more than thirty, and I'm going to die without having learned how to deal with domestic servants, for whenever it seems to me that I'm managing quite well with her, my husband isn't satisfied, and when it's obvious that I'm getting along badly with the maid, my husband complains to me that that's no way to treat a maid because after all she's a human being." You see? The contradictions are so deep.

I always say to my husband, "You don't realize that it's deeply disturbing for me to lose my freedom within my own house." I've always been a very free person. I didn't want to have my family constantly after me, blocking me. I escaped from my family by becoming self-supporting, and now when I have someone in the house, a maid, I feel like I've lost 50 percent of my freedom, really . . . for example, I have to eat at the time that the maid chooses to place my food on the table. If I tell her to wait half an hour more, she'll appear half an hour later with a long face, a frown, and that bothers me. She doesn't readily accept your having your own schedule in your own house. You always have to be thinking that she wants to take a nap after lunch; and if she's hungry at noon, then I also have to eat at noon even if I'm not hungry; and, in the end, although I don't want to, I end up falling into line. If I ask her to bake the chicken and she's too lazy and just broils it instead, that's what I have to eat. I'm not going to throw out the food I've bought. There's a whole series of little problems you can't even imagine that take on enormous dimensions when they go on day after day.

So, to go back to the beginning, if someone were to appear and ask me, "Are you happy in your marriage?" I'd say, "Yes." Because he's still someone that I'm aware is my friend; he's my man, my mate, my husband, the father of my daughter, and he's someone I can trust. At any difficult moment, with any problem, he's the first person I run to. And he's always ready to listen to me, there's never a problem about his reaction. Including in financial matters. If I need to have some very expensive treatment, any kind at all, it doesn't even have to be something really . . . crucial for me to stay in excellent health; it can be a matter of aesthetics, say. He doesn't refuse, he's extremely concerned. I even think he makes a real effort so that I feel good. Even these problems that Brazilian women have, of being very vain and wanting always to be in fashion—I don't think I'm like that; I've never paid much attention to that. I just want to be comfortable. If I want some new slacks and I think there's money to buy them, I'll go out and shop. If not, I'll go around with my old slacks, and I won't feel bad; I'll feel fine. But he's a man who makes a point of saying, "Look, you can take the money whenever you want to buy a new blouse or new slacks. I don't think you have to be calculating whether the check I give you is just for marketing. If on that day you're on the way to the supermarket and you see some pretty shoes and want to buy them, for goodness sake, forget about the groceries." So he's very open about such things, and I know that many of my friends don't have this type of freedom. He even corrects me when I say, "Give me some of your money." He says, "Mine, no. It's ours." He has a strong desire to do things collectively. That's in theory.

But in practice it's impossible, because the way he was brought up was really brutal. His life was full of conflict: his parents . . . didn't get along, they were very sick. His father killed himself, I think when Gil was about fourteen. Does he like his mother? Yes, now he does. He went from a phase of intense love and passion to hatred, which is very close. I have the feeling that the day he can see her for what she really is, he'll distance himself from her. She's a sick person who exploited him as much as possible and still does today. In every respect—emotionally, financially— she exploited him. He supported her from the time he was fifteen years old. He always paid for her to have a maid; that's why he wants to behave the same way with me. When he drank a glass of water, his mother wouldn't allow him to carry it back to the kitchen. But it was he who paid for the maid. His mother even affected his health, because she wore him down. She nearly ruined what was most beautiful in him, which was his emotional side, and I complain about this, about his coldness. She managed to convey to him—how shall I put it?—a sense of infidelity, you see. When he began going with me, he was someone who had no self-confidence, no confidence in me. She wore down the most beautiful thing he could have had, which was the possibility of being with someone without this kind of . . . conflict, of distrust. Because after all, I was no child when we began going together. I'd had a certain amount of experience. . . . I'd struggled alone to make a living, with my family as a kind of reference point, because I always got a lot of affection, and still do today.

Our wedding is an example. Let me tell you, I left Rio with just a suitcase. I had no idea what I was going to wear, what we'd eat at our wedding. I got home [to Bahia] and there was a wedding gown, flowers everywhere, enough to fill two trucks, a party all ready, guests, a tremendous banquet with who knows how many turkeys and barrels of beer, and we ate and drank the whole night. Everyone was there, relatives I hadn't seen in fifteen years showed up, bringing dozens of presents, they gave me everything. Everyone was happy, enjoying themselves, celebrating my happiness. And Gil was startled by it all, because only his mother wanted to go to our wedding, and she behaved in a ridiculous way. She didn't smile throughout the entire wedding. On the contrary, in front of my family she cried and lamented that her son had married. This hurt him, it prevented him from enjoying his own wedding.

My mother, who's seventy years old, says to Gil, "Take care of your wife, because you're really going to need her. Not now, now everything's great, wonderful, but in your old age. I'm proud to have gotten to this age with my husband and have him say that I'm a lovely and healthy old lady, and that's because he always helped me when I needed it." I understand why she says this, that we should share everything, including the housework which was always shared with my father. My mother had thirteen children, just imagine, and raised them all. When she'd stop breast-feeding one, she'd hand him over to the older kids. From 6:00 o'clock every afternoon my father would be in charge of the baby, and on Saturdays, Sundays, and holidays. My mother never got up at night to change a diaper, to prepare a bottle—only when she was breast-feeding, obviously, which is a biological matter; my father couldn't breast-feed [laughs]. We always saw our father and mother as two equal people, equally capable. I loved to be sick because I preferred my father to take care of me. I was madly in love with him, and he would make the most wonderful food for me when I was sick, better than my mother. He was an ideal father; he never disappointed me.

In my parents' home there were always maids, and lots of them, but all the children, all thirteen of us, including the males, had household chores. All the males in my family know how to cook, and very well, and if they don't do it it's because they're lazy and want to take advantage of this situation, of living in a society that allows this. But I'm constantly going to one of my brothers' houses and finding him cooking—this has happened many times. My oldest brother, for example, is someone with a . . . rather prominent social and political status. He's about to retire. He has a marvelous duplex aprtment, he has only one child, he has more money than he knows what to do with, he's always traveling throughout the world. And he's a person who's constantly in the kitchen. That's how he wants it. He even argues with his wife that she shouldn't work so hard, since he can do it himself.

So you see, it's a cultural problem, a problem of habit, of people managing their own lives, feeling self-sufficient. Personally, and this is my own opinion that I'm giving you, I think that Brazilian men in general aren't liberated and will have many more problems in becoming liberated than the women, because the women are going through an incredible process right now, and the men are surprised, shocked, and afraid of it. They can't seem to keep up with this kind of evolution in the women. They're startled, they're scared; thirty-year-old men are currently afraid of getting married. They think much more carefully than the women before marrying. For example, I can see this in my own husband's case; when I wanted to get married, I said to him, "Look, I want to get married, I want to have a child. I love you, you're the person I want to marry, but you don't want to? Then excuse me, I can't waste any more time, I'm going to look for somebody else." And he was uncertain: "Do I want to or don't I?" He didn't know what to say. And he got married with those doubts. He says that he married because I wanted to, that he wasn't sure. And afterward he wasn't sorry about it.

You see, the men are so worried about this. . . . Our friend Paulo said to me, "What did you do to catch him?" Not a thing, because I haven't changed. I mean, the changes that I'm going through are structural. God forbid that I shouldn't change; everyone changes. What I mean is this: he had an ideal kind of woman in his head, and he didn't know if signing a paper would influence me . . . to change my life project. So it was very frightening for him to have to sign a paper and afterward risk this woman changing into something he didn't expect her to be. He's much more insecure in an affective relationship than I who instigated the marriage. And in fact I knew this, I knew that I'd have this kind of problem, but I preferred it because I didn't want to think of myself as a person all alone. I wanted to have a child at about age thirty, and I didn't want to get to thirty without this prospect in view; I wanted this emotional stability. So I started on this tack about marriage, and he was frightened. I thought it ridiculous because he couldn't see that what he was afraid of was himself. He wasn't afraid of living with my questions—to this day I ask him questions. I've taken on the role of mother, housewife, cleaning woman, cook, washerwoman; and it's just as he said. I've never had problems with these roles. But I've taken them on while constantly questioning his role. I say, "Look, it's not that it's hard for me to do this, but I want you to see that it's not hard for you either, and I want you to be less of a machão, just because you're the person I chose to marry. And just as you've got an ideal woman in mind, so I too have an ideal man, but you never even ask yourself whether you correspond to my ideal." So I go right on posing questions.

Now this is very difficult. It's hard for a person to reach my age, be aware of this, and manage to live with these contradictions. I think I have to keep things light in order to manage them. Of course I'm not deeply satisfied—at heart I'm a dissatisfied person, because I also have an ideal man in mind and I'd like him to match it, not sexually, but in everyday life, in dividing work, in the family. What does family mean to me? Is it this, that I should be its slave? No. I also have an ideal kind of family in mind that I haven't attained, but I hope that my children will. Because even with a maid in the house, I tell my daughter, when she pees on the floor, "Go get a rag and wipe up your pee." And I intend to go on like this.

Even if I went back to working full-time, I don't think he'd change his role. Because he's defined himself as . . . the economic protector of the family, and he'll never leave that role. What could happen is this: I might give up a personal role that I like a lot, which is to be a housewife and mother, and I might have enough money to hire capable people to take on these duties, but I would feel dissatisfied if I didn't do at least some of them. While for him, no; for him I'd just have become one more competent person in the labor market, and he'd be proud of it. He'd be proud of being able to point to his wife's competence, just as he's proud now of saying that I'm a competent housewife . . . he's often said it's good that I'm someone with diverse abilities, since I can be a good housewife as well as a good professional. He'd be proud, but it wouldn't change his role at all. It would just be twice the work for me. And that's what was happening when we lived together before we got married. I ended up taking care of the laundry, the house, the food. That's what I was saying just last night, when he said we shouldn't talk about the past: "But obviously, you can't have a present without a past; I have to talk about the past, because my experience is cumulative." I have to say that to him, but he doesn't like it so he cuts off the conversation.

I don't think this is just his personal attitude. It's part of the intrinsic value of being a man. "Being a man!" In Brazil, maybe among Latinos in general but especially in Brazil, one of the prerequisites of "being a man" is having to take on this paternalistic role of economic protector of the family—and nothing else. The rest is simply a function of his financial situation.

He just doesn't see that my double workday is something that contradicts the whole ideology he's theoretically committed to. Emotionally, he isn't aware of it. He could even write a lovely article, a book, on this subject. But in practice, with his wife, he's not aware of it. Oh, he might even be aware, but he refuses to change his practice, because that would involve giving up the personal value he has by virtue of being male. And that's how this conflict arises, which can plague you. Possibly some of his ideas will change because of Clara, because of being father to a girl. But this contradiction isn't intellectual, it's experienced in terms of emotional values. I call it sexual deformity, a deformity in male and female sex roles. He just doesn't want to think about it . . . since if he gave it some thought, he'd have to behave differently, and that would involve changing his masculine behavior. He prefers to ignore it. And if you asked him, "Are you happily married?" he would say, "Yes, and I wouldn't want not to be married, or to be with someone else." Not that I think that's a lie. I believe it.

He has to evolve in a dialectical process, right? I think that a person's growth is precisely this, freeing oneself of these things. Personal growth means . . . as you grow, you project this growth onto the people around you. And that's what I don't understand—dialectics for me is this, and he rejects it in practice. Shall I give you an example—a really silly, practical example? We have a laundry basket in our bathroom for dirty clothes. This basket has a cover and all you have to do is grab the dirty clothing, lift up the lid and drop the clothing inside the basket. For four years I've been asking him to take the cover off the basket and drop his clothes in. Every day! And he always says, "I pay a maid to lift the lid off the basket." Such a tiny thing! He's even said, "But, darling, I'm not asking you to lift the lid! Let the maid do it. I have the money to pay her salary." I say, "But you . . . I think it's outrageous, absurd, to pay someone to lift the lid off the basket so you can throw your clothes in." You see? Lifting the lid off the basket, which is the simplest thing in the world, a mechanical motion, shakes up his masculine values. He can't be the person who "straightens up the house," because a male doesn't straighten up the house! Can you imagine?

Y E S ,   Y E S ,   I   K N O W I've talked almost exclusively about this problem. This is a problem that, right now, is troubling me profoundly. It seems to me that when a problem crops up a lot in my talk, it's because I'm trying to resolve it. It's begun to trouble me so much that I've got to look for a way out, and this is my way of starting to look for a solution.

Conceição, a tall, soft-spoken, brown-skinned woman twenty years of age, had just begun to work for Marta (preceding chapter) at the time of the interview. As we finished our conversation, Conceição asked me to play back the tape so she could hear the sound of her own voice. She sat and listened to it twice through.

12

———

I've been working as a maid since I was fourteen. My father is a mechanic, and my mother is a maid. She lives in the house where she works. My father has a house somewhere, but I don't know where he lives; it's somewhere around São Paulo. He's separated from my mother. I was two years old when it happened. I saw him once when I was twelve, and after that I never saw him again. He set up a new family. She didn't.

I used to stay with my mother at her job. Sometimes she'd pay someone to take care of me, that's how it worked. Sometimes she'd pay for me to stay with my aunt. Other times I'd stay with her at her job, and other times she'd pay a girl to take care of me. That's how it worked. And I'd sleep at those different places. I'd see her every weekend. She couldn't keep me with her because the people didn't always like it. It's hard when you have kids. I missed her, but that did no good. But I'm very close to her, I always call her where she works—it's near here.

My mother's forty-nine years old. I'm an only child. Before I started working, when I was fourteen, sometimes I'd go to school . . . or I'd stay at my aunt's house and help her take care of things. I had to repeat second grade because I was kind of weak; then I went on to the third grade and I was passed into the fourth, but I didn't go. My mother didn't earn enough to pay for my schooling; she didn't have money for the books. She wanted me to study more, to get some training, so that I wouldn't have to stick with this domestic work. I was planning to go to school at night, but I lost my registration papers and now I have to get new ones. If I can do that, I'll go back to school. You can't go without the papers.

I stayed at my first job for two years;

C O N C E I Ç Ã O

then I couldn't stay any more because it got too expensive, and my mistress was also raising the child of another maid of hers, so I told my mother that I wanted to come and live with her. But it didn't work out. The lady . . . my mother worked for her for fifteen years, but she's very difficult; she didn't want me to live there. So I found a job for myself.

My last job? I worked there for one year. I left because I had an argument with the lady, about her son . . . he was into marijuana, and I knew about it. Then I had an argument with him: I said I was going to tell his mother, and he tried to grab me. I went running out, screaming, but his mother told me to calm down and not to spread around what he was doing. I stayed on there . . . for two more weeks while she went on a trip, to the United States and other places over there; and when she came back, she came back changed, like . . . nothing I did was good enough for her . . . so I thought I'd better leave.

She always used to say as a little joke that she was going to fire me, but I'd never answer back, so she thought I didn't have the nerve to leave. Well . . . when the day came, she said that if I wanted to leave I could, and I did.

I myself found this job. I came up here one day and asked the lady if she needed some help, or if she knew anyone, and she said she needed someone. I lost my social security at my last job, because I went away for a while and then came back, and the months that I didn't pay messed it up. But Dona Marta said she'll register me now. I think that's very important because if you have INPS [National Social Security Institute], you get lots of things paid for: retirement, doctors, other things. My mother was operated on for her head, and the INPS paid for it. She had some problem with a vein in her head . . . I don't know what it was, but she had it cut open, and then she got better, but her vision still isn't quite right. And now she's back at work, at a different job, because there was too much work at the old one. The house had two stories, and she can't manage that; she can't do heavy work, just light jobs now.

At my last job I earned $60 a month. Now I'm earning $75. It's a reasonable salary and out of it I have to pay for my social security—the cost is divided half and half between the boss and the worker. The whole thing comes to $13 and something, and I pay half of that. Then I get food and other things here. This month, I got a bar of soap; I don't know if I'll get one next month. In my last job they didn't give me those things, soap, toothpaste, deodorant. Just food. No clothing, just the sheets on the bed. Clothing I had to buy with my own money. And towels they gave me. My salary's enough for me since I don't have to help anyone else. It's just for buying clothes, taking care of my teeth. But now I want to rent a room, so that on weekends, when I have a day off, I won't have to go to anybody else's house. I could go to my own room, you see. I'm not sure how much it would cost, maybe around $30 a month. I could share it with a friend.

I've only just started working here. I usually get up at 7:30, or 7:00. Yesterday was the first time she called me in the morning. I don't cook lunch—there are usually leftovers from dinner the night before. I just make the dinner. He doesn't have lunch here; it's just her. It's not a hard job, and I have lots of free time. I have one friend who lives near here, and my aunt who works up the street. I have every other Saturday off. No, let's see. . . . One Saturday I work, and have Sunday off; the next I leave on Saturday and only have to come back on Monday morning. Sometimes she asks me to stay in the evening and take care of the little girl. I like her [the child] . . . but I'm not cut out to be a nursemaid. I don't have much of a knack for it, but I don't mind keeping an eye on her.

I'd like to have children. I have a boyfriend, kind of. It's not a sure thing. I began to have boyfriends when I was very young, fourteen, thirteen years old. I've had a few since then, not too many. I've never really done it, you know . . . just . . . kind of sleeping together, but not really doing it. I've spent the night with someone, slept in that sense, but . . . I don't know . . . they tried, I tried too, but I've never actually done it. It's not really that I'm afraid . . . but I don't want to get pregnant; with life the way it is today, everything's so hard. I've never taken anything, but I know about it. I've heard about abortion, but I don't know how it's done. I wouldn't have the courage to do anything like that. I'd keep my child, even if I had to suffer, going hungry in the street with him. I'd keep him.

No, I don't want to get married . . . I'd prefer just to live together and not marry, because marriage . . . you can marry today, and tomorrow they leave you. But if you just live together and they leave, that's all right. If you're not married, your name doesn't get dirtied . . . for example, "See that married woman, now she's with someone else." That's why I think . . . marriage is . . . it's a fantasy, just illusion.

Once in a while I go to church, not too often. Nothing else, no. My mother was involved with *umbanda*, but now she stopped. I think it sets your life back—I don't know why, it just does. My aunt, for example, she went to a big center, she had a nice house and everything . . . and she lost it all; my uncle died, and now she doesn't have a thing. She was really involved in *macumba*, and she said the *macumbeiro* [leader of the ceremony] was helping her. . . . But I think he was doing bad things . . . because right now she's in a bad way. It's not that I don't believe, you see, but I think that if it works, it's to do good, not evil—but I'm not sure. My mother said it didn't work out, that after she got involved with one center her life just went backward instead of going forward.

My mother earns very little, $50 a month. She works for one woman, who lives alone . . . so she just earns $50. But she doesn't get along with her. It's hard to find a nice mistress. I don't know why . . . it seems that there's something wrong with all of them. For example, when you start on a job . . . she treats you well; then after a week you start to get to know her, you see. That's why I think it's difficult. It would be better . . . to work in a shop, for example, but I don't think I could get that kind of job. I think you have to take a course or something. Plans? Well, I'd like to go to school, at least finish grade school, because then you get to do other things . . . but I don't really have any plans.

This family? I think they're middle class, not really rich. No, I don't know why they have money more than I do, but I wouldn't want to be rich. I think poor people have love, but the rich . . . I wouldn't want to be rich. . . . I'd like to have a house . . . like anybody can have, not a luxurious house, just a roof of my own, but not be rich. I don't know why, but the rich are unhappy . . . it's like they live only on illusions. They've got all sorts of things in their heads . . . money. . . . And some of them don't like Blacks; they've got ideas like that. I know because . . . I've heard lots of people say that there are White people who don't like Blacks. My mother is very dark. I'm lighter than she is, but there are people who don't like even that. I don't know . . . most rich people . . . you see, when poor people get sick, they recover; but the rich always die of some bad diseases, some serious diseases, I don't know which. Well, the poor also die . . . but the rich are more . . . if they were brought up like the poor, eating everything . . . but the rich eat these strange foods, piles of weird things . . . they're so fussy.

I've never worked in any really rich people's houses, thank God. I don't want to. In a rich person's house you've got to work even more, you don't have time to sit down. You might have more money, but not a minute to sit down. Now the middle class is a bit better; they're a bit happier than the rich. But not as much as the poor. The rich have money and the poor have love.

Let's see, what kind of man would I like? I like them dark. I don't like White men, not for me. And he has to have some sort of job; I don't care what kind, just a job. I'd like to have children, but not now because I wouldn't be able to raise them. But if I got pregnant I wouldn't get rid of it. If I have a house of my own someday . . . then I wouldn't get rid of it.

All my friends are also maids. And they all work for White people. I've never worked for a Black family, but it would be the same thing. When Blacks get up in the world . . . I don't know. They say that poor people can't climb up.

It's true I have some freedom with this kind of job, but I still think that if I worked as a clerk in a store, for example, it would be better. . . . If I had my own home that I could leave every day, it would be better. And if my man earned a good living, I'd prefer to stay at home. But he shouldn't have to earn all the money. I'd at least want to help, to earn some money cleaning once in a while.

You know, when you're working you're not likely to have a fight with the master. It's usually with the madam; they're more difficult. As far as I'm concerned, the ideal mistress should understand that a maid is a maid . . . she should treat her with ... civility ... but some don't. They talk to the maid as if they think that a maid is an animal. Like this last one I mentioned ... she said to me that she hadn't slapped me across the face only because I wasn't her daughter, but if I had been, she'd have given me three smacks. It was like this. I was ironing the clothes, and she didn't like the way something on the pile looked. She's got this sister whose name she can't even bear to hear, and I said, "I wasn't the only one who ironed today, your sister also did," and she heard that and turned back and spoke to me. I think she was already mad because, I don't know ... because she's having so many problems with her children. She can't take it out on them, so she does on others. Well, the day she said she'd hit me in the face was a Friday, and I left that Saturday. It was a sudden fight; she said that if I wanted to go away, "Just get out!" I said I'd get my things together and go, but she said, "But first you have to finish your work, clean the house, and make lunch." I said I wasn't going to do any of it. She said, "Oh yes you will, or I'll take it all out of your salary," and I said, "Take whatever you want, money isn't my problem." And I didn't do a thing. I just got my stuff and left right then and there. And she did give me my money. I didn't even count it, you know. I was so angry that I didn't count it.

It all happened so fast. I didn't lower myself about the money. Then for three weeks I didn't work. I stayed with my aunt at her job, and with a friend at hers, sleeping on the floor. It's hard now to find work. Then I came here. I hope I can stay on here. I don't know, at the beginning they treat you all right. Then afterward you get to see, when you live with a person you get to know them. No, they don't always give you the same food they eat. For example, if they eat beef ... some don't give the maid beef, they give you something else ... eggs ... but no beef. Here I eat the same as they do.

In the afternoon, when she's out and the little girl is at school, I don't have much work. I iron the clothes ... and there's time for a nap. At night, I watch television with them.[1] I like that a lot, especially the soap operas; the one at 8:00 isn't bad. You can see what I was saying, about the rich being unhappy, especially on the 8:00 o'clock soap opera. That woman—I don't know if you've seen it, but there's this lady, Debora's mother. Well, you can see it all in that woman: she's not a normal woman, she's not right in the head, she seems half crazy. I'm not sure what it is. Well, she said she raised her daughter to be on the same social level as her, not for a lower level. That's why I think, the more the rich have, the more they want. If I had a daughter, I'd teach her what she needs to know, but I wouldn't be holding her back; that just makes it worse. Whatever has to happen will happen anyway.

I didn't have a lot of freedom when I was a kid. They didn't let me at my aunt's and the other houses where I stayed ... they didn't let me. But now, no, nobody tells me what to do anymore. Now I'm me.

Just off the main street in one of Rio de Janeiro's many North Zone *favelas* Sônia, a Black woman in her late twenties, lives with her husband and seven-year-old son. She grew up in this *favela*, above the muddy footpaths that wind away from the steep main street. This paved road is the heart of the *favela* community; small shops are located along it, as are bus stops serviced by vans that drive continuously up and down the street, providing the community with its only public transportation. Sônia distinguishes between the *favela* (shanty-town) further up the hill, where her mother still lives and where she was raised, and the *morro* (hill), where she now resides. But different economic levels are clearly visible even along the main street. Sônia has a two-room brick house with a yard, but just across the street from her, in a very large and comfortable house, lives the woman (who looks White) for whom Sônia currently does domestic work. This woman and her husband own a good deal of property on the hill and enjoy a standard of living much above that of most of the hill's inhabitants. And, only

13

a few minutes' walk further up the hill, rickety shacks crowd together. Sônia, near the paved main street, enjoys certain amenities: an indoor toilet, running water, and adequate electricity.

Over the past twenty years the number of *favelas* and *favelados* in Rio has increased dramatically. Approximately one-third of Rio's population now lives in *favelas*, as opposed to just over 11 percent in 1965.[1] A variety of levels of economic development and consumption meet in an odd patchwork in the *favelas*—where families often go to great lengths to fix up their houses. I spoke to one young Black couple (she took in laundry; he worked as a messenger in a bank) who, with the help of friends, had beautifully tiled their bathroom in the *favela* and filled it with sparkling new fixtures, including a bidet. But all the water and waste that left this bathroom flowed openly down the hillside. As one acquaintance, who had tried to organize a women's group in this community, commented: "No infrastructure."

The interview was conducted in 1983, over several days, as Sônia's schedule permitted.

SÔNIA

About two years after I started working at the cigarette factory, when I was pregnant with my son, I began to develop this problem with bronchitis. And to this day I still have it. It's a huge factory, foreign owned, and I worked there for nine years, starting in 1973. There was a point when they had about two thousand employees, in two shifts. But just last week a woman I know told me that in one section which could have a base staff of about two hundred people, right now there are only sixty. Bosses have been fired, operators, mechanics. Now there's just the minimum in each section. I hear it's because of the economic crisis.

I operated a machine that put the cigarettes into packs. There was another section that dealt with the tobacco—that's how it used to be; but by now they've changed things, in my section, too. Now it's all done mechanically, but before, there was a crate of tobacco that they'd pick up on the first floor, stick in the elevator, and send up to the second floor, where the tobacco section is. Then they'd put the tobacco into this machine, by hand, and the machine would form the ciagarette, put on the filter, and wrap it in white paper. Not now, now that's all done mechanically, from beginning to end. But it used to be that, once the cigarette was made, the same machine had a shelf, and they'd stack the cigarettes there and then send it down to my section. And in my section the machine would put them into packs, stick on the paper with the brand name, and tinfoil, and the price.

When I worked there, what I had to do was—for example, the person in charge of the cigarettes would bring them over, I'd check the labels, and straighten out the cigarettes with my hand. You couldn't have some higher than others, or some slanted in the pack; they all had to be real even. I'd press them down with my hands. Then we'd pack them up, stick on the seal, and feed glue into the machine. And then there was another machine to receive the packs of cigarettes and put on the cellophane and the pack thread. The packs would move down a conveyor belt, and further on there was an operator who did nothing but push the packs into the machine down there, and they'd come out the other side in cartons of ten packs. Nowadays that machine I was telling you about doesn't require any manual contact. But sometimes it stops because there's too much tobacco or too many cigarettes, and then the person watching the machine turns on a little light and when the light's on you can see where the problem is. And when there's a problem that the operator can't fix, then you call the mechanics to fix it. The mechanics are all men, the operators are women. On each machine there were two operators working—for example, when I was on, my coworker would be on back-up. She'd put glue in the machine, and so on.

We weren't allowed to talk during our shift—we did talk, but it's forbidden, and they don't like us to have a lot of contact. Anyway, it was very noisy, but even so we'd manage to talk. I worked eight hours a day. I'd go on at 5:00 in the morning and leave at 2:00. That way I didn't have to work on Saturdays. It was a tough schedule.

Then, when I got pregnant, I began to have this problem with bronchitis, on account of the tobacco. I was allergic to it; I still am. During the winter I feel really sick, but in the summer I'm all right. I was fired last year, and now I do odd jobs. Yes, yes, despite being allergic I went on working there. I asked them to give me a break, to change my work; but even so they wouldn't, they didn't do a thing.

Before that I tried various places, filled out applications, but they never called me. At the factory I waited for one year after applying, and I thought I'd never hear from them, but one fine day they sent a telegram. And I went, without . . . because lots of people were really eager to work there. Because they paid well, and they have this image. But once you start you see it's not like that at all. They've got this good image: it looks like an easy job, but it's not; you've really got to concentrate.

When I left last year my salary was $220 a month, a lot more than the minimum wage [U.S. $83 a month at the time]. And the meals were really terrific. They paid for a part of it—I mean, the government paid half of it, and we paid the other half. We'd get a tray with bread, milk or whatever you wanted to drink, beans and rice, salad, meat, soup. Some days they even had grilled shrimp, delicious. I ate pretty well there, but I don't really like food that much. I eat a lot of junk, sweets.

We had forty-five minutes for lunch. The rest of the day I worked on my feet. Yes, it's hard on your legs. And I had a month's vacation, and my thirteenth-month's salary. We had medical care right in the factory, or if you wanted you could go to the INPS [National Social Security Institute], because they'd accept our vouchers. But as far as I was concerned the medical part was no good: whatever medicine they gave me there never worked.

When you start working, you earn less than the people who've been there awhile, but they give you a raise every year until you've caught up with the salary of the old-timers. Then it stops, once you're earning the same. It must have taken three years, more or less, to catch up. The men, the mechanics, earned a lot more than the operators. The men who carried the crates earned a bit less than an operator, but the men who oiled the machine earned more—it was all ranked like that. There were many more women than men, and there still are. In this case, more women than men work. We were part of the tobacco-workers' union, but not everybody joined; it's not obligatory. It used to be that when you were hired you were automatically a member, but by the time I started it wasn't like that, I don't know why. The union representatives were chosen by the workers in the factory. I think the union's in cahoots with the company, and whenever we'd have a big meeting you couldn't get it out of your mind that the union was in cahoots with the company and that it let the company do whatever it wanted, so we wouldn't go to the meetings and we'd end up losing out.

I used to leave the machine to go to the bathroom, but only for fifteen minutes. When I'd start, from 5:00 to 7:00, if my coworker didn't have a lot to do she'd cover for me while I went for five minutes. I hear this sort of thing's ended now. Then, after 7:00, I could go to the bathroom. I had a fifteen-minute break. Some people used to stay for half an hour, sometimes even forty-five minutes, but that's not allowed. We didn't have any other breaks. The machines stopped only at lunchtime.

WHEN I GOT PREGNANT, what they did was this: in the fifth month they'd temporarily take you off the machines—in that respect, the boss was okay. And if someone was absent, they'd put the pregnant person back on the machine. You'd get taken off permanently only when you got really big, and then they'd give you lighter work.

I had three months of leave, beginning at the end of March. Rupert was born a month later, so I stayed home exactly eighty-four days [the legally mandated maternity leave]. When I went back to work he wasn't yet two months old. Even while on leave I'd go there to pick up my money, my regular salary, and it was always ready, just like when I was working. They're obliged to pay it, you know.

Yes, they had a nursery, right on the premises. They used to have the nursery open for just one shift, now it's two. My son went there for four or five months; then he began to have problems because of allergies. He's also got this problem. I took him out of there right away and he got better; today he's all right. Lately I've been watching him because he's started sneezing a lot. I hope it's not an allergy. He went to the nursery when he was about seven weeks old, and stayed till he was five months old. He could have stayed for one year, that's the law. And they gave me time off to nurse him. What we used to do was—for example, I had to feed him about 6:00 a.m, so my coworker stayed at the machine and I'd go; I'd stay with him from 6:00 to 6:30. Then at 9:00 o'clock I'd go down to nurse him, you see, and change his diaper. I went three times a day. But afterward, when he was three months old, I'd only go twice a day, at 8:00 o'clock and at noon, half an hour each time. Then later, when he was five years old, I found a girl to stay with him here at home. And I'd get home from work and take care of him and the house. At that time my husband was also working there, in the same factory—same section, same schedule. Then afterward we had to change because we could never find people to take care of the baby, so my husband changed his schedule and I kept on from 5:00 till 2:00.

Yes, I took care of the house, too; it was a terrible struggle. He'd help, yes, he'd help, a little, but he helped [laughs]. He was laid off after me, and now he works for a medical supply company that pretends it's Brazilian, but actually it buys the stuff abroad and resells it here as if it were produced in Brazil. His salary now is about $100 a month; it's very little, we're in a real bind. That's why I'm doing odd jobs. Just today he said to me, "Sônia, I haven't got a penny left. Do you have any money?" I said, "Yes, $8." And I gave it to him. If I hadn't put something aside, we wouldn't have had any meat. I bought half a kilo of beef in the middle of the week and just cooked half of it. I saved the other half and made it today. We've got to be really careful, otherwise. . . .

I'm pretty sure the reason I was fired was because of my problems, and the inflation on top of that. I'd been there for so long, they could fire you and keep the people who'd started more recently. Now they're not hiring a soul, just firing. About eighteen women left at the same time I did, people who never missed work, who never arrived late. But one thing is true: some of these people, though they never came in late or missed work, they didn't know how to work the machines. So that's another reason for firing them. Some others were good workers but they were kind of bossy, and they didn't want that kind of person around, see?

It was hard for me to get that job, I even had to wait a year. During all that time, I looked for work but couldn't find a thing. And then they sent a telegram and I was kind of, "Should I go or shouldn't I?" But I ended up going; I had a whole series of interviews, a medical exam, a urine exam to see if I was pregnant, because they won't hire you if you're pregnant. But once you're there you can get pregnant, you just can't have one after the other. I know a girl who stayed there for four years, and in those four years she had four pregnancies. They fired her. The way things are going at the factory, with the high rate of unemployment, what's happening is that the people there are getting pregnant. I have a friend who didn't want another baby, but she's in debt and so she had another one. I don't think that's the solution, but that way at least she didn't lose her job. While she's pregnant she can't be fired. They don't fire a pregnant worker: it hurts the company because they'd have to pay her compensation just as if she was working. Then, when she comes back she has three months in her favor [job stability]; then they can fire her. And sometimes that's what happens. I have a friend who was fired, so she proved she was pregnant. After her [maternity] leave she finished those three months, and the next day they fired her.

When I was fired, I got my [indemnity] money.[2] They paid it like they were supposed to. No, it wasn't much. Look, I worked there nine years . . . nine years and five months. But I was so sure I was going to be fired, I was so sure, that at that time I was going to school, and sometimes I'd have to leave early. My boss lately wouldn't even look me in the face, so I said to my coworker, "He won't look at me, he doesn't hand me my check personally, he always used to act up, start cussing and joking, and now he doesn't do a thing; he just stands there quietly. I know he's going to fire me." She went, "What do you mean? Of course he's not going to fire you." Until he did.

But I still have medical coverage, yes, because I went to find out about it. I went to the Ministry of Labor and told them that, to this day, I haven't been able to find another job and I can't lose my nine years of INPS. And because of that I got one more year, until next year. But lots of people don't know the law. Normally it's just one year, but if I'd worked there for ten years I'd have been allowed two years of coverage, and that's what I managed to get.

In the newspapers there are almost no job ads at all. I applied for a job having to do with medical data; I'm not sure just what the work would have been. I heard about it because a friend phoned the house to tell me. But, you know, they only give opportunities to people they're interested in. It's got nothing to do with your qualifications; it's all on the basis of who you know, and then some. If they're not interested in you, you could even have lots of skills, but you'll just go around in circles. What kind of interest? In making out, in having sex. In the factory there were girls who got fired because they wouldn't go along, and the bosses got angry and fired them. The operators were Black and White women, blondes, mulattos, and the bosses were by and large White. There was just one, for about two years, who was mulatto, but he didn't stay long. He was hard to get along with, and he didn't really know the work. Yes, they were after all the women—for sex, you know, they've got no real preference, it's all the same to them. You just have to be kind of pretty, and lively; and if you trust them, you've had it. Lots of women left because they wouldn't go along.

I W A S A B O U T T W E N T Y when I started at the factory. Before that, I did the kind of work I'm doing now, in people's houses. For a while I was a nanny, and I also worked in an office. Now I work for Dona Doris, in that house across the street. One day I wash the bathroom, another day I iron. Four days a week. I get $4 a day—it comes to a bit more than the minimum wage. No, I didn't register [as a worker—entitled to benefits] because I still have one year of INPS, from the factory; but when it's up I'll have to make the payments myself if I haven't found a regular job.

Some days I work eight hours, other days I leave early. I get home and what I usually do is wash the clothes, cook the food, clean the kitchen, take a bath, go get my son, and when I next look it's already late. So there's no time to do anything else. My son comes home from school alone, and I pick him up at my mother's; she lives on the hill, too. Some days I go pick him up early; other days I go late, because I like to catch up on my work.

Tomorrow's my day off. I'm going to see a man at a center, a spiritualist center. They say he's very good. It's this problem, bronchitis, that I told you about, and that's why I first went to a center, another one. They told me the saint was punishing me. That's why I decided to leave, because I don't like threats. It might even turn out to be true, but threatening a person makes me go away rather than get closer. Yes, I've gone to doctors at the INPS, but I've had this problem for seven years and I haven't gotten any better. At the other center they couldn't help me, but again I stopped going because they had sessions every day and it took too much time. Tomorrow's the first time I'm going to this other place. Yes, I have to pay. The woman I work for told me about this center. When I was younger I used to go to church a lot more. Once in a while I still go. Today there's a celebration going on, and I'd like to go; and sometimes I go to Mass, but not often.

I started working as a domestic when I was thirteen. I was still in school, but during vacations I'd find odd jobs because my family was always poor, so I'd take odd jobs. But it wasn't enough, so then I switched to night school. I worked during the day and went to school at night, until I finished middle school [i.e., eighth grade].

My husband and I have known each other for a long time; we used to be neighbors and, what with the dating and being engaged, we were courting for seven years. I didn't have any other boyfriends before him. We began to date when I was thirteen, going on fourteen. Then I got married when I was twenty-one. I waited that long because my father used to say that if I had a boyfriend he'd take me out of school. But later my father saw that I had a real urge to study, and I finished middle school, and after that was when I got married. I was studying to be a laboratory aide—at that time I was already working at the factory, an afternoon shift; but then I got transferred to mornings, and I had to drop the course. It was at a vocational school, a very good one. After that, I never went back to school until the year before last, and I finished last year. Yes, I liked the course I took, but it wasn't exactly what I wanted. At the time I wanted to do nursing, but I couldn't, so I ended up doing professional office support instead.

My parents approved of our marriage. At home, it was okay, but they were very strict, you see. Like when I was dating him, I couldn't go out with him alone, I had to take along my brother, even just to the movies. And I hardly ever went out. Dating the way they do now, going out and getting into trouble, I didn't have that kind of freedom. But in a sense you could say it was good, because I did get properly married.

My mother never talked about sex. When I first got my period, I knew about it more or less, but all she said was, "Be careful, 'cause if you hold a match to gunpowder it'll catch fire." And she always talked about that business of doing it between your thighs; she said you could get pregnant that way. "Don't let him put it between your thighs," 'cause of this, 'cause of that, she used to say, " 'cause you'll get pregnant." That's all she said. So I was a virgin when I married, and that's what I'd teach any daughter of mine. But I wouldn't do things like my mother did; my mother doesn't like certain subjects. I'd give my daughter lots of freedom. Oh, of course I'd want her to be a virgin until her marriage, but it might not be possible. Every mother prefers that.

I've never had an abortion, I've only been pregnant once. Well, if I'd gotten pregnant, I'm not sure . . . I think I can't get pregnant anymore; but if I did, what with these really high rates of inflation, I'd get rid of it. As soon as he was born I had a treatment with local injections. I only had three because I couldn't get used to them. I think I can't get pregnant again. The injections? Iodine-based, to dry up the uterus. But if it were now, I wouldn't start the treatment, now that I'm older, because medication made of iodine, they say it causes cancer. It wasn't an Institute doctor. I went to a private doctor to get the iodine shots. I didn't want to have more children, I still don't, but I didn't finish the treatment. The Institute doctors wouldn't help with that. There are even people who need their tubes tied and the Institute won't do it. So I went to a private doctor, and he gave me the injections, but they didn't agree with me. I only took them for three months. Each month, seven days after my period went away, I'd go there and get an injection. I'd feel really strong cramps, and my blood pressure would drop. They gave me an inflammation, and all kinds of complications. An inflammation of the uterus, and I had a discharge, which I had to get treated. So I stopped, it was making me sick.

Then afterward I went to the Institute doctor. I asked him if it was likely that I would or wouldn't get pregnant, and I told him I'd taken the injections. He said he couldn't tell me anything about it: if I wanted to go on taking the injections or some medication, fine; if I didn't, that was up to me, too. So I took contraceptive pills, and I only stopped last year. I stopped, I'm not taking them anymore, and I haven't gotten pregnant. I stopped because I didn't feel right. I felt nauseated, very nauseated. I took them for six years, trying different kinds and everything, but I didn't feel right, they make me really nervous. But I took them all that time, I never forgot, and I had normal periods. Then I decided to quit, and now I'm not using anything; but I don't want another child, one's enough—it's not really enough, but what with the high cost of living, there's no way. Living here in this house, one bedroom, a living room, kitchen and bath—it's for a couple. I already have this one [child], and there's no room for another. If I get pregnant, I'd get rid of it. You just go to a private clinic and pay. It costs about $75 now to have an abortion. I'm not sure, but I think they give you an injection. I don't know of what. I've never done it, but I know lots of women who've gone to *curiosas* [unlicensed midwives], when there's no other way, when their finances are really low. *Curiosas*, they say, do it with a sound [a probe]. Others do it with an injection. A sound's like . . . you take a papaya-tree stalk and put it into the woman's vagina, and it reaches the baby's head and kills it.

But some women get the money; a friend of mine from across the street had an abortion and got her tubes tied. She was already two months along, and they did a mini-Caesarean. She's not going to have a baby now. Catholic women also do it, but they say their religion is against it. I'm Catholic, but if one day it should happen, God will forgive me, but I'll do it, too. I go to church once in a while, and if I did it I'd confess. The priests know this happens . . . it's really common. I know women who've had lots of abortions. As far as I know, nobody in the community does them now, but there used to be some women, what do you call them, midwives, but no more. They died, you see.

My husband doesn't want any more children, either. He's just against getting rid of them. He even said so once. But if I get pregnant I'll just have it done on the sly, and I'll tell him about it later. Once he even said that if I should ever do it . . . I told him that even if the doctor told me I was in danger . . . dying doesn't bother me, maybe it's just ignorance on my part, and he said, "I wouldn't spend a penny on your funeral, if you went looking for death" [*laughs*].

WE WERE MARRIED in a civil ceremony and in church. It was in 1974; it's going on ten years [*laughs*]. We get along well, but there are times when you get fed up. . . . What? Yesterday I said I liked his being the boss? Yes, more or less, but I don't really like it much. You accept it, that's all. How do you think it should be? Sometimes I'm satisfied, not always. Lots of time men get in the way of certain things. For example, you want to buy something. I wanted a bookshelf instead of the bedroom set, I wanted to fix up the living room, but he wouldn't agree. I think that, since it's my money, I'm just asking his opinion, but since it's my money I could buy the bookshelf, but he went on and on and I ended up buying the bedroom set. No, I don't get all worked up. I don't like arguments. I don't lose my cool, but I just think my own thoughts. We disagree a lot on account of the boy, he's so. . . . I don't let my son run wild; I won't accept certain things, bad manners, I won't put up with that. So he's more partial to his father; his father puts up with more. But I complain. I think it's really important, for example, if he asks for a toy—if I can give it to him, I tell him I will; if I can't, I sit down with him and say, "Look, son, I can't do it because of this and that." Not my husband. Even when he knows he can't, he says he'll give it to him and then never does, you see?

Then my son gets angry, he says I'm bad. Sure I've talked to my husband about this, but he sticks to his guns. He believes his way of thinking is what's right. I think it's better to talk, to explain the situation to the boy.

And I wish my husband would do more at home. He helps, but he's not too happy about it, and afterward he starts to complain. I thought he should help me more, but he can't do that much either because he's going to school now. By the end of the week he's tired. He's finishing primary school now. He started school when he was a kid, but he quit. And then, from my talking on and on about his going back, he got encouraged. He began working when he was fourteen. Now he's going to night school; he's got two more years to go—at night they do four years in two—and then he'll be done. He goes every evening, he doesn't have dinner. He goes directly from work so as not to waste more money on bus fare. He gets home late, 10:30 or 10:45. If he came home first, he'd get here just in time to leave again for school. So he has a snack at work and then goes to school. It's hard. I still want to take a nursing course, but it depends on my son. He's afraid of staying here alone; he's afraid, and so I'm stuck. My mother, I ask if he can sleep there, she's not that willing. I know she doesn't really want to, and I don't like to insist.

We rent this house for $12 a month [$32 a month in January 1983 when the rent was set]. It's going up again in January. That doesn't include the other bills; I'm not sure what they are, my husband pays them. At the end of the month, he pays . . . telephone, electricity, I buy the gas [for cooking], we pay the rent. Lately I don't have any bills, just some silly little ones I'll pay off right away. He shops for food, and I just hand over some money when—like today, today he didn't have any money, so I gave him mine to go shopping, to get through the end of the week, bananas, crackers, meat.

Things have changed a lot in the past few years, lately especially. I was planning to put some money together, you know, to buy a few things, to change the furniture in the house, make it a bit more comfortable for my son [who sleeps on the living room sofa], to take him to the movies now and then. There are times I can't manage that kind of thing. But food, thank God, we've got. Nourishment, thank God. But also because I'm a person with lots of will power, otherwise we would have had to change. If he doesn't have enough, I have some, so we get by. He's earning two minimum salaries [$100 total].

For several years we worked at the same factory, the same schedule. Then he switched his work because we could never find anyone to really take care of the boy, so he switched his hours and he used to stay with him all morning. Then I found a school for the boy, private, and he stayed there. For a long time it was like that—he'd bathe him, feed him, and take him to school; then later I'd go to pick the boy up. No one else could really do it, so I'd pick him up at school. At that time I wasn't taking any classes.

I went to public school, and my son does, too. Now he's in school from 12:30 till 4:45. I pay for his books and transportation, but I don't have to pay for the school. And in the morning he has a private class, for one hour, because he's getting really low grades. I pay her $4 a month [for his lessons], for an hour a day. She lives near here. I've got to talk to her today, in fact. I've gone twice, but haven't managed to get hold of her. To see how he's doing. She teaches him the subjects he's studying in second grade. How many hours a day of school is it over there in your country? My son has classes in art, social studies, and Portuguese.

My son's name, Rupert—we got it out of the magazine *Seleções* [the Brazilian ....:.n of *Reader's Digest*]. He spent one week without a name. We were going to call him Wellington, but my husband thought it was too difficult to pronounce. Then he was reading *Seleções*, and I agreed that we should call him Rupert. But there's another Rupert further up the hill. He's about nine years old. My Rupert is seven. The other Rupert, his mother's become an alcoholic. I feel so sorry for her, just a young woman but she drinks so much she has tremors, so the father of this other Rupert took the boy away to raise him; but he doesn't pay any attention to the boy either, and it's really the grandparents who try to take care of him, but the boy's just one more castoff. He's always begging for money in the street.

Even when I was working at the factory, I always thought about a better future. I knew I wasn't going to spend my whole life there, but if I did stay, maybe they would have given me a chance, a promotion. With more schooling, I'd have more of a chance of finding a better job; that's why I went back to school. This job I've applied for, in the hospital kitchen, isn't too good, but I'd be able to move up. If I don't get it . . . I don't know, I haven't thought about it, but probably I will get it. If I don't, I'd like to go to the CIEE.[3] I'm not sure what it stands for—school and business, something like that. It's a school where you get training, and then find a job. Mostly in office work, as an office assistant, that kind of thing. I haven't been there yet, but I'm going any time now.

If I do get this job, I'm not sure what my hours would be. I just know it's written down that it's forty hours a week, maybe every other day. Depending on that schedule, I'd go on working for Dona Doris across the street. Because the salary isn't much; I think now it's at about thirty-something [about U.S. $50 a month].

No, the factory wasn't any more tiring; what I do now is just as tiring. Like last week, I really had to use my arms a lot, to wash the windows. I felt pins and needles in my arms, a kind of tingling. And at the factory it was mostly my arms, too, so it's about the same.

This job I've applied for, in the hospital, I wouldn't get more money; it's just one minimum salary, but it would be better. It would be more stable. If I get it, I won't have to worry about being unemployed. It's not much, but it's a sure thing. I'm not sure how I'll manage—it might be hard because I still have to go up the hill to fetch my son. I mean, it takes a lot of time. It might not seem like it, but it does. My mother lives near the last stop of the van. I take the van, or sometimes I walk up, I'm used to it. Now, to go down the hill, from here to the bottom, that's fast; I can walk it in four minutes. But going up takes a lot longer. It costs 50 cruzeiros [8 cents] to take the van down the hill, 80 [13 cents] to go up. But I can walk really fast, especially going down. Sometimes when I go up the hill into the *favela* really fast, I sometimes run into someone and they say, "Wow, you really get around fast!" Oh yes, I'm a great walker; I pray to God I always will be, even with all these little problems I've got—but they're temporary. As soon as I get active, I feel better.

No, no!! Even if my husband earned more, I wouldn't stop working. Honestly, I feel good working, as bad as my chores are, I still prefer it. Maybe it's just a habit by now.

Sometimes I regret having married, for various reasons. At least single women have a free life; they don't owe anybody explanations. Sure, there are some advantages to marriage, but many more disadvantages. If I could do it over, I wouldn't marry, no! I'd try to enjoy life more. Sometimes it's kind of sickening. No, I don't think it's hard for a woman to support herself, though my husband is very responsible. The little that he earns all goes straight into the house. I don't know why, but this is the way I think: it makes me crazy to see widows marry again. Not me, because I never really enjoyed my youth, I never really had a childhood. My mother was a washerwoman. She doesn't do it much anymore; now she only washes for one family, but there was a time when she did eight washings. Can you imagine? There wasn't any running water in our house. We had to carry water up the hill. Some days we got up early to go get the water. We'd go down the hill with one bundle of laundry and up with another, and then we'd get back to the house and cart more water. When I was seven I already used to give my little brothers their baths. I didn't have a childhood. I suppose that's why I think the way I do, you see, about separating some day. I'd enjoy life—one day I'd take a boat trip, the next I'd . . . I'd enjoy it all [*laughs*]. I'd go to a party one day, I'd samba the next. I'd have a ball. I might even have a boyfriend, but as soon as I'd begin to get fed up with him I'd take off; I wouldn't want that.

Oh no, I don't think I'd miss having a child. Especially now with this standard of living we've got. Everything's so expensive. It's gotten much more difficult since I left the factory a year ago, mostly because I don't have that salary, but also the cost of living's gone up. Has it ever! But we haven't changed what we eat, since I still work, I do my odd jobs. But if I didn't, it would have had to change. Yes, we all eat the same thing, only I don't eat meat. I just don't like it—beef, chicken, it's not to my taste. I like vegetables a lot more. Usually I buy a kilo of meat; that's enough for us for a week, because I only eat a tiny bit of it. Sometimes I put it on my plate and don't even touch it. I don't much like beer, but my husband does. See that mug, shaped like a shoe? That's from the last beer festival he went to. It was on my birthday in June. What sign are you?

On weekends . . . well, he watches TV a lot, but I never have time to sit down. I like it when people stop by, so I can leave off the chores, but I never really have time. . . . I go to sleep very late, even on Sundays I only get to bed at 10:00 o'clock or 11:00. I try to sleep eight hours. Last night it was 1:30 when I went to bed. I wanted to straighten up the house, but it ended up that I just couldn't. I came home from school, then I cleaned up the kitchen, washed my hair, took a bath, filed my toenails, and when I lay down it was already 1:30. Then at 8:00 o'clock I got up, but really tired in my body, and I started to wash the clothes and then I stopped.

Once in a while we go out together. Hardly ever to the movies, not lately. Because of the inflation. No, I don't watch television, because I don't have time. Television, to watch it you have to sit down and pay attention. I have two televisions, this one and the color TV in the bedroom. But I don't watch either of them, not even at night because I'm sleepy by then. I don't have time to watch it. Whenever I'm in the house I'm busy. I take a bath, I cook the food, wash the dishes, wash the clothes. Today I have clothes to wash. So there's never any time left over. What I really like is music. Romantic songs, I just love. I have a radio, and a record player—that thing there is the record player, but it's broken. Not long ago my television broke down. We got the money to fix it, just luck. Somehow, we tightened our belts and paid. And also, thank God, we don't have any debts.

Our rent's going to go up in January. I'm not sure how much, it must be nearly 100 percent, maybe a bit less. My husband's salary isn't going up, but mine just did. I asked for a raise, and she agreed. I was getting 2,000, and I asked for 2,500 a day. My husband's salary isn't going up until, I don't know, maybe October. Normally, when his salary runs out, I kick in mine. I get paid per day, and I put the money aside. Sometimes I spend it, but other times I don't. That's how we do it. The boy still wants a bottle at night—that's an extra expense. When he needs to see a doctor, I take him to a private one, but I haven't had to for a long time now. It costs $5 for an office visit. He also goes to a private dentist—the last time was in January, but I have to take him back soon. Yes, the Institute has dentists, too, but I don't want to bother with them. Last month, when I went to the Institute doctor, there was such a line! I got there at 8:00 and only got out at 11:30. That's one reason, but I don't like them because they don't do the work right either.

Especially the dentist, his work isn't good. I'd rather go privately. And sometimes the Institute schedule isn't right for me.

I like to read the newspaper, but I don't have time to read—not even *fotonovelas* [photoromances]; I just glance at them. It's a very monotonous life. Sometimes I'm disgusted with it. Yesterday I wanted to go to the beach, but I got to thinking. My nails needed doing, the polish had worn half off, they looked ridiculous. I looked at my hands, my cuticles looked terrible, so I said, "No, I'm not going." I preferred not to go. Then I went to get my nails done. The most difficult thing around here is to find someone to do your nails on a Sunday. Even if you pay it's difficult. It took quite a while. I went up the hill at about noon and only came back at 5:00 o'clock. It took a lot of time. The girl first went to make lunch, so I had to wait. I would have done them myself, but my nail clipper's broken. I asked my husband to take it down the street and get it sharpened, but he forgot. So I paid her $1.10. It's a lot, and she doesn't even charge much. There's a woman across the street who charges more than $2; she's a lot more expensive.

Carnival? Last year I went, but we stayed only a few hours. I won't pay for a seat [in the grandstands] to see Carnival. I think it's ridiculous. Carnival belongs to the *cariocas* [residents of Rio],, and *cariocas* still have to pay to see it? To see what's theirs? I think the whole thing's a rip-off. I'd never go, if it was up to me, never, unless I had a lot of money available. Here on the hill, you see people walking down in their costumes. We sometimes have blocks [of dancers who participate in Carnival] on the hill, but they're trying to stop them. For example, there was a girl here and she organized a block and tried to get some help from someone in a samba school, help for making the costumes, putting on the samba . . . and this person said they couldn't, they wouldn't let the block appear anymore. So she couldn't get the block into the street. And that put a stop to the enthusiasm on the hill. They won't do anything, and they won't let anybody else do anything either. We used to have a June festival every year, in the neighborhood organization—which stopped because we no longer have any headquarters—but this year we didn't do that, either. Where our headquarters used to be, now there's a police post.

Just yesterday my husband read in the paper that our hill is one of the best in Rio. You don't get attacked here; but I've heard that people here go to other places to steal, because of drugs—that happens everywhere. It's marijuana for the most part, I've never seen anybody using a needle here, but marijuana's everywhere.

Yes, there are always racial problems here. Always. For example, at that house where I work. He's not a racist, but if he can, kind of, put down the *favelados*— that's a kind of racism, too, and he always puts them down if he can. Anything bad that happens in the neighborhood, he blames the *favelados*. But I like this hill a lot.

Of course if I could move somewhere better, I'd go, but I wouldn't leave this hill just to move to another. I prefer this one. It's wonderful: I love the people here, they're really friendly. Years ago this main street wasn't paved. When my father first moved here the street was a mess, and he used to go to work in wooden clogs. Cars could get up only as far as that first stop, down the hill.

The most important thing for me right now? . . . Oh . . . a better job, a better situation. Then we could go to the theater, enjoy life more. I get along all right with Dona Doris. We talk; I've known her for years, even before, when I used to live near the top of the hill. I've been living here since I got married, and it's just since then that we've gotten to be close friends. I used to go for treatment of my varicose veins, so I took her to have the treatment, too, and that's how we began to be friends. I make friends very easily, and I know how to keep my friendships; but if they don't work out, I break them off. I'm not someone who gets all heated up. If I see it's not working out, I break off the relationship.

Excuse me for asking, but you said you were married before. Are you still friends with the first one? I have a friend who's separated from her husband, but she always talks to him. That's the way it should be, without bitterness and hatred and wishing bad things on him. If I separated from my husband, I'd like to go on being friends, if it were possible. But there are some you just have to stop even talking to, or talk only when necessary.

ONCE IN A LONG WHILE I'll turn on a soap opera, but I'm not too fond of them. I like to see things about fashion, how the fashion's changing. The other day I was reading something, and I saw the word "masochist." Masochist, that's someone who wants to be free, isn't that it? "Feminist"? I think that's over with. Feminists say, "I'm a woman, so the man has to pay the bills," right? Well, the way things are going, you've got to divide things up. If you go out for a beer or to grab a bite to eat, you always have to split the bill. Money's really tight now, so that's the end of that old feminism business.

Yes, I've been involved with a women's group. I used to go to a meeting at another hill, until the night my husband didn't want me to go anymore. It was great, but they didn't get very far. It didn't last long. Less than a year. I liked it because what you do is a kind of mental hygiene: each one tells about her life, you know . . . what's going on at home. I started going toward the end, and they were talking about this business of nurseries and childcare centers, debating this and that, whether men should help their wives. It was great. I agree completely about how we ought to have equal rights, but now I don't go anymore; it's been a long time. Oh, I remember, it's called the "Women's Meeting," that's where they were talking about nurseries, and they asked if we had a neighborhood organization here, and I said we did have one but it stopped functioning because we don't have any funds to construct a headquarters.

If we'd had a nursery around here when my son was little, sure I'd have put him in it, because all the money I spent so he could go to that school, I could have invested in a savings account. He went to preschool when he was almost three. I had to put him in school, plus he was real mischievous. He used to go from 1:00 to 5:00 in the afternoon. At that time, almost five years ago, it didn't cost that much. Then it doubled, not counting his snack.

It was really hard to get him into the public school. He wasn't even going to study last year, because of his age. They give priority to kids who were six years old by February, but he was only going to be six in April, and that's the reason he wasn't going to be allowed to start school. Well, by chance, there's a department store on the square not far from here, down the hill, and I was with a friend, looking at some expensive toys in the windows—I love to window-shop. We'd just left this office where a girl had told me that unfortunately my son wasn't going to get into school. I said, "My God, we've struggled so hard to pay for a private school for him up to now, then we went after a scholarship and managed to get it for him, and now he's going to lose a year?" I was furious. So we were talking, and then we stopped at the department store and were looking in the window, and a lady was there also looking at the toys. I said, "Kids don't want to know about the cost, they just want the toy." She said, "I've got grandchildren, they only ask for expensive toys." I said, "Just to give you an example, Senhora, I've just been to the school office to enroll my son, I've just come from there and they told me my son can't go to school this year." She said, "But how old is he?" I said, "He's going to be six in April, but he would have had to be six before February." She said, "And he didn't get in?" Then she took a piece of paper and wrote on it and said, "Look, I'm a secretary in that office. Don't go there today, but on Monday you go and talk to her again, and tell her that I sent you." She wrote on the paper, and that's how he got in. My son started going to school. What a break! He started school, and if it hadn't been for her, he couldn't have started till this year. So he's a year ahead for his age, but not his thinking. He's going to be eight this April, and if he passes this year, he'll be in third grade next year. What a break!

4

REVOLUTIONARIES

Célia, a lively twenty-four-year-old White *carioca*, intense in both her laughter and her political commitments, interviewed me over several days in August 1981 before she was willing to discuss her life, and especially her politics, with me. Her caution was the result of her involvement in one of the leftist political groups that functioned clandestinely in military-ruled Brazil. Célia had broken with the group in late 1980. At that time Brazil was just beginning to come out of a fifteen-year period during which only two political parties could legally exist: the opposition MDB (Brazilian Democratic Movement) and the government party, Arena (Alliance for National Renovation). From the mid-1970s on, the MDB, after nearly a decade of largely ineffective existence owing to government repression, began to grow in strength and popularity. As Brazil's economic situation worsened, the MDB, despite government machinations, gained seats in the Brazilian Congress. In November 1979, the government's Party Reform Law attempted to splinter this growing opposition. The MDB reorganized as

14

the PMDB (Party of the MDB). Arena was reincarnated as the PDS (Social Democratic Party), and new political parties emerged. The Communist Party continued to be illegal (until 1985).[1]

Célia's political group, like the Communist Party and many of the other leftist groups that survived the violent government repression of the late 1960s and early 1970s, supported the PMDB as the best hope for Brazil's redemocratization, a view reinforced in the 1982 federal, state, and municipal elections and confirmed by the PMDB victory in the (still indirect) presidential election of 1985. In 1979, the *abertura*—the period of political "opening"—began with two events: a general amnesty (granted also to the military itself for prior crimes related to its political role), which freed political prisoners and allowed many exiled women and men to return to Brazil; and the easing of the censorship that had been in force since 1968, finally to disappear in 1982. But despite the climate of *abertura*, the national security doctrine espoused by successive military governments continued to thwart

C É L I A

the free exercise of political and civil rights through a series of laws enacted in its name.[2] This was the situation when I interviewed Célia in the summer of 1981.

━━━

I have a B.A. in journalism, and I'm now doing another one in sociology. I work as a researcher on a government program. For twenty-five hours a week I earn $130 [a month], so I have to find other work, too. I also do freelance journalism, for a publisher of women's magazines—I write for a dumb magazine, about things like haircare, varicose veins, beauty and love problems mainly. And short features. A woman writes in saying she's in love with a guy who won't have anything to do with her, so we write a story on that subject. It's a magazine for lower-class women, and it's read mostly by maids and people like that. I get paid by the piece: $20 per piece. I usually do one a week, which gives me an average of $80 a month. Then I also do research for a professor. That's how I spend my mornings—my schedule's divided between classes at the university and the research that I'm doing for a professor who's hired me to help him. That's usually for a particular project—there's one he's about to start that will pay me $100 for my part of the research over the next few months. I need an average income of about $250 a month total.

I'm an only child. My mother is forty-five years old. She's a secretary. We live together, she and I. My father is forty-nine. He used to be a lawyer, but now he doesn't work. He . . . my mother is separated from him, legally separated, and he got sick and stopped working. We own our apartment. I don't contribute to the expenses because I just don't earn enough. My money isn't enough, it barely covers my own expenses—clothing, eating out, personal expenses, installments I owe, things like that. So my money is very tight, and I generally ask my mother for money. Toward the end of the month, around the twentieth or the twenty-first, I'm usually out of money. She earns $400 a month—but that's for herself, too. I mean, we don't have to pay for housing, which in Rio counts for a lot because rents are really high. Since she doesn't have to pay any rent, that's already something. But she doesn't get any money from my father, either. So it's enough just for household expenses, and she always helps me a bit. She has a boyfriend, and he helps her out, too; so there's enough for a few more things.

I'd like to live on my own, but on $250 it's impossible. But I would like to. In fact I'm hoping that next year I can live alone or maybe, I don't know, get married or live with someone. I've been thinking that it would be better to actually live alone, before marrying or living with anyone. At the very least, it would be an important experience for me. But really, with an income of $250 it's impossible.

My father lives with a cousin of his. His father left him some real estate, and he lives on the rent from those houses. I don't get along with him and rarely see him. I was eight years old when they separated. I see him maybe three times a year, but now I haven't seen him for about seven months. We just don't get on well. He hasn't worked for ages, since about the time of the separation. He's a person who . . . he's an intellectual, you see, a man who reads a lot and all that, but he hasn't done anything with his life. I'm always in conflict with him over this. A very intelligent man—he used to teach law, too—but he doesn't produce anything and, after all, he could be productive. But because of his illness, he does nothing. I mean, he uses the illness in order not to do anything. So, I have a lot of conflicts with him on this issue. He's . . . he got kind of . . . mental illness, you see. He had problems at work, then he began to drink. He used to drink a lot, and then he had some sort of mental problems and was hospitalized and all that. Then after he got out he never worked again, never wanted to do anything. And he's not crazy. He's normal, but he uses the situation a lot. To this day, "No, I'm sick, I can't work." But the truth is, he's resigned himself. My grandfather left him something, and he resigned himself to living like this. He still drinks, but not much. He's a very intelligent man, and he knows a great deal, and he's let it all go.

When they separated, our life changed in every respect, including economically. My mother had never worked, so she had to completely remake her life. In fact she became much more of a woman after she separated from my father. She was someone who couldn't see a foot beyond her own nose. A rather alienated woman, totally ignorant. She'd gone to a Catholic boarding school her whole life, left the boarding school and married my father. So she knew nothing, absolutely nothing, about life. She was the sort of woman who lives strictly within the four walls of her house. She raised me, she took care of our domestic life, and nothing else. When she separated from my father she had to struggle, and when she began to work, to get out in the world, she changed a great deal—a great deal, radically. So today my mother is a woman who, for example, fully accepts that I sleep with my boyfriend, that I run my life as I please, that I sleep out. Whatever I want to do she accepts completely. And this, given her upbringing, is an incredible thing. Which means: after she began working, struggling to build her own life, she changed a great deal, changed for the better. She even seemed to get younger and prettier; she takes better care of herself today. She is a pretty woman, she cares about her appearance, she's concerned about enjoying things more. She is not politically active, but she's no longer an alienated woman.

In a sense she encouraged me to be more independent. Economically. She always encouraged me to work, to be responsible for my own life. But naturally there's another side to this, too, which is that she wants to keep me under her thumb in a way. Clip my wings. I mean . . . she's not bothered by my independence, but she has certain ways of getting me to stay at home more. She talks to me in a kind, affectionate tone. "Oh, stay with me," and so on. She's trying to seduce me, with kindness, to stay at home with her more. She likes that. I feel it's also a way of controlling me more. But she's really a good person.

I'm not at all religious. My family was Catholic, and my mother is very religious. I was confirmed . . . I mean, until I was about fourteen I was a Catholic; and then it all started, and today I'm not religious. As I grew up I began to read more, to think about things more, and to be active politically. . . . I still admire the Church, but I'm not a Catholic. I don't believe in God. It's mainly a result of my political position, you see. I'm a materialist, which means that the faith that I had . . . well, it was demystified. But obviously there's still some Christian morality in me. My entire religious education . . . my family is very religious, so all the religious background still exists, that Christian morality still inside me crops up to this day; but it's no more than that—an attitude in relation to life . . . sometimes I see that it's rather Christian.

There's a tremendous need for us to be politically active here in Brazil. For example, when I began to get interested in politics, in '75 or '76, there was nothing out there, just nothing. We were going through a really black phase. But at school we used to organize festivals, seminars, literary competitions, and I was getting involved with people who were already active politically. I had friends, older people, who'd gone through the whole political process of '68, '69, and they used to talk to me, so I slowly got involved. In '76 I worked on a campaign for a city councilman. That was the first real work I did politically. It was a great experience, and after that I began to be active in the student movement. From there I went on to work within the university, we began to organize academic centers, councils. I was on the board of the student council, and I got invited to things that way. Now I can see that when I really moved into politics, I wasn't really aware of how things stood. But as of last year a new phase in my life has begun. Today I think I have a more clearly formulated consciousness; I already know the role of the Left here in Brazil. And I see other things, I'm beginning to reformulate my own political position, as opposed to my earlier one. We had a very closed perspective, really radical, very leftist, and I've changed.

I still want to be in the struggle, but I was part of an organization that now seems to me very leftist, very radical, an illegal organization, and I got out of it at the end of last year. I left because I disagreed with the political line of the organization on certain points. . . . For example, all these organizations are for socialism, they're all socialists. But there's the problem of how to proceed, and that's essentially what I disagreed with. How to deal with the issues. So I thought it through, and today I'm not part of any organization. I'm going through a phase of analysis of all this. I still intend to fight in another organization, to be militant, but I don't want to join the way I did the first one, maybe because I was so young, without deep understanding. This time I want to join knowing, understanding their program, their practice, their line of action—I mean, in a different way, a more mature way. I'm no longer into that radicalism I had when I was younger. Now I see my position in relation to Brazil differently. We used to think it was a question of armed struggle, right away. Now I think that's impossible. Brazil is a country that's highly visible in the Americas, and it has an enormous military power, so it's just not possible. Now I think we have to start from democratic means, such as elections for governor, for president.

But even an organization that follows such a line has to go underground. For example, the Brazilian Communist party today follows a line that's . . . let's say, it doesn't reject armed struggle, but . . . it would be very difficult for such a thing to happen. So the Communist Party today in Brazil is proposing democratic means, and it's still an illegal party. To talk about communism, socialism, anything like that, is illegal. Well, just for the communists to want to participate in the political process is already an improvement. I now believe that we have to move toward democratic means and fight through elections. I think the opposition can win, legally. I'm a member of a legal party, the PMDB, and I think that through the PMDB we're going to succeed, and we can fight for the legalization of the Communist Party here in Brazil. This is one struggle we must continue with. There's no reason why a party should be illegal. So, I rethought my views— because I used to have a rather Stalinist outlook, but practice changed it. I really believe in freedom. In this practice you go to schools, to slums, to the street, to your neighborhood. . . .

The aim of our organization was to do propaganda work and raise the level of consciousness of the masses, draw the masses toward the revolution. I think that the organization, its principles, its direction, its objectives are correct. The people there are honest, they're sincere. We live in a country that—hell, it's still a dictatorship, strong. How can people be so blind, so blind to reality? We don't have the infrastructure, it's a different reality, we can't do here what they did in Cuba. Nobody has that perspective any more: "Guerrilla warfare worked in Cuba, so let's do it here." This is another reality. Cuba's a tiny country. Brazil is enormous; it's completely different. But I think that here in South America in general this problem is still very prevalent. This business of having Cuba on the brain, thinking that the same thing can be done here, it can't. In '68 there were a number of attempts; everybody died.[3] That's why I think . . . when I left the organization I said, "I'm not inclined to get into a leaky boat," and to me getting into a leaky boat doesn't mean being killed by the dictatorship. It means leading the people into a defeat, which is what I think the Left did in 1968. More than sixteen years of dictatorship . . . the people in wretched poverty. There is a difference, though— for example, the petty-bourgeois people, if we're arrested, if we're tortured, it's awful, but we can get a lawyer; we have mothers, we have fathers, who can send us out of the country. But the poor people, the masses, the workers, if they're arrested, the family dies of hunger.

So I don't think we should mess with this sort of thing. You can't throw the people into a confrontation without having the certainty that it's going to come out right. And the organization wanted to do exactly that, without any certainty. That's what I think it was, one step forward, two back. But now we're progressing little by little. There's no point rushing in and getting mowed right down. I think there's a process . . . which is slow, slow, it won't happen from one day to the next. Well, it was with all of this repression, repression within the organization, too, our personal lives, that I left. And since I left, for example, I see a hell of an advance on my part, also as a woman. . . . I'm working, I'm doing well in my work, I like what I'm doing; I've started seeing a terrific person, who wasn't in the organization, but in another one that I think is much more open. He doesn't live and breathe politics twenty-four hours a day. He's a musician, he's involved with the arts, he doesn't like repression and he doesn't cultivate it. Because in the organization I was part of, even the people who were into art were giving it up and doing politics twenty-four hours a day.

There were many problems with the organization I used to belong to. I think that a communist organization has to provide, as Lenin said, the model for a socialist society, the basis for a socialist society. For example, internal democracy. But in fact it wasn't like that at all. The organization was a mess internally; democracy didn't exist. The people who run these organizations all come from the petty bourgeoisie. The majority of them are intellectuals, and most of them are men. These men, not all of them, but the majority, they didn't talk with the women in the organization. I mean, I was a member, so was my boyfriend, and we never talked about the problems of the organization, you see? With *his woman* he wouldn't discuss politics. . . . At meetings everyone would talk, but outside of the meetings—for example, you live in the same house, your husband's a member of the group, too, you get home, but you're part of another little cell. I had a boyfriend who wasn't in the same cell I was in. He'd go to meetings at one place and I'd be at another, and we rarely . . . when we'd meet, we wouldn't discuss Brazilian problems. He never would with me.

And this didn't just happen to me. Everyone had this experience. All the women complain about it. I think the problem is this: most of them come from the bourgeoisie and . . . they still have that *machismo* buried deep inside. So, in fact, what happens is that the woman is there running errands, doing the tasks of the organizations; but that means that intellectually she's not doing much good. You can see this within the organization in that the main positions, the leadership, is nearly always masculine.

And something else I noticed that I think is a mistake. When a woman would become part of the leadership, she'd tend to be masculinized, especially within the student movement. This is a very interesting point. For example, I myself, I remember when I began to be in the leadership of the student council within my school. It's interesting how I would prepare myself: I'd put on blue jeans and sneakers, I'd wear masculine clothes and go off to give talks, and I began to berate myself for still being vain, for dressing like a woman. As soon as you'd have a group from the same organization, you'd see the women . . . most of them dressed like men, adopting the way of speaking that men have. They tended to become masculinized. Because in fact we could only see leadership in a man. I mean, because a woman, dressed like a woman, a woman! Speaking like a woman, feminine . . . you see? In fact, we underestimated people, we thought that if we arrived there looking like women, no one would listen to us . . . that only men could succeed. So the women had to transform themselves into men, in a sense, while the men didn't change.

And when I started seeing this, I began to rebel. It took me two years to work it through. I joined that organization in '77. You see, after '64, after the coup, there began to be splits and divisions in the Communist Party, and out of these came a whole series of organizations. The one I joined was created in the late '60s. I joined in '77, and when I began to notice the strangeness of it all I rebelled. I began to notice . . . interesting, the women were masculinized and when a girl would appear, a woman looking like a woman, dressed like a woman, attractive, the men would all chase after her. I thought, "Shit, I'm pretending to be a man just to have a place in the sun!" And I began to get very upset. I stopped going along, I thought we didn't have to become masculinized, we were women and we ought to take on our role of women, that we sure as hell weren't liberating ourselves, we were simply becoming men. It's the truth, it's incredible . . . that *manner*, even today I see it in the student movement, girls got up as men, with that manner that men have. . . . I don't like it. I'm vain, I like to dress well, to put on make-up, to go out. There wasn't even time for dates.

That was another thing I criticized in the group. We were like a closed little clique; we had sex only with people in the organization. For example, if I liked a man from another party, another organization, then for sure a problem would arise. And, in fact, my first abortion was because of a fellow, a union organizer, who was in the Communist Party. I met him, and we got to like one another, so we began to date. Within my group this caused chaos. "Célia? Célia's turning reformist!" They felt they had the right to criticize my personal life, even the other women. "What? You're seeing that fellow?" And he wasn't right-wing, not at all. He was a communist who had a different position from ours; he thought things should be done by one path, and we thought by another. I mean, he was a companion in the struggle for democracy. But the things they criticized me for! We'd talked about living together, he and I. It caused a scandal, and my relationship with him was really damaged. He was more mature, older; he was thirty, and he thought it ridiculous that I was leading that sort of life. On Fridays, Saturdays, Sundays, it was always meetings, distributing pamphlets, and so on. I didn't have any life of my own, personal, emotional, affective, and I hardly had time for him and he began to resent it: "Shit, you're my woman, we want to be together. I want to see you at least on weekends." He was a union organizer, and he used to say, "Célia, your position is wrong. This is doctrinalism." And meanwhile the others were interfering in my life: "You're dating that fellow, he's just a reformist—because the communists didn't want a revolution, just reform. They used to say, "She's dating a reformist" and God knows what else, and they'd attack me.

And when, for example, within the organization I would disagree politically with something, they'd attribute my critique, which I had formulated, to the fact that I was dating a reformist and a reformist was putting these things into my head. It was all getting very complicated, and I reached a point of revolt and was furious. It took a while . . . in the middle of 1979 I began with these critiques . . . how the organization was proceeding, carrying out its political struggle. At the beginning of '80 I started to date this fellow, and lots of problems came up. We even separated because our life was getting too chaotic. I would get up at five in the morning to go God knows where. And he was someone who had even more political responsibilities than I did, and he said, "I'm not giving up my personal life," while I was. He said, "As long as you won't grow up we can't stay together"—because I thought only about the organization, it was everything to me, my whole life.

But already at the end of '79 I was getting fed up; I began to be a woman again. I started to dress the way I like to dress, to use make-up. Then when I'd arrive—it was funny, I'd arrive at meetings, at other places, even at school, fixed up, looking nice, and everyone would start, "Eh, what kind of clothing is that? Eh?"—and on and on. "Eh, bourgeoisified." And, you see, I consider this all wrong, this vision of a communist as someone who has to be in rags; it's the wrong perspective. Just because you're there, you're supposed to live in a shack and dress in rags! At bottom the petty bourgeoisie's socialization is less rigid, you see? A communist's supposed to look like a ragamuffin, the women dressed just like men. . . . There was a lot of repression within the organization. But it wasn't discussed . . . too much resistance.

I remember one time I tried to bring it up. I said, "Look, I think that all of us here have personal problems that are interfering with our politics. I think we should discuss all these problems here, all the critiques we make of what's going on within the organization, the relationship of comrades, solidarity, friendship itself." Shit, there you are with someone at your side, who works with you, struggles with you, he's your companion, right? And I remember that an aide, someone who was orienting the group, turned to me and said, "No, this isn't an analytic session. We're not going to discuss that because this isn't analysis. Excuse me, possibly I didn't hear you right." You see, a hell of a resistance to discussing something that was interfering with our organization. We tried many times. You know the result? Lots of people left the organization, men and women. In my group, *all* the women left. In my cell there were ten people, four men and five other women. Even though they were in the minority, the men dominated, because the political aide, who came from the central council, was a man . . . though he was a great speaker and he tried to involve everyone.

So, I left not only because of political problems but for other reasons, this interference in my personal life. For example, if we planned to hold a meeting on Saturday, I'd say, "No, I want to go out with my boyfriend on Saturday night." And they, "Our comrade has some petty-bourgeois deviations." Shit! I wanted to go out with my boyfriend, and they'd start with this "petty-bourgeois" business! This is a very serious problem. And then, after I left, I felt as if I'd begun to breathe again, including professionally, because while I was in the organization I was getting nowhere with my professional life. Everything I did was oriented toward the group.

The organization had a line, actually a very good line, on women. There was a congress on women, a conference that turned out a document on the problem of women. If you read it, the whole thing, it looks like a very good document, theoretically. But in practice, you see, the organization wasn't very . . . there was no democratic practice within the organization, no democracy. In fact, women weren't dealt with, they didn't have any space. The men in the organization are totally in favor of the emancipation of women—on the "woman problem," the document is terrific. It's great for women, other women, but not in my house! That's precisely it, to this day. It's a very serious problem, the contradiction these communists are living in relation to women, extremely serious.

This fellow I've been seeing, he's a great person; his head's on straight. But he's also a communist and he has these problems, too. He's a person who turned to me, the last time we broke up, turned to me and said, "In my yard the rooster gives the orders." I was amazed. I said, "Look, in that case we'd better separate. I'm no hen" [*laughs*]. The rooster gives the orders! He actually said that. He said, "Either I give the orders or nobody does." What a contradiction! I know how it is, you're terrific on the situation of women, but not in my house, get it? No way. Well, we're in a process, he and I, we broke up and now we're trying to patch it up. Two weeks ago we broke up, and this last week . . . we're attached to one another, so we began to talk. Because the problem now is this. Someone else appeared in my life, so, "What? That's the end! Another man in your life!" And I haven't deceived him or anything. I think fidelity is very important. If I want to go to bed with someone, I'll go to him and say, "This is what I want to do." Well, I went to him and told him about the other person. And, well, the man was really wounded in his *machismo*. It's a very serious problem. I see that now. He says, "No, I'm not a *machão*"; but I see his behavior when confronting this for the first time.

Now *he's* already wanted to go to bed with other women, and I handled it a different way. But when I'm the one who wants to go to bed with another man, you see? Well, it was absurd. "You want to cuckold me, to give me horns." This, in his mind, his *machismo*. And he knows this other fellow and . . . it's interesting, something I learned only recently. He met this fellow in the street and treated him very badly. The fellow didn't understand it at all, and he came to talk to me. "Shit, what's going on. Did you tell him anything? I said, "Yes, I told him." He said, "Shit, the way he treated me . . . he almost knocked me down in the street." I thought this was ridiculous. He had nothing to do with it; I was the one who wanted to go to bed with him. It's *machismo*. I mean, this is a contradiction the communists have.

This man I'm sleeping with, Paulo, I see that despite everything he really does want to change—but it's very difficult for a Latino not to be macho; even the communists are. There are those you can see will never give it up and those who do want to change, and I think he wants to. Now I'm no longer interested in being massacred by a man, stepped on, squashed by an authoritarian son of a bitch—"Either I give the orders or nobody does!"—no, I'm not! I'd rather—in fact this is what I told him: "I'll give up this relationship with you, though it's something I care about." I'd rather be without him than with him in this kind of situation.

In the organization, people's household routines vary, but most of the men don't have time to do a thing. They've got meetings morning, noon, and night. It's usually the woman who does the work, even if she's got the same political job to do, and it's usually the woman who takes care of the children. There are some exceptions, some men who share the work. I have a friend, both she and her husband do political work and they share the housework. I see it for myself, I'm often with them, they really share it. One day one cleans the house, the next the other. One day one cooks, the next the other. But most of the men leave the housework to the women. It's interesting . . . this fellow who shares everything with his wife, we were in a group one day and she said to him, "Let's go, it's your turn to cook today." And he immediately got up and said, "Yeah, let's go"; and everybody said to him, "Stay, don't go." Then he said, "No, no. I really have to go, I've got to do the cooking today." And they all lit into him: "You numbskull! You idiot! Your wife tells you what to do, she pushes you around," the whole scene. Then we started to talk, she and I: "This is ridiculous. . . ." And the men said we had feminist paranoia: "Ah, you've got it, feminist paranoia." "It's not feminist paranoia, you're extremely *machista* that's all." You see, I'd never noticed that before, but I think this kind of joking around is serious. But they didn't get intimidated. He said, "No, I really do have to go now, it's only fair." Now this fellow I'm seeing, he's great in this respect. We spend a lot of time together; I'm at his house on weekends, and we always share the work. He doesn't mind doing it. In this respect he's great.

Most of the people in the organization are rotten in bed, mostly because of lack of experience. They do politics all day long, and they don't even have time to fuck. I remember something interesting, once when we were going to Brasília, to the Chamber of Deputies for a demonstration, and in my bus there were mostly women, and we began to talk, to joke, to discuss the men in the organization. "Oh, I've already made it with so-and-so"; "Me too." And in the end we arrived at a consensus that the men in the organization weren't worth shit as lovers. . . . Let me tell you something. When I . . . I almost never used to come when I slept with those fellows. They just didn't care. For example, the fellow I'm sleeping with now, Paulo, it's incredible how concerned he is about my coming, my pleasure. But they . . . it was like an escape valve for them. They'd do it, come, and it was all over. "I'm tired, have to get up early tomorrow," and I'd be really upset. Of course there are exceptions. An older man makes love a little differently. But those boys, from about twenty to twenty-eight, chaos . . . total chaos. And I remember, it's very funny, there were women who were after the men within the organization, and the men would say, "No, I don't have time." They didn't even have time to fuck! Isn't that ridiculous? But Paulo's not like that. He's great in that respect, he's very aware. We make love a lot. But I think in fact most of those people are very repressed. They're repressed even about finding a girlfriend. You see the difficulty they have in approaching a girl, so we'd have to go after them. The women were very good, they didn't waste time talking, but most of the men were awful, just awful . . . and it was that little clique. I mean, I'd gone to bed with a lot of people that my friend had also been to bed with, and another friend, too. It became a clique. You only went to bed with men in the organization, and the men in the organization only went with the women in the organization, so everybody knew about everything, constant gossip.

There was a phase when the organization was putting pressure on everybody to get married. They didn't say so explicitly, but between the lines you could see it, because they thought that things would be easier if people were married. Dating was difficult, but if you lived with someone things would be easier. In fact, we had a friend whose boyfriend said, "Let's get married," so they did. Fine, once they were married, she began to be more demanding. Naturally, hell, he was her husband, of course she'd demand more. She expected him to be more involved at home—she got pregnant—to be more involved with the child they were going to have, and at home. Fine. This created such a conflict between the two of them that they separated even before the baby was born. In other words, in fact, marriage was no solution. Quite the opposite: it would only intensify this contradiction. I remember that at one point everybody made fun of the organization and said that its new objective, its new political position, was that everyone should get married. Between the lines this was what was happening; they thought marriage would make things easier.

Well, lots of people left politics altogether. They freaked out—they got their asses out of there and kind of went crazy, got into smoking pot and other things that have nothing to do with politics. They gave up the struggle. I think that this collective freaking out isn't the fault of the individuals. It's the fault of the Left movement as a whole, which is so chaotic that people go off in every direction. Now another large segment is continuing with independent politics, I mean, they're not tied to any clandestine group—like right now I'm not tied to a group, but I'm still in politics—and other people went into other parties, especially the Communist Party, which I think is a real alternative. It's the best of the lot; the other organizations are much worse. The Communist Party has, aside from a tradition of almost sixty years, it has a kind of maturity, it sees things in a different way. They're more cautious, they don't have this adventurism. They're not adventurers, they're more serious. They've got an organization that's much more solid, without a doubt, although they have a lot of internal confusion, too, because of political divergences, because of Eurocommunism. I don't think they expect things to change overnight politically. They realize it's a slow process. It's a great party despite the divergences, the problems.

The other day I was at a meeting—have you heard of Gregório Bezerra?[4] He's an old communist from Pernambuco. He was one of the people who was tortured a lot. I just love him. He's in the Party, and he was speaking about . . . about youth. He was talking to us, to the young people, about the importance of comradeship, of being a friend, solidarity. About our being . . . for example, if there's another militant with you and you call him a traitor, it happens a lot in Left organizations. Because he doesn't agree with your line he's a traitor. Well, he was saying that this is absurd, that this only strengthens fascism, the Right, the dictatorship. He was really emphasizing the importance of love itself, of comradeship, of . . . you and your comrade, your lover, your boyfriend. And I was watching and thinking about this and how I had tried to say that sort of thing, too.

I think it's basically a matter of experience in life. In the Communist Party there are lots of people who have a lot of experience. And in the other organizations the people are young, most of them. From '68 to now so many people left that now, for example, the leadership of these organizations doesn't have the experience that Gregório Bezerra has, or Prestes,[5] or the older people. I think this plays a part, too. Also, in the more radical organizations there are some workers, but most of the people come from the petty bourgeoisie. The great majority come out of the universities. Now in the Communist Party there are many more workers. I'm thinking about joining the Party, but I still have some doubts.

No, there's no underground organization of women only, not even one in which women predominate, but the number of women in the organizations is enormous, really enormous, It's amazing how many militant women there are now, but rarely in a position of leadership. There are some women's groups that are jokes. For example, there's a feminist group, fighting for democracy and so on, but their real problem is the orgasm; they're much more interested in sexuality than . . . but they're almost against men. And some seem more like male women. We were involved in a congress of women in which they took part, all kinds of women's groups took part. It was last year, a women's congress here in Rio. It was incredible, about three thousand women. It was on March 8, International Women's Day.[6] The congress set out all the lines in the women's movement. Childcare. Equal salaries. The whole thing. And this group participated, too. I know they created a scene, they said we all had cock on the brain. All because the husbands of the women who went formed a men's group to discuss the "woman problem," which I think is very positive, and at the end, in the plenary, they wanted to state how they saw the woman problem. I mean, it was really something—the childcare center, for example, which was set up to care for the children of the women who were attending, and the men ran it, and they prepared food for the women, you see. Then the men tried to speak, about how they saw the situation of women; and this group of women got into such a state, they said these men shouldn't speak, that this was for women only and the men shouldn't be there and couldn't speak. Some of us insisted. I said that the men should speak, and they answered that we had cock on the brain [laughs]. "Cock on the brain," that we thought only about men. And lots of fights broke out at this congress, but finally the men spoke, and they had a very good position.

There were many workers there, too, women workers, but they said, "Look, my struggle is together with my man. My struggle is with him, not apart from him. . . . In my house there's no water, no electricity, nothing. We've got to fight together with the men." I think that the liberation of women can only occur through a democratic process. You have to have basic conditions, urbanization. And yet some women only wanted to talk about orgasms. Of course that's important, too, I don't deny it, but we can't dwell on this problem while we have so many others.

I ' V E   H A D two abortions, one in 1980 and one earlier this year. They were difficult. I'm not against abortion, but I'm also not for it. I think you have to create the conditions so that people can have children. Here in Rio, for example, there are thousands of abortions a year, lots of abortions. I'm not against abortion . . . but . . . it's difficult, you see? Objectively I couldn't have those children, and I didn't want them. I stopped taking the pill for several reasons, and I got pregnant. The doctor said that I'm very fertile, because I didn't have sex during my fertile phase and I got pregnant anyway. It was . . . very difficult. I don't want to have any more abortions. This second one, I had to go on a trip just when I found out that I was pregnant. I was alone, without Paulo, and felt all mixed up, and after the abortion I had complications, I was hemorrhaging, I even thought I was going to die. It wasn't the doctor's fault, he was good. It cost $150 for a good abortion, carefully done; by now it must be more. The doctor was very good, but afterward I didn't rest, I went to a party and ended up with an incredible hemorrhage. It was difficult . . . I didn't . . . it's that sensation of having a child inside of you, it's something that touches you a lot. I was two months pregnant each time. Two months. So I felt . . . I was very . . . I felt really bad, and so did he. It was the first time anybody'd had an abortion because of him, so both of us went a bit crazy. But I still have some time left. I'd like to have a child when I'm about twenty-nine, thirty, thirty-one. Within about five years. I mean, I'll try to stabilize my life. . . .

I never told my mother about the abortions. Not because she's against it, but she would have been very worried. She knows I have sex, she knows everything. But the abortion, I didn't have the courage to tell her because I thought it would make her suffer. His mother knew, and she gave us a lot of support. But she's totally different; she's a psychologist and she understands things better. But my mother would have been too worried, and we were going through a difficult phase at home because my uncle had died, and I thought, "Not this, too, just now; she'll be very upset," so I decided not to tell her. But she's suspicious. I'll tell her later.

THE   IDEAL   LIFE   FOR   ME? Well, in general, ten years from now, I want . . . we would have had a revolution in this country, and as a result we would have a more stable life, the type of revolution that manages to get to a democratic stage. We should have managed to control poverty, managed to have a better country, with a better division of income, and so on. And personally . . . I would want to have a stable profession and be doing well in my profession. I would want to have a companion, to have a child, though I could face the life of a single woman. What I think is incredible is that women are marginalized for living alone.

But I'd like to have a companion and a child. We would both work, and share all the household chores. I can't imagine . . . I don't want to be rich, not at all, just average. In my own house, sharing the work with my husband. I think I would be happy that way. With a child. And a daycare center the child could go to. I think that's the kind of life I'd like to have. And being active politically. When I finish my degree in sociology I'd like to go on working as a researcher, with a regular researcher's salary. Currently it's about $800 a month, it ranges from $600 to $800. It's a good salary. That's my best prospect, to find a place as a researcher.

I think everyone needs to produce, to work, to do something, to be productive in one way or another. My boyfriend, for example, he's a musician. It's a very difficult field to get into. Well, I think that if I find a good job, if I work full-time and earn $800, I would be able to . . . we could live together, he and I. We've even talked about this. It would be enough for us to live on. Because he earns very little—he plays and gives guitar lessons. But, I mean, I wouldn't want him just to stay at home giving guitar lessons, not doing anything else, no. I think he has to struggle to make it in his profession, you see, he has to find places to play and throw himself into his work. I wouldn't like it otherwise. . . .

It must also be the example of my father, who is someone who hasn't done anything, and this disturbs me a great deal. Everyone has to produce something. If you like to paint, if you're an artist and like to paint, you've got to go and paint. Housework is a kind of production, but then again it's not. . . . I don't think it fulfills you, it doesn't satisfy you. For example, at home, when I do things, clean, cook, this doesn't fulfill me, and I think it's difficult for a person to be fulfilled by that kind of work. You have to try to be productive. Housework . . . it can't have first priority in your life. It's a part of your life, of course, but it's secondary. There are many more important things for you to do, to get into. I wouldn't like a man to stay at home doing just those things.

I'm in a very good phase of my life just now, because I realized what my political difficulties were about, the difficulties in the organization, and I managed to free myself in that sense. I was afraid to leave the organization, as if it were . . . as if that alone was my life, as if my life was the organization. So just freeing myself from that, well, it was a real trip for me. I managed to see the mistakes that exist within the Left, and yet that didn't turn me into a fascist or any such thing. I think I'm a communist and . . . now . . . well, that was tremendously important for me, and it set off this entire process. I mean, my process of finding a job, struggling to get a full-time position, all this. Going back to school to study sociology was a good thing, too.

Something else that gave me a great deal of strength was the break-up with Paulo this last time. I ended it because . . . without feeling insecure, you see . . . because of what he was doing . . . I wasn't paralyzed thinking it would be worse to be alone. I had the strength to separate from him. I prefer to be without him if. . . . This fortified me, too. Yes, I think I'm in a good phase, I'm growing. I think I'm maturing, I feel that I'm a woman now, and this whole business with Paulo fortified me. I feel that I'm very much a woman, and it was good for him to become aware of this, too, and to see his own mistakes as a man. That business of, "If I don't give the orders nobody does," "In my yard it's the cock who crows"— he's doing a self-criticism of all this, too.

So it's been good for me. I saw that I have the courage to do this; it wasn't negative, quite the contrary. To do what I want to do is very positive, it will always strengthen me. That's why I think I'm in a good phase: I'm standing up for myself. It's good to feel that I'm a woman, capable, struggling. I no longer feel that I have to stay nice and quiet, no. I've done things that have surprised even me, you see. For example, in relation to men, this fellow who came into my life, Carlos, there he was all uncertain and I, I simply backed him against the wall, as a woman. He was in this state of . . . won't fuck and won't get off. And I just pushed him to the wall and said, "Look, it's like this, either we fuck or I don't want to see you" [laughs]. And he turned to me—just to show you what men are like; it was really impressive, he was shocked because I'd come right out and said what I thought. I said to him, "Look, stop this business of grabbing me, I used to like little kisses when I was an adolescent. What I want now is to come, to fuck, to feel good, and I'm attracted to you, I want to go to bed with you." He turned to me and said, really shocked, he said, "You're very liberated [laughs]. I said, "Sure I'm liberated, because I'm speaking the truth," you see? I no longer have that fear of . . . I mean, we underestimate ourselves, we're afraid of going after a man, and I really am liberating myself in that respect, because I will press on and if it doesn't work out, all right. Now I press on.

With Paulo also. He says, "You're awful." I come right out and push him to the wall, and I say it's either like this or else it's not, and let's discuss it, let's see. I think that even my relationships with people are getting better because nowadays I have more confidence, I'm no longer underestimating myself, or moaning and feeling sorry for myself. I'm in the struggle and it's great, it gives me strength. You feel on top of things, in control. Now this business of Carlos saying I'm very liberated, it was really funny. Liberated? You're wild! What I thought was, "So what am I? Am I liberated or wild? Tell the truth." And I thought, "I really did want to. Why should I stay hiding, why make a fuss?" It's the same thing now, I no longer want him. Yesterday we met and he grabbed me and I said, "You can stop. I'm not interested anymore. You know that I love Paulo; our relationship was very clear." And he got scared. That's what I think is funny, because when a woman takes this position, looks at life squarely, the man gets afraid. When I underestimate myself, Paulo immediately takes over and does whatever he likes, goes after other girls, and so on. But when I take the position I'm now taking, he feels desperate, tormented, perturbed. "But Célia, you're awful!" "But I'm awful precisely because I'm taking a position as a woman. Because you like it when my position is that of a child, naturally you like it, right? Now it's hard on you to have to see me as a woman." But it's fun. It's a whole new situation.

Madalena, a woman in her early thirties, was introduced to me by friends in Rio de Janeiro who were feminists and political activists. At our first meeting, we got into a lively discussion of anarchism, a new direction for Madalena, in marked contrast, as she pointed out, to her eight years of disciplined participation in the clandestine Brazilian Communist Party (PCB), which did not acquire legal status until 1985.[1] Perhaps owing to the intercession of our mutual friends, Madalena readily agreed to meet with me on another day to talk about her life as a member of the PCB and as a lesbian.

In the summer of 1983, when I interviewed Madalena, Brazil was at the height of a recession. Even upper-middle-class people suddenly found themselves without employment, and Rio's main avenues teemed with street vendors in far greater numbers than before, a constant focus of media attention. Although she had university degrees in both political science and communications, Madalena had held only temporary and part-time jobs since her graduation. In the climate of deepening economic crisis, once again without any employment, she found herself obliged to move back into the home of her parents, long since retired from their civil service jobs as chauffeur and typist and living on pensions of $150 a month each.

———

Our family history is rather murky. My father and grandfather used to have some land in this state, but they lost it all, drinking—its a complicated story. Judging by what my father has told me, his childhood was really agitated. And so was my mother's life.

My [maternal] grandmother was Black. She worked doing laundry, and she had lots of children, two girls and three boys. I never knew my grandmother; she died when my mother was pregnant with me. My grandfather, my mother's father, I did know. Yes, he was White. He was a kind of "colonel" in his city—this was in the state of Minas Gerais—one of those landholding "colonels." There used to be lots of those in the interior of Minas, men who had a certain political influence in the area—they're called "colonels." But

MADALENA

I didn't know him as my mother's father, you see. I was aware of some kind of cover-up of their situation, of his being recognized as my grandfather. He was treated like a family acquaintance. He used to come to our house—he lived in Minas, but when he'd come to Rio he'd visit our house. I can't tell you much about my father's family, I don't know if there's some [racial] mixing there, too. My mother is *morena* [brown-skinned], like me, what we call creole. No, I've never experienced any racial prejudice at all. Frankly, I've never felt anything of that kind. At school most of the kids were about my color, or maybe just a bit whiter, so there wasn't much of a difference between us. I've never been in a country where the White race is in the majority, or where this kind of problem might exist; but here in Rio, and in the parts of the country I've visited, as far north as Bahia, I was never aware of this. I don't really know what to call myself in terms of race. On my birth certificate it says *parda* [Brown]. I've never thought of definitions, but I think that at this point, I'm not sure, I feel kind of like the predominant cultural influence in my life maybe is Black. I wasn't aware of it as a child, but that's probably what I'd say today.

My father finished secondary school. My mother started attending a normal school [for training elementary-school teachers], but she wasn't able to finish. I'm the third child in my family, the only one who's single, who doesn't have children. I have two sisters and a brother. I mean, parenthetically, I consider them my siblings, but my oldest sister and my younger brother are adopted. As far as I know—and again, our family history is rather veiled—it's interesting, it was never stated directly or explicitly, this situation of their being adopted. My aunt who was single, my mother's sister, liked kids a lot and she took [a child] to raise, and then when she died the girl stayed with my mother. Now the boy, that happened like this. My father was working in Copacabana, he used to take care of an elderly man, and one day—I remember this from stories I heard at the time—the boy was being taken around from door to door. He wasn't from Rio, as I recall, he was from the Northeast, and he was being offered house to house, and my father suddenly came home with this child. My mother felt sorry for him, too, and then there was some discussion about it, whether, he should stay or not. In the end they decided to keep him. They officially adopted him—he has the same name as I do—the whole process of legal adoption, not just raising him in our house.

I was born here in Rio. When I was about two my mother got this job in the civil service. My father was working very far away, at the house of this man, and he'd come home on weekends. During the week, maids used to take care of us. They were girls who'd been raised in my mother's house in Minas, and they used to come here to Rio, to take care of us and the house. There was a constant turnover, some would stay a year or two, some six months or three, and then they'd move on. A few of them had their own children. And that's how we were brought up. My mother would leave the house very early and get home late, and we'd stay with the maid all day long. I was a really active child and it was very hard for me to stay with the maid. I never really accepted my mother's absence.

Our standard of living, it wasn't totally poor. We had a house; we had food, clothing; we went to school. But my mother wanted to move closer in, and that's what they did. And finally they managed to buy this house they've been living in now for over twenty years. We always lived in houses, large houses, with a yard, with trees. I had a good relationship with other kids, I used to play games with them in the street, always the same group—people I get together with once in a while even today.

My mother was about forty-five or forty-six when she had me, and she was a person from the interior, from that very traditional way of life in Minas. I was brought up as a Catholic, always going to church, going to Mass, the whole business. But I think that I was happy as a child, except that today I don't much like my childhood, it seems so sad. I never had anything resembling an open relationship with my mother and father, I never had that. Perhaps even because of their age, and my mother's difficulty in relating to people. But we didn't lack affection, and I was very attached emotionally to both my father and my mother. My mother's a very strong woman, very active. In her town in Minas she loved to go out, to parties, to those regional things they had there, their folklore. And she used to work there as a secretary for the town newspaper, she took part in political campaigns, all that. When we were kids, she always liked to take us out. We used to go to the beach on weekends. My father's a quiet type, very much a homebody, too much even; but he'd go to the beach, too. One of my good memories is of those outings to the beach.

But I think I had problems as a child. Like in the morning when my mother had to leave for work, it was hard on me. As I recall, I was the only one of us to react that way. I wanted to go with her, I didn't want to stay home, I didn't like to stay with the maid. My first year of primary school, in '57, was a disaster because I'd play hooky and hang out in the street. I remember that, for about two months before the end of the school year, I constantly played hooky; I'd disappear and wouldn't even send an excuse. My sister covered up for me, too, but in the end they talked to my mother and I got a spanking. I had to repeat that grade, the first grade. My mother couldn't control what time I got home, and the maid wasn't paying much attention to me, so that's the way it was. I just wasn't involved in school. Then my mother started to keep more of an eye on me, to get after me, and I did well in school that year. I managed to adapt to some extent. Everything worked out, and I didn't have any more problems at school. But I didn't get to like it much until I was in middle school, in the fifth grade. Then I had friends; I was already an adolescent, eleven, twelve years old. But primary school [grades one through four] was a nightmare, a real disaster [*laughs*]!

No, the kids at school weren't from all social levels. In the public schools there were always mostly poorer kids. Public schools here in Brazil were always for poor kids, so there was a certain leveling, a certain homogeneity in their social composition. I never really had any problem with school; I always liked to read, comics, newspapers. I used to listen to music, news, politics, all the time on the radio—we didn't get a television till much later. My father was a *getulista* [supporter of Getúlio Vargas]. There were always magazines around, my mother always encouraged me to read. We had lots of books in the house, they would buy books.

My mother never had to pay for my schooling. I always went to public schools, for secondary school and university, too. In college, I attended two faculties [schools or departments]. I did political science at one university and communications at another. What happened was this. I took the *vestibular* [university admission examination][2] in 1970, and in '71 I began college. I wanted to study journalism, so I went into communications. About the time I started, in '71, it was a period of great repression. In fact the student movement was already at a low point, nothing going on in the schools. What did exist was a Left underground, with people who had a certain level of militancy. They were at school, too, but it was all rather hidden, and the atmosphere was really bad, even just in terms of learning. I felt something was missing, and suddenly I began to think that wasn't quite what I wanted to do. I was very concerned about social and political problems, so I said. "Well, I need a better foundation, I want to study political science."

I used to work mornings, office work. That was my first job, starting in '72, and I stayed there for just one year. I practically ran the office: answered mail, organized the work, things like that. And then in '73 I started studying political science. I had to take the *vestibular* again, because I wanted to go to another university. I could have just asked to be transferred, but it's a whole bureaucratic process and you never get it without having some connections. Things here in Brazil are done a lot on the basis of who you know—you find someone you can appeal to, who can run interference for you; but that would have taken quite a while, so I preferred to take the *vestibular* again. I passed, and I attended both faculties at once.

The great problem of the student movement here was funds, the struggle for more funds, for more places in the public schools, trying to make the state provide a larger number of vacancies. Throughout this whole period Brazil was beginning to modernize and the middle class started to go to university a lot more, so there was an enormous flood of people wanting to get into university, wanting degrees, higher education; and the competition [in the *vestibular*] was tremendous. It's like a marathon: the exams are given in Maracanã [a Rio soccer stadium with a seating capacity of two hundred thousand], and there are something like ninety thousand candidates. At that time, this was an extremely serious problem, the tiny number of vacancies for all those candidates. In that sense there's equality: everybody has to take the *vestibular*; without it you can't get in. Money doesn't help. But what does help is this: if you go to a good school, you already have an infrastructure, a base from which to deal with the *vestibular*. I took a *prévestibular*, a course that lasted for one year, after I graduated from high school. The exams were so hard because everybody wanted to go to the federal universities, which are maintained by the federal government, or to the state universities. The teaching was better in the federal universities, the best professors were there. You take the *vestibular*, and you write down your first choice, second, and so on, and then you're classified. If you do well, you get into this one; if not, you may end up being classified for a private university and, if you've got the money for it, fine. Otherwise. . . . It's not so much that there's more money for education today, there isn't. But there are more vacancies because the number of private schools, private faculties, has also increased, and they take part in the *vestibular*, too. But everyone has to take the test to get in.

What happened in the universities was this. Until 1968 lots of people stayed in the universities; there wasn't a general exodus after '64, only of people who were really activists, but not just because they were Marxists or had a progressive position, no. But in '68, the movement really took off, it became a great middle-class movement. There were enormous demonstrations, and intellectuals participated, too; and then, yes, there was a real crackdown. That was the period most closely associated with the Right, the Médici period; this was on top of the crisis with Costa e Silva.[3] All these professors were in essence retired by the school, by means of a decree-law.[4] Some of them have recently come back into the university, but earlier they were forced off the faculty, out of the professorial ranks in Brazilian universities. At the University of São Paulo a great many had to leave, and those who replaced them had no experience, or were people who out of fear had no political involvement. So there was this problem of the draining of the universities. And then I decided to try political science, because what we were doing in communications was entirely theoretical—you studied linguistics, structuralism, who knows what else, and I came to the conclusion that this wasn't what I wanted, although I did have some good professors. There was even one in our faculty who was arrested. He was politically active, and he was picked up and held for several months. We had no classes during that time. Then they released him, and there was a trial. He was acquitted. He went back to teaching, and then later he was fired. He took part in a strike at the university and, in the end, they managed to fire him.

Anyway, back in '71 there was this terrible fear at school, this emptiness. You couldn't have discussions, police agents were all around, you had to deal with that atmosphere. You had colleagues, you couldn't be sure whether they were agents or not. Everybody knew that there were professors who were informers, although there wasn't even much to inform about—the repression was so great that not much was going on within the universities in '70, '71, '73. And it was in that atmosphere, that emptiness, that I decided to study political science. I wanted . . . some way to resist. I knew people who were militants, who were aware of what was going on. The great exodus of professors had taken place in '68. By the time I started, there were good professors already, but intellectually nothing was happening, no discussion of the country's situation, of problems. You'd go to school and that was it. There was a period called *desbunde*, a kind of collective freaking out. *Desbunde* was a term invented to describe that atmosphere, that lack of confidence, apathy. That's when the hippie movement began. After '68, people couldn't see any way to really participate. Also because the academic [student] councils [within each faculty], which were our means of participating, with film clubs and other activities, all these fundamental levels of organization were cut off in '68. Right after the great demonstrations, the academic councils and student centers were shut down. Many people were arrested, many others went underground, still others went into exile.

At that time I was in secondary school, and I wasn't really politically active. I did things like being class representative and, in '67, '68, I took part in some demonstrations. In '68, toward the end of our school year [March through November], we'd go downtown to protest, and there was tear gas. The cavalry would come after us. That sort of thing. But it was good to participate. In '68 we went on strike, over repression in the school, things that weren't allowed, like short skirts and boys wearing their hair long. And some of the people who were active in all this went on to become more involved politically, and some of them were killed afterward.

Well, things quieted down at school, this was in secondary school, and my involvement was mostly limited to that. In terms of what was happening in the city, it was mainly university students who led the movement, and we secondary-school students followed along and supported them. But I wasn't more involved than that, I had no ties with any group in particular, just a general position of protest against repression on various levels. As far as authoritarian teachers were concerned, I didn't question that so much when I was in secondary school; but when I went to university, in that vacant atmosphere, then I began to be bothered by it, and by the general apathy. I had some friends who were studying history, and we used to talk about the kidnappings, the actions that leftist groups were engaged in, and in some way that fascinated me. But I already had a position about guerrilla actions, and kidnapping seemed a rather remote business. At first I supported it, because it was a form of resistance, it was a struggle, but it wasn't very clear in my mind in terms of definitions, of political positions. I knew they were on the Left, I knew about Ché, we used to read Ché Guevara, but at the university there was that emptiness—we'd go to classes, go for a drink, talk, go to the movies, that was it.

The student centers that had been shut down used to be autonomous, outside the structure of the university. The students ran their own elections. After '68, when the [Brazilian] Constitution was changed and the Institutional Acts[5] were imposed, all forms of student organization were taken over. When I started at the university, I knew the political science program was one of the best. There were a few Marxists to study with. At some of the other universities, by contrast, even if you studied philosophy you never talked about Marxism. You could study history but never hear Marx mentioned. But at my university, the atmosphere was different, even if controlled. Student councils still functioned, there was a DCE [Diretório Central dos Estudantes—Central Student Council—at the university level], and there were some groups, for example MR-8 [Movimento Revolucionário de 8 de Outubro—Revolutionary Movement of the 8th of October], in homage to Ché, that's the day he died. In '73 there was still a student movement, something was left, but repression had put an end to most of it. By '72, the leadership and lots of the people in MR-8 were all in exile. The kidnappings had stopped, bank holdups were rare, though there were some.[6]

But there were things we had no idea about—the campaign in Araguaia,[7] the PC do B [Communist Party of Brazil], the Maoist line—it was all censored. But at the university there were still student centers, and I began to take part in that. It was all very primitive. In order to put up a poster, to hold a meeting, you had to submit a memo in advance and wait, and sometimes you wouldn't get permission. To hold a conference you had to submit the curriculum vitae of each speaker. It was an enormous struggle. There were all sorts of obstacles to doing the slightest thing. And there was that fear. A friend of mine was picked up and held by the security police for a week. Then she was released. You couldn't be sure of anything. Some guys you knew really were with the police, but there were others you didn't know about. A terrible atmosphere. You'd do one thing here, another there, try to resist in some way.

Until, in about '73, things began to get clearer in my head. At school there were some people more to the Left, whose position was that we shouldn't

participate in that university structure since it was impossible to really do anything. So they created a parallel structure, which was very difficult. And then this
discussion arose, that whoever had the perception that we shouldn't take part in
those student councils, was more to the Left. But the people in the Brazilian
Communist Party [PCB] disagreed. They thought one had to be active even in this
very restricted environment, that this participation was worthwhile. And that's
how I got to know a few people and actually became involved in something more
organized. And at the end of '73 or early '74, I joined the Party. I was in a group
made up just of students at school.

The Party structure was roughly this. If you were a student, you had to
function within your university. They weren't like some other groups on the Left,
where you might even have been a student and suddenly you'd be sent to work
in a factory. No, if I worked, if I was already in a factory, probably my activities
would remain there. But I was linked to the university structure, and our nucleus
was in the university. We'd discuss politics, what we could do within the university; we'd put on shows, raise money for the student council—we got no funds, so
we had to raise money for everything we needed: paper, a stapler, a Ping-Pong
table, posters. And my work was strictly within the university. Mostly we discussed the political situation within the university.

The movement was very small, there weren't many people. In my faculty, for
example, which had nearly a thousand students, there were five or six people in
the Party. At that time, with that fear, who would want to become an activist?
People were still being arrested. Concretely, it was part of our daily life. Some of
them weren't even enrolled in the university, they just worked there. Others
because in one way or another they took part in some organization, or were
active in the student councils. In '73 one of the student leaders and his wife were
both arrested and tortured. We went on strike, and all the councils were closed
down once again. But we took a stand. We sent a letter denouncing the arrest of
our colleague. We went to the rector of the university, asking him to intercede
on behalf of our colleague, that after all he was part of the university. And the
university suspended all our activities for nine months; they sealed our offices, we
couldn't even get in. We had a mimeograph, sound equipment, everything that
belonged to us, material, tables, it was all confiscated. In '73, '74, '75, all this was still
a period of heavy repression. You still couldn't be sure of the people you were
talking to.

My own fears? Look, at that time I'd made my choice. I believed in socialism, I
believed you had to fight back in some way, and . . . that was the form that was
available to me. When I started at the university in '73, I got to know people who
thought more or less the same way, and we'd organize seminars, work together,

go to the movies, talk. It was a school that, to this day I say it was like an island, possibly even unique in all of Brazil at that time. When this fellow was arrested, we tried to do something, to organize a meeting of students from the different faculties. We'd get together and exchange ideas, and I became friendly with these people. And by that time, I'd already opted for socialism; I thought we had to struggle against the dictatorship, that we could do it. And since we were students together and were able to, we started a seminar, study groups that we ran ourselves, where we studied Marxism. That was our activism, the people in the Party.

That's how it happened, from one friend to another. You'd get to know people somewhat, you'd talk about life. I even ran into some people I'd known in secondary school, and we got to be friends, to discover affinities—we thought alike, we felt we had to be in the struggle. And suddenly you'd discover Marxism, that in order to understand our reality better you had to study Marxism. So I joined some Marxist study groups and then, from talking to me, people could feel that I was more inclined to it. And finally one day someone came up to me and said, "Look, I'm in the Party, the Brazilian Communist Party. These are our politics," and you'd get their statutes to read, and their program, their last resolutions, explaining what their line was. By that time I already knew all the lines at school, who was who, who was in agreement with which organization. Some were *foquistas*, some followed Ché, some were Maoists, others were Trotskyites, others were Stalinists. And in fact, through your experience with these people, through friendship, the work you did together at school, you got to respect these people—people confronting all these difficulties, working, studying. And then this person came to me and laid it out, "I'm in the Party, and these are our politics."

At that time, at school, there was a cell. In general they followed the resolution of the Sixth Party Congress [December 1967]; it was a time of crisis. They've gone beyond that line now, but it set out the following: at that moment, resistance was necessary. The regime was characterized as fascist, a fascist military dictatorship, and you had to fight against it. The line was that in that situation you had to form an alliance with the bourgeoisie, with liberals—you had a natural alliance with the national bourgeoisie. A distinction had to be drawn between international capital and national capital, and under the circumstances it was justified to form an alliance with some sectors of the national bourgeoisie who were opposed to the dictatorship. You had to be active at the level of the middle class, too. And the Party had also managed, even after '64, to be active within the labor movement. It wasn't much, but it was strongest in São Paulo. The Party hadn't been broken during the repression, unlike the other groups that had gotten more directly into the struggle, kidnapping ambassadors, holding up banks, rural and urban guerrillas. No, the Party didn't have such a policy. It was oriented toward the masses, and it had a more general policy.

At first I didn't really know the Party line. I knew that the Party basically didn't go in for kidnappings, it had a different line from the other groups; it wasn't a revolution-here-and-now line, creating guerrilla *focos*, that wasn't it. I first heard about this through an analysis that was being done at school, and overall I agreed with the line of the Sixth Party Congress that the revolution ought to be bourgeois and democratic. But at that time there were already important people within the Party itself who opposed this line, who said it was all wrong. And I heard about that, too. I thought it was all rather strange, but in a general way I accepted the Party based on people's behavior, their practice, which I thought for sure was correct. That was why I joined the Party.

As militants we used to have meetings outside the university, to discuss university problems, problems relating specifically to the Party as a political party, problems of repression, of maintaining a structure, of colleagues in hiding—you had to help these people, we would provide money, that kind of contribution, and maintain a more organic link that could function. And we studied Marxism more profoundly, but it was no longer that level of study we did at school, in the study group. We organized other study groups, with other people, of Marxism, of economics. The teachers were great. In the economics group they were Marxists, and we would study and try to build a more organic link. This was in '75. At that time most of the national Party leaders were still in Brazil, but everybody was in hiding, the central commitee, the state and city committees, all in hiding. And we were also active in the MDB party [Movimento Democrático Brasileiro, the only legally existing party at the time besides Arena, the government party]. We supported the MDB, we campaigned. In '74 we took part in the MDB campaign for deputies. Some of them were communists, in the Party, others weren't. In the '74 campaign we had close ties with people who already had a more progressive vision. We used to discuss all this; it was a vital part of our work, our relations with other groups, the elections, how we would campaign and for whom, all of that.

And then, early in '75, the Party suffered a great defeat. Some of the Party leaders were arrested, some were killed. After that the Party suffered enormously on the national level. A very important figure was caught; he was tortured. The Party was exposed. When this happened we got a lot of help, we had links with people at higher levels, in the state and beyond, and they helped the people in the university sector. This fellow who was arrested, he went through a lot of torture, and they asked him about the Party within the university. But he didn't betray a soul, they didn't get anything out of him, and our organization remained totally intact. But our political activities, almost all of them, became really difficult. We would meet every three months, but it got hard to find a place. We could meet only at the houses of sympathizers, people who knew we were in the Party and would let us use their houses—or in our own houses, which was very risky, but even that we did.

And the fear, to tell you the truth, there was always that fear. We were afraid. Really, inwardly, no one, no human being, manages to go through something like this without being affected psychologically. You spend every day wondering if you're going to be arrested tomorrow. You don't know why other people are being arrested.

We had a certain turnover, but finally the movement began to grow. Our work at school went on, and after '75, even in Rio, where not much had been happening, the movement began to grow again. We also had contacts with São Paulo; we went to meetings there. In '77 we took to the streets, demonstrations again. And there were strikes at school; we participated at the level of representative councils within the departments. Within the university, the university council had one-fifth student representation, and we participated in things like that. We were involved in a campaign at school not to increase the price of meals, not to increase our fees. Compared to private universities we paid ridiculously small fees, but we held rallies to keep them from being increased.

And the movement was growing, you could see it under your nose, which is why I say that the organizing work we were doing at that time was satisfying to me. You could see the fruits of your labor. You were afraid, but at the same time you really discovered what comradeship meant, you created a real solidarity, an organic connection where you were concerned with one another, learned about one another. It was an emotional thing, you see, together. At school there was a lot of support for our position. And I never missed a class. We had our representatives at all levels. The right didn't stand a chance at our school—the students were more mature at that time; now I think they're younger, they enroll at seventeen or so, but when I started they were in their early twenties, they held jobs. The Right couldn't make any headway. In engineering, in medicine, the Party was strong.

All the universities had security networks, and they would provoke us; they'd send letters to our houses saying, "Don't fall for it, don't get involved with the communists." And the Right would distribute pamphlets at school. In Brazil in '75 there was a movement against human rights violations such as torture. The Church began to speak out, and we supported it. We planned a human rights week, and the government sent in shock troops. They violated the university's autonomy and marched in. And this had enormous repercussions. The movement got larger, and the Right began to organize, too. At meetings they would throw tear gas bombs, they would take pictures of us. We fought against their intimidation in all sorts of ways. That's what the Party did, that was my life. And we had a lot of support. In fact, nothing happened to us, I was never arrested, no one in my group was. And actually our policy was correct, in the sense that we didn't leave much space for the Right. We won all the elections at school. At that point I was completely involved. In all that confusion you didn't have much opportunity to notice, to think about the structure of the Party—vertical, authoritarian. There was no time for that.

Through all that I still lived at home, with my parents. My mother sensed that I was involved, but she realized the shape the country was in. We used to talk, to discuss things. She was never totally against my participation, but she never realized that I was more directly involved. She already worried enough, and I wanted to keep her from worrying even more. Often I wouldn't come back at night, which was all right with her. She knew I had lots of activities, but she wouldn't have guessed they were of that type. So I'd sleep at friends' houses. We'd hold meetings until late, I'd get tired, and I'd sleep somewhere near the university— until I actually did move out of the house.

The first time was in '77, and I went to live with a girl—at that time I was involved with this girl, so I went to live with her and another couple. We shared a house. The movement was growing, people were beginning to talk about *abertura*, elections were coming up in '78. And I began to raise a series of questions in the Party. The leadership was in exile—after the internal collapse of '75 they all went abroad, most of them to Italy, and from abroad there was this whole discussion of the Party line, the need for another congress because the last one was already obsolete. But how should it be done? And we discussed the exiled central committee, Prestes,[8] Giocondo Dias,[9] people who were in Italy, the influence of the Italian Eurocommunists.

And all these divergences within the Party began to emerge. We had many discussions. In a sense we even had a better theoretical base for discussing the problems that were arising, and we'd talk and decide on a position, but all still very much within the structure of the Party, which was vertical, authoritarian. For example, even if you disagree with certain directions, if a resolution from a higher committee comes down, you're obliged to put it into practice. That's what democratic centralism is. And that's where my differences with the Party began. Not so much on the level of an existential questioning of authoritarianism, not that I even felt this especially—that came afterward. But basically it was a political question about carrying out our work in the elections, the problem of choosing the candidate that we would support. We began to discuss why we should suddenly support a person who perhaps wasn't the one we thought best suited for the race. Why should we support and campaign for this candidate? Conflicts began to develop over this.

Then, in '79, the movement for amnesty took hold again, and we fought for that. And then the people who'd been abroad began to return, and it was a complete mess within the Party, a real breakdown. Because the Party leaders, who'd had thousands of disagreements abroad, came back, but they never laid out these disagreements for us, never. Their documents were always more or less consistent. But the divergences existed, and we could feel, from their statements, that things weren't quite as they said. Even within the Eurocommunist position, there were divisions. And all of this began to be discussed more openly, and, along with the liberalization that was occurring in Brazil, we started to breathe more freely. It's an interesting phenomenon, because that's when these problems arose, related mostly to the organic question of the Party and its leadership. At school our position usually won. But it was a democratic thing, the assembly, the meetings of the student council. There were other currents on the Left participating, voting, and the movement was growing. You get exposed to other ways of thinking; the student council wasn't only the Party. There were other positions, sometimes there'd be differences and we'd explore them, and the students would say what they thought was most correct. That's the way it was done at our level of the Party, of a nonrepressive party politics. And you start to realize that there's space for this, for this questioning.

What's interesting is that when this liberalization began, the political *abertura* from '79 on . . . I was by then out of school and thinking about my life. Where would I work? How would my life be? After all, the revolution isn't going to happen tomorrow, and you have to think about your own life. And people, we militants ourselves, turned more toward personal questions, of our lives, of relationships, and we began to get more relaxed. No one goes through this without . . . you have a tremendous discipline. In terms of schedules, if you set up a meeting with a colleague, you have to be there on time. You have to pay attention to the smallest things, if you're being followed, and then suddenly you feel kind of paranoid, you can't be a relaxed person. Nobody goes through a dictatorship without feeling its effects. You suffer its effects, as well as those that you, by choosing this militancy, subject yourself to. So your life becomes more controlled, you control yourself more. And then all this relaxation began to occur, this *abertura*, the return of the exiles, and a euphoria started to take over Brazil in '80. It was called "*abertura* summer."

And that's when my crisis within the Party started, in 1980. It had nothing to do with my homosexuality. That was never an issue, truly. I never felt that there was a problem on my colleagues' part, there was no repression. Perhaps even more repression, more prejudice, existed within me than was actually in them. It was never an issue. The Party has a conservative position, but I never had any problem within the Party because of this. They always knew about my relationship with the person I was emotionally involved with. She was in school with us, there was no problem, they were all friends. Truly there was no problem. It wasn't discussed, I never raised the issue. It was a matter of priorities. If you're involved in a struggle like this, in a political party, you're not going to state, "Look, I'm . . . what do you think about that? We have to fight for homosexuals, for women." No. I'd avoid such a scene. You could even say it's secondary. Not in terms of my concerns, no, but in terms of bringing it up for discussion and having to take a position on it. Frankly, when you go through such a hard period, with these important political matters—after all, I was in a communist party, and I wasn't about to get into a homosexual movement, no. I was always very clear about this. But in terms of my own existence, I started having problems—this crisis of thinking that in fact it was all vertical, authoritarian, that it could be different. Or that I, too, might have a different aim in life. And the international communist movement itself raised these questions. The invasion of Afghanistan, the dissent within the movement, the Eurocommunists, the question of revolution, of other parties, of your not having any training, of the Soviet Communist Party. In short, to question what was happening. What kind of socialism is that, in the Soviet Union? All these things.

These issues eventually began to weigh on me as a person, but they still didn't have much influence on my militancy, not to the point of disruption. They weren't important. I was still a model militant, I worked tenaciously. I never doubted the significance of being against the dictatorship, never. From that point of view, my life was completely valid. But then these problems emerged, and you start noticing, reading, having other questions. Perhaps having a better comprehension of it all. It ceases to be just politics and becomes a question of life itself, of . . . I actually felt more laid back about what I wanted, about my happiness, others' happiness. And above all, the thing that really counted in my leaving the Party was still the political issue of this return [of the exiled Party leaders], this crisis in which we all began to ask questions. Possibly we were the first base in the country to question what the returned Party heads were doing, setting out their position through newspapers, through discussions, publicly taking charge without talking to us, to the bases, without laying out their differences in a document. So we started to draft documents and send them to the leadership, stating that we wanted to discuss what was happening and that the Party's position had to develop from the base, had to emerge from a collective decision, that the Party had to be *all* the militants, indiscriminately, all equal, that they had to take this into account.

And then the whole thing breaks wide open. It ends up with the people on the central committee taking one position, the Eurocommunists another, Prestes another. And in all that confusion we're never consulted, they never talk to us. We have a pretty strong position on all this. Then, in our own group, differences arise in relation to all these positions. And still another position, a fourth one, of actual dissidence, develops within the Party. It all drags on and on, and we can't handle it. We try to stay within the Party, trying to discuss this issue, trying to follow the question through, trying to discuss the national policy. Not all issues are acknowledged in the Party, in the sense of being openly discussed. There's a certain desire to impose one's political position, not based on a discussion but just opportunistically, and these were stances we condemned. So things are going from bad to worse, and I start to think, "This isn't right. What am I doing here if I can't basically agree with their line?" And there's this authoritarianism that we're questioning. We tried everything, truly, to explain our sector, our situation as leaders at the university level, our leadership as an effort to be more democratic. But there was no responsiveness to this within the Party, and to this day there hasn't been. Even now the party hasn't resolved the major question; they're all still fighting. There's a struggle now for the legalization of the party, but how? How should it be done? And all these political questions basically influenced me and went into my decision to leave the Party.

Yes, I still see them. I worked in the Party with these same people for nearly ten years. Some of them are still in it. At the moment I don't have any formal link with the Party, but politics is something that's always present in my life. I haven't given it up.

Was there a sexual division of labor in the Party? Look, let met put it like this. One of the issues we raised was the question of some people working and others thinking. Some militants think the policy through, and others do the work, carry out the plans. That kind of division exists, maybe it'll always exist. In my group the majority were men, but there were a great many women, 60 percent to 40 percent. It wasn't much of a difference. But as far as sex roles go, no, what counted was your work there, you were a militant. Yes, it's obvious that the Party reproduces the structure of our society, and we even set this out in our document. The authoritarian party undoubtedly reproduces the authoritarian structures of society and, logically, since this society is *machista*, and the masculine predominates, obviously this will have an influence. Just look at the central committee, which is the Party leadership. It must have over twenty people, and at that time there was one woman.

Now as far as homosexuality goes, which was my situation, I don't think I ever met a single other person in all my years of militancy who was homosexual and a communist at the same time, so I can talk only about my own case. As I said, on the part of my colleagues there was never any—some concern, yes, maybe even with a certain image the Party had of a communist, this moral pressure, of what people might think, society has some prejudices against homosexuals. You're a militant and homosexual; obviously there's a problem of acceptance. The Party militant has to be basically accepted by the group, integrated into the group, respected. But I never had any problem; there was no question of my competence. Nor was there a problem about acknowledging me as a member of the Party. It was just a matter of, in the organization, I never, I mean . . . I was among the leaders. And there was never any . . . I mean, it seems obvious now that maybe when I wasn't present, I can't say anything about that. Or things like friends higher up in the leadership; someone might have seen this as something negative. But I never encountered any obstacles in doing my work, not on the part of my colleagues or at school.

MY SEXUAL DEVELOPMENT? I don't know, maybe I was always . . . it's something I've thought about in a number of ways. There was a phase, when I was in that crisis over leaving the Party, it ended up as a general crisis, of work, too. I was unemployed, it was a period of transition, wanting to leave the Party and yet thinking that, no, I had to stay and see if things would improve, settle down. And, during that phase, I lived with two women. This second was the last relationship I had. I went into a terrible crisis, I started analysis, all that, and this whole line of questioning. But, in fact, for as long as I can remember having sexual thoughts, I was always oriented toward women, my sexual desire was always for women. Even in my earliest childhood, it was something very distinctive for me. I can remember things from my childhood, far back. . . . I had one or two boyfriends, childhood things, playing together. We even had little boyfriends as a game. But to tell the truth it was much more because everybody else did it, so I did, too. But I . . . I already knew I was going to have problems. By the age of ten I could tell I was going to have problems. At that point, if I'd been able to choose freely—I'm not talking about other girls, only about my own head—I'd maybe have gone to a girl and not to a boy. I mean, it's something I'm very clear about. In fact, in my life, friends to make love with, sex, to this day I've only had that with women. It's something very private that I won't give up, it's what I feel.

Precisely because of this problem, I actually waited a long time, until I was in college, before having boyfriends. And, you know, we even broke up, because I didn't feel right. It just wasn't something I could do. I got to a point where I said, "No, this is ridiculous. I'm not going to do something I don't feel. That's absurd." And because of this I was very much alone, precisely because of this. No, I didn't know any other lesbians. I had passions, I'd fall in love, but these were always platonic, distant, relationships, and I never had the courage to go up to someone, to any of these women, and say what I was feeling. Plus I didn't know anyone with whom I could even talk about it, as a friend. I couldn't open up in that way. I was always a very reserved person, because of this problem and other things. So I got emotionally involved with someone only rather late. My first adventure, the first time I had the courage to reveal myself, it was with a cousin of mine. It didn't lead to anything. I told her, but nothing happened. She felt something, though not quite that on her part, but it was very important for me to reveal this, finally to say what I felt. I managed to work it out within myself very calmly, and I was finally able to tell another person, and after that it got much easier.

I was about twenty then; but, even after that, it took another three years or so to have a reciprocal involvement, to meet someone who could face this with me. And what was important was that this person was a friend, we already had that friendship, and it never crossed my mind . . . although maybe there was something homosexual influencing our relationship, but nothing explicit, not on her part either. She was the first women I was really in love with; she was just ending a relationship, in fact with a fellow I knew, and we had met, I was a friend of his. And one day . . . I said, "Well, I'm going to have to bring this up, because she's someone I like, someone I know, so why not talk about it?" And in fact it worked out, and something began to develop. It was the longest relationship I've ever had; it lasted four years. We lived together, we were students, and we worked to support ourselves. I was living at home, in my mother's house, when a job came up, so we were able to move in with this couple, and we decided to live together. She'd already left home by then and was living alone in a room.

It was a pretty traumatic experience, her moving out of her house. It was in '75 . . . we were at her house, talking. I used to go to her house. Her brother knew already, it wasn't a problem, there was only her brother and her mother. One day we were in her bedroom. We were kissing when her mother walked in, and it was a really unplesant scene. [Her mother] left the room and Celina said, "I'll go talk to her." She went into the living room, and her mother asked her what it meant. Celina said, "Mother, I want to talk to you." I said, "Let's talk this over," and she said, "No, I just want to talk to my daughter. Get out of here." And I left. It even got a bit violent. Her mother actually attacked her physically, she hit her. She locked her in for a day and wouldn't let her leave the apartment. This was on a Saturday night, and we'd arranged to meet some place on Sunday to discuss what to do. She didn't show up, and I said, "Something's happened," and I went to her house. She was at the window upstairs when I got there, and she was signaling to me. It was all crazy. She threw down a piece of paper saying that her mother had kept her shut up inside the house. She was waiting for her brother to get home— he'd been away for the weekend—to see if he'd give her the key so she could leave the house. And there I was downstairs, desperate. I went up. I rang the bell. Her mother didn't answer. This was on Sunday. She'd been locked in the whole time, all Saturday night and the following day. I went to the house of a friend who lived nearby and told her what was happening. I asked her to try to intercede in some way. And she went upstairs, but [the mother] wouldn't answer the door. We spent the whole night there; we slept in the hallway outside their apartment, waiting for her brother, but he never showed up, he never came.

Then, in the morning, Celina had a class, and her mother let her leave to go to school. It was a horrible thing, and we said, "What are we going to do?" "My mother wants to take me to the doctor, she's having a fit, she hit me, and I can't talk to her because she comes at me and attacks me. I'm going to end up hitting her back to defend myself if it goes on like this. I'd better get back home, Fernando's coming back this afternoon. I don't know what I'm going to do, how we can handle this situation." And she went home. Her mother was calmer by then, but she insisted they go to the doctor. So they went to an analyst. And the man said to her [mother], "Look, Senhora, you're the one who is sick!" [*Laughs.*] Her mother had some problems, too: she was separated from her husband, they hadn't lived together for a long time, their relationship was very difficult. And the doctor said, "She doesn't need therapy, Senhora. I think at the moment you're the one who needs it."

This was in '75, and that horrible atmosphere continued. Celina managed to move out of the house only at the end of the year. Then in '77 we started living together, with this other couple, and her mother never mentioned the matter again. I don't know whether she accepted it. Later, when we separated, in '78, she got involved with another girl almost immediately and started living with her. Her mother must know, obviously.

Why did we separate? Look, there was nothing else to do, our relationship had already deteriorated quite a bit. We no longer had the same feelings. In the end, there was no longer any reason to stay together, to be in a relationship, so we decided to separate. But to this day I'm still friends with all the women I've been involved with. You see, that's something very good that remained. I love them all, I care about them a great deal, and they care about me, too. We can really talk, we always want to hear how the other one's doing, about work, emotions, how life is going. It's a very good thing.

Now, in terms of the actual relationships, this business of roles, it's like this. Celina, the first really heavy relationship I was involved in, she'd never been with a woman. But it was hard for me, not for her. I had a problem about security, problems in my head, and it was very difficult for me to overcome them within a relationship. That issue you raised, about the way authoritarian structures are reproduced, it also happens within homosexual relationships. Social roles are defined, and as aware as I was of this—it's something we used to talk about a lot, something we were very conscious of—it was hard, really hard, for me to absorb this, to interiorize it and feel at peace, so that I could say, "No, this doesn't really matter." I had to go through the experience of living with another woman, I had to have another relationship, which by the way was also fairly chaotic, to get to the point I'm at today, of having some peace of mind. I changed a lot, and I had to work at it, to question myself, to make a real effort. Because it's not enough to know things in your head, about your behavior, in order to have this peace of mind.

And prejudice also enters into it, to the point even that I couldn't accept, couldn't see a homosexual relationship as a perfectly ordinary thing, as something not abnormal. All that took some time, you see, and at the base of it was my own insecurity, maybe my desire to be like everybody else. And I realized suddenly that I wasn't, that I didn't have a relationship like other people's. It was different because we were homosexual. That's why I think it's important for people to be in a group, in a movement. It's important to see other people who are also in a homosexual relationship, because it's very hard to live, to be different, in a context in which you're the only one who is different. It's *very* hard, it's something that . . . it's like a constant demand on some level, a demand by other people. And even . . . something I always wanted to do but never managed was to walk down the street holding hands, you see, with the people I liked and loved. I wanted that. So I felt resentful, and I'd dump it all on the relationship in a way that was totally wrong and destructive. It's much easier to have a relationship with someone who's already opted for this, who's already had some homosexual experience, who's already loved someone of the same sex in the past. At least for me this was very important. As equals, not on the level of sex, but as equals because it's a good thing, you feel that you're not alone, not in the wrong.

No, I was never in a group. There were some people at school who I knew were homosexual, but they had classes in the morning and mine were always at night. Once somebody even came up to me when I was in a bar and said, "Look, there's going to be a demonstration of homosexuals on Independence Day"—I think this was in '78. But I didn't even go. Here in Rio there have always been bars where homosexuals, women and men, hang out, but I never really went. I never wanted to get involved. I thought it was the kind of thing where they had their own slang, that it was like a ghetto, a special kind of group, and I was never into that. I already had a group, another group, where one way or another I was accepted. Then later I used to see announcements in the newspapers about groups in São Paulo—there are more groups in São Paulo than here.[10] At the university level, too, there are groups of lesbians, but I never had any contacts with them. With my friends, obviously, in one sense I was a complete outsider, but in another sense I was very much a part of a group and I didn't need to have these other contacts. I knew about the girls in the morning session, but only after I left school did I actually become friends with one or two of them, and we remembered one another and even laughed about it, "Oh, I always wanted to get to know you more," that sort of thing.

In a way I was a very tough person, and yet I always had that insecurity, those inner problems that I never discussed with anybody. I discussed them only with the person I was going with, never with anyone else. With our friends we'd talk about our relationship, but never in terms of this matter of homosexuality. It just wasn't something to be discussed. Although, you know, I think it would have been important to have had some more support, and I never did. But then, I was a very rigid person. The Party involved discipline, you had to be such and so at school, so that everybody could see; and despite my crises, my special problems, my insecurity, I always gave people the impression of being very self-sufficient, very secure. I was always concerned that—no, I wasn't concerned, I just was like that, I still am: "If you want to accept me, fine; otherwise, that's fine, too, this is what I'm like." That's the way I was, take it or leave it. Even when I opted for this radical position, I never tolerated any interference, never.

Then, after I broke off with Celina, I got involved with someone else, but it ended badly. She's never gotten in touch with me again. What's done is done. And right after this messy relationship, when I'm in this state of crisis, with this closed way of seeing things, of seeing my own life, homosexual relations, I meet another woman who's also coming out of a very messy relationship with a fellow. She'd never had any sort of homosexual experience, and we decided to live together. This was toward the end of '79. We lived together in '80, '81, that whole period. It was rather difficult, too—because I was unemployed, I was at a crisis point with the Party, with my own life, questioning everything. That's why this last person was so important in my life. We talked, we went into things deeply, we fought, we had very good moments and very bad moments.

But my head got bent out of shape because she was supporting me. You see, when I went to live with her I was out of work. At first I said, "No, I won't go." She said, "That's ridiculous. I'm supposed to wait till you find a job so we can live together, so we can have a real relationship? This doesn't make any sense. So long as I can afford it, I don't see why this should be a problem." I agreed, but in my head it *was* a problem. And there was another problem, the matter of roles. After all my earlier experiences I was finally questioning all that, I was trying to change, trying to get out of that craziness. But it didn't work out either. We lived together for two years, and all that time I was out of work. After I graduated in '78 I never found a regular job, just part-time work, a month here, a month there, doing research, surveys, things where you're paid by the hour, by the day. And it was never enough to live on. When I started working, when I was living at home, I always had enough money to pay for my own clothing, my books, transportation. I ate and slept at home, I didn't have to pay rent, so it was enough. And when I lived with Celina, we divided everything, we each paid half. But with Valéria I couldn't do it. She had to pay the rent alone, buy the food alone, that sort of thing. It was very unpleasant for me. It still is.

No, Valéria never tried to dominate because of the money. I took care of the house, I did the cooking and all that, but there wasn't any role division—it was just I had the time to take care of those things since she was working, and I could deal with the shopping, the house, all of that. And I was still in the Party, still going to meetings until '82. She wasn't in the Party; none of the people I've been involved with were.

After about a year I got more regular work, but still it was a temporary job, with a large project researching the problems of rural laborers. They liked my work and started paying me regularly, every month, but it was just enough for my personal expenses, not so much that I could rent an apartment. In fact, even when Valéria and I broke up, I still kept on living there for a while. Then it got to be too much, and I moved into a house with several other people and we split the expenses. But then, a few months ago, the project ended and, when I saw that I wasn't going to have enough money even to pay the rent, I moved back into my parents' house, and that's where I'm still living.

Now I'm waiting to hear about a job. It's really hard with a degree in the social sciences, but since I also have a degree in communications there's a possibility of a job, as a production assistant at a radio station where I have a friend. They're just waiting to hear about the funding.

My family? They must know. It's obvious. They've never seen me in a relationship with a man. My mother knows, my father, my family, they all know, but we never talk about it. It's not a problem; they never butt into my life. They don't know that I was in the Party; it was never discussed. This is the kind of thing where I've never put up with any interference. All this time that I've been unemployed, I've never run to them for help. They support me, but they never question me about my life. And there are lots of other things we never talk about. I've never talked with my sister about her marriage, which is shit. And we've never discussed the fact that my brother and sister aren't really our siblings. There's a kind of pact about unsaid things, things that don't need to be said. I understand it, it's something deeply painful. Why open old wounds, knowing you were rejected by your father or mother, that you never knew your parents? It must be very hard for them, but they've never mentioned this subject to me.

Would I like to live with another woman? Not right now. Let me tell you why. This last relationship, she was very important to me, it was a very strong relationship. They all were, with a lot of companionship, a real sharing. And when I left that relationship, in this crisis, I was very depressed and I said, "Now I'm going to try to get my head together, to let some time pass. I don't want to leave another relationship like this." And right now I feel very calm about all this; it doesn't seem so important. I can't tell you that in the future there'll never be a man in my life. If it happens it'll be perfectly natural. Having a child has never crossed my mind, I've never wanted to have children. You have children with someone you love and, since I've always loved women, it's impossible, so in my mind that's always been settled. But if I happen to fall in love with a man, I think I might have a child, but then again I might not. It depends on what happens in one's life. I like children very much. I have nieces and nephews, and a godson. But if I fall in love in the future, I guarantee it'll be perfectly calmly, because I've learned a lot.

I have a deep respect for other people, which I didn't used to have. I always wanted to impose my views, my way of living or seeing the world, and all that's gone. Today I'm much calmer. I accept a man or a woman who gets involved with a man or a woman, this doesn't make the slightest difference to me now. I have dreams, I have a utopia, I have plans, but that doesn't mean that the plans I make, the projects I have, have to be exactly as I imagine them. And I've grown calmer, I've changed. When you live with another person, there are *two* people, and it'll never be exactly the same as one. People have to recognize this, to feel their feelings. I'm not the only person in the world. I'm not the only source of pleasure. Nearly two years have passed since we separated. I went through a phase, you know . . . to end a relationship that you think is going to last your whole life, this doesn't mean life has ended, no. Life goes on, in everything. You die, the world goes on.

5

GOOD GIRLS

Branca was nineteen at the time of the interview (1981) and had a child a year and a half old. She was working in Recife as a "dancer" in a club, a depressing place in which a few young women wearing only G-strings and absent expressions on their faces moved mechanically to thunderous music from a juke box, while a half a dozen fully clothed men looked on and, now and again, left the bar to join one of the women in a dance. I invited Branca to go out for a beer. She got dressed (which seemed to restore the expression to her face), I paid the exit fee, and went to an outdoor café down the street. There, over the din of passing vehicles, I explained to Branca what I was doing. At her suggestion we went to her room in an apartment house a few blocks away, so that we could converse quietly and with the prospect of making an audible tape. Branca lived in a room that measured approximately 8′ × 12′. It contained one bed (on which we sat and talked), one dresser, one closet, and several piles of boxes from which household goods—pots and pans, sheets, towels— peeked out. Playing nervously with a matchbox, Branca told me her story in

16

fits and starts. Later, as we were parting, Branca said, "It's good to talk, even if it's not with a real friend, just for once to get it all out to someone who really listens."

Branca describes herself as *morena clara*—light-skinned *morena*. She has wavy brown hair, dark eyes, and golden skin. Her mother's mother, she told me, was Indian, and her mother's father was Portuguese.

———

My father was responsible for my mother's ruin, and so was I. He died when my mother was pregnant with me. They were going to marry, they really were, but there wasn't time. When she got pregnant she was very young, she just got caught.... She gave herself to this boy, and her family made a big fuss, but they'd already decided to get married, and then he was killed in a car accident. This happened here in Recife. Well, that complicated everything. My mother had to shoulder the responsibility all alone, for the pregnancy. My aunt caused her a lot of grief, my grandmother, too, and my grandfather. Sometimes she couldn't even eat. She

BRANCA

went on living at home, but pregnant. She went through a lot with my grandparents, she really suffered. So then, when I was born, she couldn't really care for me, I think because she'd had no help, no support. So she couldn't help but pass it on to me, that lack of support. She never gave me much support.

Well, her sister is married, my aunt, and Mama, as soon as I was born she gave me to my aunt to raise. This was in the maternity ward. But when I was three years old, my aunt died, so she put me in a neighbor's house. She resented me, you see, so she took it all out on me, all that resentment, for my father having died, for her having such bad luck. She couldn't love me. So I stayed with this neighbor, my aunt's neighbor, who lived nearby. And then . . . at a certain point, I was going to go to school—I was a bright girl—and when I was about nine I needed to register so that I could go to school and my foster parents had to get my real mother's consent for this. And that's how I found out that I had a sister, that my mother had another daughter, by another guy. I didn't know her, and I hardly knew my mother; she almost never came to visit me—or I don't remember, I was just a child . . . So they took me there and I just went crazy over my little sister, she's a year and half younger than me. I didn't have any other kids to play with and we got to be good friends, and then a particular moment came when I was going to have to separate from her. We had to go to court . . . I'm confused about it . . . but the time came, and the judge asked me, "Do you want to live with your foster parents or with your mother?" And I was so thrilled about my sister that I said, "I want to live with my mother." I was . . . I didn't know what lay ahead of me . . . and I went there.

Then, little by little, my mother . . . I . . . even as a child, I began to notice that she didn't like me. She said bad things about me to my cousins, and she would quarrel with me. I'd ask for her blessing, and she wouldn't even answer. I suffered a lot. She didn't send me to school, nothing. She didn't care. If she had some clothing to give to me or my sister, she gave it to her, she wouldn't divide it between the two of us. And so I grew up resentful, bitter. Then, when I was fourteen, my oldest cousin, who lived with us, decided to enroll me in school, and so I began to study. I went for just one year. But I was very badly treated. My cousin was very demanding, I had to do this for her, and that and the other thing. She'd hit me; she used to slap my face in front of my mother, and my mother never did anything about it. I'd already run away from home once. One time I went downtown with her, and I pretended that I didn't know the way and got lost, on purpose. She couldn't find me, but later a policeman heard about it on the radio and he took me home again.

Then, when I was around sixteen, I went to . . . my sister used to go to a house . . . my mother used to sew for a lady, a woman about thirty years old, pretty and rich. My mother was sewing for her and didn't know anything about her private life. And she, this woman, was very attached to my sister—she's blonde and pretty, my sister. And she ended up living with her, like a friend. She used to take her out, everywhere, you see. And she was . . . she took drugs, she smoked pot and . . . she'd fix girls up with men, you see. And my mother didn't know about it. So my sister stayed there, like I said.

One day I went to pick up my sister to go to a party at a club, at six o'clock, and I got there . . . and we set out on foot. And on the way a boy . . . in an enormous car, stopped the car and called to us. My sister knew him by sight, from the club that she'd been to with this woman who, like I said, arranged for dates. She didn't know what kind of life he led; she just knew his name. So we got in the car to go to this club at six o'clock. He went to the house of a friend of his, spoke to him about something and then we went on, and he took the wrong turn, so he wasn't going toward the club. He was driving along another road where there were just woods, the road, no houses, nothing, and a few minutes later his friend appeared. We tried to get out of the car, we tried everything, you see. We begged him not to do what he wanted to do, that we were virgins, everything. My sister cried, "For the love of God" and everything else; she said she would tell on him, but it was no use. His friend who was with him, he had another car . . . we went running when he stopped the car to talk to his friend, but it was a deserted road, dark, away from the main road, there was no way out. So they raped us, both of us. They had a gun. One held the gun and then handed it to the other one. Both of them used us.

And from that day on I've felt cheated. I couldn't tell my mother, and I couldn't do anything about it. Because I was the older one and my mother never liked me, so she would have blamed me, she'd have said it was my fault for accepting a lift. My sister was living in that lady's house, so for her it was all right; she didn't have to face my mother, nothing. I ended up running away from home. And I began this life. That was three years ago, I was sixteen.

Then, in order to eat . . . I didn't have any training for anything. I didn't know what life was about. That same lady started me turning tricks. The first man in my life was one of these tricks, and afterward I got pregnant. . . . I love my daughter, I really love her. But I don't even know who her father is. I love her a lot, really I do. Next year I'm going to go to school, to see if I can get some kind of vocational training so I can work. I've only had one year of school. I've tried to do other work. I worked in a store for a while, in a pastry shop, as a clerk, but I broke a piece from a machine there and they took it out of my salary. It cost almost as much as my whole salary, which was the minimum salary, $65; that was a few months ago. I couldn't continue because they were taking it out of my salary, and I was going to spend every day for the whole month just working for them. So I left and came back to this life that I'd given up. I found this job in the club, and here I am.

I don't want to live like this, but I just don't have any choice, because that's . . . all I know how to do. I don't have schooling, so I can't get a job that pays decently. And I have to earn more because of my daughter. I don't have a man to help me, I don't have my family. There's nobody I can count on. So all the money I make is to pay for things for my daughter, the food that I eat, and clothing.

I rent this room, in this apartment. It costs $40 a month, and I pay for the utilities, the laundry. And also for my daughter. She lives at my mother's house—that cousin of mine lives there, too, and takes care of her. Right now I'm trying to buy some furniture so I can move into a house, with my daughter and a maid. My mother doesn't want to come too. You see those things there? I'm just buying things bit by bit, pots and pans, sheets. I go to see my little girl every day, almost every day. It's because . . . I get up late. Some days I have lunch, take a shower, and get there at about four and stay until six when I have to go to work.

I work five days a week, and get Tuesdays and Sunday off. From 7:00 in the evening until 2:00 a.m. You saw, it costs $5 to get into the club, and then it's up to me whether I want to go with a man or not. Sometimes it's difficult to decide; sometimes if I think the person looks all right, then I go. I talk to them, I say what I want. If he thinks it's too much money, that's fine, I don't leave. I set the rules. Look, to go with someone you don't even know, and all the rest, it has to be worth it, doesn't it? If they want to give me what I ask, fine. What I earn at the club is very little, so I have to get extra work. At the bar I get $70 a month, barely enough for the rent here. Tonight there wasn't much going on. If a bunch of clients show up, and there are, say, only four girls for eight men, they'll leave and look for other places with more girls. If two men arrive, with four girls there they'll stay. Tonight a lot of the girls are off, so there's not much happening. It's hard to say what I earn altogether. If I ask for $20 or $30, that can be for the whole night, or not. I can't cook here, so I always have meals out, and that's $5 less. And I have to pay a washerwoman because there's no place here for me to wash my things. And every week I spend $20 just on food for my daughter—I buy her food myself. Some days I earn enough, other days I don't. It's really . . . it's awful. Once I leave, I don't have to go back to the club that night, because the customer has to pay the exit fee to leave with me, just like you did. That's now $10. I usually go to a motel by the beach; they're all okay, the place doesn't matter.

The cost of living is going up from one day to the next! Sometimes I buy milk for my little girl for . . . let's say $2. The next week it's already up to $2.25. Right now it's $2.23 for a can, and I buy two little ones. Sometimes I buy one big one for $4 and one little one, for two weeks. Other times I buy two little ones for the two weeks. And yogurt. One small container of yogurt is 40 cents, just one. And I have to buy eight, that's eight times forty. I have to buy apples. One apple is 30 cents. You see how crazy it is. Buying three apples, eight apples . . . there goes the money. I buy lots of fruit for her, I buy it as I get the money. At home I take care of all the bills for my daughter. Rice, vegetables, greens, fruit, I do it all. Even detergent, soap to wash her clothes. You go to buy something one day, and the next the price is up. Lunch around here costs $2. Every day I spend $2 for lunch, and at night I eat a sandwich. When I can't stand it, I have a real dinner. It's awful. Each time I go to the doctor I pay $20, per visit.

I used to work in another club, not nude dancing, just a club for making contacts. We'd sit there, drinking and talking, and they had rooms right on the premises. They would charge for the room and the drink, and the money that the clients gave us was ours. And then there are the *caftinas*, the women who arrange a man for another woman, and they charge both the man and the woman. I fell into that, as soon as I left my mother's house. With those people who, instead of giving me a job, set me up to turn tricks. And I was just sixteen. . . . By the time I saw, it was too late. I wasted my time, and now I'm a mother. . . . I tell my mother that I know who's the father of my child, but I don't. I try to fool myself, you see? I didn't know anything about contraceptives, but now I take the pill and I go to the gynecologist every few months. Married women only go twice a year, don't they? I have to go more often, because of this life, but I've never caught anything.

So, after two months working in that shop, I came back. Because it's just not enough money. If you live in your mother's house, you have support, you don't need to pay so much to live, for food, everything, so it's all right. But if you live alone, facing life all alone, without anyone to help you, then the minimum salary just isn't enough. You know what's causing prostitution here in Brazil? It's society, because the salary you can earn isn't enough. If you don't have schooling, it's not enough unless you're single and don't have children. Do you want to see a photo of my little girl? [*She takes a small album from a box under the bed.*] Her name is Michele, she's everything to me. I really wanted to have a girl. In this photo she's only seven months old; now she's one year and eight months. Here's a book I'm writing for her—see, there's the date of her birth. I filled in all those blanks. I can read, and I can speak some English, too, . . . here I'm going to put a lock of her hair, and more photos; there's a lot to do still. I got this book from Avon. I bought some talc for her, and this album was a bonus. I was expecting a little boy, the baby I got rid of, it was a boy, just this big. So I would have had a boy and a girl . . . if only I could have kept him. But I was hemorrhaging. The doctor wanted to give me some medicine to keep it, but I couldn't bring it up anyway, so I preferred the abortion. I would have had to rest, and stop working, and I couldn't because of my finances, so the abortion . . . I would have lost him anyway if I'd kept on working. So I had the abortion, a few months ago. But I want to have other children. I want to have a boy, not now though, many years from now, when I've finished school. . . .

I'm going to take courses next year, you know, accounting, English, and shorthand. Just those, to see if I can get a better job. I can't really go back to school—there isn't enough time, I've lost so many years—but I can take a private course. If you pay, the teaching is better, and then I could work as a receptionist in a hotel, or as a secretary. Maybe I could earn around $200 or $300 a month. At least it would be a fixed income, whereas now sometimes I earn more, sometimes not. And with an honest job I could find a man who would see me as a person, as people, and take care of me and my daughter. At my job I never will . . . where can I find a man who'll understand me rather than sponge off of me?

In the past three years I haven't met a single man I liked. I don't know . . . before I was raped I did like them, when I was a virgin. But my mother never let me go out. And afterward, I had that anger against men. I haven't managed to like a single one. I only think about their money, just that. You know, the only person I really care about is my daughter. I don't want her to go into this kind of life and, if it depends on me, like I depended on my mother, she'll never have to because I'll give her all the help and support I can, and freedom—but with limits, you know. And she'll be able to go to school. I'll open her eyes to what life is, like a friend. Not like my mother opened mine. She didn't open my eyes; on the contrary. If I had a boyfriend, then I was doing something wrong, I was . . . doing something ugly. And she'd yell out loud that I was this and that, and the neighbors could hear. . . . So, without meaning to, she steered me toward this. When she found out that I wasn't a virgin anymore, she wanted to know who it was, and I couldn't say, because my sister would have killed herself if I'd told. To this day, she still has all my mother's support; my mother never found out what happened, though she knows she's no longer a virgin because my sister herself showed it by her behavior. She turns tricks, but it's because she wants to. My mother would support her—she still sews in a boutique—if she wanted. Even the money my sister gives to my mother, she then spends on clothing for my sister though she says not to, that it's to fix up the house.

Why does my sister do it? I think it's her fate, you see. She made friends with these influential people, that woman I was telling you about, and so she got into it. If I were her, I'd want to enjoy my youth and my freedom. As soon as you have children, your freedom's all gone. What you do depends on your child. If you want to travel, you can't. And even if you're not financially tied, you feel morally tied to your child. So, if I were my sister, I would work, study, study and work. And be a good girl, not forced to go out with this guy and that, just for a money. She's pretty, really pretty, she's lovely and young. She's seventeen years old; she's going to be eighteen in a few months. She should enjoy life while there's still time, shouldn't she? So I think she's doing it because she wants to.

And she's on drugs, she smokes pot. Thank God I don't; I tried it a few times, but I didn't like it. When I left home, one of the people where I lived used to smoke and she offered me some; and I felt like a terrible failure, I felt horrible. It seemed that I was to blame for everything that happened. Whenever I smoked, I felt that I shouldn't have been born. A thousand bad things would go through my head. When I'm not on those things, then I feel good, I feel marvelous, I feel capable of looking life in the face, but if I smoke pot I feel as if I'm dying, something awful. I don't see any rose-colored world on that stuff. I see clearly. I don't think I'm very likely to get addicted to anything, only cigarettes. I drink when I feel like it, not every day, just once in a while. One, maybe two or three shots, but I don't drink much.

Right now my relationship with my mother is good, because I really tried to show her that I wasn't any of those things that she imagined about me. I think that I set the best example for her when she rejected me when I was pregnant, and when she used to hit me and lock me in my room when I'd get home late. I was always trying to find money to help at home, and I would get in late and she'd yell at me, and she'd shout things at me that the neighbors could hear. But I wasn't angry at *my* daughter, and I didn't try to get rid of her. On the contrary, I got even more attached to her. When she was born, my mother still didn't like her much, but little by little I brought her closer to the baby, you see. Secretly, I'd find her with the baby . . . and little by little she got to love her like a grand-mother. But not me. I was the one who was really responsible. . . . I can forget to eat, but not that I have a daughter, no. When she's sick, I stay with her in the hospital, everything. A bad person, a bad mother, that I'm not. I think that my mother finally saw that I'm really not that, even though she was. So now she's my friend, she talks to me. She just doesn't want to live with me, because . . . she's still not a complete mother to me; but she's already a friend, she talks to me and gives me her blessing. Before, she used to avoid even mentioning my name. It was horrible.

Sometimes I wonder if I should have been born. I was seventeen years old, I was pregnant, the baby's there, a good little imp, but. . . . What I was really afraid of was her being born and my not having any help and having to be out in the streets with her. But thank God I managed. She's so cute.

I'm going to get out of here. I don't have a place in mind yet; I'm still looking. Or maybe I could rent an enormous room in a rooming house, big enough for me to put my things in. I've bought a hotplate; it's over there. Here are some cups, a coffeemaker, other things. . . . At my mother's house there's a set of pans that I already bought. Lots of things. But there's lots more still to buy. I could pay the same rent as here, $40 a month, but a house is cheaper than an apartment. Here in the city, apartments are very expensive. This one costs $300 a month; it's got five bedrooms, two bathrooms, three other rooms, the veranda. He rents out to other people.

This course I want to take, it's about six months. Shorthand, six months; typing, three months . . . and, what do they call it? I'm going to specialize in secretary . . . secretarial . . . two years. Then, in three years I can do it all. Three years. In three years I can get out of this life. I can take this course in the afternoon.

There are men, clients, who go to the club and ask me, "Do you work?" and I say, "You think I can work, with the schedule I've got here?" Or they say, "Do you go to school?" And I say, "Good God, where can I find the time to go to school, working days, working nights?" The day isn't long enough, twenty-four hours aren't enough to do all this. But I've got to find a way.

A T T H E C L U B I get tired; I'm there from 7:00 to 2:00 *a.m.* every day. When Saturday comes around, I'm exhausted. Sometimes I go with a man early, sometimes I don't go at all. Other times it's already 2:00 *a.m.* on my way out. I need the money, so I have to liven up. Sometimes I'm so sleepy I'm half-dead, but I don't even have money, sometimes, for lunch the next day, so I have to go.

You know, with this kind of life I'm leading, I just can't get to like any of these men. It's . . . I don't know . . . they want sex, fine, but they don't want any responsibility. And especially once they know I work nights, right away they have no respect. He'll go to bed, take me out somewhere, but he won't want any kind of commitment, or introduce me to his family. He considers me a deviant, you see. So I have to coldly face how they are. My idea about them is this: if you're not their little wife safely at home, or their fiancée, then . . . we . . . to them we're just objects, sex, pleasure. So I look at them in the same way—as a way to make my living. I pay them in the same coin, and I don't feel love for any of them. All kinds of men, young, old, married, single, every kind. But if I'm not working, then he can't know anything about my past or my life, and he can get to like me like any woman, like a person, not like a woman who turns tricks, who he knows makes it with anyone, does it for money. And sometimes they even ask for money. No one's ever asked me, and I've never given any, and I never will, God help me. I think it's horrible. A woman has to have some dignity. To get to the point of giving money to a man!

Sometimes they go with me and they want to do it different, you see. There are women around who did it different, and others don't. I never do. With me it's only the normal way, the usual. So then, if I have to tell them no, they don't always want to listen, they want to hit me sometimes; but I can always manage to talk to them, to say, "Look, you can only do this if the woman likes it, and I don't. And money won't get me to do it." I talk to them, friendly; they may not want to go to bed or pay me . . . but I'll never let anyone hit me. After what I've been through, nothing could be worse. Can you imagine having to face a stranger in the woods, without any defense, he's got a gun, and even he didn't hit me, he didn't do anything. He just made it, not from the rear or anything, just the normal. So I think that I've already been through the most dangerous part, because my virginity was taken, it was stolen. All right, so whatever's still to come is the least of it.

The other girls at work? Well, most of them, you have to be careful. Just to say, "Hey, how are you?" to chat a bit, that's all right, but some of them like to fight, they're violent. They gossip about each other's lives, and sometimes they're violent; it doesn't take much for them to hit someone. I've only been there for a month, and there's already been some trouble. One woman wanted to beat up another one because she was gossiping. I try to stay out of it, but there've been fights. So I look at it this way, I try to talk to all of them the same, I don't like to get too close—they don't even know where I live—but I also try not to make enemies, because the women you meet in these kinds of places are poison mostly. They like to set one against the other, to badmouth people, to say that this one's got a better build and that one's ugly. At all levels, from the highest to the lowest, they're always like this, and there are always arguments. They don't try to be friends to each other. They think that to be a friend, to admire another woman, is just not done. To them a friend is someone to go on a binge with, to gossip with, to go out and get high and play around with. Even here when I live, there are two other girls here with children, just like me, but they never think that what someone else earns is by their own sweat. I have to have someone do my laundry, you see, I have to lock it up. I can't wash it here any more and hang it outside, because I'm not like them and I get very upset. Instead of being a friend, they steal things. I don't talk to them, not even about our children. No, I don't have other friends. That's why the only day I have much contact with people I like is Sunday, tomorrow . . . with my mother, my little girl, that's all. Real friends I don't have.

On Tuesday, my other day off, sometimes I spend the day with my mother, and sometimes at night I go to the club, to see if I can earn some extra money, but I don't take my clothes off. Or I stay at home. If I don't need money, I go to sleep early. I wake up late, at noon, or 1:00 o'clock. I can't wake up early because I don't have an alarm clock. I don't need one anyway: I don't need to be anywhere, so I sleep late. Then I get up, take a bath, and have lunch down the street, and then sometimes I go home and "Holy Virgin, how's my little girl doing?" Sometimes I go to the doctor, sometimes I don't do anything, just stay at home. Or I go to the movies, alone, or I go to the beach, always alone.

I'd like to meet a nice fellow, but I don't think they exist. At least in the life I'm leading, they don't exist. Only if I get out of it. In this atmosphere I'm in, there's no friendship, no love. There's just prostitution—money, sex, nothing else. So as long as I'm here, my life will always be really primitive. I'm not going to have friendship, because I don't want to be friends with someone who'll badmouth me, or who'll rob me or be dishonest with me, and that's what I usually meet.

The men that I meet, here in Brazil, they don't try to understand. They think we're prostitutes, that that's what we are because we want to be. They just want to . . . how can I explain it? They want to judge, to judge us, not to help. At least those I've met, those that I thought I could have liked, they only wanted to judge me, never to give me any support. They never say, "Let's find a place to live, let's live together; you work and me, too, we'll get someone to take care of your little girl." No. The moment they learned that I had a little girl and lived alone and was leading this sort of life and wanted to get out of it, they'd immediately start to treat me with less respect, they'd want to see me less often, and only want to go out with me if it was straight to bed, never to the movies . . . so the relationship would cool down. That's why I'm telling you, so long as I'm in this life I'm not going to meet a serious man. And what I want is a serious man. I don't want a man to stay with me just on weekends or late at night, not at all. A waste of time.

Who wouldn't like to get married? I want a man who's young, like me, and who would work . . . let's see, he should earn at least three minimum salaries, that would be $200 or so a month, because I'd work, too. I wouldn't mind being a housewife, though I don't know how to cook or do anything [*laughs*]. But I'd rather keep working. I don't like to stay in one place for too long, I get bored easily. I like action, activity. I can't bear just to sit still.

I don't think I have much background for talking about marriage, because until now my experiences have been short and there hasn't been much . . . much dialogue, you see. But I don't know . . . I think the man should come home every day, both of them should come from work, they should have dinner at home, she'd make dinner and he'd help, he'd treat her very gently, and on weekends the three of them, the kid, too, would go out. That way, life wouldn't be boring or routinized. The problem with most couples is that the husband goes to work, the wife stays at home, and when he gets home she's there. Every day the same thing. Then on weekends they both stay home, in the house; that cools things off, their relationship. I think it should be like this: both of them working, not staring at the other's face every minute [*laughs*]; and, on weekends, grab the kid and go to the movies, or do something different. That way you can be married and it would still be like dating at the same time. Lots of holidays, or else it gets lukewarm.

They ought to agree about things together. For example, I buy some clothing, you see? And he doesn't like it, but he knows that I do, so he can't try to tell me what to do, because I think I'm free. I live with him, I love him, but that has nothing to do with my clothing. He should feel secure; he knows that I love him, and he should have confidence. Or, if it's buying new furniture, they should go out together and see if the furniture is nice, if not, "Let's get some other kind."

One shouldn't buy it if the other doesn't like it and wants something totally different. They should try not to get angry, so both can be satisfied. Nobody should be ordered around; I don't think anyone has the right to tell somebody else what to do.

FIDELITY IS VERY IMPORTANT... but... men have always been that way, haven't they? Never satisfied with just one woman. The woman, well, if he satisfies her, she doesn't need to go looking for somebody else in the street. A woman is more romantic, she doesn't really connect with a man unless she likes him. She knows that the man she really cares about is the one who lives with her. So she doesn't do it just for sex, but for love. But the man isn't very romantic; for him, the woman is more of an object than a woman, so I think he does have the right to have more sex, more sexual freedom, than the woman. Yes, I do, so long as he respects his wife and she doesn't hear about it. That's very important. But the fact that he's on the make in the street, that's all right. It's always been like that; it always will be. Just so long as he doesn't let her know about it. He has to respect her and pay attention to her above all else. Let him do what he likes when he's out, that's okay.

If I had a son? . . . The men I meet, they have their own homes, they're fathers, they're sons, they're brothers. So there, in this atmosphere I live in, they're able to release something that was all bottled up inside them and that they couldn't reveal at home. I think that's all right. If he goes there, sometimes he's violent, but he can control himself; or when he makes it with a woman, he's just acting like a man, isn't he? So long as at home he's a good son, is studious, let him be a bit wild. So long as he's obedient, too, that's fine. I would want my son to be normal, like everybody else. Now, my daughter, I don't want her to be like I was. I grew up too fast, in too short a time. . . . I want her to enjoy her childhood, her adolescence, to have a good time, without thinking that the world is some sort of monster with seven heads, or that it's all rosy-colored. That's the way I want to bring her up. And I'd like her to be a virgin when she marries. I didn't lose mine because I wanted to. It just happened. My mother should have understood me, should have helped me and accepted me. Or even if she'd given me—which she didn't—some education, I might have done it knowing what it was all about, that it was wrong. Okay, then she would have had some reason to blame me, but she still should have supported me, because she's my mother. But she didn't do it, you see; and, as it happened, she didn't give me any support. So it doesn't matter if virginity was important to her. What matters is *why* I lost it, you see?

I'm Catholic. I used to go to church a lot, but now I'm just not in any condition to set foot in a church. I feel as if I'm sinning, leading this life and going to church the next day. I prefer to pray at home, to talk with God and not go to church. I feel that people are staring at me and are judging me, you know.

I ' V E   H E A R D about the women's movement, but frankly I don't really know what the point is. I don't know . . . truly . . . I don't know what the aim of these feminists is, because . . . look, let me put it this way. The shape we're in, speeches, strikes, appeals for help won't do a thing. We have to do things for ourselves, not by counting on other people, other women. As far as I can see, all that is just an effort to . . . how do you call it? It's all theory, you see, that business about having equal rights with men and bla-bla-bla; it's all theory, because in practice the world isn't really going to change from what it is. It is the way it is and that's the end of it. That's the rule, you see? That's what I think. Our life is a game and all the rules have already been drawn up, all we can do is follow along nice and quiet. There's no point wanting things to be different. I don't think that's going to help at all, that feminist movement, it won't help. I mean, people getting together, talking, having meetings, making suggestions about how to act to improve what's happening. . . . It could improve, but it won't be set right, it just won't be set right, you see. Sometimes people can be wonderful, can be terrific, just by wanting to. But for me . . . I don't know, I want so little, so very little. I just want a small house, my daughter with me, and a man to help me, so I could take a job that doesn't pay much but that's honest, during the day, and have a normal life like other people.

━━━━

W H E N   I   S A W   B R A N C A again two years later, she looked well and told me she was earning more money than ever—in the midst of economic disasters all around her. She had again tried working in a shop for a few weeks, but she couldn't stand the long hours and tiny salary and was back at her usual job. She had had one miscarriage and one abortion since our last meeting.

Alice, a sweet and slender twelve-year-old with large brown eyes and wavy dark hair, is in the fifth grade at school. Her mother is forty years old and works as a seamstress. Alice, her mother, and her fifteen-year-old sister live in a one-room apartment in a skyscraper on a main avenue in the Copacabana section of Rio de Janeiro. The two girls have bunk beds in the small room at one corner of which is a tiny cooking area. Their mother sleeps on the sofa and works at her sewing in the same room during the day. They have many friends in the building, mostly single women who would rather have a tiny apartment in high-status Copacabana, close to the beach and to elegant shops and restaurants, than a larger and cheaper apartment in some other area of the city. It was at a birthday party for one of these women that I first met Alice. She was the only child at the party.

Alice was rather shy and tended to limit herself to short comments. As a result, this was an interview in which I played a far more active role, asking follow-up questions about her vague answers, trying to draw her out. It was also one of the few interviews that I

17

approached with a fixed notion of what I was primarily interested in: how Alice made sense of gender roles.

We began our talk sitting on the stairs in the corridor outside her apartment. When we got chased away by a janitor, we went back into the apartment. Without my asking, Alice's mother stopped her sewing and left the apartment so that Alice and I could talk in private.

———

J ust the three of us live here—my mother, my sister, and me—we rent this apartment. My parents are separated, but I see my father nearly every day. My mother's the one who supports us, but he helps out once in a while: he gives us some money, or he buys something and gives it to us; he brings food. But mainly it's my mother who takes care of the expenses. Yes, we go to church, on Sunday and sometimes during the week, too.

A brother? For some things it might be nice to have a brother, but not for others, because he'd get in my way. . . . If he was younger, that might be okay, but not older . . . because my older

A L I C E

sister already pesters me, about things that I want to do but can't, and I think I also bother her, just because she is older. My mother says she doesn't want my sister to go out alone, so she has to take me with her, and I can tell she doesn't like it. She wants to go out alone with her friends and not have to take me along. So if I had a brother it would be even worse. . . . He'd upset my mother even more, and . . . there are times when I have to obey my sister, so I'd have to obey my brother, too, and I wouldn't like that. It would be nice to have . . . someone my own size, or a baby brother or sister to take care of—I like kids a lot. But older than me, one is enough.

I think I was about seven or eight when, you know, when I began to notice that I had to do things that girls do and not boys. I was always with boys and girls in a group, never just one boy or one girl. But boys . . . boys play soccer and girls don't, and they do lots of other things different, too. I never played soccer, I never wanted to, I just don't like it. I don't know how to explain it but . . . girls play with dolls, and they fix themselves up and things I like that. Boys don't. With them it's cars, ball games, and all that. No, I never wanted to play the kinds of games boys play, not even when I was four, five. Never ever. There was always this difference. In my [public] school we're all in class together, but some things are different. The girls accept it. . . . Like when you see the fights, I never . . . whenever there's a fight in the classroom I always leave the room, so I won't get scolded or have to take a note home. That's what I try to do, to always kind of keep my distance. I don't like it when I see them doing things that are wrong. So I just keep away in order not to be hurt, too; that's what I always do. But with the girls it's not like that. I always hang out with the girls because I think that's right. But when I see that a girl's . . . going wrong . . . is going to lead you down the wrong path, then I keep away from her. I have one close friend at school and I always sit with her, not with the others, and I don't turn around a lot in class. When I have some work to do with somebody else, it's always that same girl I do it with. I don't have any real close friends among the boys.

When I grow up I want to have children, two, a girl and a boy. . . . I like girls a lot, but I also like boys, to take care of. I'm planning to do lots of things, but I won't do what many women do—leave my children at a friend's house while I go to a party or to the movies at night. I'm . . . I'm going to do everything so that it all comes out right. I don't want to do anything that's wrong. And I'll work, too, if I can, and take care of my children, too. If I can't manage that, then I'll find a nanny for them, or, I don't know. . . . It's more important for a woman to have a job than for a man, I think. You see, most men don't want anything and . . . well, I guess for some people it's better for the man to work than for the woman. But when I get married, I don't want one of those husbands who goes, "Oh, let me take care of everything, you don't need to work," I don't want that. Me and him, we'll both work, we'll both work outside the house, and then when we come home we'll share the work, I'll do some things and he'll do others. Though maybe when we get home I'll do all the housework by myself. That would be fair, too, so that the children could live in a clean house. And then, if anybody came for a visit, everything would be neat and clean. If possible I'd like the children each to have their own room, and I'd have to clean their rooms, too. They'd play and leave all their toys lying around, and when I'd get home from work I'd straighten up, put everything back where it belongs, so it would all be nice and neat. Yes, I think I'll get married. I can't imagine being like these women you see today who seem to live in the street. Every day they've got a new boyfriend. At that birthday party upstairs, where we met, the women at the party, most of them weren't married ̣ı̣ı̣ı̣, but they're all right, I don't mean that. I mean those girls that are always hanging out in the street . . . some man invites them somewhere and off they go. . . . I don't think that's a good thing for them to do. But my friends here in the building, they're different. They go to work, come home, watch some television.

If I don't get married, I'll at least have some kind of pet of my own, like Valmira who lives downstairs—she doesn't have a boyfriend, but at least she has a kitten, you see? That way you can . . . can have some fun. But actually I think I will get married, I intend to. Nineteen or twenty, up to twenty-one, would be a good age. And the boy ought to be about twenty-two or twenty-three. The age would depend on what kind of person he is. He could be older or even a bit younger, but . . . I'd rather he was one or two years older. I don't know why [*laughs*]. Sometimes I wonder . . . but I think it's better that way, to tell the truth. For example, my father is a year younger than my mother, but I don't know if that had anything to do with it.

My earrings? I had my ears pierced this year. I always wanted to have it done, but I thought it would hurt, and only this year I got up my courage and did it. Sometimes I wear the same earrings in both ears, but now it's the fashion to wear different ones [*laughs*]. I've always loved jewelry. These [five] rings I'm wearing. . . . I have others, too, but my mother fights with me if I wear them all at once. It's good to fix yourself up, to wear a bracelet, or a ring at the very least. I think it's pretty. Some girls don't like it, but most of the girls I know wear some kind of jewelry. Maybe it gives them more appeal, I'm not sure. Yes, it's important for women—but not for men, for a man wearing a watch is enough. But a woman wants to wear a bracelet, a little ring. Men don't need to be as attractive as women, a bit less is okay. Why? . . . because . . . I think that a man doesn't need these things to go out, to be able to . . . I can't explain it, but he just needs to look neat, to have a bit of style. But a woman needs a lot more. Women have to fix themselves up more than men; it's more difficult for a woman because she's not . . . she's got to fix herself up because she's not the one who's going to make the first move when she sees a man. It's the man who's got to come up to the woman out there. And for him to come up to her, she's got to be well dressed, all fixed up. And when the man's a good man, and wants a woman just for himself, to marry and everything, then he's not going to want one who's messy. He's going to want a good girl, who knows how to fix herself up. But nowadays some of these men don't care what they've got, they just want one more woman, anyone at all.

Let's see . . . what else does a woman need to know? She has to know how to fix herself up; she can't be casual about these things. She has to be careful. She also has to work and earn money so she can live and take care of herself. The things I like in my girlfriends are for them to be studious and not messy, and to be a good friend, too. To help their mothers at home. Lots of things. To know how to take care of the things they have, and to appreciate them. It's different for boys, they're always playing, doing what boys do, but they should do what's right, too, and not do bad things. They shouldn't fight. They should study, too, and not do wrong things. They should really try to be good. And lots of other things, too.

No, the girls I know don't do the same things the boys do, and I don't think they should. You see, the boys . . . they know more, they have to know more, they have to know . . . how to react in a certain way, but women can't react that way. For example, in the street. Every day the man has some place to go. He goes to a bar and talks to his friends. But not the woman. I mean, the right sort of woman isn't going to leave her house and go to a bar to talk to the men. If she wants to? I don't know . . . then she . . . I don't know, the boys are always—I don't know how to explain the difference, but I think that boys have always got to have more freedom than girls. When the boys go out, they go to a friend's house, they go to play in the street, to play ball. But the girls are more . . . they also go out in the street, but they're not going to do the same things the boys do. They'll go to chat with the other girls, they'll sit on a bench . . . it's just different. I don't think I know any girls who want to do the things boys do. I might have known some, but I dropped them when I saw that they didn't want to do girl things. I think there was one like that . . . but she wasn't really a friend.

Y E S ,   M Y   M O T H E R has talked to me about sex. And once in a while the subject comes up at school. I don't know everything, but I know a lot already . . . but it wasn't just from my mother. Some of her girlfriends also tell me things; sometimes I spend the day with them. It's an interesting subject, but not for children. I haven't gotten my period yet; there's time for all that. I like my age. I think everyone who's ever been this age must have liked it. I just want to be a good girl and not do things that are wrong. Well, let's see . . . I can think of lots of things a girl shouldn't do, like going out at night in the street, like lots of them do around here, and staying alone with the boys, though there are some girls who think it's all right to do that. I always want to stay in what seems like a safe place, the right place, not the wrong one. And always go in the right direction and do the right things. It might be interesting to do some things . . . like travel around the world on a ship, but since I can't. . . .

What kinds of things might I want to do [*sighs*]? I'd like to live in a very peaceful place, where there wouldn't be holdups and pollution, where I could live peacefully. I wish there wouldn't exist all this business about the bomb. . . . I wouldn't mind a place that was cold, but it shouldn't be lonely or sad, and there shouldn't be holdups and attacks, or the kind of poverty you see around here with people sleeping in the street wrapped up in newspapers—that shouldn't exist. But here, for example, here at home we're not rich, but we're also not poor. We have a place to live, my mother always finds money to pay the rent, and at least . . . we have what we really need, there's always something. But there are people going hungry, who haven't got a thing to eat. No one should have to go hungry.

I'd like to find a place where everyone could earn a bit of money. And I'd like to be a doctor, or a secretary. Because a doctor gets to take care of people—it's a good job, isn't it? And a secretary because . . . or maybe a bank teller would be nice. I haven't really decided. I'm not sure, but I'd just like to find a good job where I earned enough and liked it, too, not a job you have to do just to earn money. I'd like to earn a good salary and like the work I'd be doing, too. And I'd want to continue to work after getting married, but that would depend on the salary he earned. If it was enough to support the household, that might be all right. Then I would have time to take care of the house, my children, and I'd find some way of filling my time. But I think that a man who works has a more interesting life . . . he can get more out of life, because he's outside the house so he . . . but the woman, if she's going to be a housewife, she has to stay at home, she has to do everything at home and just stay there, stay home. But not the man. He goes off in the morning and comes back at night. I think it's better to work outside the house.

But at home I think the man has to be in charge, the father . . . because, for example, the mother doesn't work, she's a housewife, so he's the one who's putting food on the table. Now if the woman works, too, it gets more complicated, and it's hard to say who should be in charge. But if she just works in the house, she's not earning money, right? He's the one who's trying to provide things for the household. If she wants things for the house, most of them the father has to provide. He's got to earn the money to buy the food for her to prepare. . . . But in some things he depends on her, too. I can't explain it . . . it's not that men are smarter—some women are smarter than men, and some men are smarter than women. I like to decide things for myself, so I don't think that in my house there's going to be this business of a head. When it comes to taking care of the children, for example, it's the mother who decides what to do because the father's out working and the mother's the one watching the children. When the baby's small, the mother gives it baths, feeds it, so for those things she's in charge. Here at home my mother decides everything. If my father showed up and told her what to do, she wouldn't put up with it, because he's not supporting the family; my mother is, she's doing it all by herself. If I wasn't working I could accept my husband's being the boss in some things, but not in others. I'd be taking care of the children and he wouldn't . . . and if I didn't have children and didn't have a job, I'd stay home alone and take care of the house, which wouldn't be as interesting as having a job or children. But first I'd like to go to university. It depends if I'm good, good at exams. If I do well I could go on studying. I like school, I like to study.

I'm not sure what sort of job I'd want my husband to have [*laughs*]. Maybe manage a bank—that's a good job, isn't it? He could earn enough. A doctor's a good job, too.

I F   I   T H I N K of my life in the future, when I'm twenty, say, I imagine I'd be working, and my husband would work, too; and if I had children and continued to work, I'd find someone to stay with the children, and when I'd come home from work I'd take care of them. I'd love to have a little girl. . . . Girls are . . . you can dress them up more when they're little . . . and girls go along with the things their mothers do, but boys, no, boys don't want to have anything to do with their mothers, you see. That's why I'd prefer to have a girl.

6

ENTREPRENEURS

18

Ana Maria is a White woman in her late thirties who inherited a large sugar mill in the Northeast. Inheritance laws in Brazil give (legitimate) daughters and sons equal protection. Under the old Portuguese marriage regime of complete community of goods, a surviving spouse retained half of the couple's joint estate, while one-third of the estate was inherited in equal parts by all the legitimate children (who could not be disinherited). Only the remaining third could be freely disposed of in a will.[1]

I visited Ana Maria's sugar mill one weekend in August 1981; thereafter, I interviewed her in the coastal city in which she now lives, several hours' drive from the rural area where her estate is located. Her husband, a tall and somewhat autocratic figure, manages the mill, while Ana Maria deals with—as she calls it—"the social side." She was uncertain of the size of the estate and the number of employees, but some months after our conversation she sent me a data sheet with the following information.

The property is more than 10,000 hectares in size and includes more than 20 separate plantations that provide the mill with sugar. More than 2,000 agricultural laborers (male) live permanently on the plantations, and at harvest time nearly 800 temporary workers come to provide the additional needed labor. All of these people earn between one and two minimum salaries, as do several hundred of the mill operatives and a few dozen foremen. Above them are about 70 mill operatives and supervisors earning between two and five minimum salaries, 20 men earning between five and ten, and, finally, another 20 who earn more than ten minimum salaries. The permanent workers have close to 5,000 dependants living with them, and the migrant workers bring with them over 1,500 more.

About half of the plantations are still without electricity, and most do not have running water. Each plantation has approximately 60 houses and a school, and each family has a small plot of land whose crops supplement the laborers' salaries. Agricultural laborers' wives or companions also work cutting cane, as do children who, at eight or nine years of age, begin to perform lighter tasks for which they receive a smaller wage. All the permanent

ANA
MARIA

employees are officially registered workers, thus eligible for federal and regional social and medical benefits.

This is the world for which Ana Maria expresses a sense of responsibility, a world she must perpetually balance against the smaller realm of her own life and family. When she speaks of "the mill," Ana Maria usually means the administrative and technological seat of the estate, at which the mill itself and the family's large and comfortable house are situated.

———

Originally, the estate was a sugar mill constructed by my great-great-grandfather. And then it passed into other people's hands, and eventually my grandfather bought it back—that was some years before I married. He owned other things, too—a textile factory, real estate, and some businesses, but not a mill. When my grandfather bought the mill back, my husband, who's an agronomist, went to work there. He was very young then, he'd just got his degree in agronomy and had gone to São Paulo for further training—this was before we got married; he spent several months in one of the modern sugar mills there. Then when we married I moved to the mill and, although I used to visit it before that, it was something totally new to me—the people, the way of life. I didn't even realize such a way of life existed. I was just a girl, really, and I could see these extremely serious problems. I couldn't sleep nights . . . I didn't feel comfortable knowing there were people there—for example, having babies, which was something I really wanted, and they were having them at home with an untrained midwife. That was a great shock to me. The people had this image of the owners, they were ashamed to come to us. Then I invited a midwife from a hospital to go to live at the mill, and I began to do deliveries with her, to go to people's houses for deliveries. And I realized this was also a way of getting closer to the people there, and in fact they started to worship me because I'd begun to help them, delivering babies with the midwife. It wasn't easy at first . . . they wanted to be closer, but they were ashamed, and the best way I could find to get in touch with them was to go along with the midwife—because nobody expected me to show up, to help. And I'd talk to them as usual, and this tie of friendship got established, and after that I was able to sense what their needs were, what their lives were really like.

I didn't go to university. I took a teacher-training course, but then I went to live in the interior of the state, and the roads at that time were really awful. It was a shame because I was ready to take the *vestibular* [university admission examination] in pedagogy, and I've always been sorry I didn't do it. But I wanted to have a child right away. I was nineteen when I married, and I knew it would be hard for me to get to school because the roads weren't what they are now—it used to take an hour to get to the city, and you'd often get mired in the middle of the road. So it would have been quite difficult for me to coordinate it all. But it's something I've always regretted. I would have loved to teach, and I've really missed that at the mill. I could have been a lot more useful there if I'd done it. I wish my family had advised me better, because I was only nineteen and in a way I was still a child.

My father is a lawyer. My mother never started university, she married even younger than I did—she was only seventeen. I have three brothers; I'm the oldest. You see, my grandfather had two children, my mother and a son who was never really well. And when my grandfather got old, he divided up everything he owned, so that the businesses went to my mother and the real estate to my uncle. And then my mother realized that it wouldn't work to have things in the hands of a group, so she decided to divide everything she had among her four children. My brothers didn't get along too well, and my husband didn't get on too well with them, either, so it was clear they wouldn't be able to act as a group. My father is a very good person, but he's not an entrepreneur; that's just not his way. Everybody's born different. Well, my mother sensed this, and she determined to do things the best way possible. So, my brothers still hold shares in the mill and we pay them dividends, but the control is in our hands.

My grandfather ran everything for twenty years, while my husband, who was the agronomist there, was working his way up. After a while he became the manager. Twenty years. It's a long time, he moved up slowly, and he took charge of the mill while my grandfather still owned it. But my grandfather always had the last word. And then, a few years ago, we took it over and now the last word is ours. If there's not enough money, we're the ones who have to wheel and deal to get it. Any problems that come up are ours. Including all the social problems. My mother was always intensely interested in that side of things, and from the time we were small we got used to that, but now she no longer wants to be involved in that: "Oh, that's over for me, you've been prepared, now you deal with it. It's not just the mill that's in your hands now, but also the social side." She was pleased when I hired a social worker. This side I got from her, ever since I was little. Before, when they had the textile factory, she started a youth group there. You should have seen how concerned she was if someone got sick! She never said no to anyone, and even if she couldn't solve the problem, she always listened. She guided us in that direction and it stuck, because my other brother—I'm not very attached to him, although I am to the other two—even he is very sensitive to this social side.

When my grandfather still ran the mill we didn't go there much, because my mother didn't go often. When I was little we lived near the [textile] factory, but that wasn't like the mill at all; it was an urban reality, very different—it was another world. But after my marriage I lived at the mill for twelve years, while my grandfather was still in charge. My husband was running things, he worked right there, and I was living there, too, so the people looked upon me as their mistress—I mean, they knew I wasn't the owner yet, but they treated me as if I were.

I'm not sure how many plantations there are, more than a dozen—I can get you the figures if you like—but they all belong to us, and they provide the mill with sugar. Each plantation has an administrator, a person actually responsible for that plantation. Then there's the supervisor, who's in charge of about three or four plantations. I started working with the people when I went to live there, and we've improved things constantly since then. I hope we go on doing that. About seven or eight years ago, we created a representative, that's what he's called— that's quite apart from the supervisor—and he represents the agricultural laborers. He's responsible, say, if a person falls sick. Since my husband and I can't talk to all the people on all the plantations personally, we talk to the representatives and work together with them.

Most of the laborers live on the plantations, but during harvest time, when you have to cut the cane quickly and there's more work, lots of people come from the backlands. No, I'm not sure of the size of our property, or the number of people who work there—but I can get all that data for you. There's a special name for the temporary workers, I just can't think of it at the moment.[2] Anyway, they come in September and they stay until the mill finishes all the work, which is usually about June. Then they return to the backlands where they have a small plot of land. But in the backlands they live only on what they plant, and they can earn more by cutting the cane, so they like to come to us.

It's changed a lot since the old days. There used to be far more of these temporary workers, but my husband doesn't want to do things that way any-more. He thinks the whole enterprise has to be better organized, with all the workers officially registered. Otherwise, if an accident occurs, or if there's some problem with these workers, it's a lot harder to get it settled. So, from the business point of view, it's better for all the workers to be registered, even the agricultural laborers. Now when they come they get a contract for a fixed period of time. It didn't used to be like that; there was no contract. But it's better for the business that it be done this way. Still, it's very hard, because the cane cutters work for only three and a half hours a day. They get up very early—they've got the habit—they go out to cut the cane, they cut it, and they go back home and don't want to come out again. For the rest of the day they drink. It's been like that for a very long time, it's an archaic mentality. But today they could earn twice as much—and this is something we're trying to set up, aside from the social work, to improve the business, to shape a new mentality.

I'm not sure what they earn now, I think it's a bit more than the minimum salary. I've heard my husband say it's between one and two minimum salaries. If they worked two shifts—I mean if they went back home, washed, had lunch, and went back to the fields, they'd earn a lot more. But they haven't got this frame of mind, because they've never been to school, and the older ones—poor things—they drink a lot. Nobody's ever worked with them. So, as a result, we've got to have many more laborers than we actually need. That's the reality of the plantations. Now at the mill, no, there they work eight hours a day. The difference in salary used to be much greater, but it's not anymore. Now there's a union, they're all organized, all the laborers, and they've gotten a lot of things through their union. It's one union of all workers in the sugar industry, and the union sets the salaries. For each kind of job there's a fixed salary, and you're obliged to give them exactly what was decided on.

At the mill there are only men working, it's not like in the fields where there's work for their wives. It's very heavy work at the mill, so it has to be that way. For women there's work as teachers, and we have a little hospital at the mill, with a midwife and a lab technician to test feces and urine, things like that—those are the only women. The hospital is for everyone, the field laborers and the men at the mill, everyone who's part of the estate.

I'd say we're medium-size. We're not one of the largest mills in the state, nor are we among the smallest. There's a fair amount of land, and that's necessary in order to have the raw material to mill. There's no point in upgrading the equipment if there's nothing to mill. So it's very important to plant more cane and increase the crop. My husband doesn't want to raise cattle or plant anything else. He has to plant sugar cane so that the mill can process it.

My husband likes being in charge, of course. For example, in my grandfather's time the mill was remodeled, and my husband thought they should take out a large loan and really do what was needed to modernize, so that it could compete with the other mills, all of which were doing that. But my grandfather was very . . . he had an old-fashioned mentality and was extremely responsible in that sense. He would never . . . he'd only take out a loan if he could really pay it off, you see. He didn't have the mentality to be in debt and not know what he was going to do next. So he borrowed a little money and didn't do a complete renovation, and the result is that we're finishing doing it now, in order to increase production.

My husband goes to the mill on Wednesday mornings and comes back at night, rather late, at about 10:00 o'clock. And then he goes again on Fridays and generally stays until Sunday. I usually go then, too. I lived at the mill until my oldest son was in second grade. Then, although we had a primary school at the mill itself, you always want the best school for your children, don't you? So my son went to school at the mill until second grade, and then we came here [to the city], and since then he's been in a very good school, and he's doing fine there, thank God, except that just recently I hired a tutor to give him some extra classes. I have four children, three boys and a girl who's six years old. The boys are fifteen, twelve, and ten.

HOW CAN I DESCRIBE my life here in the city? I have my house, and now that the children are bigger they're all in school. When I'm in the city I spend a lot of time at home, but since I'm constantly looking after the social side for the mill, there's always something for me to do. Sometimes the social worker calls me from the mill with a problem, sometimes I have to contact some government agency. Since that's what interests me, there's always something I have to take care of. . . . At least once a week I spend a morning or an afternoon resolving problems with the social worker. Because the problem she deals with, you've got to straighten them out right away.

Aside from that . . . I stay at home, I go to my children's school when necessary, but I don't do much else. You see, with four children you constantly have to . . . one needs some help with schoolwork . . . it's hard to coordinate it all, and for everything to run smoothly you've got to be there, on the spot. I think we should bring up our children ourselves. I have trouble accepting . . . it's an old problem we've got, of having servants to do things for them, and I think it doesn't prepare the children for life. But here in Brazil it's difficult to change this attitude because how can you get your child to understand that . . . you want him to do things in the house even if you've got someone there to do it? There's no way he can understand, and to break through this—how can I put it?—this kind of structure. . . . In other places, where they don't have servants, the kids have lunch at school, so that's already much easier for the mother—they just have breakfast and dinner at home. But here, everything—I mean, the husband comes home for lunch, too, and the children, so you really need someone to help out at home.

The house we live in now—I got the land as a present when I married. Then, when I lived at the mill, I used to spend weekends with my grandmother, at her house. Actually it was a hotel that my grandfather owned at the beach, so I'd stay with her at the hotel. But after my third child I thought it was getting very difficult to stay at the hotel, although she was really good to me, so then we bought a small house at the beach. After that my husband built a house, our own house, but we rented it out to an American executive for several years, and then, when we finally came to live in the city, that's where we went.

Right now, let's see, I have three servants who live with me: a cook, a cleaning woman, and that girl you saw at the mill—she used to take care of my daughter when she was a baby. She could perfectly well do all the cleaning now, too, but she doesn't like it much and, since she's a good person, when I go to the mill I take her, not the others. Just one person in the house isn't enough, so I've kept all three on. Then there's a washerwoman who comes in twice a week and washes the clothes. No, there's no washing machine. I don't have one because I thought that . . . you see, whatever they get their hands into . . . they're not very handy. The iron breaks. If you buy an electric blender, it breaks. If it were just up to me I'd have one, but their level is so low that it would break in an instant. And also I felt that it's not that much work, because nowadays if I really thought it was necessary I could buy one. I couldn't have before, but now I'm more relaxed about money, but I don't really feel like it. It's not a chore that's that hard for her to do. I mean, if it were me, I'd really feel it [*laughs*], but she, she does it perfectly happily, singing. She's never asked me. She could have said, "Senhora, wouldn't it be possible to buy a machine?" Now the cook, she's on a higher level, and she asked me for an electric mixer, which I bought for her since I felt sure she would appreciate it and take care of it.

Their salaries, let's see . . . they've only been there about six months, there's a constant turnover. I pay my servants well. I pay the cook about $110 a month, and the cleaning woman $80, and the girl gets $50—she gets less because, even though she's been there the longest, she doesn't make much of an effort. She could have learned to cook a steak, for example, on the maid's day off. She could help out a bit, but she doesn't want to earn more, or to learn anything either. I've even discussed this with her, you see, and she knows that she earns much less than the new ones who've just started, but she just doesn't want to. She's about sixteen or seventeen, and she's going to school nights.

Then why don't they stay? Look, I was surprised that this last cook left because she was really popular at home. She was on a much higher level than the others—since I pay more I try to find a better level of servant, you see. But she got involved with a painter who was doing some work at the house. She was over fifty, and he was a boy of twenty, and she fell in love with him [*laughs*]. She didn't actually go away with him, I think she felt ashamed. She told me she was sick, she said she had a bad pain in her head, so I sent her to the Institute and went on paying her salary for a month. I was about to make an appointment for her with a private doctor because I was really worried, but then the others told me she was with this painter and was in no hurry to come home because she was having a great time. Well, I was still paying her, so I went to her house and discovered that—I mean, she really had been sick earlier, but at that point she could have come back to work. I set a date for her to come back, but then she preferred not to work.

Yes, I did say she lived with me, but she had a little house of her own that she rented. You see, at my house this is the system: they sleep there and every two weeks have time off. She can leave Saturday afternoon, after making lunch, and come back on Monday. Perhaps if she'd talked to me about this love of hers I wouldn't have gotten upset. Not that she could have gone to her own house every day, because in general when they go home every day they start getting into the food. They consider themselves honest so long as they don't take objects from the house. It seems to me that taking food, things like that, doesn't weigh on their conscience. My washerwoman is a very honest person, she'd never take a piece of my clothing. I don't lock up anything in the house, I think it's offensive for a person to work in a house where food is kept track of, and I've never, ever, locked anything up. But I notice that at times they've gotten into something, and they seem to do this without thinking it's wrong. Perhaps they need it at home, really need it, and they see that there's more than enough at my house. But it would be better if they'd ask me, and I would give it to them. I mean, if I have lots of bananas and someone tells me she doesn't have any at her house, I'd give her some. I give them to the night watchman—I forgot to mention that he also works here; but he doesn't live with us, he works for a company.

Yes, I live surrounded by people, but I manage. For example, when I feel the need to be alone, I send the children and my husband to the mill for a week and I don't go. I take care of myself [laughs], oh yes, I do. My house is a very open one. My husband's the kind of person who makes friends easily, and the house is always full. My children also bring lots of their friends; they often have some friend sleeping over. At times it gets to be too much, and you feel really worn out. When that happens I just say, "Go to the mill, take the children. I'm staying here today." But he doesn't really like this; he complains about it. He goes along, but he thinks it's terrible. And also when I'm not home for lunch. He says a woman should do what she likes, because he always supported me at the mill, with the social side. That part is fine, he doesn't mind that at all. But I feel that my presence in the house—for example, if I want to take a class or go out somewhere, if I go but am back at dinner time, that's fine; but if I'm not there, he doesn't much like it. I do it, but he doesn't like it at all, I can feel that he's hurt and. . . . How ridiculous! When he comes home at whatever hour he pleases!

HIS FAMILY wasn't rich like mine, but that never created any problems because he had the same level of education. And now that he's . . . that he and I own the mill, there's no difference at all, although I think I ought to be more involved with the mill, the accounting part, the actual work. But I don't seem to have much vocation for management. I take after my father. I don't like it, it's not my talent, but I feel that I ought to be more involved. Why? Because it's my responsibility, too, as well as his, you see. I think it would be more responsible of me, whether things turned out better or worse. Yes, he'd like me to, also, he's suggested it, but I don't feel capable. I mean, to just stand there like a lizard with its head swaying from side to side, no, that I won't do. Although why couldn't I learn, if other people do? I just need someone to start to teach me. But I don't really want to. I think the real reason I haven't done it is that I don't really like it, and I'm afraid of going there and just lying around like a lizard. But I feel like I'm doing the wrong thing and I *ought* to be more involved, because our responsibility is equal. I mean, what if something went wrong while my husband was in charge? If we lost the mill. . . . It's not really the money that worries me, everybody likes to have money, but that's not it. What really affects me is that my children might one day want to be a part of it. Their father talks to the boys about it already, he takes them around the plantations.

When I was growing up . . . I was very close to my grandparents. Not so much to my father's family because my other grandfather died when I was still a baby. But my mother's father lived at the mill, and we lived in a small town not far away, and every Sunday we'd go to the mill to spend the whole afternoon. I was always very attached to my grandmother, much more than to my mother. Funny, isn't it? I just felt much closer to her. She was from the South; her people were in the government, very learned and capable people. She met my grandfather in Rio and married him. She married very young. My grandfather was an engineer, and after a while they came to the Northeast. He didn't have all those businesses yet, nothing, and she told us that the first real toilet in the town was in her house. She was someone who was . . . intelligent. She respected my grandfather, she thought the world of him, you could feel that. And she was very open, very affectionate. My mother is rather cold, incapable of giving anyone a hug.

No, we don't address our parents formally anymore. What do you mean? You heard my son address me as "Senhora"? Now that you mention it, it's true, he does occasionally call me "Senhora," but he's the only one of the four who does that, I'm not sure why. I never addressed my parents that way. It just varies from one family to the next.

As I was saying, my mother's a rather cold person, but with a really strong personality. My father's a very good person, but in our family the real power was my mother. I'm not sure why, I just never got along well with her. It wasn't that she was very rigid, she wasn't, but she had these very strong beliefs about religion. My grandmother was much more open, much more. She would talk things over with us naturally. I just felt good with her, and she was very affectionate; my grandfather, too. When I got married she almost became my husband's mother-in-law.

My parents brought us up with a very strict and traditional education. Marrying virgin. Marriages could never be undone. She always used to say, "It's in sickness and in health. Think twice before marrying"—because she was Catholic, and in our religion you can't divorce. So that's how it was, more or less that tone. But she didn't want me to marry young, not at all. She never felt she was raising me just so I could marry when I got to, say, seventeen, no. I could have led whatever life I wanted.

School was very important in my home. But I myself began to date very young, at fourteen, and then I fell in love and I didn't want to go on studying. But school was always taken very seriously. I even learned English. Since my family was rich, I had an English governess who lived in the house for two or three years. But I had a horror of speaking English, because I felt that I was different from other children and nobody else had a governess—though she didn't really interfere in our education at all. She just gave us lessons and talked to us in English. But we could run around alone—she wasn't our nanny, more like a tutor. But even so I felt different from the other children, and I hated it. I went to school just like the other children, but then at home I'd have English lessons in the afternoon. I don't speak English well, although I ought to, considering the time I spent studying it. I can make myself understood, but I can't write well. Today I think it was great to have studied English, it's an advantage when I travel, so I think my mother really did the right thing. But, at the time, I thought it was awful. I was terribly ashamed. I used to hide it, I wouldn't tell anyone I knew some English, I felt that bad about it.

My mother did talk to me about sex. If I asked her she'd say, "Tomorrow I'm taking Communion, so I'll explain this to you today." She did talk about it, but always in a rather formal tone and always linked to religion, never as something natural. I had a very poor notion of sex. Not that this hurt me; it didn't damage me at all in my sex life, except perhaps in the sense of some problems about guilt. Lots of guilt. Aiiiiii . . . incredible! When I was small I used to dream about guilt. But when I began to date I didn't really feel guilty, only when I'd do something bad [laughs]. I was scared to death of getting pregnant. In those days that would have been the end of everything. I didn't really have much information, I just knew what was right and what was wrong, but in a very formal sense—that it could only happen once you were married. In fact, while I was dating I went wherever I wanted, but always with a third person along. When I became engaged, that began to be tougher.

I can't tell you if I was a virgin when I married, truly. Because I had a bit of sex with him, so I can't really tell, but it wasn't a problem for me because . . . it was only with him, and we were already engaged. Before him I had lots of boyfriends, and we'd pet and so on, but just the way children do. With him it was really . . . something more, a passion that we both felt. We met when I was fourteen, and after we'd dated for two years or so he wasn't attracted to anyone else and neither was I. But I couldn't do anything wrong, so there was this problem of having a really bad conscience, a terrible fear of pregnancy, although, ironically, after I married I went for years without getting pregnant.

Each of my pregnancies was different emotionally. The first because it wasn't easy for me to get pregnant, so it was a great feeling, and the last because it was a girl. Each pregnancy was an incredible feeling. Having children was extremely important for me; I always wanted to have a large family. Now I think it's time for me to get involved in other things, and I have other responsibilities at this point. But when you have a small child at home, nowadays . . . I'm not much in favor of the mother working when she has a small child. A mother's care—even when you have money and could hire a nursemaid, no one can give the child what the mother gives. I'm in favor, for example, if the woman wants to work, she can do that once the child is about . . . like my little girl, she's six years old now and goes to school already. The first five or six years are fundamental in a child's life, fundamental. That's my opinion. And I also think children are very important. I married wanting to have children.

I don't use the pill. I keep track of my cycle, and I use an American product, a spray, during my fertile phase. I've never wanted to have my tubes tied. Not that I made a vow, nothing like that. If I had some health problem, I'd have them tied; and I've had three Caesareans—which would justify a tubal ligation. But I don't have any health problems. My uterus was fine, there wasn't anything wrong . . . but the Caesareans . . . I don't know, the children wouldn't be born. My husband says I'm so attached to the children that they don't want to be born [*laughs*]. The delivery date passes and I still show no signs of labor, even with induction. The doctor doesn't know how to explain it, because I'm completely normal. It's odd, but they don't come out, so it has to be done with a knife.

M Y   H O M E isn't at all like my parents' was. I don't have a strong personality like my mother. I'm a more gentle type, more pliant, more affectionate, more inclined to talk. I have my father's temperament. He was a very good person, but he also didn't have this affectionate side that I've got. I've always found it strange that at our house we'd kiss our parents only if we were going on a trip. Isn't that odd? Just on that day we'd give them a kiss, and my father would give us his blessing. Never at other times. But we felt fine at home, as I told you. It wasn't at all strict, not even my mother . . . although . . . she was very clean, that's something I never liked about her. She was very strict about cleanliness, things like clipping your fingernails. And she was very tidy. I never managed to tidy up my closets the way she wanted, so she used to do it for me. And even when I married, the first time I went to visit her at her house, when I got there she wanted to empty out all my suitcases. Neither I nor my husband liked that, you see. That's why I preferred to go to my grandmother's house; she didn't pay much attention to those things at all. She was very neat, too, and yet we could run around barefoot and so on. But my mother—she was very organized. That's the term: organization. And to this day I've never sewn a button on right, nor have I ever managed to really tidy anything up very well. To this day, I have a real horror of tidying up, and I can't seem to do it. My husband is tidy, and he cares about these things a bit, but I just can't.

O C C A S I O N A L L Y, on Sundays or when it's necessary, I cook, and I enjoy it. At the mill we have a cook, and a servant who's a boy—because there are two houses to care for [the main house and a guest chalet]—and a cleaning woman who also does the laundry. The boy who waits at table is part of the regular staff, and there's another one who usually works at the mill, but when we're there he comes to the house because I worry a lot about the children playing in the pool. And he also takes care of the water in the pool. The house was large and not well divided. There weren't enough bathrooms, and usually when we go to the mill we take my children's friends, we take family, and it's more comfortable if you have a better house. So last year we remodeled and had the chalet built, and that's when we had the pool put in. We thought it was very important for the children to like being there. In the chalet there are five guest rooms. During the week, for example, our lawyer sometimes stays there, and the social worker sleeps there, too.

As for other employees, now there's a resident doctor, Lauretta, and there were others before her. Since long before my husband took over the mill we've had a resident doctor. And before that the doctor used to come two or three days a week; he'd come and go. And there are two midwives who also live at the mill. Now the social worker—ideally she should live there, too, but normally she can't because she's married and has a child. There's another girl who did this work before her, though without a degree, and she still lives there. The social worker comes on Monday mornings and goes home at night. On Tuesdays she spends the day here in the city, dealing with government offices, taking care of all the problems that come up. Also, when people are sick and can't be cared for properly in our little hospital, or if some special medication is needed, she makes the arrangements. And when someone's here in the city because of an operation, she visits them in the hospital. On Wednesdays she's at the mill, and she stays there till Friday. On Friday night she goes to her own house. It's a full-time job. Right now she's earning about $550 a month. The other girl—the one without the degree—she's earning a lot, because she gets $550, too. I mean, she began with a certain salary, and it's constantly increased, and she wouldn't have accepted it if we'd tried to lower it. But she's earning a lot more than she needs. Ideally we should have one social worker earning more and living at the mill permanently.

Now the social worker with the degree, she also holds meetings at the plantations. She works with those representatives I mentioned to you. She visits all the communities on the plantations and sees what's really going on. She just recently started, so first of all she's getting to know the area where she's working. And the services that already exist—she's trying to energize them for the moment. The schools, the parents' and teachers' groups, everything that touches the lives of the people there. She's in contact with them, and she deals with it. I mean, she clears it with my husband first. Because we have some funds . . . they're insufficient, but you're obliged to spend a certain percentage per sack of sugar on social work. The government determines this, but for a person who wants to accomplish something, the funds aren't sufficient. You're free to use the money on whatever you want, on housing. . . . At the mill, for example, the social worker says we're spending a lot on health. Ever since she started working there, she's been complaining: "You're really laying it on where health is concerned, but I want to get into the housing aspect." But there's not enough money. You want to do things, but there just isn't enough.

We put in a lot of extra money, though, a great deal. The teachers are paid by us, the whole medical clinic, the doctor, the midwives. The doctor earns, to the best of my knowledge, about $600 a month, and gets a house, too. The teachers live at the mill, too. Yes, they're all young women. If they marry local men, they stay and keep on working. The teachers earn $120 a month; I know because recently we had a problem with the salary. They work morning and afternoon, but they teach the same class—I mean, they have the same preparations twice. At the mill, there are three or four first-grade classes—that's the grade that has the most children. The classes are small, not more than thirty-five, so she teaches thirty-five in the morning session and another thirty-five in the afternoon. At first it was difficult to get the teachers to accept this, teaching mornings and afternoons, because in the public schools they taught just half a day, although, if I'm not mistaken, they've recently switched to two sessions, too.

When I first moved to the mill, the schooling was terrible because the teachers didn't even have middle-school entry exams. There used to be a course that you had to take, like a mini-*vestibular*, in order to get into middle school. And the girls didn't even have that—so they had just four years of primary school, no more. Then I brought someone in to teach the teachers, to see which of them wanted to study further, and I organized a van to take them back and forth, and they all went back to school. Now I think we have about twelve teachers in all. Six or so live at the mill, and the rest . . . no, there must be more than twelve. Because the majority of the teachers are hired by the mill; but sometimes we can get one from the municipality, and we always take advantage of that so that none of the plantations should end up without a teacher.

But then another problem comes up: the teachers from the municipality usually want to do whatever they like in the school, things that aren't right. For example, they miss classes. But at the mill it's not like working for the government, where sometimes you're a friend of the mayor and he arranges some special leave for you for weeks on end. If you offer them more training, sometimes they're not eager to participate. But now they do go to school longer, not like when I first went to the mill. Now it's another reality. Everybody, even the children of the mill workers . . . it's something that pained me at first, and I'm encouraged because now they all want to go to school and are making an effort to learn. Some of them even get scholarships and go to school in the municipality, which is some distance. They go at night and come back at 10:00 o'clock, and sometimes they get bogged down because the road is still bad. The percentage of kids who go to school is very large now, but when they finish this middle-school course, they're still not capable of, say, working in an office at the mill—because they're still illiterate. Yes, even once they've finished middle school, often they can't write a letter. And now we've having a really serious problem, because they feel that since they've gone to school they don't want to work anymore cutting cane, which they consider to be an inferior sort of job, and yet they aren't fit for work in an office, either at the mill or in the city. So they feel discontented, and there's nothing they know how to do. With a tremendous effort some of them learn 'tilografia [dactilografia, i.e., typing]. Can you imagine!? They don't know how to write, and they want to learn 'tilografia, as they call it [laughs]. And all this is going to create an extremely serious problem with manpower. This is very worrisome. Professional training here just doesn't work, neither in the city nor at the mill, much less in the backlands. And they feel very disappointed. With a poor father who's made an effort to send his son to school, and when he finishes what can he do? He doesn't want to come back to the sugar cane, and he's not capable of finding a better job anywhere else. So what happens? Sometimes they go to São Paulo; it's much bigger, and sometimes they manage to find a job—but not in an office, nothing like that. They learn some sort of trade there, in order to work, to be a chauffeur, something like that. This is a very serious problem, I think.

ON THE PLANTATIONS everybody works, the men's wives too, and they earn the same as the men. Only among the mill workers do the wives stay at home, but on the plantations, no, almost all the women work, and even the children once they get a bit older. Sometimes they skip class because they want to help their fathers in the fields.

No, they don't pay for their houses, we provide them, and the light and water. They don't pay for anything. The houses near the mill—near that field where they were playing soccer when you visited—that's where the mill workers live. The houses further away, those aren't as good, they're in very bad shape. But, for example, mud houses, the kind made with palm leaves, where you find the *barbeiro* [insect that transmits Chagas' disease], that sort of thing we don't have. If anyone puts one up, my husband has it torn down immediately because we know that the *barbeiro* causes a horrible disease. But the houses are in very bad shape, it's true.

For some time we've been constructing lavatories on the plantations, with the help of the state social welfare agency. The state government provides various things, medications; and up to a certain age, if you're pregnant or have a child, you receive a food basket. That's taken care of by the other girl, the one who's not actually a social worker. She gives classes in how to feed and take care of children, all that. And she's organized it and done it very well, which is why she's still there. Now I'm not sure if this is good or bad, because I think this motivates these people to have more children, you see, because they want to stay in that program and keep on getting the food basket. It's a good deal, especially these days with the cost of living so high. So I'm not sure, but I think they may be motivated to stay in the program and not mind if they're expecting another child. But, on the other hand, it really is a good thing; it provides great help.

The social worker also talks to them about contraception. Many of them want it, although it's mostly the people at the mill who've already got some notion about having fewer children, because they're somewhat better educated than the men on the plantations. Now on the plantations most of them don't want contraception. Their wives have fourteen children, and they feel like men only so long as they're making babies. It's very difficult to change that mentality, it moves very slowly. But the women on the plantations are very free, I think. Since they work, too, they don't depend on the men. At the mill, they do. You see, there's one reality on the plantations and another at the mill, and the women of the plantations have a lot more freedom than those who live at the mill. Even if their husbands leave, they just go right on in their own houses, there's no problem at all. They have whatever children they want. They find another man, they've no difficulty finding another one. Now at the mill, they have problems. Since the woman doesn't work she has to put up with her husband, she has no one else to live with. I mean, if the husband takes another lover—I know of several cases like that—she has to stay with him. She has five or six children by him, so she's not going to be able to find employment anywhere else. She's got nowhere else to live, so she has to bear it all. And as the level rises the situation gets worse. For example, the personnel in the office . . . they have more money and therefore more lovers. And it . . . it hurts, to see this. Although it also happens that the women at the mill betray their husbands. We end up knowing everything. Everybody talks: "So-and-so was at such-and-such a house last night"; everybody knows.

Not too many people marry formally, either in the Church or in a civil ceremony, but maybe they're more likely to have a civil ceremony. Even so, there are few. Most of the girls lose their virginity at a very young age. They actually have more sexual freedom than middle-class women, since it's not a problem for their fathers and mothers. They don't feel that weight of responsibility that we do. And then the girls can work, too, on the plantations, so they manage.

These home remedies that the women use to abort, they just don't work. They take some medicine that's bad for your liver, but even so it's not enough to make you abort. I think they should avoid pregnancy instead. And nowadays the attitude is changing in the sense that some of them want to have their tubes tied, and this is done. I support that, yes, when it's someone with lots of children. If rich people can do it, why shouldn't these people, too? But INPS [National Social Security Institute] doesn't cover it, so you can't go there and say, "I want my tubes tied." You have to find a private doctor and pay. At the mill, because we've had friends who were doctors, when it was really necessary they've done it for free, in a hospital. But it's a favor, not something to which the women have a right.

And now, when the laborers get old, they have pensions. This is very recent. It's called FUNRURAL [Rural Worker Welfare and Social Security Fund].[3] It's really good these days, because before, when an old man who'd been working for years couldn't work anymore, his son wouldn't have wanted to take care of him at home, he'd just be a burden to them. But now that they get a pension, there's no question about their staying on. In general the children continue working, and it's to their benefit and to the old people's for them to stay because of the pension money. It didn't used to be like that. When I first went to live there, the old people would be kicked out by their children.

The people at the mill, I always say they're very intelligent people, and they learn. My husband has some people there—one who began as a tractor driver and today is an excellent topographer. You see, he managed to do it. But I don't know that much about the mill. . . . One year, when I was living at the mill, I wanted everyone in the fourth grade to get some training at the mill, but I got into a conflict with one of the foremen. I used to send the girls to the medical clinic to learn how to give first aid and do stool tests. It was a great idea, and even today there are some people doing well here in the city because they learned how to work at the mill. But it was something that could function only if I was there all the time, so it went on for a while and then it stopped because I really had to be on the scene every day to talk with one person and another, with the head of a section, and so on. If someone wasn't working out because she was undisciplined, I'd move her to another section, you see. And today there are people who have good jobs here in the city on account of this.

M Y   H U S B A N D   never goes into the plantations armed, nor have I ever been afraid. We've never had that sort of problem being the owners. But among the workers there are problems with alcohol and fights. There have been murders, too, of men and women, but not out of jealousy. People separate and someone else moves in, that isn't a problem. It's more out of drunkenness, the crimes that do occur. They're not premeditated, just things that happen out of the blue, and they use their *peixeiras* [knives]—they work with *peixeiras*, and if they get overexcited or something, somebody gets killed.

There's a police post at the mill, and a soldier from the municipality comes to the mill. He can arrest people; he can do whatever he, as the government authority, thinks best. Generally I have a talk with his whenever he's there. Because I won't allow anyone to be beaten, I mean in my own area—what's going on elsewhere I don't know. The people have a horror of being arrested and taken into town. They say they'll be mistreated there. If it's nothing very serious, the person just has to spend the night at the police post at the mill, as punishment, and he's released the next day. If it's serious, he has to be taken into town. But I always talk to the soldier first, so that nothing happens that I think shouldn't be going on—not while I'm there and can do something about it.

What can I tell you about politics? I loathe politics. Both sides, on both sides you see these people rise up, always wanting to take advantage of their power. Whether they're the government or the opposition. I think it's a ... horror. I wouldn't be in politics for all the money in the world. This social work I can be involved in, but I would never confuse it with politics, never. Now my husband thinks we ought to be involved, that he himself ought to ... run for some office.[4] He thinks that good men are fleeing, no one wants to get into politics these days. I don't know which party he'd be in. ... It's really difficult now because the government's so bad. What we see is these men's total bankruptcy. That's what he thinks, too. But we're afraid of the opposition, afraid that everything will veer completely to the other side. Communism, you see. Because there was a time [before the 1964 coup], a really bad time for the mills. They even shut the mills down for a week, because of strikes. It was tremendously damaging, production fell drastically. We were well liked at our mill, so nothing happened to us. But if the people get really worked up, you can't tell what might happen.

Still, I can't imagine that I'd have wanted any other sort of life. I accept this responsibility. The more you receive, the more you're obliged to give, to do. But it does feel like I have a lot of responsibility. And my husband does, too; he hasn't been spared this, either. Oh yes, we have the same values, we agree about how things ought to be done. Now, my husband's temperament is rather different. He's, well . . . let's say, he likes lots of people. He's very outgoing. How can I explain it to you? He talks a lot, he tells stories. It's just his nature to be that way; mine isn't. For example, I never say, "I'm going to the mill." I never say that, I never use the mill. I always say, "I'm going to the country" or "I'm going to my house in the country"—that's just my way of being.

T H E   R E S P O N S I B I L I T Y for the house is mine, in the city and at the mill. Even as far as money goes, I deal with everything. And where the social side is concerned, I'm very strong. There are women who don't have the strength to fire a doctor, to hire another one. If I want to do more with housing, to work with the social worker on this, which is what I've concluded lately, then I have the strength to carry it through.

The finances are like this: we have a joint account, but in general I tell him first. I have my own salary from the mill, about $1,000 a month of my own. I don't need to explain to him what I do with it. I've always had that, much less at the beginning, but I've always had a bit of money of my own. Even when I was single I used to have some. It wasn't much. Given our social status, it was very little even for those days. I wasn't raised as a rich girl who was given everything. No. I was raised like everybody else, having to be careful about money. My mother also wasn't raised like rich people. We were brought up to be normal. Today I'm a bit more relaxed about money. This $1,000 is mine; it's not for food or anything else. If I want to give it to charity, I do that. If I want to buy dollars for a trip abroad, I buy them. He doesn't even know what I do with it.

But apart from this, I generally say to him, "I'm going to need so much." I never go to the office and just take the money I need—I mean, I do take it, but I always tell him first. And then I take it myself, it's not he who gives it to me. But I always make him aware of it. He's never been tightfisted, even when I wasn't so . . . when I had much less, he never locked things up. My house has always been an open one. Food . . . the servants eat exactly what I eat, their rooms are the same as mine—except they don't have air conditioners, but they have fans to keep the mosquitoes away. They have electric showers [to heat the water]. I mean, there's no . . . they talk to us like anybody else. I mean . . . for example, they do eat separately, that they do, but their quarters and the way they relate to us are all as equals.

Now in this respect I don't think I'm succeeding with my sons. They treat the maid with a lot of condescension. They think it's her obligation to make them a sandwich. I'm worried about this, I think they're very self-centered. I don't know how to explain it, how my parents dealt with us. Of my three brothers, one doesn't behave that way, and the others are rather self-centered. And yet we were all raised in the same house, and we always had this example. A servant was never . . . for example, in my husband's family, which is of a lower level, I've noticed that servants are treated much worse than in my family's house. I don't know . . . it's just different. Maybe having more makes you feel more of a responsibility. At home there was always a lot of respect for the people who worked there. On both my father's part and my mother's. And even my grandfather and grandmother were like that, too. I remember, for example, the chauffeur who worked for my grandfather. My grandfather was the head of the establishment, he was everything, you see, but he never made the chauffeur wait for him. Never. Or said, "You're working this Sunday." No, he respected that individual. He would call him only if he genuinely needed him. And then he'd give him some other day off. In my husband's family I don't see that sort of thing. Well, as I said, we were never raised like rich people, like people who had everything, never. If someone needed to take a trip, for health or some such thing, it was gladly given, but we never had much money on hand. We used to take the bus, like all the other kids. In my time that wasn't usual for girls of my social level, but my parents tried not to give us that kind of education. I already feel some anxiety about doing these things wrong with my own children. But I think example is everything, and it's no use preaching something you don't do. At home they do get this example, both from my husband and from me. I just hope it sticks.

I can only tell you about my reality, the way I was raised, and my mother says that in her family, no, there was never this business of the masters going after the poor girls on the plantation. That didn't exist in her family, although it might have elsewhere. And she already had the plantations—not the mill, but the plantations. She says she doesn't ever remember hearing about anything like that. My sister-in-law, Margarida, says that my family is different. We don't have the mentality of the rich around here. It would be totally out of the question for my sons to try to take advantage of a girl. Totally. My mother, too, she always showed us this . . . because my brother who's still a bachelor, for a while he was seeing a waitress who worked at a hotel. This didn't shock my mother in the slightest. She's a person who is—different. She said, "Look, who cares if she's a virgin or not? What matters is if you care for one another and if you want to go on together." She's more concerned about the person's basic honesty than about anything else.

But one thing she'd never accept is divorce. And I'm not in favor of it, either, not in any circumstances. I think when there's the possibility of divorce, young people marry already thinking they've got other options. In marriage you build, the two of you build it, and that's why I'm against it. But separation, that's something else, because you can reach a point where you can't bear any more, and I don't think there's a law in the world that can keep you at the side of someone you don't love once you've reached the conclusion that you don't want to anymore. In that case, it's right. Now, the way I was raised, I could never take another husband. And my mother . . . if by chance one of her children should want a legal separation, that child and the grandchildren would always be welcome in her home, with open arms. But the second partner, no. That's what she always says. I don't know what would happen to me if I. . . . And on the religious side, too; I couldn't do it because my religion doesn't allow it. But on the, let's say, the human side of things, I don't know if I could bear it. . . . I think I couldn't bear to go on without another husband.

Words pour out of Lúcia with extraordinary speed and intensity. Her eyes flash, her hands move as she talks. She is a dark-skinned Black woman (with some Indian and White antecedents) in her mid-forties who gives the impression of containing more life than her small body can bear—and so it comes out, in dynamic speech and gestures, in more work to be done, in the dramatic story that she spins. Lúcia had been described to me as a "self-made woman." Born into poverty in a rural area of the Northeast, she had created a very successful hairdressing salon in the city through her own labor and persistence. The interview took place in 1981 in her home, a large new house, which she had decorated with artifacts from the Northeast—pottery, woodcuts, paintings, basketry. Lúcia has two children in their twenties from her first marriage, and now lives with her second husband and his two children. When the interview ended, Lúcia offered some advice about my hair.

Macaxeira [sweet cassava], just what you're eating right now, that's what's grown

19 in the part of the state where I was born, in a small town in the interior. My mother worked on a farm, she had four daughters, and it was really hard for her with five people to support, counting herself. I came to this city all alone when I was seven. I left my mother; I was only seven. Mama couldn't send us to school because she was having such a hard time. We were living on a farm, part of a sugar mill. Well, Mama was doing farmwork with the four of us, to support us, and we all had to help Mama, and she couldn't even buy notebooks . . . but I really wanted to go to school. I couldn't. I had just one year of schooling. So Mama said this to us, that since we couldn't go to school, we had to work, because there wasn't much money, not enough for us to live on. And I was the youngest child, the baby, the last daughter. Well, I . . . I actually did go to school for one year. The second year I managed to get into a public school, but I couldn't do the homework because we didn't have kerosene to burn in the lamp. This is probably the saddest story you'll ever hear. To see the woman I am today . . . the things that have happened to me!

LÚCIA

Well . . . Mama was a farmworker, and I used to burn corncobs to read my lessons by; that's why to this day I'm studying, to this day. . . . In one semester I'll have a degree in education, in vocational counseling, pedagogy. I work and I go to school. You see, my will power wasn't crippled, despite all the problems.

So I went to school for one year. Then I came here. In the town where I was born there was a produce market, and I had a godmother who owned a store and Mama took me, made them my godparents. I don't know whether it's the same thing in your country; after baptism there's confirmation, so Mama had me confirmed. This lady was a very good person. She always wanted me to stay with her in the city, but I was so little, Mama didn't want to let me go: I was her youngest daughter, her baby, very spoiled. Even though Mama was poor, she gave us lots of affection, four daughters, five females counting her. Without a father. My father deserted us. I never knew him because he left Mama. I was about a year old, and Mama was pregnant with a brother who died, so there were just the four of us, and I was the youngest, the littlest. I don't know anything about my father, just some things Mama told us about his type. But, even so, I've missed having a father. I longed for one, I complained about not having a father. Mama was everything to us, Mama was good.

So it happened like this. Mama took the girls, her daughters, my sisters, and it was like this. We all went out to work, and Mama said, "I'm going to keep you with me, 'cause you're the littlest one." But I said, "Mama, let me go, too, I need to work." I hated the farmwork. I thought that Mama and I, nobody . . . there wasn't enough . . . so I had to plant corn, beans, manioc, sugar cane. I was following in Mama's footsteps. I had a lot of, what do you call it, adult experience, but I didn't like it. And I used to say, "Mama, when I grow up . . ."—I was a scrawny little thing, you can see that even today I'm petite, I'm 5′ 1″—so I used to say, "Mama, when I grow up I'm going to go away." She'd say, "Never, because you're my littlest girl." Well, one time I went to my godmother's house with Mama, to do the marketing, and I said to Mama, "Mama, let me stay here in my god-mother's house." But she wouldn't. Then, another time, Mama was at the market and she met a man. He said, "How are you, Senhora?" Mama said, "I'm fine, thank you," and I was hanging onto her skirt. Then he went, "Senhora, you wouldn't have a girl I could take to the city to work as a maid?" And Mama said, "No, I don't, all my girls are working. I only have this little one, my youngest daughter, and I love her, I'm never going to let her leave." I just let Mama talk, and the man told her the kind of work he had in mind, as a domestic. And I said to him, "Senhor, wouldn't you like to take me with you?" I was only seven years old. Then Mama said, "No, I won't allow it." I said, "You see, I just don't like living here. I love my mother, but I want to live in a bigger place, where I can work. . . .

I like children a lot, I could take care of a child because I like them and I know about them." Then the fellow said, "No, not you, you're too scrawny, you might drop the baby."

This is how I came to the city—but there's so much to tell. I had a very difficult life. Mama went through a lot with us, really a lot. To give you an idea, this is a parenthesis. Before I offered to come here, we had some terrible times. Mama used to live on a little plot of land, and sometimes she had to take us all to sleep in the brush, hiding us, because she lived in a tiny shack and at night there were these men, bandits, who'd open women's doors and . . . they knew that Mama had four girl children . . . all little. So Mama would take us out of the house and we'd sleep outside, covered with a tarpaulin, so they couldn't get to us or to Mama herself. This was before that visitor. There are other scenes, too, primitive pictures I have in my mind, from before that. Well, afterward, Mama came to live on the farm, and things got better because it was more civilized on account of the tough administrators.

Well, conclusion: the fellow said he wouldn't take me, and I said, "No! Take me with you. I really want to leave Mama, not that I don't love her, but I don't want to do farmwork, I don't want to go hungry. I want to go around pretty, clean. . . ." He said, "Interesting that you should say this. I really could take you home to my wife." I said, "Any house, I don't want to stay like this." "Look, I'll take you to a lady who has a new baby, but she might not want you since you're so small." I said, "Take me there. Tell Mama where it is, and she can fetch me later if they don't want me, but take me." And the fellow did. We arranged it for a week later. Mama said, "I won't let you go, I won't let you." I begged her, I cried a lot, and "Go, go," finally she let me go, and that's how I went away.

When I got to the house of this lady—she was from Bahia, the wife of a lawyer who was a congressman and everything—she had four children, all very small, too, just slightly different ages, and she set me to take care of the littlest boy. I liked children, and I took care of him for the lady. The girls would get in the way, and I'd play with them more than work. What I really wanted was to play, but I also tried to learn everything. After one year, I knew how to cook. I cooked, I cleaned, I did all the housework, although I was still a child. Later I met a . . . my first husband there, in that house. I was still a girl; he was much older and was already working as a janitor in an office building. My boss, who was a lawyer, knew him, and when I first saw him he was a married man, married in the Church, with four children, very different from me, and I was fascinated by him. I think it was because of not having had a father. I fell in love with him and dated him for many years. My mother didn't want me to get married because she saw that it really wouldn't work out. But I wanted to marry him and I did [in a civil ceremony]. I was always capable of making my own decisions, even when I was a child and moved to the city, and when it came to marriage I married the man I wanted. I got married, and my mother said all right. And we had two children.

But . . . before I got married, I had left my job as a maid and looked for another job. Then I met a lady who had a beauty salon, and a friend of mine—I think this is funny—a friend of mine said, "Why don't you come with me to the beauty salon, to see if we can get jobs as assistants?" "But I don't know how to do hair, what would I want there?" And she said, "Look, just stick by me, I'll ask for you." I was staying at a neighbor's house then; I had no place to live. Mama couldn't watch out for me, she had no way of doing anything for me, so I had to do it all myself. At that time I didn't even have a birth certificate. I registered myself later so I could get married and work. . . . On the farm we didn't even have birth certificates. Life was difficult.

Well, we knocked on this lady's door, but she didn't want me, she wanted someone who knew the work. I said, "I don't know it, but I can help you with housework, I know how to cook"—I could do very good regional cooking by then—"I really know how to cook, I can do lots of things," I said to her. "If you want to try me out with any kind of work, I'll stay." She said, "All right, we'll give it a try. If it works, you can stay. I need someone hard-working." So I went. I and my friend. The first day I began to work there, I arrived and immediately started to straighten things up—I'm good at decoration, I have a talent for it. Well, she got to like me a lot, and one day she called me over and said, "Look, tell your friend not to come anymore. You can have her place; you're much handier and could become a real hairdresser, but she can't." I said, "No, I don't know how to do anything." "That's not true," she said, "You've got what it takes, you were born with good hands." I said all right. I needed a job and I stayed. I spent many years there working, living with her and working there. At first I didn't get any wages, she just gave me food, and with my tips I supported myself and my mother. I helped support my mother with that job, and also with my earlier job as a maid—although I didn't earn any money when I was little and went to work in that house where I met my boyfriend, my fiancé. Whenever she'd give me something I'd say, "Don't give it to me, send it to my mother." I always wanted to work to help support my mother. So when . . . this woman said to me, "Come live here and I'll give you your food," I said "Fine," and I went to live there.

Then I started to do hair. . . . I worked in the salon and did the housework, too. She was single; there were just the two of us living there. She wanted some company, too. I was already engaged then, and I told her I was engaged, that I wanted to get married. "Don't get married, not to this man, he's not right," but I was in love and wanted to marry. I was so . . . I don't know, it was puppy love, I married really in love. I spent eight years at this hairdresser's house, dating my husband, and after eight years she still didn't want me to get married, but I did. I was already over eighteen, earlier I couldn't have done it, but I went to the registry and got married. My first marriage was in . . . I'm terrible at dates and that date I've wiped out of my mind because it didn't turn out right. But I was about twenty. I lived in a very simple house, of mud. Have you been to the slums? Then you've seen those mud houses [daub and wattle]; it was one of those. I lived there, and I continued working in the beauty salon. Eight and six . . . fourteen, right? I worked another six years in that house, fourteen years altogether, eight single and six married. During that interim my oldest child, a son, was born. So I was working, with a child. Which led to more problems. My husband wasn't much good, not at all. Apart from being irresponsible as far as he himself was concerned, he would act that way to me, because that's what he used to say: "If you've got, you can give; if you haven't got, you don't give anybody anything." And he wouldn't even take care of himself. I felt lost, because of having a child and myself, too. But even so I didn't lose heart.

I started to work more, to be even more productive and to be more *myself*, to take more responsibility for myself. I could already see that I had my mother to take care of, I had my son, I had myself, and him, too. Despite his age, he didn't give me any security. My passion was for a mature man, but he didn't give me security. He wasn't the man I wanted, but I didn't complain, I didn't get upset about it, and I didn't even judge him. I spent nineteen years married to him. . . . For fifteen years I lived with him as a wife, and for about five years I withdrew and didn't want anything more to do with him. I spent those years living in the same house without any sort of relationship. And by then I'd had another child, my daughter. . . . You see, while I was living in the house where my son was born, I was actually taking care of him at my boss's house, in the salon. Then, when I got pregnant again, she said that she didn't want another child at her house because it was a beauty salon and my child was getting in the way. I could see what she meant. Now I was a terrific employee, she adored me, I didn't have a single fault as an employee; but as a mother I had a terrible time because it was so hard to work with two children, there was too much to do. Even today, in this part of Brazil, this is a serious problem.

So this is what I did: I built a better house. I left that tiny mud house and built a house in a better spot. I myself built the house, I and the father of my children, my husband. We built the house, so that we were living closer to the salon. That way I could work more, and it was easier to take care of the children. I used to take everything to work, even their food. When I got pregnant she said, "I don't know about your staying here, with this child . . . and another one," you see. I hadn't had another child in four years; my son was going on four. I tried to do everything to satisfy her, so I said, "It's no problem, I'll find a way. Don't worry, I know what I need to do to be a good worker. I'm not going to change your administrative structure, I'll change *my* way of living." So I found a lady to take care of my daughter, and I would take my son to the salon. She liked him; he was her godson.

And then ... when my daughter was two years old, I asked her to settle accounts with me. Then I bought a house in the center of town, a small house. I rented out the one that I already had, the little one that I built—it was a good house, not as bad as my first one because it had brick floors, a tile roof, and a garden. You see, I'd been working in the salon from 7:00 *a.m.* to noon. I had an hour or an hour and a half to rest, and then I'd take my son and give manicures in people's homes. The money that I earned from doing nails I used to keep in a tin can, and I earned a lot of tips. And also, she'd begun to give me a salary; when I got married she gave me a small salary. It wasn't even the minimum salary in this part of the country, she gave me about half of that, and my husband earned less than the little I did. But, even so, I managed to save money and build a house so as not to have to pay rent. Then, when my little girl was born (and as I told you she said she couldn't have her in the salon) then I thought about leaving and working at home. But it was way out of the way, the clients wouldn't go there, even though the house was nice. It was suitable for clients, although it wasn't fancy, but it was too far. There wasn't any transportation, there weren't sidewalks, it was a rather drab neighborhood. So I thought of buying a house in the city.

I saved the money in a condensed-milk can, you know the kind. Later I'd open it and go to the savings bank and count the coins and save up to buy a house. It took years. I saved money my whole life. The simplest clothes, I only had two or three things to wear, but I never cried, never complained. I laughed; I was very well liked by the clients, I got lots of presents, lots of tips. When my children were born they got presents, almost their entire layette, soap, everything. And my terrible husband. My husband was a chronic gambler. He had lovers all over the place. His own money wasn't enough for his lovers, and he would take the money I was saving for the marketing. A terrible kind of marriage, terrible ... he would beat me.... He didn't consider me as a spouse at all ... but rather ... as if I were ... I think he loathed me. At least judging by the way he behaved, I don't think ... I never got in his way as a woman, but I sensed it. Still I couldn't act, because I was in a process, kind of starting out, adapting to things, and it took me a long time.

Then I bought my house in the city and settled things up at the salon. I always solved my own problems. So I said, "Dona so-and-so, I want to give you notice," and she said, "What do you mean? Aren't you my favorite employee?" I said, "Didn't you say when I had my second child that you didn't want me in your house? Because my children caused problems for you, which is true. For you and for me, too. I can't bring two children to your house every day. I think it's a crime, Senhora. You don't want me to go because I'm a good worker, I contribute, but it's very difficult for me, and since I see how difficult it is I want to give my notice." She said, "I won't let you go, you can't leave. Bring both your children." I said, "I can't bring the children, because they can't both sit quietly anymore. When I set one down, the other jumps up. It wouldn't work. And I have a bit of money." She said, "You haven't got a place to fall down dead in. Where can you go?" I said, "That's no problem, I'll manage." But I really didn't, and my man doing nothing, nothing and nothing. I had about 500 cruzeiros, 500! This was nearly fifteen years ago. Well, I had a friend, a lady who was a good friend of mine; her husband worked in a bank. No, I had only 250 cruzeiros, the house cost 500, so I needed another 250. I said, "I'm going to take out a loan, and pay for it with my work, so I can buy this house in town. That way I can stay with my children, set up a dressing table, give haircuts and support my children until. . . ." You see? And that's what I did. She didn't want me to go, but I said it was what I wanted: "I want to and I won't give it up." She was very sad, but she finally gave me what she owed me. And I left.

I bought the house. I borrowed the money. Well, to pay for the house was a disaster. I'd skip lunch, feed my son, take him with me to people's homes, to make a bit more money. That money, no one could get it away from me. It was just for the house, and for medicine for the children. I didn't have any [social security from the] INPS, I didn't have anything. I always worked a lot. I would start working at 4:00, 5:00 in the morning. Then when I bought the house in the center of town, I moved in, set up a hair dryer and a cheap dressing table, and when I opened the door in the morning there were about twenty people waiting in line. I couldn't believe it, but that salon where I'd been working was the best in the city, all the "misses" came there, the First Lady [the governor's wife], and so on . . . and I had a reputation as the best hairdresser, my work was highly valued. So I looked at them all and set to work. I used to carry water on my head to wash their hair, a can of water this big, because there wasn't any running water, but I was always laughing, joking. My children used to help me.

LOOK, LET ME TELL you something: in a sense it was very easy because I'd been doing it for a long time, and I saw that I was going to win out. I just gathered up my courage. . . . My little girl went to kindergarten nearby, and I enrolled the boy in school. I would cook my food in the morning. I was already working for myself, but after a year I bought another house, I moved the salon to a house closer to my children's school. I could hardly sleep; you can't imagine at what hour the clients would begin to arrive, at dawn, and I'd take care of eighty people a day. I had some helpers. A niece and another girl, but I did everything, from pedicures on up. And I did good work. I learned how to make wigs; I learned it all alone. I took a stick—I saw this in a magazine—attached it to a chair and began practicing with strands of hair. I became one of the best wigmakers here in the Northeast, I sold wigs outside the state, too, to Rio de Janeiro, São Paulo. I learned how to dye natural colors. On Sundays I'd go to buy hair for the wigs. . . . Then I bought a car, and a house, and I went on buying; then, after a few years, [a famous company] from Paris was taking a group of hairdressers to France, and I went to Rio de Janeiro as the best hairdresser from this part of the country, and they invited me to go to Paris to take an international course.

I was already at my peak, after a few years on my own. I had my own house, I had a nice little Volkswagen, everything was going well. But I left my husband to himself. I couldn't take care of his life, too, because I had to take care of my own. We were still living together but he . . . I was establishing myself, I had two children and myself to take care of. And my mother. My mother already had her own house by then, she had food, she had everything. I brought her here to the city, took her out of that farm. As soon as I could, I brought her here. She had a tiny house, but it was her own.

So I said, "An invitation to go to Paris? But I don't know any French." They gave us three months to decide. I wanted to take the course, so I said, "I'll learn French, just the basic words." I didn't even know what French was at that time. But, "Paris, I'm going." I wrote and found out about the fees. I sent the money through a bank in Rio de Janeiro; I enrolled in the course. I wrote to the newspaper that I was going to Paris to take a course. The first world championship, the first group of Brazilian hairdressers who left for Europe—and I was there, I went to Europe with this caravan. Not even knowing what it was. I went to Rio de Janeiro without ever having been there before either, just got on a plane, and pouf! What an incredible thing!

Well, I went to the French Institute, at night, two hours of classes at night, after work. I took my son with me, he'd sleep in a chair, and I'd study, audiovisual, and I learned everything, I learned to speak French fluently [*laughs*]. And so I was off to Paris. I arrived in Rio de Janeiro, at the airport, and everyone was waiting for me and off I went again, to Paris. Paris, Spain, Italy, London, I went to these four places, the world-famous centers, technical centers. I learned, I studied, I had teachers. I already knew a lot, but I didn't have a technique—in Brazil there isn't a lot of technique. For thirty days I studied. I thought it was fabulous, and when I came back the house was jam-packed. Thirty days. I left the kids with some friends, and I went. I left them and I went. When I got back, I had international diplomas and more technical skill. I took first place in everything, I made friends. . . . I was another person by then, I dressed with a different soul, a different standard.

Then I said to myself, "I'm going to build a bigger house, this one's too small." The house I was living in was good, it already had an indoor toilet, but it was in the center of town and was as small as an apartment. I enlarged the salon, I redid the walls—I myself tore down the walls. I decorated it; I wanted to receive my clients with more of a show. I almost never had to pay for work, never, because I did everything that I possibly could myself, with honest labor, and everybody knew it. Then . . . two years later, another professional trip, another invitation. This time to Luxembourg. Paris and Luxembourg. I was traveling like crazy by then. To sum up, I made five international trips in a row. The most brilliant courses. I trained in world-famous cities, in the technical centers of the world. The only one I didn't get to was Tokyo—I was planning to go this September, but now I'm not going. Then, I thought that I ought to . . . I built a new house, a mansion. This time I didn't build it, I contracted it out, without a loan. My husband still gambling, but even so I'd managed to save money. I built a house that today . . . it has two levels, with gardens, a beautiful house, today it's worth nearly $100,000. It's all marble, a mansion. It's twice the size of this one. Then I moved to that house, and I already had an Opala, that's a Chevrolet [laughs].

Then I said, "Now I'm going to go back to school, I want to prepare for the *vestibular* [university admission examination], I'll go to night school." It was a two-year course. I did it in one year. There were eight subjects. I passed all of them, and I took the *vestibular*. I studied all the subjects for nine months and passed. And I was still working.

By then I had an established firm, independent, with its own building, my own car, everything. And my children were in a good school, the best school in town. I had totally altered my sights. Failure was no longer a possibility. I was one of the best wigmakers. Shows, newspapers—I was involved in everything that had to do with the best in hairdressing. It's been less than two years since I got back from Germany, I won a prize as the best hairdresser in the regionals, I won a prize. And I've been studying, going to the university. I haven't finished yet because it's very slow. I study three subjects, at night. I work during the day, so I couldn't study days. I'd been working from 4:00 in the morning to 7:00 at night, without stopping for lunch, just right through. Then I started to suffer from exhaustion. I'm hypertense, because my organism can't do otherwise, I pushed too hard, I'm hypertense, and I had a nervous exhaustion, I couldn't . . . I was like a machine that's always on.

Then, at home, I said, "I want a separation." This was in the big house already; I'd done the international trips. I recognized that he wasn't a husband, that I'd taken the wrong turn. I talked to him and I said, "I don't want to go on living with you. You have to change your life, and I'll change mine. We have to separate." He didn't want to.

My biggest problem wasn't . . . it wasn't having to sleep in the brush, as I told you, it wasn't being a farmworker, it wasn't being a maid, it wasn't working and living in my boss's house. My biggest problem was the separation, which involved litigation, the courts. And he . . . I felt like a thing . . . an object that belonged to him, and he didn't want to let me go because I was doing so well in life and he wasn't going to let go. He did nothing; he'd stopped working. He spent his time gambling, with women, girlfriends, illegitimate children. But he didn't want to leave because he had a high social profile on my account. I had an enormous "social visibility," so he didn't want to leave me. He said, "Only with a lawsuit." So I started it, I did it. He didn't want to, didn't want to. And, you know, this is horrible . . . it was a repulsive procedure. He didn't treat me like a human being, he treated me in the most miserable way, and it became . . . a very dirty separation. I already had assets that today would be worth about 20 million cruzeiros [U.S. $200,000 in 1981]. You know in how many years? In ten years of working on my own. I wanted to divide the estate, but he didn't want to; he wanted it all. That's why I went to court and put these assets in their hands. Let the law settle it. I wanted to keep the children, and he said no. The separation took so long; it was a very dirty business. He used the radio, the newspapers, to defame my name, to say incredible things about me as a professional. He didn't use my real name, but always my professional name.

The financial part I won in the separation. Everything. I didn't lose a thing. My children were already older and could speak for themselves. My son was eighteen and my daughter fifteen. He could make up his own mind. Legally, here in Brazil, at eighteen, not for all purposes but for some, young people can speak for themselves. Well, the children stayed with me, but it took the police to get my husband out of the house. I lived with the police for two months, protecting me, because he wanted to kill me. Then I had enough. I said, "No more, I'm going out, even if I have to die." And I took the car and started going out alone. Well, my separation was ratified, but to this day I have no illusions about being divorced, because this marriage . . . it's still up to the law. I have the use of my property, but . . . the entire estate . . . there was still the problem of his four children, because he registered them before marrying me. Community property, here in Brazil, it's been amended, but before, whatever you brought into the marriage, you . . . you had the right to. I didn't bring anything . . . and he contributed very little. Most of the time he simply lived off of me. I wouldn't have had any rights as a Brazilian woman, but there's a new code in Brazil, the Statute of Brazilian Married Women, and now a woman, if she proves she did something with her own sweat, her own work, has more rights. And my lawyer, she . . . there are two of them, a couple, and they worked with this code, defending the woman's work. The Married Woman's Statute.[1] This is used often in the South, in Rio de Janeiro, in large cities, but in small cities the women are generally submissive to their husbands and don't have a say in the estate. It's not easy for a woman to do what I did, but in my case it was possible because I could prove that I had created these assets, with witnesses and everything.

So I won. They approved my separation; they gave me my property, and I put it all in my children's name, for their use when we both die, I and my husband. That way he couldn't gamble it away. He used to hock everything and gamble. He did it with the car, the house, land. He used a false identity and sold some land from a ranch. So, this property, these assets, I had to put in the name of the children, so it's still in the courts. It's mine, but they haven't given it to me yet because we're now in the process of divorcing. It's so difficult, this problem of division . . . but it's all mine.

This is what happened: I won everything in the separation, but I lost my son. My son couldn't remain my friend, because he thought I shouldn't have separated. My daughter is still my friend, but my son isn't. That's why I'm living here, because my son didn't want to live in that house with me; he said it was disrespectful to his father. I thought it was better to leave. Once again I made a decision. I found a man, this one I've been living with for five years. He's my husband now; he's very good, he works hard, we get along fine. We set up this household, and we've been living here for five years. And my work continues to go marvelously well. I've made other trips. After moving here, I traveled to Germany. I took an international course. I won prizes, and my life is going marvelously.

Well, this is just a small part of my story. It's so incredible because I had no one to care about me, to help me, only to destroy. And to be able to do all this, well, it takes a lot of drive to succeed. I've never been especially attached to money, to goods. I gave everything to my children, and my son kicked me out, because the house I had built, the large house I told you about, is in his name, and he said I couldn't live there anymore. This house is my own. I bought it to live in with my new husband. I can adapt . . . wherever I am, I adapt. I set up my furniture and my house, I set up my life and go on and on, and I feel fine. I have an easy time adapting, changing with life, it's impressive. So long as I don't impinge on others' rights, I'll pursue my own. Legally, as I said, and I get along and I feel fine.

I've never complained because my children live in a house better than mine ever since I've been living in this simpler house, never. But my son, no, no . . . he spent two years on the outs with me; my daughter spent six months. Then they started talking to me again. My son is twenty-five years old, he's going to be twenty-five, and he doesn't work. He's gone to school, he has everything, the best clubs, he lives extremely well in that luxurious house, he has his own car—they each have their own car, given by me; I pay for the car, the gasoline, their allowance. . . . They live in high society at my expense, and they didn't want me to live with them. Explain that to me. I don't exist for them. My daughter may still change . . . but my son, no. He's twenty-five, he's entering his prime, though they say that maturity is made of mistakes, and he's certainly still making them. But how can he not have an idea of how things are? He just says no. Look, it's decadent that I can't cross my son's threshold with my [new] husband, when everyone in society visits us, likes us. My husband is a marvelous man, a man with a great deal of character. I'm close with his two children. Just look, my husband has a son, he's fifteen, and he hugs me, he walks arm in arm with me throughout the house. And my husband's daughter, she's a lovely girl, she kisses me, hugs me, sleeps with me, clings to me, she really loves me. She's not here right now because she's with her father, working in his bar, and her brother is there, too, working, helping. The boy respects me, and he's affectionate; I've never had to fight with him. They've been living here with me since I started living with their father. It makes a big difference.

And I can't walk by my . . . my ex-residence, with my husband, because my son won't stand for it. But everything he wants I give him. My daughter already comes to visit, when she feels like it, but she doesn't call me on weekends, only when it's time to get her allowance or to make a trip and she wants to pick up money for the trip. I don't understand it; I brought them up right, extremely carefully, with love. I love children. I never beat them, never punished them. My daughter went to live for a while in the United States. She's even been to Disney World. She's traveled through all of Brazil, north and south, she knows it all. They've gone to Manáus, Fortaleza, Rio, and São Paulo—it's like strolling on the beach to them. She lived in the United States on an exchange program; I supported her there for six months. She has a degree in English, she's an English teacher.

But that wasn't enough to please them, you see. I set up a business for my son, so he could work, because there's not much employment here for young people, so I set up his own business for him, in construction materials, cement, bricks, tiles, so that he can work selling them. I gave him a car. A month ago I gave him a new car. My daughter has one, too. He used to have a big car but, because of the price of gasoline, I got them smaller ones. I pay for their marketing. I have an old servant who's been with them for ten years; she helped raise them. She and her husband live in an apartment behind the house. There's a watchman, a gardener; I pay for them, too. Everything they want I give to them; their father didn't give a thing. Because he couldn't. He was no good, he got poor all over again. I think that . . . I don't know why my son doesn't love me. I never complained, no, I stood up to everything. . . . But I think it's all very relative, I have no reason to complain, because when I lose one thing, I gain another. I've gained two children. I have my children, I don't forget them and I care about them, but these kids that I'm raising now are wonderful children, sweet, they give me so much affection that sometimes I don't even feel the lack. . . .

M Y   M O T H E R   died five years ago. She was always cheerful around me. She worshipped me, she couldn't believe all the things I'd done. I helped all my sisters; all of them live well today, all of them. They're very attached to me. Only my son doesn't love me, and yet he did love me, so much that he didn't want me to marry again. It's a different way of being, a different way of loving, and I respect it.

Am I satisfied? As I said, I've adapted. When you adapt to something, you're satisfied. I'm not all alone; I have a man who cares for me, who's a wonderful companion. He's not here now because he's working—as I said, he works in the bar at night—but he's a very good companion and so are the children. My own children may not love me, but they care about me, and at least they respect me and can have confidence when they see my attitude—because I didn't relinquish my rights. I thought I had the right to a companion. So I am satisfied, I'm not sad about all this, not at all. I'm doing well, very well even. I stop by the house, I visit them like a friend, like a sister. I'm very concerned about them, I don't want them to go without anything, so I take care of everything for them. And I don't have any regrets at all. But for middle-aged people, my age and up, there are still so many taboos. My children . . . one of the taboos I still have to bear is with my son. But I couldn't have stayed with his father, I couldn't, if I'm the woman I'm telling you about. I don't regret anything I've done to this day. It takes me a long time to act. I spent several years separated, and finally found someone who suits me. I found someone just in time. But if it doesn't work out, I'll leave again. I didn't promise anything to my children. I tell them, I won't stick with it if it's no good for me. Nobody has the right to hamper anybody else's life. Each one comes and goes in his own good time. One thing we're born with is freedom. So long as we respect the freedom of others, we have to have our own freedom. Isn't that true? So I'm fine.

But you can't be independent if you're not economically independent. I think that's 80 percent. What is independence? Independence is a structure. When it's economic it's two structures, because a woman's independence isn't in marrying, in feeling like a woman, in having a degree. You can have a degree and be an adult and not have any independence, in which case you're not independent. I think this is superimportant in a woman's life. She must be economically independent, she has to have the same economic level as her husband, or better. And if it's not the same, at least it should come close. She mustn't be too far below, and if she can she has to fight to reach a higher level, at least of equality, because we can do this. That's why I've shown you my strength and my past . . . and today I don't raise my hat to anyone. . . . I don't have a college degree yet, I just have technical knowledge, the general knowledge of my line of work, but I've got where I wanted. It's good you asked me about that, because I think it's of the greatest importance, and I've educated my daughter so that she could be independent of a man. Dependent on love, yes, but economically dependent, never [laughs]!

I haven't changed; I still work from Monday to Saturday, without fail. I work twelve hours a day. I had six assistants, right now there are two, but I have a team of new assistants ready to start this week. I don't want to work less, no, not in the least. Because my work has never worn me out. It's never caused me to shed a single tear; I've never had any disappointment or problem with my work. Thirty years of work. I've been working in this line for thirty years. I've never shed a tear and never gotten tired of it. I get there laughing and I leave laughing. On the contrary, whatever problem I have, when I go up the stairs at work, when I find the work there, it puts me in a better mood. It doesn't wear me out. It's a companion, it refreshes me. Of course physically I get worn out, and my mind sometimes tires a bit—but I myself, I'm never tired, never. Ever since I was a child I've been very hard-working. I have a lot of skill, a lot of facility, for work, and this makes life much lighter. And I like it. I'd give up anything for work, anything in order to be able to work, no matter how great the object. My work is the most important thing I have.

My own experience has influenced me . . . well, all experience is valid, isn't it, for people to broaden their perspective, and I think mine was very valuable. Everything we can learn, everything that broadens us, is very good. My own experience was important for me . . . and today I get along very well with my employees. I'm very demanding of the people who work with me. I demand a lot, not brutally but by giving them incentives, and I succeed. For example, when a new employee comes, she doesn't know anything. So I observe her for a while, and I see what she's best at. And then, starting from what she can do, I try to improve on it, pointing things out and talking to her. Sometimes when they want to quit I tell them right away, "If you leave here you'll run into other problems elsewhere, so it's better for you to have this problem, which you already know about, here—because elsewhere it may be worse. Besides that, I'll help you however I can." I give them carfare when they don't have enough money, since sometimes they don't earn much, I give them food on the job. I do things differently at work, it's much more social, so that they'll stay. And they do stay, they stay eight years, six years, ten years, with me. They earn the minimum salary when they begin and, as they learn, their salary increases and they earn extra, depending on their schedule. They make a good living. And my clients keep coming back—about 50 percent are old clients, and 50 percent are new.

Here at home I have a governess, and there's also one at my children's house, both of them salaried. Here I only need one because one is enough. She also cooks. The marketing, I do. I go to the market, to the grocery store, I do my own accounting, I take the books home with me. At home, my husband kills chickens, he washes the dishes, he dries, he sets the table. . . . The only thing he doesn't do is wash the clothes, but the rest we share. And if it were necessary, he'd do laundry, too. When we don't have a maid, we do the work together, hand in hand. I think that everything should be mutually divided, education, economics, everything. What is a couple, if not to share things? There's no gender in housework, there are just chores to be done.

In the Northeast, we're brought up like Greek women, one man to a woman. But if a man doesn't give his sexual favors to that woman, she even has an obligation to betray him—but not betray with falseness. She should tell him, and decide what she wants to do. It's like this. If we're all made out of the same matter, in the same way, we have the same feelings. Only our sex is different. Then why shouldn't our feelings, our needs, be equal? But you see, Brazilian men, men from the Northeast, are constantly betraying their wives. Again and again. They're really deceitful, and they do it on the sly, hiding. However bad the marriage is, they don't want to lose it. I'll tell you why . . . you may not know this. They don't have the money to support the women, but they have lots of women because here, statistically, I think there are many women to every man. There aren't enough men for all the Brazilian women.[2] I think that about 80 percent of Brazilian men have more than two women. Now, some women also deceive their husbands; there are lots of Brazilian women who betray them secretly. And I don't think they should do it secretly. They shouldn't be cowards, unable to take a stand. To live a hypocritical life, I don't think that's right. But a woman here, if she tells her husband such a thing, she's as good as dead. Lots of women die if they betray their husbands and are found out, and if the men hear something like that, even without proof they still might kill them. There was something in the paper a couple of days ago, a mother with her two children—her husband killed her. She had two children, one about ten and the other two years old. Just because she was in a car with a man. Her husband appeared and shot her in that car, right in front of their children, in cold blood. Let's see if he even goes to jail for it. It's incredible how limited the women are in their rights. Sometimes what they need is a plate of food, not sex. They don't have affection, money, an allowance, any way of making a decision. I have several friends like that. The husband deserts them, goes to live with someone else, leaves them at home, and then brings food and leaves it on the steps. She doesn't even go out to buy her own food, and she won't go to court for fear of losing that food. Do you know why? Because she's not economically independent, that's what it is. Economic independence is important because then she'd have a way out when a man leaves her ... men are always doing that to women here. Brazilian men aren't so great. Or the women stay for fear of what people will say, or to be near their husbands even if they have nothing to do with one another, with no tenderness, no affection. I mean, various factors make a woman stay in this situation like a coward, and I don't think it's right.

I've been asked to participate in a feminist group, but I don't because I don't have time. I'd like to, though. Women should get together and have their own movement. And say what they want done. Because not only men do things. We have to do everything, too. But if you have the psychic strength, you can find material means. There's a lot of space for the things that need to be done. Brazil has hardly done a thing; there's so much still to do. If only the people wanted to ... but Brazilians are very accommodating. When you want something you have to fight for it. I've gotten where I have because I fought. Not by taking other people's rights, but by fighting for my own. People in Brazil have the ability to do lots of things. In the government, for example, anyone can enter; there's room to do things, you pay your taxes, you have good references, and there's no problem, everybody progresses. But I think Brazilians don't work very hard, so when one or another does it seems like a phenomenon. They're intelligent, but they're rather accommodating, because we've all got an indigenous part to us. We have those indigenous origins, and they say that the Indians were like that, with that sluggishness that Brazilians have.[3] But there's so much to do in Brazil, everything you do is valuable, everything that's done. You work with what you've got. If I weren't a hairdresser, I'd be something else—I'd be a good cook, I'd have a bar, like my husband, and make good food. There's a lot to do in Brazil, and if you don't do it, it's because you don't want to.

Tell me—this was just a summary of my whole life. What will they think in your country when they read this? Will they think I'm crazy?

Cristina, a forty-four-year-old White woman, together with her brother **20** inherited an engineering firm from their father. After spending eighteen years primarily as a housewife, she began to work in the firm as her marriage was breaking up. She is now one of four directors, as well as the major stockholder, in her company. Her salary alone places her among that tiny group of privileged working women who earn more than twenty times the minimum monthly wage.[1] Cristina attended Catholic schools and has a degree from a university in Rio. She now lives in an apartment in Rio with her two children, a boy age sixteen and a girl age thirteen. The interview was conducted in August 1981 in Cristina's elegant office in the commercial center of Rio.

———

U ntil a few years ago I'd never been directly interested in this firm. My father founded the firm when he was a young man. After my parents died, my older brother took it over. Then about five years ago he died, of lung cancer, and control of the company passed into my hands. But during that time I was doing other things. I gave music lessons, I did a bit of writing. I knew the directors, and the firm seemed to be in good hands, so I just never paid much attention. Then, about three years ago, our marital situation started to get really bad, which finally led to a separation about a year ago. And I thought it was high time I began to take a deeper interest in the firm, since I could see we were headed for a separation, and since the firm was going to be mine—in fact, it already was mine—and I wondered what I would do once we separated. So, about two years ago, I began working here. I wanted to see first-hand what it was like, so I began to do one job here, another there, to get acquainted with the firm, about which I was totally ignorant. I'd never dealt with the business at all.

That's how I took on this job. I realized that I really had to be more active, at work, in something that's mine. Plus I didn't have much choice, since I was responsible for my children, you see. I moved to a rented apartment, and having this work provided me with a good salary, which really gave me a lot of independence.

C R I S T I N A

My work as a music teacher and the other things I'd done had never really been enough. So there were these two motives. The situation arose from our separation. Probably, if we hadn't separated, I wouldn't have gotten to the point of really having to take a position. Perhaps I'd never have become aware of the importance of my being here. But it *was* important for me. I think that—although it was very ... you know, a separation is a very wearing business, especially because I'd been married for eighteen years, it's a long time—but I think one gain from the separation was that I really became aware that I had to join the firm, continue the work my father had started, with a lot of trepidation and, of course, a lot of insecurity at the beginning, because I was a woman and had rejected all opportunities to work here, so I didn't understand it, and I still don't understand everything really well. I still don't have an abstract image of what this firm is. There are three other directors, and they've helped me a great deal.

We have about thirty-eight employees here in the office. And until recently I didn't know anything about it, I didn't know what a promissory note was, I didn't understand anything about business. I had my own sphere, you see, I was involved in music, literature, it was another sphere altogether, nothing to do with this. But I thought it was important, since my brother was dead. Who would take care of my interests? I don't have a mother, I don't have a father, I don't have any other brothers or sisters ... and I was separating from my husband. So I had to get more into this myself. And here I am. And I feel good about it.

Housework alone isn't at all gratifying: to stay in the house, taking care of your children, the maid. I never liked that, I was always doing one thing or another. But now the responsibility here is enormous. Every time I sign something, that makes me responsible for the financing ... I have the impression that now I'm really working, in the sense of having more responsibility than when I'd give a few lessons, although that, too, was gratifying. But I think that the weight of the responsibility is far greater here. It's a greater challenge, too, since it involves a woman, which still isn't normal in Brazil, for a woman to own a business. I think only a tiny minority reach such a level. And I did, not through my own merits, obviously, but through an inheritance.

But, however it was, this is very satisfying for me because it took some courage—that's really what it is, you see. You get fearful of what will happen to you. It's not like when you write an article and that's fine, or you give lessons, and at the end of the month you get paid. Here the involvement is much more direct. And also the contact with the personnel in the office. What's interesting is the way it happened: I started here not as a director, although everyone knew who I was, but I came and sat down at that desk outside and worked there. So I started by having direct contact with the employees' needs, and now I'm on the other side, as the boss. That's an extremely difficult thing. By being on the employees' side, you see that . . . generally speaking their view is that every boss wants to cheat them, that's their philosophy, that's what's normal: the boss is there to exploit them, the boss is the one who's rich, that's their idea. And you more or less adhere to that when you're on that side, but when you cross over to this side, you see how difficult it all is. My God, given an economic system like ours, with the terrible economic situation that Brazil is in right now, it's incredibly difficult to coordinate these two things. I mean, the owner of a business, within a capitalist system, what is he? You have to aim at profits, there's no point saying you don't. You do. That's the reality. This is a business. It has to show a profit. So you get this into your head, but without turning into some bastard entrepreneur, and it creates a lot of conflicts.

And that's what I'm trying to resolve. In fact, it created quite a confusion in my head. I said, "My God, now I'm on the other side." You have to deal with all sorts of corruption, bankers, financing, all these work contacts. There are always people who urge you to earn more, to get money on the side. You can't do anything officially without having to reach into the cash register—to get even the simplest paper. You're told, "It'll cost so much," and you've got to hand over the money. There's a total contempt, a total lack of interest on the part of the dominant class for the class that's subordinate to it. Then, add to this all the economic problems of the firm, which also have to be considered. You can't just be a goody-goody, sometimes you have to be bad. The firm has to be the main thing. And this orientation, in which the firm is the main thing and the person serves the firm, this creates a lot of conflicts in your head. There have been times, in the last year . . . for six months business was very bad, and then you come to the conclusion that you have to fire people. Just today I read in the paper that more than six thousand people were laid off at an automobile factory. Here, obviously, it's in terms of five or six people, but the problem in your head is the same. Whom should you let go? Who's earning more? Are they earning more because they're good? But the payroll has to be reduced because not enough money is coming in. How can costs be reduced? By reducing the payroll. How to fire people, say you don't want them anymore? That's a matter which has an enormous influence on your relationship with the person. You have an interest that you have to protect, which is the interest of the firm, in detriment to the relationship the firm has maintained with that person for many years, and now you really have to fire them and say, "Look, it can't go on, I can't pay you anymore." This was very difficult for me, to start doing this. In the end there was no other way. You do it because . . . there just wasn't enough work.

Until now it's been all right because we recovered, and now several of the people who were let go have already been rehired. That's the way it is with a small firm. It ends up being kind of a family; everybody knows everybody. There are people who've been here since my father's time. So you get into a very personal situation, not like a large firm in which the owner doesn't even know the employee's names. Here everybody knows everybody's problems, knows so-and-so's pregnant, that one has two children, another one lives way out somewhere and the bus fare's going up. You get involved in all these problems that everybody has, and at the same time you have to keep in mind the firm's interests, which generally conflict with the interests of the personnel you employ. It's a complicated business, you see.

I have no choice but to accept my role as owner. It's not something you can do halfway. I can't say, "I'll settle for less because I want to go against the system." No, that doesn't work. I think that unfortunately the system and the regime are set up in this way. Of course, once you're the owner, you can control things. Your aim isn't only profits at the expense of everything else. But, you know, you end up making a series of concessions, or you say, "Look, I'm not cut out for this, I don't want to be in charge, I don't want to be owner of a firm because this conflicts with my way of being."

I only started working as a director last year, so it's all very recent, and only now do I feel that I'm on my feet. If you ask me whether this is exactly what I want to be doing, perhaps it's not even. First of all, the work isn't really creative. It's rather mechanical, a permanent commercial transaction. You deal with various organizations, with money, with the bank; at the end of the month there are so many bills to pay, there's not enough money, you call up, postpone some—it's work of this kind. Intellectual creativity, in the sense of really creating, there's very little of that. You see, I was used to another kind of work, a more creative kind, which gave me enormous personal satisfaction. Well, that's gone, that's a thing of the past. There's no time left for anything, hardly enough even to read a paper. Your leisure time gets very limited.

But a very good thing happened: I've gotten to like being at home. I like to arrange the plants, clean out a drawer, practice my music. There's a lot that's good in all that, and I'm actually calmer than I used to be. I always used to be anxious about planning things for the weekend. I think there weren't enough satisfactions during the week, and so on weekends I had to get out, go to the movies, a concert, have dinner out, do some sports—which I like—run, go to the beach. I needed that to round out the weekend. But now, no. I love staying at home, and on weekends I can spend more time with the children, because during the week I'm only with them in the evening. So, that side . . . it's a man's life, you see. Women here normally have other duties. But the housewife side of my life really does leave a lot to be desired, because I leave at 8:00 *a.m.* and don't get back till the evening. But it's all working out very well. The children were used to a very easy lifestyle. I lived in a house with four servants, so they'd get home and drop their clothes, one item here, another there, and they'd call out, "So-and-so, get me a glass of water," famous Brazilian style. But now they both make their beds, straighten up their rooms. I have just one maid to take care of everything, and everybody helps. When the maid's not there, they do the cooking themselves. So, even for them it's been very good, because they've seen that things aren't so easy as they'd got used to before.

Generally, here in the office, the people who earn more go out to lunch, and the ones who stay here bring their lunch box from home—they earn less, they have less purchasing power. Like that girl who just served us coffee, she's a cleaning woman, and some of the others work in accounting. The girls who work in accounting earn about $200, between $200 and $300, in that range.

I didn't have to change salary policy; that was never a problem here. Equal pay was an old policy of my father's, completely equal pay. It's by job, sex has nothing to do with it. If there had been a problem, of course I would have changed things. In fact, we even had an example not long ago. There was a boy here, his job was to open the office, clean up, make deliveries, go to the bank . . . a kind of office boy. He left, and then a girl showed up, an office girl, looking for a job, and my secretary said, "There's a girl here who wants to take Seu [Senhor] João's job," and everybody else said, "What? A girl? No!" And I said, "Why not? She knows how to get to the bank. If there's a package to be delivered, I believe she's even stronger than Seu João"—because he was nearly tubercular, poor fellow. He had five children and was as thin as a rail. He left to get medical treatment—"She's strong, she can carry more than he did, she's presentable. Why not?" But it always comes up, you see. A woman had never replaced an office boy before. An office boy has to be a man, why should you hire a woman? But I don't see any problem with this, and here she is, doing everything Seu João used to do, as well or better. Obviously, some jobs require greater strength. But in general I think it's exactly the same, and everything's working out perfectly. And as far as employing women—because sometimes companies don't want to hire women since they may get pregnant and then we have to give them three months' leave—here, thank God, we've never thought in such terms. There are many women working here. One of the engineers is a woman. There used to be another one, too, who left recently. In accounting there are several women.

But there aren't many women in my kind of position in Brazil. Most of the time I have to deal with men, which until now hasn't been much of a problem. I haven't had that much contact because I haven't been in this position for very long. And I haven't always taken on this task. I mean, for example, if we have to ask a bank for some financing, there's someone here who's already dealt with the bank manager, so he usually takes care of it. I haven't often had the opportunity to do this myself. Little by little I'm getting there, but I believe there will be a reaction on their part. I think they'll look at me strangely at first, they'll try testing me to see whether I really understand what's going on. I've dealt with the bank manager, no problem, but many of the other aspects of the firm are still in the hands of one of the other directors. Of course it will be different for them to have to deal with me instead of with a man in his sixties. It *is* different.

Women who earn less just because they're women, who don't have the opportunities that men have, because they're women—perhaps this is the result not precisely of the dictatorship, but of an entire process related to work, an entire system rooted in *machismo*. With the *abertura*, women's very participation within the political process, actively struggling for their rights, will be easier. They'll have much greater opportunities for fighting for their rights, as professionals, as workers, as peasants, in a regime that allows them to organize, to organize their own unions, their own affairs, and to speak up, to have a representative who can fight for their interests. I think the dictatorship has gone against everything I believe in. I don't see any way in which the dictatorship has brought any kind of benefit, really. My son's generation, for example—he was born the year after the military revolution of 1964, so he's a person who has no idea what a democratic process is. Absolutely no idea. He knows by reading about it; but at school, in the world, he hasn't got the slightest idea of what a democratic process is, in which you have an active voice, you defend your interests, you vote. To him, a vote is an abstraction. I myself voted for president of the Republic just once in my life—once, can you imagine!

Now things are beginning to explode, and whoever wants to can really gauge all the evil that these years of dictatorship have wrought, down to our very homes. Not only in social terms, which are obvious, but within the home itself, because the dictatorship goes right into your home. It creates conflicts. You feel the futility of participating in anything since you can't vote, you don't elect any representatives. You see social distinctions increasing all the time—hunger, misery, unemployment. Brazil is a country undergoing development, but you go to the backlands, you go to Pernambuco, Paraíba, and you see the bleakest poverty. You don't even need to go that far. Right here, too, urban life. And you're totally powerless to do anything about it. How? What can I do? Become a terrorist? Throw a bomb? That's not the way. Whatever I can do is so little. And all these obstacles—you feel revolted just because you know that there's no way you can act on such a situation, not even indirectly. It makes you frantic. It makes you dissatisfied with your nonparticipation and it all ends up reflected within your own household. That's why I think the dictatorship influences us in our homes. It's very serious. I think that everyone has to face this and see that there's only one way out, which is a return to the democratic process. There's no way to survive in a regime such as this one.

T H E   S E P A R A T I O N   from my husband was a very difficult period. Just imagine, I was twenty-five when I married, and when we separated, last year, I was forty-three. We'd been married for eighteen years, not counting the time I knew him before—that would make it well over twenty years since we'd met. Nearly half of my life, you see. And that weighs on you in an extraordinary manner, because even when you've reached the conclusion, after a long struggle, that continuing together is impossible in terms of your own personal needs, when you see that you really have nothing to do with the other person's life, still there's a whole series of emotional ties, of dependencies. . . . Whenever I talk about this separation, I compare it to a diseased limb that you've had to cut off, and yet you always go on missing it. I think I'll always feel this cut. I can't imagine how I . . . even if I were to marry again . . . but the Sérgio part that's gone from me was a part of me, and it was very painful, although it had to be done. Exactly like surgery, something's diseased and it's got to be cut out.

The whole process took three years more or less. First he left and I stayed, then he came back home and we tried again. It didn't work. . . . There were about three years of effort that, unfortunately, finally resulted in our realizing that there was no other way. It was more difficult for him to leave the house than for me, and I saw that if someone had to go, it would have to be me. I said, "Look, I'll go. If I wait for him to leave, he'll never do it." He kept saying, "Oh, I'm leaving tomorrow, or the next day, I'm looking for a place." And finally I said, "I'll go," and I did. But it was very difficult, especially when I'd get home. I used to say, "Oh my God, what have I done?" And at about the same time that I left, I started working here more seriously. I'd begun to think about that long before. The first time I came to work here was about a year earlier, when one of the secretaries went on vacation. They always have to find a replacement, and I said, "I'll come in instead." So I did the secretary's work, answered the phone, typed letters, the whole job. And when she returned I did other jobs for a while. The following year I decided to come back, and it was at about that time that we separated. It was horrible then, because I'd spend all day here and, at the end of the day, I'd go back to a new apartment. It was all rather complicated.

For a while you project things . . . you do everything to make it work, but then a moment comes when there's no other way out: "It's so bad on this side and I don't know what I'll find on the other side, but I'm going to try, because it can't be worse than this, though it might be just as bad." That's what causes the fear, that leap in the dark; you don't really know how you're going to react. You try to provide yourself with certain safeguards. You don't know too clearly what will happen, but I think you must have the courage to leap over the wall. And for me, as a person, I now feel much more fulfilled, calmer and happier, than I used to be. Naturally, since I was going through a crisis. There was a time when my marriage was marvelous. It really was perfect then: to have a companion you love, your children, your home . . . emotionally you feel complete. But weighing in the balance the very bad moments we had and how I am now, I think I was right to do what I did. Not only in terms of my personal life, but also professionally. I think this really was what I ought to have done, and I don't regret it.

And I'm going to get a divorce. It used to be called a *desquite* [dissolution of the conjugal bond, but not of the legal state of marriage], but since the divorce law was passed [1977—allowing one divorce per person] it's now called a "consensual judicial separation." The judge has to approve it, just like the *desquite*, and three years from that date you can apply for a divorce. And if you just separate, I mean without any legal procedure, you can file for divorce five years later. Well, I've already been separated for about a year, so two years from now I intend to file for divorce. As long as we're already legally separated, the divorce will just make it more definite. I think it's a very important law that benefits women, and the family in fact.

If I were to marry again, I think it would all be very different. Not that I got married too young—I was twenty-five—but I went into it full of illusions, that's really the word. I thought I'd never have another problem; marriage would provide everything—a person to give me support, to give me money, to guide me. In fact, I think all this weighed on our relationship. I relied too much on Sérgio, I transferred everything from my father to him. Maybe I didn't cooperate in establishing a companionship, two people together, each with a separate identity, with work, with interests. No, I was a dependent person, and I think that if I were to marry again, this side no longer exists, because now I'm independent, even economically, financially, so it would be a joint life, but of two separate people. It's hard to maintain your individuality in a relationship with another person, but I'm much better equipped for this now.

I was part of an in-between generation, kind of sandwiched, because I was programmed for marriage. A profession? That was secondary, the important thing was to marry. But in the middle of the road, this whole process of women's evolution began: of identity, of one's value, as a professional, as a person. And I only caught this bus once it was in motion, it was already in the middle of the road. So you think, "My God, what can I really do? What are my rights? Should I leave the house, leave my children? Can I fight for equality?" After all, I had a different past from this. I think, even in the minds of men at this stage, suddenly they don't know what they can demand, what they can concede. I was the one who always conceded, who tried not to displease the other person. That's the way a relationship was: you had to adapt yourself to what the other person expected. For a marriage to work, the woman had to conform to the ideal that her husband had of her: domestic, faithful, a good mother. She couldn't arrive home after he did because it was understood that when the man gets home, his wife is already there all smiling, pretty, to greet him.

Among my friends' marriages, I mean those that have lasted, people who've stayed married for fifteen or twenty years, I would say that 90 percent of them are marriages of convenience by now: "Ah, I've been married for so long, but I'm just no longer interested in sex." You see? That's how it is . . . people who don't work, and so they're constantly on top of their children, they start to live their children's lives. But they won't separate, either: "What for? He's all right, he doesn't drink or gamble, he doesn't bring women home . . . so let's continue," because it's more convenient. There's a lot of adaptation of this kind, especially because women of my generation had no professional training. And then suddenly you've been married for twenty years. You're going to go out to work? To do what? You're forty years old, what can you do? You don't know English, you don't know French, you don't know how to type, you don't have any training—what are you going to do? How can you separate and go on receiving money? To do that, you've got to have really strong motivation, the man has to be a real horror. So you adapt instead. Economics has a lot to do with the continuation of such marriages. If these women had a profession that would give them the freedom to say, "I want out, I'm going to rent an apartment," as I did. . . . But to ask the man, "Look, I want to leave this house, but you've got to pay my rent" or "I'm going back to Papa's house," to leave your children, who by that time are adolescents— it's very complicated. I think women of that age, my generation, weren't prepared for any personal accomplishments, either in terms of rewarding work or in simple economic terms. They're dependent on their husbands, so what can they do? They adapt. And they separate only in extreme cases.

M Y   H U S B A N D always wanted to paint, but he started right in working as a lawyer and he didn't have free time in his schedule. But he's changed jobs, and I learned recently that he's started to paint again. I think he's finally going to have what he's always wanted. Now he no longer has the burdens he used to have, professionally, and also because I support the children. He contributes a little bit— he pays for their school, and he gives a small sum each month—but he doesn't have to give me alimony, which means his responsibilities have decreased a great deal as far as the family is concerned. And now he'll be able to devote more time to what he loves, which will be very good for him. But our relationship right now is really bad. In this whole process of separating, we haven't managed to remain friends, unfortunately. We have to give it time, first of all because of . . . his temperament, actually. He's very possessive, jealous, domineering, authoritarian, a paterfamilias. It never crossed his mind that things could happen the way they did.

The fact that I took on this position, that I left, all this hurt him a great deal, and our relationship got very bad. There's still a lot of friction—as bad as when we were together, if not worse. We communicate only when strictly necessary—about the children—which I regret. I'd like to be able to stay friends with him.

And then there's all that business [*laughs*] that makes your blood boil. . . . I think that men . . . I don't know . . . I'm a great admirer of women, I think we criticize ourselves more . . . women are always criticized, and so you're more open to criticism than men. A man has that superiority, so he can't admit his faults, his mistakes. "I was always perfect, it's all your fault," that kind of thinking, although it's not stated. "I'm the one who was always great, an exemplary father," and he gives ten reasons why everything should have worked out. Well, it's much harder for someone to accept a separation if he hasn't accepted his role in a bad marriage. It's like a punishment. He says, "You wanted it, you did it, you destroyed it"—he's even used the word "destruction." Yet he wanted the separation, too; he just never took the initiative. And when I did, that wasn't quite the way he wanted it—he wanted it all to have been his initiative. And when he saw that I really left, then he began to question why I'd done it. "Isn't it obvious why I left? For three years we've been fighting nonstop. I can't take it anymore. It's no good, this relationship is impossible." But since he hadn't faced this, suddenly he felt shocked, as if we were on our honeymoon and out of the blue I'd decided to leave. The minute you don't accept what's happening, you start to blame the other person, to attack, to wound, because you feel injured. He feels like the injured party, as if I'd really destroyed everything, something he'd constructed all alone and suddenly I'd destroyed it.

He's so . . . he's not taking it well. He goes on believing it was an act of destruction—as he said, "twenty years out the window"—when it's not! I haven't thrown out anything that happened! I think we had some wonderful times, I really married him out of love, exclusively. He was from a different background, he was from a poorer family—a whole series of things that went contrary to expectations. I had to fight against my family's pressure, since my father, my mother, thought it wouldn't work out. In short, I faced all of that because I loved him, because I thought it *would* work, and suddenly when it begins to go sour, we're not going to erase all that was good. We had wonderful times of real closeness. We have two children, born of love. I always really wanted to have children, I never rejected them. But in the end we were living together for a long time only through them. You see, suddenly it began to go wrong. We never tried to analyze it, but I reached the conclusion that there wasn't much communication between us. We talked without understanding one another. We talked a lot, but in fact we said very little.

Sérgio's always had many friends, he's a very social person. Our house was like a club, always full of people. He's the sort of person that, if he likes you, he asks you thousands of questions, he invites you for dinner, he invites you to stay for the weekend, and one week later you're an intimate friend, he knows everything about you. That's the way he is [*laughs*]. Now, I'm more reserved. I have some close friends, but not many. Something happened to me that.... My analyst—my analyst is a woman—she was telling me that this isn't just a problem here in Brazil or in Rio de Janeiro, it's global, it's a universal problem. When a woman separates, the couples who were friends of theirs withdraw. It's odd; I don't know whether it's because we become rather threatening, or whether these people at heart want to do the same thing but, since they haven't the courage, they start to reject you a little. Then suddenly everybody's disappeared. I got to thinking about it: what you're really used to is having relationships as a couple. And it takes some time to make new friends who are single or separated. You're used to socializing as a couple, at least in our group it was like that, everybody married. And when these couples withdraw, suddenly you're all alone. It's odd.

I was really sorry when our friends withdrew, especially the women. There's a couple, friends whom I've known for years and years, since long before I married, close friends. And the other day I went to their house for dinner. She's expecting a baby, they already have one child who's nearly grown up and now she's expecting another one. After dinner, he said he would take me home and she, with that belly, with her feet swollen, so heavy, she insisted on coming along. You see? I said, "Oh, you don't need to come, you're tired, go to bed." "No, I'm coming." She forced herself to accompany me home. Before, when I was still married, her husband gave me a lift home lots of times. But I think she felt insecure, she wanted to come: "What might they do on the way?" That's the way she looked at us. I thought, "My God, I'm nobody's rival, I don't need this." But it seems to bring out this insecurity, and so people withdraw.

So I can't say that I have very close friends. . . . I have friends I'm just beginning to get to know, because among the couples there's not a single one left. But a really intimate friend, no, I don't have any yet. And then, I've been changing, too. There was a time when I was very . . . I'd come up, discuss my problems, seek that intimacy. I used to think that to be really close you had to know *everything*, to tell *everything*, and now I think that's not quite the way it is, you see. I think there's a certain reserve I should maintain. To be close I don't need to tell that I had my nails done. So I'm even restructuring this, my idea of friendship, with a certain reserve because I got rather . . . rather wary, unsure. How close can I really get to a person, without dominating her or having her dominate me, without creating a neurotic relationship? But I'm still looking for new people.

Y E S, I W A S a virgin when I married. In my time, the problem was formulated in this way. To begin with, the pill wasn't widespread yet, so there were two fears. First, the fear of becoming pregnant, and second—I'm talking about my own social class, obviously—there was a great fear that if you went to bed with your boyfriend, he might not respect you as a person and might not marry you. Since marriage was projected as the ideal situation, there was the fear that you would be devalued in your boyfriend's eyes if you went to bed with him. The men themselves drew this distinction between the girls they took to bed and those who would be their wives in the future. It was a very hypocritical business, because in fact we did everything, all kinds of petting, of intimacy, we just didn't lose our virginity. Everything, kissing the breasts, masturbating one another, anal intercourse—all of this was done, but that one place, no. There you had to maintain a virginal hymen until your wedding night. It was completely hypocritical, because what did it mean? And aside from this, obviously, the fear of pregnancy, because very few people took the pill at that time; it wasn't like today. There were these two fears. And I played that game, precisely that way. So, I had *almost* complete relations with Sérgio; however, I say that I was a virgin when I married because in fact he hadn't broken it, you see?

The hymen was broken on our honeymoon, *comme il faut* [*laughs*]! Incredible hypocrisy, wasn't it? And I had a boyfriend before him, I went out with him for four years, and it was the same thing, the same kind of relationship. Nowadays, I occasionally run into him, rarely, but when I do I feel a kind of emotion that sends me right back to my adolescence—only and exclusively, I think, because I never went to bed with him. It all stayed at half-measures, and so I still have this emotional reaction of something incomplete, solely for that reason, because I don't really know what kind of person he's become or anything about his life. But whenever I see him, I feel as if I'm back in that time. . . . Today this problem has really ended. My daughter is too young, but the daughters of my friends, in the sixteen- or seventeen-year-old range, schoolmates of my son, about his age, they've all had intercourse already, or almost all of them; they take the pill.

But can a woman go on taking the pill her whole life? Legalizing abortion is a measure that would be extremely beneficial for women. They must have this option of deciding whether the pregnancy suits them or not. I had my tubes tied when my daughter was three years old, ten years ago, because the pill wasn't agreeing with me. I didn't want to have more children, I was already thirty-four years old, I thought two children were enough. And so I had a tubal ligation, which is also illegal. I mean, I think that when a pregnancy is life-threatening, then, yes; but, even then, I think it has to be approved by a medical board. So, public clinics don't do tubal ligations, only a private doctor does. Obviously, if you're going to your own doctor, he'll take care of all the paperwork, he'll say he has to remove a tumor, and then he'll do it. And charge you. So long as you can pay, everything's all right. If you have to rely on the state for this, forget it.

I remember that I was kind of hesitant about it; it's such a definitive, irreversible step. But I think it was great, because I'm not poisoning myself with the pill and I have a totally free sexual life, without this kind of worry. At this stage I wouldn't want to have an abortion or have to keep on taking the pill. This gives me considerable freedom; I think that's very good. The sexual relation itself is less stressful because you no longer have that fear of pregnancy, or any other problem. But it's still against the law.[2]

Sexual pleasure is extremely important, and it ought to be equally important for men and women. But that's a whole other story. Women, for example, women of my mother's time, were so poorly prepared for marriage that they practically didn't even know what pleasure was. For them it was more of a conjugal obligation, and [a means] to have children. And periodically the man would seek his pleasure . . . outside the house, with lovers, with prostitutes, and so on. I think that nowadays this is unacceptable. A balanced relationship has to have this, too, mutual attraction, and also the space to discuss problems that might come up.

I wouldn't say that men here are already concerned with their women's orgasms, but I think it's beginning, it's a subject that's finally on the agenda. I believe men are struggling, too . . . becoming aware of the importance of both partners being equal, that they have to see this from her point of view, too. It seems to me that at least among a certain sector there is concern about this, they're attuned to this, and it can even be discussed.

No, there wasn't really any open discussion about clitoral orgasms. We heard about it through the Hite Report. But the other day I was reading, I forget who it was, a woman who did some research with various types of women, a peasant, a worker. Well, she said this: for the upper-class woman, everything's fine. She enjoys sex, she has an orgasm, and so on. Which doesn't mean there are no problems. But the real problem is for women who have no way of saying that they don't have orgasms. And among a certain category of women, they don't even know what sexual pleasure is.[3] So, to point out the difference between vaginal and clitoral, that's another level of knowledge altogether, and if it's discussed at all here in Brazil, it's only in minimal terms, among a tiny segment of society that doesn't really count.

Here in Rio a tunnel separates the North Zone of the city from the southern. You go through the tunnel, and on the other side ideas are completely different. Now, judging by the women I know [in the South Zone], those who have remained married, many of them cheat on their husbands in the afternoon.

They've been married for twenty years, and there's always some sort of opportunity, but it's done in such a way that it doesn't interfere with the marriage. And I think that once they do this, they accept that their husbands do it, too. Now, what absolutely does not exist is any openness on the part of men for facing up to their wives' infidelity. Women—it's not that they accept it, but they've already incorporated the fact that men have always betrayed women and can always say to them, "That's got nothing to do with my relationship with you. You're the woman I love, the mother of my children." This is almost accepted inwardly, even if rationally it's not, but culturally it's already accepted. But, with men, it's very unlikely that they'll accept infidelity, very unlikely—in all classes, I think. It's still an established thing: she's married, she has to be faithful. Their attitudes are so different: the women are already accustomed to being betrayed, while the men go on fooling themselves that their wives are faithful when, in fact, sometimes it's obvious they're not.

And they're also very jealous. It's that feeling of ownership. Brazilian men— they still think in terms of possession: "That woman belongs to me. After all, she's taken my name. So she belongs to me, and she can't deceive me or betray me. She can't be different, can't go against the patterns that I've set up for making her mine." Infidelity—it's funny, but it often seems that for a man . . . it's a matter of what other men will say. The worst threat to a man is to be considered a cuckold. In fact, among many of my friends, they let their wives travel, what she does elsewhere is no concern of his, it's in another country and no one is going to know. But if we just have a beer on the corner with a man friend, "What will people say?" They have a cuckold complex, you see. The worst form of insult for a Brazilian man is to be called a cuckold. The only thing worse is Italian men, who still believe in cleansing their honor with blood, although this happens here, too; a lot of women are killed, and there's always a problem about jealousy at the root of it.

My own feeling is that fidelity is important so long as it's a voluntary act. In a good relationship, the chances of your wanting to betray your partner are very small. It's the result of some dissatisfaction, so I think it's better, before the betrayal, to investigate the source of this dissatisfaction. It's better, but it never happens like that. Sometimes the woman doesn't have the courage for this, and maybe she's right, because a man can rarely face this squarely and see that it's really a joint problem, which they can solve together. He'll get hateful, call her a whore, create enormous difficulties at home. He'll want to leave her, to separate.

Oh yes, I would marry again. But I really like living alone; I think I'm even becoming addicted [laughs]. The other evening, I was with a friend of mine. We were at her house and we went into the kitchen, cooked up a dish, and then sat on the bed and watched a soap opera. That's something I do alone, too. And sometimes I get home, put on a nightgown, and go to sleep. There are other times when I want to go out. You regulate your life strictly according to your own wishes. When you have a husband, it's all different, isn't it? But now I'd have other demands, and I don't know whether . . . whether these demands would interfere much in a relationship. If the possibility of a second marriage arose, all this would have to be brought up. This freedom that I've acquired with great effort, it would be very difficult for me to give up certain liberties, even small ones such as wanting to go to sleep when you feel like it and not having to wait for the fellow to be there so you can go to sleep together.

Still, I don't think that I could spend many years alone and happy, not completely alone. I think I have a great need to give and to receive. You might not be unhappy or feel totally isolated in the world because of not having a man, but to feel complete, no. Right now I'm very. . . . Coming out of one marriage, it's hard to think about another, although I see this as a future possibility. It's difficult for a person to be happy, fulfilled, all alone. Because you can have great friends, but I think that you'd miss that special person. But for the moment, I'm still kind of vaccinated [*laughs*], you see . . . and I haven't give this a lot of thought.

Of course, my possibilities are also fewer now. Not so much because of the way I've changed. I think the real factor here is the availability of men in the "market," so to speak. I'm at an age—I'm forty-four, I have two children—and I have fewer possibilities within the Brazilian system than if I were twenty-three and had no children, no question about it. Because, look, men my age are usually married. Or else they're separated and so doubtful about life that they prefer a young girl to start all over with. Age has a lot to do with this. I'm not afraid, but I see that it counts; or, if I am afraid, it's a kind of inner fear, which isn't quite the same thing. And then the changes I've gone through also play a part. Men are a bit frightened of mature women, of women who are professionally successful, independent. With adolescent children, in terms of reconstructing a life, I think it's difficult, but I still have hopes. I wouldn't want to spend the rest of my life alone, no, not at all.

In a traditional marriage, to the extent that the man is responsible for supporting the household, with a woman who is dependent on him on various levels—some of them don't even have a checkbook, you know; they ask for money just to go to the hairdresser—in this traditional setup, he does end up thinking he's the most important person in the household. Because he's responsible for that entire family. In a sense he's even right, because in fact he is more important, he's the one who supports them. Hence the preoccupation with earning more, with providing his children with a more comfortable life. I think that the ideal would be to realize that this isn't good even for the family itself. The woman should help him with this task. Because it's a very heavy burden; now I can see that for myself. When you get to the end of the month and everything depends on you, it's a very difficult thing, so it's normal for that person to actually feel more important. But if a man gives this a bit of thought, he ought to see that, as a person, this has nothing to do with anything else. As a person responsible for a household, he might think of himself as a superman, since he's carrying his wife and children on his back, sometimes his mother-in-law, the maid, too. But the day he fails, all that is over.

The kids today have a very different idea of marriage. The girls no longer go into marriage as a dependent relationship, and even if it turns out that she doesn't want to work, or doesn't need to, this inner sense remains. It's so different from the old attitude of unloading everything onto your husband. It's a very different inner attitude. I'm speaking, obviously, about young people of my class. What goes on in the rural areas of Brazil, I don't know. It could be that they persist in seeing marriage as a solution to all a woman's problems: she'll just cook and bring up her children. But among the young girls I know, if they go into a relationship, it's not likely to be from above to below, with the husband giving the orders. I see this a lot in my son's girlfriend—the serenity with which she reveals who she is, what she wants, what she needs. She's confident. She doesn't have that concern *just* to please him, but rather to be herself: "Look, that's the way I am; I like this, I don't like that; I don't want this, I want that." My daughter is developing in this direction, too. Very equal, much more equal than in my time when there was a pattern for a woman, a behavior pattern that you tried to more or less fit yourself into. You had to put up with everything and fight to keep your man. Now there's no fight at all. Relationships start and stop much more calmly than before.

I have great hopes for these young people; I think that things are really changing for the better. For example, the boys can have a girl as a friend, a real friend, pure and simple friendship. The other day, my son was there at home with a girl, they were sitting on the sofa holding hands, and afterward I asked him, "Are you dating Júlia?" He said, "No." I said it was just that they were so close on the sofa, and he said, "No, she's my friend, she's a very affectionate person." Well, what I think of as dating behavior, for him is not. His own experience is restructuring these things, knocking down some prejudices that his father had. He's doing things differently from all of us, and I think it's a change for the better.

It is possible to give up sex roles, but it's difficult. You learn these things so young, you're socialized in this way, conditioned to play this role, and you end up incorporating it. Sometimes these concepts of weakness and strength that are identified with women and men can even lead to uncertainty about your own sexuality. Suddenly you begin to feel strong; you say, "I feel as strong as a man." And then you start to ask yourself questions: "Wait a minute, am I ceasing to be feminine?" I went through this, and I still do: "And my sexuality, what's happened to it? Do I have to be fragile and protected? What's going on?" It's considerable work to decondition yourself from associating strength with masculinity. You can be a woman and be strong, but it's a very deeply rooted thing, this idea: a man is strong, he's the one who acts, who imposes, who earns, who leads. That's why I always bring up the subject of discipline. It's an inner work that you have to undertake to disassociate these things which have been linked together for centuries. You're almost born with it: "Don't do that, that's not nice for a girl to do"—this is very common—"A little girl doing that?"

But, as I told you, there's less of this with my children's generation. Though it still goes on, in some respects—more, for example, in relation to beauty. The girls do gymnastics in order to have a nice body. Well, that's fine, but in relation to sexuality there's still the same standard, of a pinup girl. You know: "Wow, look at that!" This still exists. Which means the woman still has to be pretty, elegant, with a small waist, firm breasts; there's still all of this. So, they study together, they talk about things, but this image, of the woman-as-object, still exists.

When I was an adolescent, you wanted to be pretty to please the boy. You saw yourself through his eyes, you wanted to be attractive for him. Not just average attractive either. If you were fat, you went on a diet, you tried to look as attractive as possible. Maybe all this is just the sexual awakening of adolescence, and afterward it falls into place. At least it should, but our problem seems to be that this persists, that women don't affirm themselves in any other way. They have only this, this struggle for beauty, for youth.

But, judging by my children, boys aren't less vain than girls. My son is constantly in front of the mirror. He's sixteen, and he gets up at 6:30 to prepare himself for school. Just this morning, I was still half-asleep, he put on a sweater and started asking me, "Should I wear my collar inside or out?"—at 6:30 in the morning! First he put it inside, didn't like it that way, pulled it out, combed his hair, then brushed his hair. He's incredibly vain. He likes clothing, he works out, he thinks his body is beautiful. He stands in front of the mirror exactly like a woman, no difference at all [*laughs*]! He's worried because he's getting some pimples; he's worried about the girls.

Things are evolving; men are taking on certain tasks. I think that caring for the children will be more equally divided in the future, and not just a mother's obligation. When my husband and I separated, we talked about who the children would stay with. I didn't feel they necessarily had to stay with me. Well, if they were really small, then yes . . . I'd have more opportunity to stay home with them. But they were already adolescents, they knew how to take a bath alone, eat alone, take the bus, they were already mobile. So it was something that was questioned. But what happened was this. I told my husband, "I don't think they necessarily have to stay with me." He said, "Oh, then let's ask them." And this raised a hellish problem, because they couldn't make up their minds. I think it was too heavy a problem for them, that they thought choosing one of us would imply disrespect for the other, so they were confused. My son said, "Oh, I don't know, I think I'll stay here till I finish high school, then we'll see." And my daughter said she wanted to stay in both houses. I said, "That won't work, you have to decide on one. Naturally you can always go to the other, but you have to have one place; otherwise, where would you put your books, your clothes? You have to have a place." But they absolutely refused to take a stand. I saw that this was confusing them, so I said, "Look, I'm going to decide. You're staying with me. I'll rent an apartment near your school, and you'll stay with me. Besides, I need you, too, and your father has to travel a lot." I decided for them, and it was obviously a relief to them. It was too much responsibility to put in their hands. They were hesitant to hurt either of us.

Of course I talked to my husband first. He never really made much of their staying with him, but I insisted we talk about it. I didn't think it was fair, since they were already grown, to demand that they stay with me. I thought he had the same right, although I really wanted it the way it is now, to have them with me—I've always been very attached to them. Sérgio was always a good father, to the extent that he participated—but at a distance, you know. He's the kind of father who doesn't know the doctor's name, and if you ask what grade they're in, he knows more or less, but he's never dealt with their teachers, never. All those ties I maintained, and I would have missed them greatly, so I really preferred that they stay with me. Anyway, it's an open question—whenever they want, they can go to live with him. If one day they say, "Look, I feel like living with my father," I may feel horrible about it, but I'll say, "Fine."

WHEN I THINK of my past, I don't feel like the same person. I don't know how to define it, but I was completely different. I had, let's put it this way, I had within myself all this capacity to transform myself into what I am today, but it was all inside. And I didn't know that I had this capacity; it emerged slowly, as I pressed on. With each step I became more aware, of what I wanted to do, to be, to become. Now, when I compare the woman I am today with the woman of five years ago, I don't even know how to say who I was. I was lost in time.... Five years ago, what did I aspire to? What was my life? I don't know, and today I do know.... I'm struggling to learn still more, to know myself more, but at that time I didn't even want to know myself through analysis, or to have a personal identity. There were some things that I felt weren't quite right, but I didn't even know how to determine what was causing my dissatisfaction. Today I know, I may not know everything that I like, but at least I know what I *don't* like. What I want,

I may not always be sure of, but I already know how to say what I *don't* want, you see. And I think that, on balance, I've done well. But it's difficult, it leaves marks.

Another point: before, my main concern was our home, and I only did other things if they didn't interfere much. Today, no, it's this right here that's dominant at the moment, and although I hope everything's fine at home, that they've had their lunch, that they're studying—still, I'm not there, you see. So they have to manage on their own. Mama isn't home anymore.

Sometimes I think, "One year has passed and, my God, so many changes in such a short time!" But I already had them all prepared, all coiled up within me. It's like a butterfly coming out of its chrysalis . . . you never know when the right moment will come. There are times when you crack the shell open a bit, or it even starts to open by itself, and there you are with your little wings still folded up—not flying yet, but able to fly.

INTRODUCTION

1   William McKinley Runyan, "Life Histories in Anthropology: Another View," *American Anthropologist* 88:1 (March 1986), p. 182. See also Runyan's *Life Histories and Psychobiography: Explorations in Theory and Method* (New York: Oxford University Press, 1984).

2   The 1960s and 1970s were a period of intense rural-to-urban migration, which transformed Brazil's population, especially in areas other than the impoverished Northeast, from a predominantly rural-based one to a predominantly urban one. In 1984, 73 percent of Brazil's population of approximately 131 million was estimated to be urban (see *Economic and Social Progress in Latin America. External Debt: Crisis and Adjustment* [Washington, D.C.: Inter-American Development Bank, 1985 report], p. 210). P. A. Kluck, in his chapter "The Society and Its Environment," in *Brazil: A Country Study*, ed. Richard F. Nyrop (Washington, D.C.: American University, Foreign Area Studies, 1983), p. 128, summarizes: "Migrants, regardless of how lowly their urban occupations or how minimal their earnings, were financially better off than they would have been had they remained in the countryside." Women were more likely to migrate than men, since young women were readily able to find employment as maids in urban households. One-half to three-quarters of all female migrants began urban life in domestic service, and then, as their length of residence in the city increased, they were more likely to shift into work in industry or the social sector or to get married (which, it should be noted, merely meant that their domestic service moved from the public, wage-earning sphere to the private, unremunerated sphere). The proportion of women in remunerated domestic service declined to between 25 percent and 40 percent among migrants with ten or more years of urban residence (p. 128). The economist Heleith Saffioti, in her book *Emprego Doméstico e Capitalismo* (Rio de Janeiro: Avenir Editora, 1979), pp. 10, 16–17, and 49, notes that between 1872 (when the first Brazilian census was conducted) and 1970 the percentage of the economically active population engaged in the primary sector (agriculture) fell steadily, as is invariably the case in industrializing societies, and more so among women than among men. A corresponding increase in the number of women engaged in the tertiary sector (services) has occurred, and it is above all to the large cities that rural women are drawn in their search for employment as unskilled labor. In the 1940 and 1970 censuses, the percentage of women in the secondary (industrial) sector was nearly identical (10.6 versus 10.5), having risen to 15.6 percent in 1950 and dropped to 12.5 percent in 1960.

NOTES

3   Micaela Di Leonardo, *The Varieties of Ethnic Experience: Kinship, Class, and Gender among California Italian-Americans* (Ithaca, N.Y.: Cornell University Press, 1984), p. 41.

4   Calvin Pryluck, "Ultimately We Are All Outsiders: The Ethics of Documentary Filmmaking," *Journal of the University Film Association* 28:1 (Winter 1976). My thanks to Professor Mark Jonathan Harris, of the School of Cinema-Television at the University of Southern California, for sending me this article. A more detailed discussion of ethics appears in my article "Ethical Problems of Personal Narratives; or, Who Should Eat the Last Piece of Cake?" in *International Journal of Oral History* 8:1 (February 1987), pp. 5–27, in which portions of this introduction first appeared.

5   See, for example, Claire Robertson, "In Pursuit of Life Histories: The Problem of Bias," *Frontiers* 7:2 (1983), pp. 63–69; Gelya Frank, "Finding the Common Denominator: A Phenomenological Critique of Life History Method," *Ethos* 7:1 (Spring 1979), pp. 68–94; Lawrence Watson and Maria-Barbara Watson-Franke, *Interpreting Life Histories: An Anthropological Inquiry* (New Brunswick: Rutgers University Press, 1985), who provide a critical review of the development of life history research in their first chapter (and to whom I am grateful for allowing me to see their manuscript in page proofs); and L. L. Langness and Gelya Frank, *Lives: An Anthropological Approach to Biography* (Novato, Calif.: Chandler & Sharp, 1981).

6   See, for example, Marvin Harris, "Referential Ambiguity in the Calculus of Brazilian Racial Identity," *Southwestern Journal of Anthropology* 26:1 (Spring 1970), pp. 1–14, who gathered 492 different racial categorizations in five different states; and Roger Sanjek, "Brazilian Racial Terms: Some Aspects of Meaning and Learning," *American Anthropologist* 73:5 (October 1971), pp. 1126–1143, who describes 116 racial terms gathered in a village in Bahia.

7   Florestan Fernandes, in *The Negro in Brazilian Society*, trans. Jacqueline D. Skiles, A. Brunel, and Arthur Rothwell (New York: Columbia University Press, 1969), discusses the "myth of racial democracy" and the "prejudice of having no prejudice" in Brazil. Fernandes considers it justified to speak of Brazilian racial "tolerance" but distinguishes this from absence of prejudice and racial equality. For a comparison of Brazilian and North American racial attitudes, see Carl N. Degler, *Neither Black nor White: Slavery and Race Relations in Brazil and the United States* (New York: Macmillan, 1971). Degler introduced the idea of a "mulatto escape hatch" as the key feature setting Brazilian racial attitudes apart from North American racism, but this has since been disputed. See also Thomas Skidmore, *Black into White: Race and Nationality in Brazilian Thought* (New York: Oxford University Press, 1974).

8   For a discussion of this subject, see Dennis R. Preston, " 'Ritin' Fowklower Daun 'Rong: Folklorists' Failures in Phonology," *Journal of American Folklore* 95:377 (1982), pp. 304–324.

9   See, for example, Vincent Crapanzano's review "Life-Histories," *American Anthropologist* 86:4 (December 1984), pp. 953–960.

10   Dennis Tedlock, "On the Translation of Style in Oral Narrative," in *The Spoken Word and the Work of Interpretation* (Philadelphia: University of Pennsylvania Press, 1983), p. 51. This important volume collects Tedlock's essays from the previous fifteen years.

11   Two essays dealing with literary analysis of oral testimony are Elizabeth A. Meese, "The Languages of Oral Testimony and Women's Literature," and Alice T. Gasque, "An Analysis of the Oral Testimony of Edna Anderson," both in Leonore Hoffman and

Margo Culley, eds., *Women's Personal Narratives: Essays in Criticism and Pedagogy* (New York: Modern Language Association of America, 1985), pp. 18–26 and 78–85.

12   Tedlock, "Learning to Listen: Oral History as Poetry," in *The Spoken Word and the Work of Interpretation*, pp. 107–123

13   *Antologia Poética de Manuel Bandeira*, 2nd ed. (Porto Alegre: Editora do Autor [1961]), p. 79. The poem was originally published in Bandeira's volume *Libertinagem* (1930).

14   The Russian formalist Viktor Shklovsky developed the notion that the function of art is to "defamiliarize" or estrange the viewer or reader, to restore freshness to deadened reactions by prolonging perception. Poetry does this, for example, through its difficult formal structures and deviations from everyday language. See his essay "Art as Technique," in *Russian Formalist Criticism: Four Essays*, trans. Lee T. Lemon and Marion J. Reis (Lincoln: University of Nebraska Press, 1965), pp. 3–24.

15   George Dickie, *Art and the Aesthetic: An Institutional Analysis* (Ithaca, N.Y.: Cornell University Press, 1974).

16   Marialice addresses her mother in the formal polite mode, as "Senhora," rather than in the informal "você."

17   Walter J. Ong, *Orality and Literacy: The Technologizing of the Word* (New York: Methuen, 1981), chap. 3, "Some Dynamics of Orality." Ong's comments, which I have utilized in this section, refer to "primary oral cultures," that is, those that have not been touched by writing. Still, it is intriguing to note how many of his (and earlier scholars') observations about oral cultures indeed apply to Marialice.

18   This section of Ong's argument closely parallels Carol Gilligan's views about women's morality in contrast to men's. Gilligan argues that women, unlike men, construe a moral problem as one of "care and responsibility in relationships rather than as one of rights and rules." Following Nancy Chodorow's work in *The Reproduction of Mothering: Psychoanalysis and the Sociology of Gender* (Berkeley: University of California Press, 1978), Gilligan sees males as primarily concerned with the role of separation in defining and empowering the self, whereas females express the "ongoing process of attachment that creates and sustains the human community." See Gilligan's *In a Different Voice: Psychological Theory and Women's Development* (Cambridge: Harvard University Press, 1982), pp. 73, 156.

19   Given the constant devaluation of the cruzeiro during the period in which I was conducting interviews, I have translated all cruzeiro figures into roughly equivalent dollar amounts throughout this book. Although this is a very imprecise measure of the Brazilian economic situation, the women themselves often describe their condition in terms that clearly convey how far their money will go.

At the end of February 1986, in a major overhaul of the Brazilian economy, President José Sarney introduced the Plano Cruzado, a one-year plan to control inflation, nearly 400 percent annually at the time, by eliminating indexation (see note 23, Chapter 3, and note 1, Chapter 5, below), instituting a price freeze, adjustments in wages and other contracts, and establishing a new currency, the cruzado—worth 1,000 cruzeiros. The daily devaluation of Brazilian currency against the U.S. dollar was stopped—but only temporarily. The minimum wage was increased by 33 percent and frozen at Cr 800 (U.S. $58), and workers received a further 15 percent bonus to offset the effects of inflation before the package went into effect (*Latin America Weekly Report*, 7 March 1986). Furthermore, whenever accumulated monthly inflation reached 20 percent, a wage increase was automatically triggered. Among the immediate effects of the plan was an increase in purchasing power, which quickly led to shortages since domestic output could not keep up with demand.

An extension of the Plano Cruzado, known as the "Cruzadinho," aimed at curbing consumption, was introduced in late July 1986. This imposed a 25 percent tax or surcharge on international sea and air tickets and on the price of dollars for foreign travel, a 30 percent tax on the price of new cars, and a 28 percent tax on gasoline (*Latin America Economic Report*, 31 July 1986). In late November 1986 an economic austerity package called Plano Cruzado II was announced, implementing severe tax and price increases and causing President Sarney's popularity to plummet and public protests to take place (*Latin American Weekly Report*, 11 December 1986 and 8 January 1987).

Early in 1987, in the face of continuing widespread shortages, inflationary pressures, and the foreign payments crisis, Brazil suspended interest payments on $68 billion of its $108 billion foreign debt. For the background on this decision, see Celso Furtado, *No to Recession and Unemployment: An Examination of the Brazilian Economic Crisis*, trans. Sue Branford, intro. Teresa Hayter (London: Third World Foundation, 1984). By mid-1987, with the collapse of the Plano Cruzado and in a climate of rapidly increasing inflation and unemployment, Brazil was again heading toward a major recession and hyperinflation, with the annual rise in prices estimated at 800 percent (*New York Times*, 13 June 1987). Despite government announcements that prices could be increased only once a month and then by a maximum of 80 percent of the National Consumer Price Index, they were actually being increased at least once a week, sometimes twice (*Latin American Weekly Report*, 11 June 1987). In mid-June 1987, a harsh new austerity plan, dubbed "Novo Cruzado" or "Plano Bresser" (after Finance Minister Luiz Carlos Bresser Pereira), was announced. It imposed a ninety-day freeze on prices and ended the inflation-linked "trigger" for automatic wage adjustments, which, since March 1987, had been set off every month (*Latin American Regional Reports: Brazil*, 9 July 1987). Widespread popular dissatisfaction and protest resulted from the erosion of wages and increasing unemployment (*Latin American Weekly Report*, 16 July 1987).

20   Agnes Hankiss, "Ontologies of the Self: On the Mythological Rearranging of One's Life-History," in Daniel Bertaux, ed., *Biography and Society: The Life History Approach in the Social Sciences* (Beverly Hills, Calif.: Sage Publications, 1981), pp. 203–209. Hankiss writes: "The image of the self is never just a simple reflection of the experiences related to the self: it always includes a specific response to the 'Why' of the development of the self. Everyone builds his or her own theory about the history and the course of his or her life by attempting to classify his or her particular successes and fortunes, gifts and choices, favourable and unfavourable elements of his or her fate according to a coherent, explanatory principle and to incorporate them within a *historical unit*. In other words, everybody tries, in one way or another, to build up his or her own ontology" (p. 204).

Hankiss carried out a survey to find out "how the mythologically rearranged image of the subject's childhood was related, within the image of the self, to the image that the subject had of his present life" (p. 204). The interviews I conducted tend to bear out Hankiss's generalizations, although I believe that the four predominant strategies she outlines are too rigid. They are (i) the dynastic strategy: a good image of one's childhood, leading to a good present image of the self; (ii) the antithetical strategy: a bad image of childhood leading to a good present image of the self; (iii) the compensatory strategy: good childhood, bad present image of self; and (iv) the self-absolutory strategy: bad childhood, bad present image. On the importance of a "core self," see the excellent article by Jane Flax, "Re-Membering the Selves: Is the Repressed Gendered?" in *Michigan Quarterly Review* 26:1 (Winter 1987), pp. 92–110.

21   Maria C. Lugones and Elizabeth V. Spelman, "Have We Got a Theory for You! Feminist Theory, Cultural Imperialism, and the Demand for 'The Woman's Voice,'" *Women's Studies International Forum* 6:6 (1983), p. 593.

22   Clifford Geertz, " 'From the Native's Point of View': On the Nature of Anthropological Understanding," in *Local Knowledge: Further Essays in Interpretive Anthropology* (New York: Basic Books, 1983), pp. 55–70.

23   See Paul Zumthor, "The Text and the Voice," *New Literary History* 16 (Autumn 1984), p. 75.

24   Louis Althusser, "Ideology and Ideological State Apparatuses," in *Lenin and Philosophy and Other Essays*, trans. Ben Brewster (New York: Monthly Review Press, 1971), p. 162. He goes on to elaborate: "all ideology represents in its necessarily imaginary distortion not the existing relations of production (and the other relations that derive from them), but above all the (imaginary) relationships of individuals to the relations of production and the relations that derive from them. What is represented in ideology is therefore not the system of the real relations which govern the existence of individuals, but the imaginary relations of those individuals to the real relations in which they live" (pp. 164–165).

25   In several of the life stories that were told to me, I was struck by the emergence of this theme, so important to Marialice, of being a "good girl." Here we see ideology in flagrant conflict with experience, but this is perfectly comprehensible: in the face of hardship or misfortune, women search for survival strategies. One such strategy can be discerned in this clinging to the notion that if they just manage to be good enough, or if they have small and safe aspirations, the very traits their society claims to reward in women, things may in the end work out all right. See Part Five, below, for two more stories with this theme.

26   *The Autobiography of William Carlos Williams* (New York: Random House, 1951), pp. 361–362.

1   SISTER DENISE

1   *Latin America Weekly Report*, 26 April 1985. In a speech later in 1985, President José Sarney described the problems that he, as the first postmilitary president, faced: "I have inherited the greatest political crises in the history of Brazil, the world's largest foreign debt, Brazil's largest-ever internal debt, the highest inflation, the largest 'social' debt, an active labour movement and despair. . . ." He cited statistics indicating the massive redistribution of income that had occurred during the military's rule: in 1960, 50 percent of the country's

population held 4 percent of the national wealth; by 1985, this was down to 3 percent. Conversely, the richest 10 percent of the population had increased its share of the national wealth from 39 percent to 51 percent during the same period. Forty-five percent of the land was held by one percent of the people in 1985. Thirteen million people were unemployed that year, and 6 million underemployed. Sarney concluded: "The poor are getting poorer and the rich, richer" (*Latin America Weekly Report*, 2 August 1985). See also note 23, Chapter 3.

2   *Latin America Regional Reports: Brazil*, 8 February 1985. Anthony L. Hall, *Drought and Irrigation in North-East Brazil* (Cambridge: Cambridge University Press, 1978), argues that the Northeast's social and economic organization is as much responsible for the region's hardships as is the drought. On land reform, see note 10, below.

3   Before 1971, primary education in Brazil consisted of four years of compulsory schooling. This could be followed by an optional four years of middle school (*ginásio*). The 1971 education reform combined primary and middle school into an eight-year program that is free and compulsory for children between the ages of seven and fourteen. Despite extensive expansion of the public school system in the past two decades, to this day the number of public schools in Brazil is inadequate and compulsory attendance impossible to enforce, especially in the rural areas. Although nearly 75 percent of Brazil's population now live in urban areas, approximately 4 million of the 7 million school-age children *not* attending school in 1983 were living in rural areas. There is also a staggeringly high dropout rate: in 1983 approximately 24.5 million children started first-level schooling (the primary cycle of eight grades), while the number starting second-level schooling (grades nine through eleven) was less than 3 million. The greatest dropout rate, nearly 50 percent, occurs between first and second grade. The Ministry of Education and Culture acknowledged, in September 1983, that of every thousand children enrolled in first grade, only 170 would complete eighth grade. A further problem is that, with a few notable exceptions, public schools in Brazil have a poor reputation, and those people who can do so prefer to send their children to private (often Church-affiliated) schools. Among public school teachers, according to the 1980 census, 41 percent earn less than one minimum salary and 72 percent less than two. See *Almanaque Abril '86* (São Paulo: Editora Abril, 1986), pp. 695–697; and also Fay Haussman and Jerry Hoar, *Education in Brazil* (Hamden, Conn.: Archon Books, 1978). In 1980, more than 95 percent of primary-school teachers were female, as were more than 77 percent of secondary-school teachers. In higher education, however, the figure dropped to 42 percent (up from 30 percent in 1970)—but this is in fact an extremely high rate and reflects the acceptance of teaching as a "woman's profession" even at the higher levels. Salary discrimination exists in this profession as elsewhere: only 14 percent of all female teachers earned more than five minimum salaries, whereas 51 percent of male teachers did. See *Mulherio* 6:20 (1985), p. 14. Traditionally in Brazil, education has not been considered important for females. Although female school-attendance rates have increased enormously during the past few decades, women, but not men, are still likely to lose, in the course of their later lives, such literacy as they acquired in school. And illiteracy is directly associated with low wages and high fertility. As regards higher education (see also note 2, Chapter 15, below), between 1968 and 1978 the proportion of university students in Brazil as a whole went from 0.3 percent to 1.1 percent, with a much higher rate of increase among women than among

men. See Carmen Barroso, *Mulher, Sociedade e Estado no Brasil* (São Paulo: Editora Brasiliense/UNICEF, 1982), pp. 57–66.

4   The *comunidades eclesiais de base* (CEBs) began in Brazil in the 1960s and have vastly increased in number, especially in poor areas on the peripheries of the cities and in the rural zone. In 1980 there were an estimated 80,000 base communities throughout Brazil. See Maria Helena Moreira Alves, "Grassroots Organizations, Trade Unions, and the Church," *Latin American Perspectives* 11:1 (Winter 1984), pp. 73–102; and her indispensable *State and Opposition in Military Brazil* (Austin: University of Texas Press, 1985), pp. 177–182, for an outline of the organization and functions of CEBs. Alves argues that the CEBs "have been the schools and the seedbeds of participatory democracy" (*State and Opposition*, p. 182). The CEBs are an offshoot of the Second Vatican Council's call for the Church to come to terms with the contemporary world and of Brazil's own Movimento de Educação de Base (MEB, Movement for Basic Education), a Church-sponsored, government-financed adult literacy program that was active in Brazil's poorer rural areas in the early 1960s. Like Paulo Freire's educational philosophy, expressed in the phrase "education as the practice of freedom" (also the title of a 1967 book by Freire), the MEB, after the 1964 military coup, was accused of being "subversive" and was suppressed. See Emanuel de Kadt, *Catholic Radicals in Brazil* (London: Oxford University Press, 1970). See also note 5, below.

5   The Church in Brazil has undergone sweeping changes over the past twenty years. Scott Mainwaring, in *The Catholic Church and Politics in Brazil, 1916–1985* (Stanford, Calif.: Stanford University Press, 1986), pp. 14–15, states that, since the early 1960s, "lay and grass-roots movements have played an important role in the transformation of the Brazilian Church. Well before liberation theology appeared, Brazilian lay movements and progressive pastoral agents at the grass roots had already reflected on the major themes that would be systematized by the new theology and had introduced a conception of faith linked to radical politics. Several of the most famous Latin American liberation theologians . . . have recognized that these grass-roots and lay movements shaped their theological reflection. Later, after repression had destroyed the radical lay movements of the early 1960's in Brazil, pastoral agents in the communities began to innovate. The first base communities, the early discussions about pedagogy among the popular classes, the early work with the Indians, and most of the other major innovations in the Brazilian Church started at the grass roots." Repression against the Church after the 1964 coup, Mainwaring says, was a key factor in the Church's transformation.

The National Conference of Brazilian Bishops (CNBB), founded in 1952 and led initially by Dom Helder Câmara (subsequently archbishop of Recife and Olinda; see note 7, Chapter 5, below), is the social and political arm of the Brazilian episcopate; it issues documents and organizes grassroots activities and pastoral plans for enacting the conclusions reached in the bishops' synods (see Alves, *State and Opposition*, p. 154). After the 1964 coup, the leaders of the CNBB initially supported the military. In the late 1960s, during a period of severe political repression in Brazil, some bishops, prodded by a young activist clergy, began to modify their public stance. In 1969 the bishops took thirteen documented cases of torture to then-president Emílio Garrastazu Médici but were rebuffed, an event that marked a turning point for the Brazilian Church, most of whose "moderate" bishops joined in arguing that the regime's national security doctrine was in opposition to Christian teaching. In the 1970s, as the negative consequences of Brazil's developmentalist policies grew clearer, the Church became more active on behalf of the poor. The social activism supported by much of the Brazilian episcopate has brought it into conflict not only with the Brazilian government—especially before the 1985 return to civilian and democratic rule—but also with the Vatican, culminating in the Vatican's criticism of liberation theology in September 1984 and in its subsequent imposition of a one-year teaching and writing ban on the Franciscan friar Leonardo Boff, a leading Brazilian theologian. In early 1985, Archbishop José Ivo Lorscheiter, then president of the CNBB, stated that, with a new government about to be elected, the Church could cede its political role (*Latin America Regional Reports: Brazil*, 4 January 1985 and 31 May 1985). But by mid-1986, in the face of the new government's failure to implement extensive land reform, the CNBB was resuming its activist stance (Alan Riding, "Civil Rule Fails to End Brazil's Church-State Rift," *New York Times*, 7 July 1986). See also note 10, below.

6   Infant mortality in the Northeast of Brazil is much higher than in the developed Southeast. During the recession between 1980 and 1985, which coincided with the worst drought of this century in the Northeast, infant mortality rates soared. In the Northeastern state of Ceará, for example, infant mortality rose from 140 per thousand live births in "normal" times to 250 per thousand in 1983 (*Latinamerica Press*, 22 September 1983). In early 1985, the overall infant mortality rate for Brazil was estimated to be 68 per thousand live births, while in the Northeast as a whole it was 107 per thousand, rising to 300 per thousand in some areas of the Northeast (*Latin America Regional Reports: Brazil*, 8 February 1985). This should not, however, be viewed merely as an inevitable consequence of climatic conditions. Charles H. Wood, in "Infant Mortality Trends and Capitalist Development in Brazil: The Case of São Paulo and Belo Horizonte," *Latin American Perspectives* 4:4 (Fall 1977), pp. 56–65, analyzed the relationship between the increase in infant deaths and the decline in real wages of low-income groups that resulted from the government's policy of economic expansion in the late 1960s and early 1970s. The ongoing deterioration in working-class standards of living as capitalist development was pursued would, he argued, continue to result in increased infant mortality rates. Nancy Scheper-Hughes, in "Culture, Scarcity, and Maternal Thinking: Maternal Detachment and Infant Survival in a Brazilian Shantytown," *Ethos* 13:4 (Winter 1985), pp. 291–317, reports that approximately 1 million children under the age of five die each year in Brazil, mostly from parasitic infections interacting with infectious disease and chronic malnutrition (p. 292). Arguing that infant mortality is a problem of political economy, Scheper-Hughes notes that mothers in the Northeastern town she studied would selectively neglect their weakest children, motivated by both pity and the pressure of scarce resources. She calls this "maternal deprivation" and links it to material and emotional scarcity.

In addition to the increase in infant mortality and death from starvation caused by the drought of the early 1980s, a further problem is the long-term health consequences of the drought. In 1983, a World Health Organization medical team estimated that an entire generation of *nordestinos*—3 million people—have had their growth drastically affected by the lack of water (*Latin America Regional Reports: Brazil*, 21 October 1983).

7   In the 1982 elections, after years of dwindling support, the progovernment PDS,

for the first time since the military coup of 1964, lost the support of the majority of the Brazilian electorate at the state and federal (but not at the municipal) level. The PDS ended up with 43.1 percent of the valid votes in the Chamber of Deputies: in the most-developed areas of Brazil it was resoundingly defeated, but in the poor states of the North and Northeast, which have always been the PDS's greatest electoral stronghold, the PDS was able to win 62.5 percent of the votes for Federal Chamber of Deputies. The year 1982 was also the first since 1965 that state governors were directly elected by the people. Twelve PDS governors were elected (of a total of twenty-two), and nine of those twelve were elected in states in the North and Northeast (*Latin America Regional Reports: Brazil*, 11 February 1983).

8   Brazil's 1891 Constitution prohibited illiterates from exercising the franchise. This stipulation was finally abolished through a constitutional amendment, approved by the Brazilian Congress in May 1985, which enfranchised some 20 million persons (*Latin America Weekly Report*, 17 May 1985). MOBRAL (Movimento Brasileiro de Alfabetização) is a much-criticized government program initiated in 1970 to provide basic literacy skills to adults and later expanded to include children.

9   In 1985, ten years after the start of Proálcool (Programa Nacional do Álcool), which aimed at providing an alternative source of fuel that would decrease Brazilian dependence on imported oil by converting sugar cane into fuel alcohol, the government of President José Sarney cut the subsidies on which the program depended, making its future uncertain. At that time, 83 percent of the country's trucks and cars were reputedly powered by fuel alcohol (*Latin America Weekly Report*, 8 November 1985). The subsequent fall in oil prices made fuel alcohol less competitive and further threatened the program (*Latin America Weekly Report*, 21 February 1986).

10   In October 1985 the government decreed into law a land reform program to distribute more than 40 million hectares of land to 1.4 million landless families by 1989. But members of the armed forces, conservative politicians, and large landowners created vociferous opposition to the program. After many delays and revisions, President Sarney began to implement a much-modified agrarian reform in May 1986, aiming at resettling 150,000 families in 1986, a goal that the government later announced could not in fact be met (*Latin America Weekly Report*, 18 April 1986, 16 May 1986; *Latin American Weekly Report*, 9 October 1986). President Sarney gave his assurance that he would not retreat from the land reform program (*Latin America Weekly Report*, 26 June 1986), but relations between the Church, which has set agrarian reform as its principal social demand, and the government have become ever more strained on this issue. In October 1985 there were an estimated 10 million landless peasants, and one percent of the population owned more than 40 percent of the land (*Washington Report on the Hemispheres*, 15 October 1986).

It was later estimated that only about 2,500 families were in fact resettled by the end of 1986 (*Latin American Regional Reports: Brazil*, 23 April 1987). Violence has repeatedly broken out as armed groups organized by rural landowners attempt to drive squatters off idle lands and to attack and intimidate their supporters. Millions of people are reported to have been expelled from land they have lived on over the past ten years (*Latin America Weekly Report*, 21 August 1986). In 1986, the number of people killed in conflicts over land came to 272, of which about 200 were landless peasants—this according to figures issued by the Ministry for

Agrarian Reform and Development. While the root cause of violence in rural areas is conflict over land, it has spread into cities, where police and squatters engage in violent clashes. The important 1985 book *Brasil: Nunca Mais*, available in English as *Torture in Brazil*, trans. Jaime Wright, ed. and intro. Joan Dassin (New York: Vintage/Random House, 1986), an extensive survey and history of human rights violations between 1964 and 1979, showed that nearly 90 percent of the political prisoners during that period were from middle- or upper-class families—which explains the support these sectors gave to the fight for human rights. Today, by contrast, such violations are committed against the poor, and as a result there is no protest by middle- and upper-class individuals (*Latin American Regional Reports: Brazil*, 4 June 1987).

11   BEMFAM (Sociedade Civil de Bem Estar Familiar) is a private family-planning organization founded in 1965 with grants from the International Planned Parenthood Foundation. It has set up community clinics and distributed contraceptives (above all, the pill). Only in the mid-1970s were the pronatalist policies of the Brazilian government reconsidered and slowly modified, initially to a "laissez-faire" position that recognized the right of couples to make decisions about family planning. By 1980, however, with a deteriorating economy, the government had drawn up a broad family-planning program under the rubric of "responsible paternity." As the minister of social welfare declared, "No one is against population growth and the occupation of our national territory," long associated with one another in Brazilian consciousness. However, "what we do not want is that the price for this should be 700 children dead out of every 1,000 born, as happens in the region of Gameleira in Pernambuco" (cited in McDonough and DeSouza; see below). BEMFAM, meanwhile, had entered into hundreds of formal and informal agreements with state and municipal agencies. Toward the end of 1986, the government's long-awaited family-planning program was to be put into effect, to help the uncoordinated private efforts operating hitherto, which had reduced the birthdate from more than 3 percent in 1970 to 2.4 percent in 1980. The Brazilian minister of health announced in 1984 that the government was finally implementing a full-fledged program of integrated health care for women (PAISM), intended (among a series of broader health measures) to ensure that information and means of family planning are available to those in need so that they can decide for themselves. In fact, however, as of late 1986 the program was just beginning, on a very small scale (*Veja*, 21 January 1987).

Officially the Church in Brazil continues to condemn "artificial" methods of contraception, as set forth by Pope Paul VI in his 1968 encyclical *Humanae Vitae*; in practice, however, there is much disagreement about this issue among both clergy and laity. See *Latin America Regional Reports: Brazil*, 14 August 1986; Peter McDonough and Amaury DeSouza, *The Politics of Population in Brazil: Elite Ambivalence and Public Demand* (Austin: University of Texas Press, 1981), pp. 4–7; and the special report "O Direito de Evitar" in *Veja*, 21 January 1981.

Fertility began to decline among the "modern" groups and regions of Brazil as early as 1960, and after 1970 declining fertility spread to the Northeast. Between 1950 and 1970, rural birthrates remained steady, at about 7.7 births per woman, and then dropped by 1.3 births per woman during the 1970s. See Thomas W. Merrick, *Recent Fertility Declines in Brazil, Colombia, and Mexico* (Washington, D.C.: World Bank, Working Paper no. 692, 1985).

Women's groups in Brazil have criticized government intervention in the area of fertility control—whether in a pro- or antinatalist stance—because, either way, women are treated as tools of government priorities, lacking the information and means to make their own decisions (Branca Moreira Alves, "A Conquista do Corpo," *Veja*, 20 February 1980, p. 3). In particular, antinatalist policy directed at the poor is often seen as a means of avoiding the more basic problem of distribution of income. A focus on overpopulation, it has been argued, implies that this is the cause of poverty, whereas it is rather an effect of poverty. As Carmen Barroso wrote in *Mulherio* 5:21 (1985), p. 8, the feminist position has to be reiterated constantly if women are to combat the debris of authoritarian ideas still present on the issue of fertility control "on the part of those who think we ought to have many children in order to populate the Amazon and [on the other hand] on the part of those who want to control poverty and urban violence by means of sterilization of our uteruses, without considering the right of the woman over her own body." See also note 11, Chapter 5.

    12   Abortion, an extremely controversial issue in Catholic Brazil, is illegal except when practiced by a physician in order to save the pregnant woman's life or in cases of rape (Articles 124 to 128 of the Penal Code). Self-induced abortions are also a crime, although they carry a lighter sentence. Nonetheless, in the early 1980s it was conservatively estimated (extrapolating from data on hospitalization following illegal abortions) that 3 million abortions are performed in Brazil every year, most of them in unsound conditions (*Veja*, 21 January 1981, p. 53). One recent article mentions the figure of 3 to 5 million illegal abortions per year, and states that one in four Brazilian hospital beds are occupied by victims of these abortions (*Veja*, 17 June 1987, p. 146). Women's groups in Brazil have in recent years demanded legalized, state-funded abortions as well as better life conditions so that women can have the children they desire. The first prochoice demonstration in Brazil took place in Rio de Janeiro in January 1980, during the course of a criminal trial for abortion. See Frente de Mulheres Feministas, *O Que É o Aborto* (São Paulo: Cortez Editora, 1980), pp. 47–50, and the various articles on abortion in *Mulherio* 3:15 (1983) and 7:30 (1987).

    Despite a national day of struggle for the legalization of abortion in 1984 and extensive feminist agitation on this issue, the subsequent three years did not bring any progress. On the contrary, in mid-1987, as the work of writing a new constitution for postmilitary Brazil proceeded, it appeared that abortion, the object of a "holy war" by Church lobbyists, would be addressed in the new constitution, only to be altogether prohibited, an enormous setback in women's struggle for legalized abortion. The feminist activist Comba Marques described as "ingenuous" feminists' supposition that the abortion issue would not be raised in the Constituent Assembly, thus avoiding a constitutional prohibition, broader and more difficult to overturn than the present legislation. Women's groups attempted to prevent this outcome by organizing a popular initiative for the legalization of abortion via a petition that, were it successful in obtaining 30,000 signatures, could be submitted to the Constituent Assembly. See Santamaria Silveira, "Aborto: Momento de Decisão," *Mulherio* 7:30 (July 1987).

    In 1980, 30 percent of pregnancies in Brazil ended in miscarriage or illegal abortion. The public health-care system is reported currently to spend 40 percent of its obstetrics budget on the treatment of complications from self-induced or illegal abortions (*Latin America Regional Reports: Brazil*, 14 August 1986). In the late 1970s it was estimated that 340,000 women die every year from complications of clandestine abortions—the majority of which are sought by working-class women who have them under the worst medical conditions. Medical care subsequent to abortion was required by 44 percent of women who had abortions (see O Que É o Aborto, pp. 15–16). A 1987 study, sponsored by the National Conference of Brazilian Bishops, reported that, at 4 million a year, the number of abortions in Brazil surpassed by 200,000 the number of live births, and that 400,000 women die each year as a direct result of clandestine abortion (Latin American Regional Reports: Brazil, 17 September 1987). The maternal mortality rate—through complications of pregnancy, childbirth, and puerperium—was 134 for every thousand live births, according to one 1979 study; that is, nine times greater in Brazil than in developed countries (see Carmen Barroso, Mulher, Sociedade e Estado no Brasil, p. 96). For a brief, general survey of women's status in Brazil, see Sisterhood Is Global, ed. Robin Morgan (Garden City, N.Y.: Anchor Press/Doubleday, 1984), pp. 77–88. See also note 11, Chapter 5.

2   CAROLINA

1   On Afro-Brazilian religious practices, see the introduction to Chapter 4.

2   Three kinds of marriage exist in Brazil—civil, religious, and common law (amasiado)—of which only civil marriage, at a minimum age of sixteen for women and eighteen for men, is recognized by the state. The fact that an individual can be married in either a church ceremony or a legal ceremony (neither church nor state recognizes the other's jurisdiction) also means that a marriage in one jurisdiction could be followed by another marriage (to another individual) in the other jurisdiction. Only those married both in church and civil ceremonies would have no alternative but to divorce or live in a subsequent common-law marriage. Since divorce was prohibited in Brazil until 1977, people often merely separated and started living with new partners in more-or-less socially sanctioned unions. Women's groups have been arguing for the rights of women and children outside of the legally sanctioned civil marriage. Like divorce, legal marriage is very much a function of class. It was recently reported that two out of every five couples in Brazil are not legally married. A subcommittee of the Constituent Assembly writing a new constitution for postmilitary Brazil has proposed doing away with the concept of illegitimate child and unwed mother (Veja, 3 June 1987, p. 32; see also note 1, Chapter 19).

3   VERA

1   See Latin America Regional Reports: Brazil, 8 February 1980; and the books by Carlos A. Hasenbalg, Discriminação e Desigualdades Raciais no Brasil (Rio de Janeiro: Edições Graal, 1979) and, in collaboration with Lélia Gonzalez, Lugar de Negro (Rio de Janeiro: Editora Marco Zero, 1982).

2   Fúlvia Rosemberg, "Pirâmide Racial," Mulherio 4:19 (1984), p. 10.

3   Fúlvia Rosemberg, "Racismo no Sistema Escolar," Mulherio 6:25 (1986), p. 18.

4   It has been argued that this distribution of material rewards and life possibilities is not the result of lingering prejudice in a formerly slave holding society, but is rather an essential feature of capitalist development in Brazil (Gonzalez and Hasenbalg, *Lugar de Negro*, pp. 89–97). More recent analysis of racial inequalities in Brazil, showing the poor position of Black and Brown women (in comparison with Whites and also with Orientals, who surpass Whites in all economic measures in Brazil) is available in Sueli Carneiro and Thereza Santos, *Mulher Negra* (São Paulo: Nobel/Conselho Estadual da Condição Feminina, 1985).

5   Rosemberg, "Racismo no Sistema Escolar."

6   Denise Natale, "Domésticas, Tentando Sair da Cozinha," *Mulherio* 5:21 (1985), p. 22. On the still higher salary brackets, see the introduction to Chapter 20.

7   *Latin American Regional Reports: Brazil*, 27 November 1986.

8   Natale, "Domésticas, Tentando Sair da Cozinha."

9   June E. Hahner, "Women and Work in Brazil, 1850–1920: A Preliminary Investigation," in *Essays concerning the Socioeconomic History of Brazil and Portuguese India*, ed. Dauril Alden and Warren Dean (Gainesville: University Presses of Florida, 1977), p. 101.

10   Thereza Martins, "Ainda na Base da Pirâmide," *Mulherio* 5:21 (1985), p. 21.

11   Lélia Gonzalez, "E a Trabalhadora Negra, Cumé Que Fica?" *Mulherio* 2:7 (1982), p. 9. A related issue is the economic hardship experienced by Black women heads-of-families. Official figures for 1980 recognize 15.6 percent of all families as headed by women (up from 10.8 percent in 1970). The majority of these families are at the lowest income levels, with 23 percent of them having, in 1980, an average monthly income below one-half the minimum salary. Women heads-of-families who are Black work more than their White counterparts and, as we have seen, are concentrated in the least prestigious and worst remunerated jobs. See Cristina Bruschini, *Mulher e Trabalho* (São Paulo: Nobel/Conselho Estadual da Condição Feminina, 1985), pp. 66–70.

12   Sueli Carneiro, "Trazer a Negritude ao Novo Feminismo," *Mulherio* 5:21 (1985), p. 17. Against this view, however, Fúlvia Rosemberg, in "Education: Democratization and Inequality," a paper prepared for the Conference on Worldwide Education for Women, held at Mount Holyoke College, South Hadley, Mass., November 4–7, 1987, argues that, at all levels of education, salary differentials between White men and Black men are smaller than those between White men and White women. According to this reading of the statistics, then, the hierarchy of privilege in Brazil is as follows: White men, Black men, White women, Black women.

13   Ines Castilho, "Implacáveis Amores Brancos e Negros," *Mulherio* 5:21 (1985), p. 18. Castilho reports on some research showing that nearly 37 percent of Black men with eight to ten years of schooling and more than 43 percent of Black men with eleven or more years of schooling marry White women. Among White men with comparable levels of education, the rate of marriage to Black women is low—only 8.7 percent and 4.8 percent respectively.

14   Carneiro, "Trazer a Negritude ao Novo Feminismo."

15   INAMPS (Instituto Nacional de Assistência Médica da Previdência Social) is the medical branch of Brazil's social security and welfare system. It provides clinical, surgical, pharmaceutical, and dental care to urban and rural workers registered in the INPS system

(see note 3, chapter 5, below) and their dependants, to civil servants and their dependants, and some special medical assistance programs to the needy population. The medical services reorganized under INAMPS in 1977 were previously under the jurisdiction of INPS. Many of the women I interviewed in 1981, however, still referred to the INPS as the source of their medical care. Others said "the Institute."

16   The very word *mulato* is a racial insult: it means "young mule"; hence, an animal of mixed parentage.

17   Since 1934, the Brazilian Constitution has affirmed that all are equal under the law (see note 1, Chapter 19). In practice, however, continued discrimination against Blacks eventually led to the 1951 passage of the Afonso Arinos Law, which spelled out penalties for racial discrimination in public places.

18   The Partido dos Trabalhadores (PT) came into being in 1979 when the government's Party Reform Bill attempted to fragment the opposition by dissolving the only two political parties (known as the "Yes" and the "Yes, Sir" parties) that had been legally allowed since 1965. A series of complex regulations governing the formation of new political parties was imposed in an attempt to destroy the opposition MDB (Movimento Democrático Brasileiro, or Brazilian Democratic Movement), which had acquired considerable strength and was likely to win control of the Congress; the ploy, however, backfired. What followed was a period of intense political organization by opposition groups. Among other political parties that emerged was the PT, led by Luis Inácio Lula da Silva ("Lula"), which, by the end of 1981, had become the third largest party, with strong ties to grassroots movements, *comunidades de base*, and peasant and union activists. The opposition MDB reemerged from this reorganization as the PMDB (Partido do Movimento Democrático Brasileiro), while the government party Arena resurfaced as the PDS (Partido Democrático Social). See Maria Helena Moreira Alves, *State and Opposition in Military Brazil* (Austin: University of Texas Press, 1985), pp. 214–220.

19   The Frente Negra Brasileira (FNB, Brazilian Negro Front), founded in September 1931 in São Paulo, brought together a variety of Black groups and within a short period of time attracted thousands of members. It started its own newspaper, *Voz da Raça* [Voice of the Race], in 1933 and became a political party in 1936. After Getúlio Vargas's 1937 coup, which inaugurated the authoritarian Estado Novo (New State), the FNB was outlawed. It then became the União Negra Brasileira (Brazilian Negro Union), under the presidency of Raul Joviano do Amaral, and managed to continue its activities until May 1938—the fiftieth anniversary of the abolition of slavery in Brazil. The FNB, with activities on both a political and a cultural plane, was the first major Black movement in Brazil after abolition. See Florestan Fernandes, *The Negro in Brazilian Society*, trans. Jacqueline D. Skiles, A. Brunel, and Arthur Rothwell (New York: Columbia University Press, 1969), p. 214; and Gonzalez and Hasenbalg, *Lugar de Negro*, pp. 22–23. With the establishment of Vargas's Estado Novo in 1937, Black activism was suppressed, to reemerge in the 1950s—only to be once again disrupted, this time by the 1964 coup. In the mid- and late 1960s, Black cultural organizations began to be active in Brazil's major cities. A national organization, the United Black Movement (Movimento Negro Unificado, at first called Movimento Unificado Contra a Discriminação Racial), was created in June 1978 (see Gonzalez and Hasenbalg, pp. 43–66, for its history and activities).

20   On the myth of racial democracy, see note 7 to Introduction.

21   On *candomblé* and *umbanda*, see the introduction to Chapter 4.

22   In 1984 a gigantic Carnival amphitheater was completed at a cost of $8 million. "Samba for Profit" is the new slogan of one winning samba school and the strategy now openly pursued by many Carnival entrepreneurs. See *Latin America Regional Reports: Brazil*, 15 March 1985, pp. 6–7.

23   As part of the system of indexing designed to control inflation, a policy of wage control was inaugurated after the military coup. Wage adjustments, based on the National Consumer Price Index (see note 1, Chapter 5, below), were made once a year until August 1979 when they were changed to twice a year. The government's 1979 wage law was supposedly redistributive downward, but, as pointed out by Alves, *State and Opposition in Military Brazil*, on whose work this note is based, that legislation had only a limited "Robin Hood effect" since it did not involve capital or profit rates. Rather, it redistributed income from the middle classes to the lower classes, but without affecting the higher-income groups. Although it increased dissatisfaction among middle-class professionals, the measure succeeded in the short run in reducing tensions among the lowest-paid workers and resulted in fewer strikes in 1980 by those workers (p. 202).

At the end of 1982, owing to the economic crisis and a supplementary loan made by the United States to Brazil (which allowed Brazil to close its accounts for the year), this wage policy came under increasing attack and was then modified in January 1983. The extra 10 percent that had been added to the Consumer Price Index twice a year in calculating salaries was removed. Only the lowest-paid workers were to receive adjustments, equal to the increase in the cost of living. All others suffered losses. Furthermore, the Consumer Price Index became ever more divorced from real increases in prices, with the result that all workers suffered a loss in real purchasing power.

In July 1983, as part of an agreement with the International Monetary Fund, the government attempted to introduce a decree-law limiting all raises after August 1983 to 80 percent of the already "purged" Consumer Price Index. This is the prospect that Vera is incensed about. It was the focus of public outrage and protests from July through October of 1983. When the measure came to the floor of Congress for a vote, forty-five members of the government party sided with the opposition and the decree was defeated, marking the first time in fifteen years that the Congress refused to approve a decree-law. See the account of this struggle in Alves, pp. 236–248.

Between 1968 and 1973, during the years of the "economic miracle," economic growth (thanks primarily to the industrial sector), as measured by the gross domestic product, occurred at an average yearly rate of more than 10 percent, while inflation averaged only 20 percent during the same period. It was during this time that Brazil's foreign debt began to increase dramatically: it went from $3.9 billion in 1968 to more than $12.5 billion by 1973 (and stood at $108 billion in mid-1987). Alves's book cites several measures of the pauperization that occurred in Brazil. The "productivist" ideology of the military was geared neither toward an immediate increase in the standard of living of the majority nor toward fulfilling their basic needs, but, rather, toward attracting foreign investment so that sufficient capital would be accumulated to allow Brazil to reach the "takeoff" stage; such growth was seen as the necessary condition for advancing Brazil's objective of becoming a world power (Alves, pp. 106–107). Income concentration was a part of this strategy, with the result that a major redistribution occurred between 1960 and 1976. The income share of the poorest 50 percent of the economically active population dropped from 17.71 percent in 1960 to 11.60 percent in 1976. The next poorest 30 percent of the population suffered a similar drop. The middle 15 percent increased their share slightly. But the richest 5 percent increased their share of the gross national product from 27.69 percent in 1960 to 39 percent in 1976 (Alves, pp. 106–111).

Meanwhile, the evolution of the minimum monthly salary indicated a consistent drop in the real minimum wage during this period. A study by the trade unions' think tank, DIEESE, pointed out that, using the gross domestic product as a yardstick, national income in Brazil rose from a base of 100 in 1940 to 485.05 in 1986. The minimum wage, however, fell in dollar terms from $98 to $68 (in March 1987). Official figures released by the IBGE (Brazilian Institute of Geography and Statistics) indicate that 17 million workers, or one-third of the Brazilian labor force, is on the minimum wage. Since, as the DIEESE notes, each worker earning the minimum wage is supporting 3.11 other people, approximately 70 million Brazilians are living in absolute poverty (*Latin American Weekly Report*, 19 March 1987).

In terms of the amount of worktime needed to buy a basic market basket that would sustain a family of four for one month, the condition of the minimum wage earner declined by nearly 50 percent between 1959 and 1978. Whereas in 1959, 65 hours and 5 minutes were needed to purchase the minimum food basket, at the end of the "economic miracle" years, in 1974, 163 hours and 32 minutes of work were required to purchase the same basket. Thereafter, necessary worktime began to decline for a while, so that in 1978 the food basket required 137 hours and 37 minutes of work, but in 1979 it was back up to 153 hours and 4 minutes. In July 1982, according to *Almanaque Abril 1984* (p. 713), a worker receiving the minimum salary in São Paulo would have had to work 136 hours per month in order to purchase the food basket; one year later, in July 1983, 171 hours were needed.

A further indication of the absolute poverty of much of the population was a 1975 parliamentary study estimating the number of Brazil's abandoned children to be nearly 2 million (85 percent of whom were in the North and Northeast), and the number of needy children to be more than 13.5 million (75 percent of whom were in the North and Northeast). At that time Brazil's population was approximately 105 million (Alves, pp. 111–113). In late 1986, government authorities estimated that six out of every ten minors lacked basic necessities, and one in ten was homeless, while 7 million were described as "abandoned" (*Latin American Regional Reports: Brazil*, 27 November 1986). See also note 19 to Introduction.

4 ÂNGELA

1   See IX *Recenseamento Geral do Brasil–1980. Tabulações Avançadas do Censo Demográfico: Resultados Preliminares* (Rio de Janeiro: IBGE, 1981), vol. 1, pt. 2, p. 11.

2   Maria Isaura Pereira de Queiroz, "Religious Evolution and Creation: The Afro-Brazilian Cults," *Diogenes* 115 (Fall 1981), pp. 1–21, from whose work most of this introduction is taken.

3   Roger Bastide, *The African Religions of Brazil*, trans. Helen Sebba (Baltimore: Johns Hopkins University Press, 1978). Bastide criticizes Afro-Brazilian religious practices for inadvertently serving to deflect political activism and protest.

4   Queiroz, "Religious Evolution and Creation: The Afro-Brazilian Cults," p. 20.

5   NORMA

1   INPC (Índice Nacional do Preço ao Consumidor) is the National Consumer Price Index, computed by government statisticians. Indexing was a system of monetary correction initiated shortly after the military coup, by which an adjustment for inflation was added to wages, rents, taxes, bonds, etc. In theory, indexing was to provide an objective and automatic adjustment for past inflation. But, in practice, the indexing formula was manipulated for policy purposes. See Darrel R. Eglin, "The Economy," in *Brazil: A Country Study*, ed. Richard F. Nyrop (Washington, D.C.: American University, Foreign Area Studies, 1983), pp. 173, 222. Maria Helena Moreira Alves, *State and Opposition in Military Brazil* (Austin: University of Texas Press, 1985), p. 68, points out that the government's wage-control system set only the *maximum* indexed increase that could be given to workers once a year, but did not set the *minimum*, which was decreed periodically by the federal government: "Over the years, the wage policy [wage-squeeze policy] has consistently underestimated the anticipated inflation rate as well as the rise in productivity [two of the three factors in the formula used in calculating wage levels], such that wage levels have fallen significantly in real terms" (pp. 52–53). See also note 19 to Introduction and note 23, Chapter 3, above.

2   According to Brazil's 1943 Consolidated Labor Code (Consolidação das Leis do Trabalho, or CLT), every firm employing more than thirty women between the ages of sixteen and forty is obliged to maintain a childcare facility (*creche*) for infants being breast-fed (up to six months old). Very rarely, however, is this done. In 1985, for example, only 3 of the 273 São Paulo metallurgy plants that should have done so in fact maintained childcare facilities; see Thereza Martins, "Ainda na Base da Pirâmide," *Mulherio* 5:21 (1985), p. 21. Women's groups have pointed out that even if the law were respected, it would cover only 2 percent of the female labor force. The rest of the economically active female population (27.49 percent of the female population over ten years of age, according to the Brazilian census of 1980) either are not officially registered workers or work in smaller firms or as domestics and rural workers. Even where the law is respected, women may find it difficult or impossible to take their babies long distance with them to their places of work or wherever the firm has made an arrangement with a childcare facility (not usually near poor women's residences). In addition, the law does not oblige the firm to inform employees about the arrangements, thus "phantom" childcare facilities can exist, where many different babies are supposedly registered for the same slot, in apparent compliance with the law. The women's movement has in recent years made childcare a high priority (although there is regional disagreement about the importance of this issue) and has achieved some success. See *Mulherio* 1:4 (1981), p. 12.

The CLT stipulates insignificantly small fines for companies found not to be in compliance with the law. In 1983, however, two feminist lawyers achieved a historic victory in the fight for childcare facilities for workers: they won a case brought by an employee seeking compensation for the childcare costs she incurred while working at a firm that did not maintain childcare facilities as legally required. The firm was ordered to reimburse her. See Adélia Borges, "Agora Nós Vamos Apelar," *Mulherio* 3:12 (1983), p. 23.

3   INPS (Instituto Nacional de Previdência Social) was established in 1966, unifying prior pension plans and providing accident insurance through a worker's compensation program. It includes disability and accident insurance for registered workers, pension plans, survivors' benefits (dependent children, too), and maternity benefits for registered workers. INPS is a contractual system, in which benefits are scaled to correspond to contributions from workers and employers. Until 1977 it also included medical coverage, but this is now under the auspices of INAMPS (see note 15, Chapter 3, above). James Malloy, whose book *The Politics of Social Security in Brazil* (Pittsburgh: University of Pittsburgh Press, 1979) provides a description and history of the system up to the mid-1970s, explains that the general term *previdência social* refers to a "system of state-enforced obligatory insurance," covering all persons in the designated groupings and financed by compulsory contributions from covered individuals, their employers, and the federal government (pp. 4–5). The Ministério da Previdência e Assistência Social (MPAS), created in 1974, formulates policy and implements the various programs that comprise the system. Subordinate to it is SINPAS (Sistema Nacional de Previdência e Assistência Social, set up in 1977), which is made up of seven entities including INPS and INAMPS. See Jaime A. de Araújo Oliveira and Sonia M. Fleury Teixeira, (Im)*previdência Social: 60 anos de História da Previdência no Brasil* (Petrópolis: Editora Vozes/ ABRASCO, 1986).

4   Article 391 of the 1943 Consolidated Labor Code stipulates that a woman's employment may not be rescinded on the grounds that she has married or become pregnant. Article 392 stipulates that pregnant women are forbidden to work for four weeks prior to and eight weeks after delivery, as determined by medical certification. During this time, the woman is entitled to her full salary or, if this has varied, to the average salary of her past six months of work, as well as to all accompanying benefits and rights. She may, if she chooses, return to her employment thereafter and is in any case guaranteed three months of job stability. In 1974, legislation was passed transferring all costs of such leaves to the INPS. Nonetheless, losing one's job because of pregnancy continues to be a major problem, as is preferential hiring of unmarried women. Article 396 ensures nursing mothers of the right to two breaks of one half-hour each during the workday for the purpose of nursing a child up to the age of six months. Obviously this provision can be implemented only if a firm maintains childcare facilities on the premises or very nearby—or if the worker lives next door to the firm.

5   Carmen Barroso, in *Mulher, Sociedade e Estado no Brasil* (São Paulo: Editora Brasiliense/ UNICEF, 1982), p. 119, mentions this "humiliating monthly proof of nonpregnancy" as a continuing practice in many firms.

6   Humberto de Alencar Castelo Branco, Brazilian president from 1964 to 1967. Born in 1900 in the Northeastern state of Ceará to a traditionally military family, General Castelo Branco was hand-picked by the military officers who led the 1964 coup and was formally

elected president by a purged Chamber of Deputies. He governed with emergency powers acquired through a series of Institutional Acts (see also note 3, Chapter 14, and note 5, Chapter 15). As president, Castelo Branco's chief priorities were to reform the Brazilian economy, control inflation, and combat the "communist threat." To this end he instituted austerity measures, including wage freezes and concessions to foreign firms. During his presidency a reform of the electoral process was introduced that provided for indirect elections by Congress of the president and vice-president (this lasted until 1985) and that dissolved existing political parties, replacing them with a two-party system made up of the government party, Arena (Aliança de Renovação Nacional—National Renovating Alliance), and the opposition MDB (Movimento Democrático Brasileiro—Brazilian Democratic Movement). Under Castelo Branco's rule hundreds of politicians, labor activists, academics, political activists, writers, and many others were stripped of their political rights. In January 1967 his puppet Congress ratified a new constitution giving the presidency increased powers and further centralizing public administration. Castelo Branco served until March 1967 when he was succeeded by Costa e Silva, who had been elected as the unopposed Arena candidate. In July 1967 Castelo Branco died in a plane crash. See *Dicionário Histórico-Biográfico Brasileiro, 1920–1983*, ed. Israel Beloch and Alzira Alves de Abreu (Rio de Janeiro: Editora Forense-Universitária, FINEP, 1984), vol. 1.

7   Dom Helder Câmara, one of the most famous leaders of the Third World Church, was born in 1909 in Ceará and was ordained in 1931. Although he belonged to the right-wing Integralist Party of Plínio Salgado during the 1930s, his views changed considerably during the following decade. By the time he was made a bishop in 1952, he had become a progressive prelate. With support from the Vatican, he founded the National Conference of Brazilian Bishops (CNBB) in 1952 (see note 5, Chapter 1, above) and used it as an instrument to bring the Church as a whole around to his progressive views. In 1955 he was appointed auxiliary archbishop of Rio de Janeiro, where he worked directly on behalf of the poor. In April 1964, almost simultaneously with the military coup, he was named archbishop of the See of Olinda and Recife. Shortly thereafter, he was defeated for reelection as secretary-general of the CNBB by Church conservatives who feared the anger of the military regime and saw an opportunity to institute a less progressive form of Church activity. Dom Helder, however, continued to be outspoken. At the opening of a seminary in May 1965, his speech emphasized the problems of underdevelopment and the need to train priests to aid in development; he spoke specifically of the need for a new socialism and defended bishops, priests, and layworkers against accusations of communism. In March 1966 he refused to celebrate a Mass to mark the second anniversary of the 1964 coup. Laymen who tried to work with him were harassed by local authorities, and priests who were involved in his projects were harassed and sometimes expelled from the country. In the summer of 1968 Dom Helder announced the launching of a nonviolent resistance movement and became an ever greater target of anticommunists. He was threatened with house arrest and, after the tightening of the regime with Institutional Act no. 5 in December 1968 (revoked in 1979), which suspended constitutional guarantees and routinized the extraordinary powers taken on by the national security state, he was subjected to strict censorship. Press control regulations were instituted specifying that Dom Helder's comments and activities could not

be divulged by the media, his photograph could not be published, and no mention of him (other than by way of attack) would be made. Harassment continued: his house was machine-gunned; he and his aides were attacked in the news media and received threatening phone calls; and in 1969 a close aide was brutally murdered, apparently as a warning to Dom Helder and his collaborators. All word of him continued to be banned from the Brazilian press, radio, and television for more than a decade. He remained active in the Church, however, and led a group of bishops who continued to press for human rights and to deplore terrorism, imprisonment, and torture. During the 1960s and 1970s he was several times nominated for the Nobel Peace Prize. In February 1984, at age seventy-five, he announced his retirement as archbishop of Olinda and Recife, but he has continued to be an active spokesman for social reform, especially land reform. See *Dicionário Histórico-Biográfico Brasileiro*, vol. 1; and Scott Mainwaring, *The Catholic Church and Politics in Brazil, 1916–1985* (Stanford, Calif.: Stanford University Press, 1986), p. 96.

8   Gilberto Gil, a native of Bahia, was one of the young musicians (most of whom came from the Northeast) who became popular and politically active during the late 1960s. "Tropicalism," as the post–bossa nova music of this group was called, combined traditional and popular music, jazz, rock, Caribbean, and South American elements. It also incorporated political protest and criticism. Gil was imprisoned during the government crackdown in early 1969 and was exiled later that year, spending some time in England. In early 1987, he became head of the Department of Culture of the city of Salvador (see Julian Dibbell, "Party Politics," *Village Voice*, 31 March 1987, p. 71).

9   The Revolution of 1930 marked the end of the Old (First) Republic that had been initiated in 1889 upon the abdication of Emperor Pedro II. Getúlio Vargas, after failing to win the 1930 presidential election, led a coup and took power in November 1930. He was supported by the so-called *tenentes* (lieutenants), nationalistic junior officers in rebellion against the federal government. This is the event to which Norma is referring. With the collapse of the Old Republic, the state of Pernambuco became even more divided politically. By 1933 a right-wing coterie had emerged in Recife that attacked the reformist administration of Governor Carlos de Lima Cavalcanti. For a while Vargas supported Lima Cavalcanti, but, after the quickly suppressed left-wing revolt of 1935 (in Recife and elsewhere), conservatives demanded that communists and progressives be rooted out of the government. On 10 November 1937, the day of the promulgation of Vargas's authoritarian Estado Novo, he formally removed Lima Cavalcanti from office. See Robert M. Levine, *Pernambuco in the Brazilian Federation: 1889–1937* (Stanford, Calif.: Stanford University Press, 1978), pp. 83–89. Norma is saying that her father's career in the military suffered because of his support of the progressives in this struggle.

10   Norma addresses her mother in the formal third-person form, as "Senhora," rather than in the informal "você."

11   A 1942 law prohibits physicians and hospitals from dispensing information about any treatment that prevents pregnancy or interrupts gestation. However, the Medical Code of Ethics stipulates that sterilization can be performed in exceptional circumstances following consultation with and approval by two physicians. Legal barriers to sterilization are not in practice insurmountable, but, as with other methods of fertility control such as pills,

IUDs, and condoms, the inability to arrange and pay for services limits access to sterilization more than legal restrictions do. See Barbara Janowitz, Joann Lewis, Deborah Clopton, and Milton S. Nakamura, "Post-Partum Sterilization in São Paulo State, Brazil," *Journal of Biosocial Science* 14:2 (April 1982), pp. 179–187. It was announced in 1981 that sterilization would be covered by the health-care system when medically indicated. The minister of social welfare (Previdência Social) stated that INAMPS (see note 15, Chapter 3, above) had in fact already sponsored medically indicated tubal ligations and vasectomies, with the agreement of the patient, and that in the preceding year alone 3,000 tubal ligations and 3 [*sic*] vasectomies had been done in this way. See the article "O Povo Aprova," in *Veja*, 7 January 1981, which reports on a Gallup Poll conducted in São Paulo and Rio de Janeiro indicating that 71 percent of the interviewed people try to plan their own family. There are also reports that, after 1965, sterilizations were increasingly performed by the INPS (see note 3, above) among the poorer segments of the population. See Carmen Barroso, *Mulher, Sociedade e Estado no Brasil* (São Paulo: Editora Brasiliense/UNICEF, 1982), p. 95. The CNBB (see note 5, Chapter 1, above) claimed in 1980 that BEMFAM (note 11, Chapter 1) had sterilized 2.7 million women in various areas of Brazil since 1973—with the approval of local state secretaries of health, but without informing the women of the type of operation they were to undergo (*Latin America Regional Reports: Brazil*, 12 September 1980).

As regards vasectomy, a 1976 study conducted in the São Paulo/Rio de Janeiro areas indicated that 88 percent of the men surveyed did not know what it was and, once it was explained to them, said they would not submit to such an operation. They considered fertility control a woman's responsibility. See Heloneida Studart, "O Comportamento Sexual do Brasileiro," *Manchete*, 3 April 1976. But vasectomies have in recent years become more popular, to the point that vasectomy clinics such as Pro-Pater (a nonprofit outfit in São Paulo, funded by a New York–based organization through U.S. AID), which performs 4,000 vasectomies a year, has taken to advertising in the pages of the major Brazilian weekly *Veja*. INAMPS will do vasectomies, but on the sly and paid for by the client; or private doctors can be found to do them. Either way, the state turns a blind eye—when not openly colluding. Yet sterilization is illegal in Brazil, according to Article 129 of the Penal Code, and can be punished with one to eight years' imprisonment. See Rita Freire, "Xô Espermato-zóides," *Mulherio* 6:24 (1986), pp. 12–13.

Research conducted among women in Rio's *favelas* in the early 1980s revealed that 41 percent of them used no method of contraception. Of the nearly 5,000 women interviewed, 99 percent knew about the pill and 36 percent used it; 91 percent knew what tubal ligation was, and 14 percent had had it done; 84 percent were aware of IUDs, which 3 percent of the women used. The researchers concluded that greater access to modern contraceptives must be provided. See *Jornal do Brasil*, 30 October 1983.

There is a very high rate of delivery by Caesarean section in Brazil. According to the World Health Organization, a Caesarean rate of between 7 percent and 10 percent of all births is considered clinically justifiable. In Brazil, however, the rate is three times that and, in some hospitals, reaches 45 percent (see Barroso, p. 96). The Caesarean rate rises along with income level—from 16.6 percent for women with incomes of up to one minimum salary to 57.6 percent for women with incomes of more than ten minimum salaries. On the other hand, in 1981 one-fourth of all parturient women in Brazil had no prenatal care at all—and the same pattern (more medical intervention/assistance the higher one's income) was apparent. *Mulherio* 5:21 (1985), pp. 8–10. See also notes 11 and 12, Chapter 1, above.

12   *Latin America Regional Reports: Brazil*, 16 September 1983.

6   GLÍCIA

1   João Baptista Figueiredo, the last military president of Brazil, was born in 1918 in the city of Rio de Janeiro. He was chief of Brazilian Intelligence during the presidency of General Ernesto Geisel (1974–1979) and was chosen to succeed Geisel in 1979, for a term to last until 1982. His term was later extended to 1985, when, as the culmination of the *abertura* process, the opposition PMDB defeated the government candidate in an indirect presidential election that brought back civilian government. The president-elect, Tancredo Neves, died before his inauguration and was succeeded by José Sarney, who, as vice-president-elect, became president.

2   On 30 April 1981, following several years of right-wing terrorist attacks aimed at impeding the *abertura*, a bomb exploded in a car outside Riocentro, a convention hall in Rio de Janeiro. Inside the hall, 30,000 people were gathered for a May Day concert organized by the Left. Two military officers, allegedly under orders of the Army Intelligence Service, were in the car. Despite evidence of military involvement, the Army opened and closed an inquiry that depicted the two military men inside the car as victims of a left-wing plot. This episode demonstrated the deep divisions within the military between opponents and proponents of liberalization. See *Latin America Weekly Report*, 11 October 1985; and Maria Helena Moreira Alves, *State and Opposition in Military Brazil* (Austin: University of Texas Press, 1985), pp. 221–222. During the summer of 1981, many of the women with whom I spoke brought up the Riocentro bombing, always in the context of their assumption that the government was implicated and that the truth had been suppressed.

7   DOROTÉIA

1   Until recently, women in Brazil rarely enjoyed the de facto protection of the law in cases of violent crimes against their persons. In 1980, the women's movement, which had been gaining strength in Brazil since the mid-1970s, began to make stopping violence against women a central issue and rallying cry. Very quickly, and with virtually no funds, SOS-Mulher (SOS-Woman) centers spread throughout Brazil. These centers, usually run by feminist activists who volunteer their time, have dealt with problems of beating, rape, murder, and threats of murder suffered by women. Under the influence of European and North American models, some activists' early expectations were that rape would become the dominant issue addressed by this part of the women's movement. In the early 1980s this seemed not to be the case: few Brazilian women were willing to publicly announce that

they had been victims of rape. See "SOS-Mulher do Rio de Janeiro: Uma Entrevista," in *Perspectivas Antropológicas da Mulher* 4 (1984), pp. 109–137.

The major issue that did emerge, around which organizing took place throughout the country, was the murder of women, usually by husbands or lovers. Using the slogan *Quem ama não mata* ("Those Who Love Don't Kill") and organizing public demonstrations and pickets wherever trials for such murders were occurring, the women's movement drew attention to the extent of these crimes against women (more than 700 such murders were recorded in São Paulo alone during one year in the early 1980s) and to the complicity of the law in these acts. A significant change in public (and judicial) consciousness resulted. To take one (notorious) example: in 1976 in Rio de Janeiro, a playboy named Doca Street killed his lover, Ângela Diniz. At his first trial, in 1979, he was virtually acquitted. Using the hitherto acceptable legal defense that Doca Street had acted in "legitimate defense of his honor"—which has allowed countless men to murder women with impunity—his lawyer portrayed Doca as wounded in his masculinity because Ângela Diniz, who had decided to end their relationship, had supposedly threatened to betray him in the future. As a result, Doca was given a two-year suspended sentence. At his second trial, in 1981, the mood was different. Feminist activists organized, petitioned, demonstrated—and Doca Street was condemned to fifteen years in prison (Heleno C. Fragoso, "A Condenação de 'Doca,' " *Mulherio* 2:5 [1982], pp. 6–7). Writing in the light of such successes, the feminist journal *Mulherio* (6:20 [1985], p. 3), in its evaluation of what ten years of the women's movement (1975–1985) have achieved, noted that no lawyer today would dare use the bizarre notion of "legitimate defense of one's honor" as a defense against a murder charge. But anecdotal evidence and newspaper clippings sent to me from Brazil suggest that the celebration is premature.

In the past few years, police precincts run entirely by women and for the defense of women have been set up, the first in 1985 in São Paulo (a leader in women's activism in Brazil, it was also the first state to create a state council on women, in 1983); there are now several dozen such precincts throughout the country. On its opening day, the São Paulo precinct dealt with 130 cases, and during the first month it dealt with 3,000. About 20 percent of these cases have involved sexual crimes, and the great majority of reports have been of violence and threats of violence against women, almost always from husbands and lovers. See Maria Teresa Horta, "Ruth Escobar: 'Eu Sou uma Feminista,' " in *Mulheres* (Lisbon) 98 (1986), pp. 6–8; Alan Riding, "Brazil's Battered Women Find Haven from Abuse," *New York Times*, 14 September 1985; and *Latin American Regional Reports: Brazil*, 19 October 1986.

PART THREE: "WOMEN'S WORK"

1   A word of warning is necessary here about the difficulty of obtaining reliable statistics on women. As several Brazilian scholars have noted in a review of the 1975–1985 "decade of women," even existing data are often contradictory (*Mulherio* 5:21 [1985], p. 4). In relation to employment, this problem is discussed in Zulma Recchini de Lattes and Catalina H. Wainerman, "Unreliable Account of Women's Work: Evidence from Latin American Census Statistics," *Signs* 11:4 (1986), pp. 740–750. This article does not include 1980 censuses.

Feminist researchers, however, have begun to influence data collection in Brazil; see Neuma Aguiar, "Grupo de Pesquisa 'A Mulher na Força de Trabalho,' " in Projeto-Mulher do IDAC, *Mulheres em Movimento* (Rio de Janeiro: Editora Marco Zero, 1983), pp. 188–189, and also her valuable "Research Guidelines: How to Study Women's Work in Latin America," in *Women and Change in Latin America*, ed. June Nash and Helen Safa (South Hadley, Mass.: Bergin & Garvey, 1986), pp. 22–33. The statistics I cite in this section, as elsewhere in this book, are unreliable in their specifics, with different sources often providing different figures. The general trends they indicate, however, are clear. As June E. Hahner points out, in "Women and Work in Brazil, 1850–1920: A Preliminary Investigation," in *Essays concerning the Socioeconomic History of Brazil and Portuguese India*, ed. Dauril Alden and Warren Dean (Gainesville: University Presses of Florida, 1977), pp. 87–117, "Statistics on total female employment, even if accurate, cannot tell us many things about the status of women" (p. 115).

2   Cristina Bruschini, "Desvendando uma Trama Invisível," *Mulherio* 5:21 (1985), p. 20; and Aguiar, "Research Guidelines," p. 30.

3   See Marianne Schmink, "Women and Urban Industrial Development in Brazil," in *Women and Change in Latin America*, ed. Nash and Safa, pp. 136–164. For discussions of the logic of women's representation in the labor force at different stages of Brazil's economic development, see Heleieth I. B. Saffioti, *Women in Class Society*, trans. Michael Vale (New York: Monthly Review Press, 1978), pp. 179–196, who analyzes how capitalism increases gender division and produces greater economic dependence in women while making them serve capitalism's interests; Felicia Madeira and Paulo Singer, "Structure of Female Employment and Work in Brazil, 1920–1970," *Journal of Interamerican Studies and World Affairs* 17:4 (1975), pp. 490–496; and Elsa M. Chaney and Marianne Schmink, "Women and Modernization: Access to Tools," in *Sex and Class in Latin America*, ed. June Nash and Helen Icken Safa (South Hadley, Mass.: J. F. Bergin, 1980), pp. 160–182, for an analysis of the worsening of women's economic status as modernization gets under way.

4   Thereza Martins, "Ainda na Base da Pirâmide," *Mulherio* 5:21 (1985), p. 21.

5   *Latin American Regional Reports: Brazil*, 27 November 1986.

6   Carmen Barroso, "Ascensão e Queda da Funcionária Pública," *Mulherio* 7:29 (1987), p. 8.

7   Martins, "Ainda na Base da Pirâmide." Martins states that about 20 percent of all wage-earning women are domestic servants; close to 25 percent is the figure mentioned in *Latin America Regional Reports: Brazil*, 25 April 1986.

8   Cristina Bruschini, "Trabalho Feminino no Campo: Invisível?" *Mulherio* 6:25 (1986), p. 10. See also note 2, Chapter 18, below.

9   According to Alda Marco Antonio, labor secretary for the state of São Paulo (the first woman to hold this position), as quoted in *Latin American Regional Reports: Brazil*, 18 September 1986.

10   Hildete Pereira de Melo, "Somadas, Divididas, Multiplicadas e . . . Diminuídas," in *Mulheres em Movimento*, p. 176. These figures refer to the late 1970s.

11   "The Isolation of Domestic Servants," *Latin America Regional Reports: Brazil*, 25 April 1986; Heleieth Saffioti, *Emprego Doméstico e Capitalismo* (Rio de Janeiro: Avenir Editora, 1979), p. 21; "Domésticas, Tentando Sair da Cozinha," *Mulherio* 5:21 (1985), p. 22.

9   CARMEN

1   Women's political participation, in terms of voting, has increased substantially in recent years, even given the often symbolic value of voting under the dictatorship. From 35 percent of the general electorate in 1975 (12 million voters), women moved to 46 percent (26 million) in 1985. A corresponding increase occurred in number of women elected (which, however, continues to be extremely small). In 1974 only one woman was elected federal deputy; in 1982 there were eight. Women representatives in office went from 0.3 percent to 1.7 percent during this period (and these women almost always came from the opposition parties). In addition, during the dictatorship, women candidates were elected as a result of the political prestige of their spouses or other family members who were prevented from running for office by the frequently used expedient of simply depriving critics of the government of their political and civil rights. More recently, despite the adoption (at least verbally) of women's issues in political platforms, the number of women at the leadership level within political parties has continued to be insignificant. At the ministerial level, only 7 of 175 leadership positions in the various ministries were held by women in 1975 and, ten years later, the figures had increased to 13 out of 216 positions— that is, to 6 percent from the earlier 4 percent. Yet Brazilian women were the fourth in the Western Hemisphere to win the vote, in 1932 (a victory written into the 1934 Constitution), after an active campaign led by Bertha Lutz. The establishment of Getúlio Vargas's Estado Novo ended electoral politics, and of course women's participation, until 1946.

The more recent return to democratic rule, in 1985, led to a concerted effort on the part of women's groups in Brazil to see that more women were elected (in November 1986) to Congress, since this body formed the Constituent Assembly charged with drafting a new, postmilitary, constitution for Brazil in 1987. See "Conquistas e Derrotas," *Mulherio* 5:21 (1985), p. 3; Fanny Tabak and Moema Toscano, *Mulher e Política* (Rio de Janeiro: Editora Paz e Terra, 1982); Fanny Tabak, "Women's Role in the Formulation of Public Policies in Brazil," in *Women, Power and Political Systems*, ed. Margherita Rendel (New York: St. Martin's Press, 1981), pp. 66–80; and June E. Hahner, "Feminism, Women's Rights, and the Suffrage Movement in Brazil, 1850–1932," *Latin American Research Review* 15:1 (1980), pp. 65–111, as well as Hahner's more extensive study, *A Mulher Brasileira e Suas Lutas Sociais e Políticas: 1850–1937* (São Paulo: Editora Brasiliense, 1981). See also note 6, Chapter 14, below.

2   Even among those Brazilians who did know the word "feminist," it often had negative connotations, as seen in Chapter 6. The very growth in acceptance of the term in recent years is a measure of the success of the women's movement in Brazil. To take one example: in her 1974 book *Mulher: Objeto de Cama e Mesa* [Woman: Object of Bed and Board] (Petrópolis: Editora Vozes), Heloneida Studart, a journalist, novelist, politician, and one of the founders of Rio's Centro da Mulher Brasileira (Brazilian Women's Center), allowed an apology in the guise of an introduction written by Lauro de Oliveira Lima to appear in her book; he takes pains to assert that Studart is not a "feminist," is not preaching rebellion, and

that she is, among her many other talents and activities, an "exemplary mother." By 1982, however, Studart was saying, "I am a feminist. It's a word I'm not afraid of" (in *Mulherio* 2:8 [1982], p. 8).

12   CONCEIÇÃO

1   In many households, I have observed maids watching television with their employers in the evening. Often the maids sit on the arm of a sofa or lean against a doorjamb; that is, they maintain a deferential distance and are not fully integrated into the group.

13   SÔNIA

1   *Latin America Regional Reports: Brazil*, 8 February 1980. For a description of *favela* life, see Janice E. Perlman, *The Myth of Marginality: Urban Politics and Poverty in Rio de Janeiro* (Berkeley: University of California Press, 1976).

2   The Fundo de Garantia por Tempo de Serviço (FGTS, or Time-in-Service Guarantee Fund), enacted in September 1966, eliminated the job security provisions of previous labor legislation that had provided for indemnity payments to workers fired without just cause from positions they had occupied for one to ten years, and guaranteed job stability after ten years of employment unless the employer could prove in court that the worker was guilty of serious misconduct. The FGTS greatly reduced the cost of firing workers and of hiring replacements at lower salaries. The indemnity that workers receive under the FGTS when they are laid off comes from an account in their name into which employers deposit 8 percent of the monthly wage. This account is then drawn on when the worker is fired, thus eliminating the need for the employer to come up with large sums when cutbacks or plant closings occur. The FGTS system has been attacked for providing an incentive to fire workers prior to a new contract date. As Maria Helena Moreira Alves points out, in *State and Opposition in Military Brazil* (Austin: University of Texas Press, 1985), pp. 67–69, "The state's wage-control policies [up to the mid-1980s] owe their effectiveness to the general insecurity of the job market and the new threat of mass layoffs. The combination of controlled wage-indexing and the FGTS provide an ideal cheap labor market for capital investment." Alves discusses the role of the FGTS in supporting Brazil's wage-squeeze policies and drive for capital accumulation during the dictatorship. James Malloy, in *The Politics of Social Security* (Pittsburgh: University of Pittsburgh Press, 1979), p. 126, points out that the resources acquired through the FGTS went into the National Housing Bank (BNH, Banco Nacional de Habitação), created in 1964, and were used to stimulate the housing and construction industries: "The FGTS became an important source of savings and investment funds which probably redounded mainly to the benefit of middle- and upper-income groups."

3   CIEE (Centro de Integração Empresa-Escola) is a private nonprofit organization

that works together with public services and private organizations to promote better collaboration between schools and private companies. The CIEE provides job training, information on courses and professions, professional guidance, and technical help and orientation, preparation of résumés, etc. See Francisco de Paula Ferreira, *Dicionário de Bem-Estar Social* (São Paulo: Cortez Editora, 1982), p. 72.

14   CÉLIA

1   The Brazilian Communist Party (PCB, Partido Comunista Brasileiro) which was legalized in 1985, was founded in 1922 and banned from Brazilian politics for most of the time since. It is not to be confused with the Communist Party of Brazil (PC do B, Partido Comunista do Brasil), a Maoist and later pro-Albanian group that, in the wake of the Sino-Soviet split, broke away from the PCB in 1962 over the issue of how socialism was to be pursued in Brazil. The PCB advocated a peaceful route to socialism, whereas the PC do B endorsed armed struggle. See also notes 3, 4, and 5, below, and Chapter 15.

2   On the creation of Brazil's "national security state," see note 3, below, and note 5, Chapter 15.

3   During the presidency of General Artur Costa e Silva (1967–1969), a period of severe political repression was inaugurated in Brazil, one that continued throughout the presidency of General Emílio Garrastazu Médici (1969–1974). In an effort to consolidate its own power and to continue attracting foreign investment, and faced with mounting protests, strikes, and demonstrations at home in 1967 and 1968, the military government resorted to increasingly dictatorial measures. Maria Helena Moreira Alves, on whose book *State and Opposition in Military Brazil* (Austin: University of Texas Press, 1985), pp. 95–137, I have drawn for this note, describes the period as a "third cycle of repression." The first cycle, in 1964, focused on purging individuals with political links to past populist governments, particularly that of João Goulart, president at the time of the military coup. Violence during the first cycle was directed against workers and peasants only, in an effort to eliminate possible sources of resistance to the military. The second cycle of repression, initiated in late October 1965 with Institutional Act no. 2 and continuing through 1966, attempted to finish the purges in the state bureaucracy and electoral offices, but without resorting to direct widespread use of violence. In December 1968, a third cycle of repression was introduced with Institutional Act no. 5 (lasting until 1979), which gave the president power to close Congress and state and local legislative bodies, annul the mandate of any elected official, and suspend for a period of ten years the political rights of any citizen. This act suspended constitutional guarantees (including habeas corpus for individuals charged with political crimes against national security) and consolidated the military's control of the news media and the nation's political life. As traditional outlets of protest were effectively eliminated by the government's repressive apparatus, some parts of the opposition took up armed struggle.

Although total participation in the various guerrilla organizations in the entire period 1969–1974 has been estimated to have been around six thousand, the government termed this activity "civil war" and used the existence of groups committed to armed struggle as a justification for the most violent state repression in Brazil's history. As organizations involved in armed struggle became more active in attacking banks (to finance their operations) and engaged in ambushes to acquire arms, the government responded with mass arrests, beatings, and torture. Nor were known guerrillas their only targets. Major military mobilizations—government terror campaigns—also occurred in the countryside, aimed at an unarmed rural population. Torture in particular became institutionalized. The National Security Law (Decree-law 898, of 29 September 1969, slightly but not significantly modified by President Ernesto Geisel in December 1978, then replaced in 1983 with milder legislation), which gave the state complete discretion in defining just what constituted a crime against national security, allowed an individual to be held incommunicado and without the filing of charges for up to twenty days of "preventive detention." Torture was usually the first stage of the proceedings, and it became a part of the fabric of Brazilian life during this period. Fear of arrest was great, and even political conversation was stifled. The guerrilla struggle rapidly turned into a largely defensive action, characterized by kidnappings of foreign diplomats to be exchanged for political prisoners.

By mid-1973 the armed struggle against the military in Brazil had been effectively defeated, the underground political opposition was in disarray, and the whole strategy of armed struggle had fallen into question. By the end of 1973 the Left had learned to concentrate on the official opposition party, the MDB, as a focal point for organizing opposition to the dictatorship. See James Kohl and John Litt, Urban Guerrilla Warfare in Latin America (Cambridge: MIT Press, 1974), pp. 29–170. See also note 5, Chapter 15, below.

An analysis and description of the repressive apparatus that functioned in Brazil between 1964 and 1979 is to be found in Brasil: Nunca Mais (Petrópolis: Editora Vozes, 1985; in English, Torture in Brazil, trans. Jaime Wright, ed. and intro. Joan Dassin [New York: Vintage/Random House, 1985]). This volume summarizes an exhaustive study of the military's human rights violations. That study, prepared under the auspices of the Catholic Church and funded by the World Council of Churches, was carried out in secret over a five-year period. It is based exclusively on records of political trials held by the military courts between 1964 and 1979.

An important contribution to the history of Brazilian women during the dictatorship is the oral history Memórias das Mulheres do Exílio, ed. Albertina de Oliveira Costa et al. (Rio de Janeiro: Paz e Terra, 1980). For analysis of this collection of testimony by Brazilian women who went into exile after the military coup occurred, see Angela Neves-Xavier de Brito, "Brazilian Women in Exile: The Quest for an Identity," in Latin American Perspectives 13:2 (1986), pp. 58–80.

4   Gregória Bezerra, a Brazilian Communist Party (PCB) leader, was born in 1900 in Pernambuco. He was a career military man who joined the PCB in 1930. Repeatedly arrested and imprisoned (1917, 1935, 1948, 1957), Bezerra became involved in the peasant movements of the early 1960s; he was arrested again in Recife in 1964 after the military coup, tortured, and publicly dragged through the streets of Recife with a rope around his neck, clad only in his shorts. He was among the fifteen political prisoners freed in September 1969 in exchange for U.S. Ambassador Charles Burke Elbrick, who had been kidnapped by a leftist group. Bezerra went into exile in Moscow and while there became a member of the central

committee of the PCB (1977). He returned to Brazil in September 1979, upon the granting of a general amnesty. Bezerra supported Luis Carlos Prestes (see next note) in Prestes's fight with other PCB leaders. He died in October 1983. See his *Memórias, Segunda Parte: 1946–1969* (Rio de Janeiro: Editora Civilização Brasileira, 1979), pp. 193–250; and *Dicionário Histórico-Biográfico Brasileiro, 1920–1983*, ed. Israel Beloch and Alzira Alves de Abreu (Rio de Janeiro: Editora Forense-Universitária, FINEP, 1984), vol. 1.

5   Luis Carlos Prestes, born in the southern state of Rio Grande do Sul in 1898, was an army engineer who for nearly forty years led the Brazilian Communist Party (PCB). For his role in what came to be known as the "Prestes Column," a group of about a thousand soldiers who held out in the Brazilian backlands for nearly three years after the failure of their 1924 revolt of reform-demanding military men, Prestes gained the nickname "Knight of Hope." He went to the Soviet Union in 1931, secretly returned to Brazil in 1935, and was arrested in 1936 after another abortive uprising. After Prestes's arrest, his German-born Jewish wife, Olga Benário, also a communist activist, was deported back to Hitler's Germany (she was seven months pregnant at the time), interned in a concentration camp, and killed there by the Nazis in 1938. Prestes was named secretary-general of the PCB while in prison. Like Gregório Bezerra, Prestes was imprisoned until the general amnesty of 1945, which followed the end of Vargas's Estado Novo. In 1945, when the PCB was legalized (for the first time, apart from a brief period in 1927, since its 1922 founding), Prestes was elected as a federal senator. Within two years, however, the PCB was again banned and remained so until 1985. While continuing to be active, Prestes went underground from 1947 to 1958, at which time charges against him were dismissed.

After the military coup of 1964, he was deprived of his political rights and once again went underground. In 1971 he went into exile in Moscow, returning to Brazil in 1979 when the military declared a general amnesty as part of the *abertura*. In the period of his absence from Brazil, especially after 1974, when President Ernesto Geisel's policy of liberalization (*distensão*) allowed electoral victories in Congress for the opposition MDB (which the PCB supported), the PCB went through the most violent repression in its entire history. Between 1974 and 1975, ten members of the central committee disappeared. Others are known to have been tortured. In the period 1974–1976, between 700 and 1,000 members of the PCB were arrested. The Party newspaper, *Voz Operária*, which had been clandestinely published since 1964, ceased to circulate, only to resume publication from abroad in 1976. The remaining members of the central committee had to go into exile, with the result that the Party suffered a complete breakdown in organization. Reassembled abroad, the leadership of the PCB continued to disagree, and a struggle for power broke out between Prestes and Giocondo Dias. Once back in Brazil after eight years in exile, Prestes continued his criticism of the PCB and its "tendency." In May 1980, the central committee of the PCB named Giocondo Dias as secretary-general of the Party, replacing Prestes. Continuing political divergences between Prestes and the PCB leadership eventually led to his ouster from the Party in early 1984. See *Dicionário Histórico-Biográfico Brasileiro*, vol. 4; Ronald H. Chilcote, *The Brazilian Communist Party: Conflict and Integration, 1922–1972* (New York: Oxford University Press, 1974); and Alan Riding, "Brazil's Red Knight of Hope: Unhorsed but Undaunted," *New York Times*, April 4, 1984.

6   For a discussion of the early stage of the contemporary women's movement, see Marianne Schmink, "Women in Brazilian *Abertura* Politics," *Signs* 7:1 (1981), pp. 115–134. Despite its rather dramatic early congresses, at which conflicts developed between feminists and political party activists, who were often seen as trying to take over the meetings and use them for their own organizational purposes, the women's movement developed rapidly all over Brazil. For a sketch of the development of feminist activism in Brazil during the United Nations' "Decade of Women," see Maria Lygia Quartim de Moraes, *Mulheres em Movimento* (São Paulo: Nobel/Conselho Estadual da Condição Feminina, 1985), pp. 1–33. This volume is one of seven, published by Nobel in 1985 under the sponsorship of the Conselho Estadual da Condição Feminina de São Paulo, which together take stock of the position of women in Brazil. The titles of the other six volumes are *Mulher e Trabalho, A Saúde da Mulher, Mulher Negra/Política Governamental e a Mulher, Os Direitos da Mulher, A Educação da Mulher,* and *Creches e Pré-Escolas.*

Eva Alterman Blay, in an editorial examining ten years of the women's movement in Brazil (1975–1985), notes that, in the military Brazil of 1975, to actively pursue adherence to Brazil's own labor laws or denounce violence against women was enough to brand a woman as subversive and hence endanger her. But this did not keep women from speaking out and organizing—against the high cost of living, in favor of amnesty, of childcare centers, of lives free from masculine violence—but always within the context of the ultimate goal: the reconquest of democracy. "The great difference in the '80s," Blay writes, "is that democracy and the gains demanded by women are no longer thought of as two separate moments, but rather are now seen as equally important and concomitant." The creation in 1985 of a National Council for Women's Rights (CNDM) and of state councils on women's condition, she notes, have moved the women's struggle into the executive structure and into political parties (*Mulherio* 6:20 [1985], p. 2). The political scientist Fanny Tabak also has written of the importance of women's work within political parties, at the same time that they must guard against the co-optation of their energies and issues by parties not genuinely committed to promoting their demands (see her "Women and Authoritarian Regimes," in *Women's Views of the Political World of Men,* ed. Judith Hicks Stiehm [Dobbs Ferry, N.Y.: Transnational Publishers, 1984], pp. 101–119; *A Mulher Como Objeto de Estudo,* ed. Fanny Tabak [Rio de Janeiro: PUC, Divisão de Intercâmbio e Edições, 1982], and her *Mulher e Política* [Rio de Janeiro: Editora Paz e Terra, 1982]).

The National Council for Women's Rights, set up by the federal government, is linked to the Ministry of Justice but is financially autonomous and run independently of it. Dealing with legal aspects of women's issues, the CNDM aims to "promote in political circles the elimination of discrimination against women, guaranteeing conditions of freedom and equal rights as well as their full participation in political, economic, and cultural activities" (*Latin America Regional Reports: Brazil,* 18 October 1985). The CNDM was very active in promoting strong representation of women in the Constituent Assembly. In the November 1986 elections, twenty-six women (including one Black women, representing the PT [see note 18, Chapter 3]) were elected to the Federal Chamber of Deputies, surpassing the total number of women—fifteen—elected in the past. These twenty-six women, forming 4 percent of the Constituent Assembly, are not, however, one political bloc, although there is a heavier representation of women among the small leftist parties. In addition, thirty-five women were elected as state deputies. See Fátima Jordão, "A Bancada Feminina na Constituinte: Maior e Melhor do que Parece," *Mulherio* 7:27 (1987), p. 13. See also note 1, Chapter 9.

15   MADALENA

1   On the Brazilian Communist Party, see notes 1 and 5 to preceding chapter.

2   The *vestibular* exam system was created in 1911 as a means of screening candidates for secondary-school graduation diplomas. As the secondary school system expanded uncontrollably in the following decades and as standards were lowered, the *vestibular* became a university entrance examination. The 1961 Law of Directives and Bases, Brazil's first general education law, made the *vestibular* compulsory for university entrance. Applicants always outnumbered vacanies, however, which turned the *vestibular* into a device for limiting the number of admissions rather than serving as a selection process. Both content and grading were manipulated to achieve this aim. The privately owned and operated *prévestibular* courses became a buffer in this system, preparing students for the highly competitive *vestibular*. Starting in 1971 the Ministry of Education and Culture began to "reform, modernize, and equalize the system of access to higher education," as explained by Fay Haussman and Jerry Haar in their book *Education in Brazil* (Hamden, Conn.: Archon Books, 1978), p. 87, from which this summary is taken. Arbitrary passing scores were abolished as the *vestibular* was transformed from an eliminatory examination into a classifying one, by which only as many candidates "passed" as there were places available. This "resolved" the problem of passing candidates for whom no available spaces existed and the concomitant threat of law suits when these candidates legally pursued their rights to university admission (p. 129). During the period between 1968 and 1972, the number of secondary school graduates grew at an average annual rate of 13.7 percent, but the demand for higher education far exceeded this figure. In 1968, for example, nearly 215,000 candidates applied for college admission, of whom nearly 83,000 passed the *vestibular*. By 1973 there were more than 532,000 applicants, of whom 318,000 passed (pp. 88–89). This expansion resulted from the rapid increase in the number of private, isolated faculties, which are often substandard (p. 129). By the mid-1970s, overexpansion of higher education facilities had occurred and supply exceeded demand, with freshman places going unfilled (p. 134). In the mid-1980s, there were sixty-seven universities (institutions with at least 5 separate faculties) in Brazil and more than 700 isolated faculties. Of the sixty-seven universities, forty-seven were public and hence charged minimal matriculation fees.

In an attempt to meet the middle-class demand for higher education (a major avenue of upward mobility), educational resources, after 1964, were poured into higher education rather than primary and secondary. But these resources were not evenly distributed throughout Brazil. Instead, higher-education facilities, like primary and secondary, were concentrated in the developed Southeast and South of Brazil, where 90 percent of all higher-education institutions are located. The government policy of low-cost expansion fostered the growth of humanities and other faculties that were less expensive, because less dependent on technology, at a disproportional rate. See P. A. Kluck, "The Society and Its Environment," in Richard F. Nyrop, ed., *Brazil: A Country Study* (Washington, D.C.: American University, Foreign Area Studies, 1983), pp. 134–135, 148–150. In the mid-1980s, between 70 percent and 75 percent of students attended private universities, with poorly qualified and poorly paid teaching staffs and inadequate facilities, indicating the military government's failure to establish an effective private university system. The remaining 25 percent attended federal universities, in which the highest level of teaching is found. See *Latin America Regional Reports: Brazil*, 10 February 1984. See also note 4, below.

3   On the Costa e Silva and Médici periods, see note 3 to the preceding chapter.

4   Decree-law 477 of February 1969, which curbed the political activities of students as well as professors, was applied against 215 persons (all but 5 of whom were students) in 1969 and against 38 more in the following four years. Thereafter, although it fell into disuse, it continued to function as a threat against any dissension within universities. "[I]t provides for the expulsion of students, professors, and staff for disciplinary infractions of a 'subversive' nature. This covers a multitude of serious crimes as well as innocuous misdemeanors, plus the 'intent' to commit them. Anyone found guilty by university authorities of any of these infractions can be expelled and, if he is a student, *prevented from rematriculating at any Brazilian university for 3 years*. If the culprit is a professor or administrator, he cannot be reemployed at any university for a period of 5 years.... [D]ecree-law 477 retains its function as an insidious academic curb. Communism, marxism, and all types and shadings of leftist ideology became taboo in Brazil after 1964" (Haussman and Haar, *Education in Brazil*, pp. 132–133, their emphasis).

5   Brazil's national security state came into being with the First Institutional Act, drafted in secret and published on April 9, 1964, just seven days after the coup. This act defined government authority as stemming not from the people, but from the de facto exercise of power. As Maria Helena Moreira Alves explains in *State and Opposition in Military Brazil* (Austin: University of Texas Press, 1985), pp. 31–34, Institutional Act no. 1 laid the groundwork for the restriction of individual rights and of Congress's powers and began the transfer of legislative power to the executive. This was followed by more than a dozen additional Institutional Acts over the subsequent five years, which consolidated the power of the dictatorship. Meanwhile, the Constitution of 1967 incorporated the important shifts in power embodied in the Institutional Acts, which thus lost their exceptional character of measures based on *revolutionary* power and took on the force of *constitutional* power. Alves explains (pp. 77–79): the 1967 Constitution, which was highly authoritarian, nonetheless reflected the basic contradictions within the system, for it ensured the implementation of measures designed to destroy the enemy within, as mandated by the doctrine of internal security; at the same time, it included the Bill of Rights—a major victory for the opposition—which reflected the goal of restoring democracy that the national security state claimed to defend. This contradiction, in turn, led to the institutional crisis that culminated in the promulgation of Institutional Act no. 5. See also note 3 to the preceding chapter.

6   On armed resistance to the dictatorship, see note 3 to the preceding chapter.

7   Araguaia is an area in the Amazon where, in the early 1970s, the government

used some 20,000 soldiers to terrorize the peasantry and wipe out 69 guerrillas who, following Régis Debray's ideas, had tried to set up a *foco* there. Substantive information about the campaign came out only in 1979. See Palmério Dória, Sérgio Buarque, Vincent Carelli, and Jaime Santchuk, A *Guerrilha do Araguaia*, *História Imediata*, (São Paulo: Editora Alfa-Omega, 1979), no. 1; and Alves, *State and Opposition in Military Brazil*, p. 120ff.

8   On Luis Carlos Prestes, see note 5 to the preceding chapter.

9   Giocondo Alves Dias, born in Bahia in 1913, was active in the Brazilian Communist Party (PCB) starting in 1935. The most important communist leader other than Prestes during the period of the dictatorship, Giocondo Dias replaced Prestes as the PCB secretary-general in 1980, and was himself replaced by Federal Deputy Roberto Freire in 1987 (*Latin American Regional Reports: Brazil*, 23 April 1987).

10   Gay activism emerged in Brazil in the late 1970s, as part of the *abertura*. Most of the writing on homosexuality in Brazil, however, has related to men, and lesbianism continues to be a taboo subject, according to Miriam Martinho Rodrigues, of GALF, the Grupo Ação Lésbica-Feminista (Lesbian-Feminist Action Group, in São Paulo), which has been in existence since 1979. GALF publishes a paper polemically entitled *ChanacomChana* [CuntwithCunt], which first appeared, briefly, in 1981 and which was revived and expanded in 1983 (Rodrigues, mimeo.). It now appears three times a year.

18   ANA MARIA

1   Muriel Nazzari, "Women and Property in the Transition to Capitalism: Decline of the Dowry in São Paulo, Brazil (1640–1870)," paper presented to the Meetings of the American Historical Association, Chicago, Illinois, December 1984.

2   The term Ana Maria is searching for is *bóia-fria*, literally meaning "cold grub." *Bóias-frias* are temporary farmworkers, whose numbers grew as Brazil's economic situation worsened from the mid-1970s on. Overworked and underpaid (usually paid by output), they are not registered workers and thus have little legal protection. In recent years, however, they have been organizing and pursuing their rights. See Inês Castilho and Reinaldo Pinheiro, "Vento e Fogo no Canavial," *Mulherio* 4:17 (1984), pp. 11–14. Cheywa Spindel, in her recent work on the sexual division of labor in rural areas of Brazil, notes that between 1970 and 1980 women's participation in agriculture, principally in the form of temporary seasonal work, increased by 133 percent, whereas men's participation grew by only 5 percent. This signified a massive increase in the exploitation of women, the vast majority of whom receive less than the legal minimum wage, lack workers' benefits, and are not unionized (cited in Shelley Baxter, *Feminist Theory, State Policy, and Rural Women in Latin America*, Working Paper no. 49 [Notre Dame: Helen Kellogg Institute for International Studies, University of Notre Dame, 1985], p. 16).

3   FUNRURAL (Fundo de Assistência e Previdência do Trabalhador Rural) went into effect in 1970 to extend health and social security coverage to rural workers, although its benefits were not so extensive as those received by urban workers. It was subsequently incorporated into the INPS/INAMPS system (see note 3, Chapter 5, above).

4   The path Ana Maria's husband is thinking of following is the traditional one that has, in the past, made owners of large rural estates the most politically powerful individuals in their area.

19   LÚCIA

1   The Brazilian Married Woman's Statute (Estatuto da Mulher Casada) is the name usually given to Law no. 4.121 of 27 August 1962, which introduced into Brazil's Civil Code a series of changes in women's rights under the law. A brief history of married women's legal status follows.

Traditionally, married women's access to the public sphere was through their husbands, to whose authority they were subjected. Shortly after the establishment of the Republic, Decree no. 181 (24 January 1890) defined a married woman's status as auxiliary to her husband in the family unit. This then became the basis of Article 240 of the 1916 Civil Code, by which customary male privileges and rights were explicitly articulated and written into law. The 1916 code confirmed the special incapacities and limited freedoms of married women, who were placed on the same level as minors. The husband was the head of the conjugal unit and, by taking on his name, the wife also took on this secondary status. Only in the absence of her husband, under stipulated conditions, was the wife recognized as head of the family, and upon the husband's return his status was restored. Interestingly, the 1916 Civil Code recognized in women the same capacities as in men, and explicitly stated that this capacity became restricted by the act of marrying, in order not to "obstruct the management of the family," which is in the husband's hands. A married woman's incapacity, in other words, rested in her husband and the institution of the family, which imposed a hierarchy on the two sexes. Among other features of Article 242 of the 1916 code, women could not, without their husbands' authorization, accept or relinquish an inheritance, act as guardian or trustee, or exercise a profession. None of these restrictions applied to married men. As head of the household, it was up to the husband to determine his wife's relationship to property and to employment outside the household.

Brazil's 1934 Constitution eliminated some of these prohibitions and affirmed that all are equal under the law "with no distinction of birth, sex, race, one's own or one's parents' professions, social class, wealth, religious beliefs or political ideas" (Article 113-1). But the Constitution of 1937, which established Vargas's Estado Novo, eliminated the phrase "with no distinction of sex." The liberalizing 1946 Constitution, after Vargas's ouster, merely stated: "All are equal under the law" (Article 114-1). Article 153-1 of the current Constitution, which dates from 1967, states: "All are equal under the law, without distinction of sex, race, religious creed, and political convictions."

In 1943, with the Consolidated Labor Code, women gained the right to employment without the authorization of their husbands, although husbands were entitled to prevent wives from working if they judged this damaging to the family ties or to the woman. Thus men and the state continued to prevent women from having access to public life, as is pointed out by Maria Valéria Junho Pena, from whose book *Mulheres e Trabalhadoras: Presença*

Feminina na Constituição do Sistema Fabril (Rio de Janeiro: Editora Paz e Terra, 1981) parts of the above summary are taken.

The 1962 Married Woman's Statute once again altered women's status in the direction of greater equality with their husbands. No longer were married women considered relatively incapable of acting juridically, akin to incompetents, savages, and minors. The husband's leadership of the conjugal unit, while confirmed, is now to be carried out in "collaboration" with the wife. In cases of conflict, the husband's will prevails, and he continues to be the legal representative of the family. Within ten days of a marriage, the husband can have the marriage annulled if the wife had already been "deflowered." The husband is obliged to support his wife, and he has control of their joint and the wife's particular possessions (except when there is a prenuptial agreement stipulating the separate maintenance of the property with which each enters the marriage). But—and this was a major change—he no longer has control of her earnings. The 1962 Married Woman's Statute, in other words, recognized assets acquired by the wife through her own labor, independent of her husband's profession, as falling under her own jurisdiction. Thus Lúcia's problem was to prove that she had indeed been the sole creator of the family's assets, so that they would not fall under her husband's jurisdiction.

A draft version of a *new* Married Woman's Statute, designed by two feminist attorneys, Silvia Pimentel and Florisa Verucci, was published in November 1980 and has since been the basis for discussion of this part of the projected new Civil Code. Pimentel and Verucci's version attempted to eliminate many, but not all, aspects of the Civil Code now prejudicial to women. But even this proved too much for the Brazilian legislature. In 1984 the Chamber of Deputies approved a new Civil Code that altered women's status in a few particulars. This proposed legislation is now in the Senate. Its key feature is that the husband would cease to be the legal head of the household, which would now fall jointly under the direction of husband and wife. From this change follows a number of others: the husband would no longer have sole control over the couple's assets; place of residence would be selected by both partners; the husband would no longer be able to claim abandonment (and custody of the children) if the wife left the household for a few days—both partners would thus be able to absent themselves from the household for professional or personal reasons. An effort to alter the term *pátrio poder* (*patria potestas*—the sweeping legal authority exercised by the oldest male in the family in ancient Roman law) to "parental authority" did not succeed; however, *pátrio poder* would now imply a somewhat altered function since the man would no longer be the sole head of the marital unit. See Silvia Pimentel and Florisa Verucci, "Esboço de um Novo Estatuto Civil da Mulher" (mimeo., 1980); Pimentel's outline in Projeto-Mulher do IDAC, *Mulheres em Movimento* (Rio de Janeiro: Editora Marco Zero, 1983), pp. 53–66; and *Mulherio* 4:19 (1984). Women's rights in Brazil are also currently the subject of debate as the Constituent Assembly drafts a new constitution for Brazil, to be completed in early 1988. Despite the Assembly's opposition to abortion (see note 12, Chapter 1), the new constitution is expected to improve significantly women's position in Brazil. Anticipated changes include the following: women will acquire the same rights as men have within the family; marriage will cease to be the only recognized form for constituting a family; the juridical categories of "unwed mother" and "illegitimate child" will cease to exist; divorce will be possible after two years of separation; the state will undertake to guarantee family planning; any form of abortion will be illegal; all forms of artificial insemination will be illegal (*Veja*, 3 June 1987, pp. 32–33). See also Postscript, below.

2   As mentioned in note 2 to Introduction, in recent years there has been greater female than male migration from rural to urban parts of Brazil. The 1980 census allows one to calculate that, in Lúcia's city in the Northeast, men constitute approximately 46 percent of the urban population, while women constitute nearly 54 percent. In Brazil as a whole, according to the 1980 census, 49.67 percent of the population was male, and 50.33 percent female.

3   Lúcia was the only woman (among the sixty I interviewed) who in any way mentioned the fact that the indigenous population of Brazil played a part in shaping Brazil and its present population. It has been estimated that between 2 and 5 million Indians lived in Brazil at the beginning of the sixteenth century. The process of colonization itself, with its attendant diseases, violence, and deracination, drastically reduced this population. See John Hemming, *Red Gold: The Conquest of the Brazilian Indians* (Cambridge: Harvard University Press, 1978). The National Indian Foundation (FUNAI) estimates that there are about 220,000 Indians left in Brazil today. In 1982 the first meeting of indigenous Brazilian leaders (I Encontro de Lideranças Indígenas do Brasil) took place and that same year a Chavante chief, Mário Juruna, was elected to the Chamber of Deputies, becoming the first Indian representative in Congress. These events marked the beginning of more active defense by Indians of their interests.

20   CRISTINA

1   Approximately 0.4 percent of all working women earned more than twenty minimum monthly salaries, according to 1985 figures, as opposed to 2.4 percent of all employed men. See *Latin American Regional Reports: Brazil*, 27 November 1986.

2   On women's reproduction rights in Brazil, see notes 11 and 12, Chapter 1, and note 11, Chapter 5.

3   See the important study conducted by Rose Marie Muraro, *Sexualidade da Mulher Brasileira: Corpo e Classe Social no Brasil* (Petrópolis: Editora Vozes, 1983), which received a good deal of publicity in Brazil even before its publication. Muraro explores the extent to which perceptions and experiences of one's own body and sexuality differ by class and region throughout Brazil. In terms of Cristina's comment, Muraro did indeed find that wealthy women invariably said they always had orgasms—but also said a woman should pretend to have them if she did not. Urban working-class women said they sometimes had orgasms, sometimes not. But poor rural women for the most part said they experienced no sexual pleasure and had sexual intercourse because their husbands wanted it.

Following twenty-one years of military rule, Brazil today is undergoing a period of transition to democracy. As I write, at the end of March 1988, a constituent assembly elected in November 1986 is approaching the final stage in the creation of a new constitution.

Since achieving its independence from Portugal in 1822, Brazil has had seven constitutions, three of them drafted by constituent assemblies during periods of political upheaval. Women have not participated in the drafting of these constitutions, despite the fact that Brazilian women have, from the middle of the last century, been active in movements for their own emancipation.

In the constituent assembly of 1934, which had 214 members, two women were nominated to advise the commission that was to prepare the preliminary drafts, and two others, Bertha Lutz and Almerinda Gama, were elected to the constituent assembly itself. The constitution of 1934 was the first to establish the principle of isonomy, declaring that all are equal before the law, without distinction of sex, race, occupation, religious creed, or political conviction. It also guaranteed women the right to vote, and established the first legal protection of women's work, thereby sanctioning demands that had been voiced for nearly a century.

The authoritarian constitution of 1937, conferred by Getúlio Vargas after his coup d'état, maintained the principle of isonomy. After the revocation of this document in 1945, a constituent assembly was convened to create a new constitution in a climate of freedom and euphoria much enhanced by the sense of relief that came with the end of the Second World War. But not one woman was elected to this assembly, and the constitution of 1946, although more advanced in many respects than previous constitutions, reduced the principle of isonomy to one lapidary phrase: "All are equal before the law."

The constitution of 1967, drastically amended in 1969, added nothing that might benefit women, for it was imposed by the military government that had taken power in 1964 and whose authoritarianism intensified in 1969.

Although the 1986 elections brought twenty-six women into the Chamber of Deputies, none was elected to the Senate. Despite the apparent increase—only

POSTSCRIPT
by
FLORISA VERUCCI

eight women had been elected in 1982—women's representation in congress, 4 percent of the total current membership of 559, continues to be insignificant.

Women are mentioned in constitutional texts in primarily two areas: with respect to the principle of equality before the law, and in relation to the social order, whether directly as citizens and workers or indirectly as family members. The principle of isonomy articulated in the constitution of 1934 has been reiterated, while social rights have been gradually expanded. Equality, however, has referred to nothing more than equality before the law.

In the light of this history, the work of the constituent assembly that has been meeting since February 1987 seems highly innovative. The assembly has already approved one important change, corresponding to the proposed Equal Rights Amendment in the United States. An article in the chapter on fundamental rights affirms: "Men and women are equal in rights and obligations, in terms of this constitution, and it falls to the state to guarantee the implementation of this clause." This represents a great leap forward in equal rights, the enforcement of which will in the future depend not merely on the actions of the state but also, greatly, on the initiative of Brazilian women themselves, the subjects of this right. Another important innovation is the inclusion in the constitution of the principle of punishability of any form of violation of fundamental rights and freedoms, including discrimination against women.

In the proposed clauses relating to social rights, preliminary balloting has already led to the assembly's approval of progressive measures. Maternity leave has been extended from 90 to 120 days, paternity leave of 8 days has been introduced, and obligations of firms to provide free nursery and preschool care for their employees' children and dependents have been extended up to six years of age. These matters continue to generate heated discussions, with considerable pressure being applied by syndicates and groups on the left of the political spectrum.

Unequal salaries and differential criteria for employment of men and women have been prohibited in the texts of constitutions ever since 1934, and these prohibitions will certainly appear in the new constitution, although such laws have seldom been enforced in practice. Among other changes regarding the work force is the reduction of the work week from forty-eight to forty-four hours, and the extension to domestic servants of all benefits received by other registered workers, including the right to the legally mandated minimum salary.

As a member of the Provisional Commission for Constitutional Studies, created by the Presidency of the Republic to prepare a preliminary draft of the constitution, I tried to introduce into the discussion issues relating to the democratization of the family. These include:

— separating the notion of family from that of legal marriage so as to protect in the Civil Code rights originating in concubinage;

— equality of rights between men and women within the family;
— restraints on domestic violence;
— equality of rights of all children, independent of their origin, including adopted children;
— introduction of family planning as an individual right and not as a means of population control, limiting the state and private entities to the provision of information and access to contraceptive devices;
— extending to adoptive mothers all social rights pertaining to maternity.

All these issues now appear as articles in the constitutional project under debate. Their approval, however, cannot be taken for granted, for in the process of final voting some of the amendments will certainly be opposed, and their intent modified, by conservative groups.

Like the rest of the country as it observes the work of the constituent assembly, Brazilian women await the final results which will certainly bring significant advances, consolidated at the level of the constitution, in their juridical condition.

Even if other objectives will not be attained, the inclusion of the clause affirming the equality of men and women in terms of rights and duties is sufficient, in my view, to facilitate the passage through the normal legislative process of a new body of laws that will assure its implementation.

We can also expect the formal principle of equality to alter in a fundamental way traditional legal protections afforded to women, who are today still considered as dependents from the juridical, economic, and social points of view.

São Paulo
March 1988

Translated by Daphne Patai

Florisa Verucci, feminist lawyer, writer, and jurist, is the author of A Mulher e o Direito (Women and the Law, 1987), and co-author, with Ediva Marino, of Os Direitos da Mulher (The Rights of Women, 1985). Together with Sílvia Pimentel she drafted the New Married Woman's Statute.

INDEX